ACCLAIM FOR ANDREW BURSTEIN'S

America's Jubilee

"A snapshot of a nation in transition. . . . An excellent work."
—*Booklist*

"Burstein opens a window in 1826 showing the politics, business and everyday lives of Americans." —*The Oregonian*

"A captivating book about how the people of 1826 marked that fiftieth Fourth of July." —*The Dallas Morning News*

"Gives the reader valuable insights into the everyday rhythm of living in America in 1826." —*The Roanoke Times*

"Spirits readers back to the 1820s. . . . [A] well-documented look at people and events of the era."
—*Fort Worth Morning Star-Telegram*

"[An] eminently readable re-creation of post-revolutionary America. . . . Burstein seizes the patriot in us very quickly."
—*The Orlando Sentinel*

"An affecting portrait. . . . Burstein's evocative reconstruction shows Americans pausing to consider where they had been and where they were going." —*Kirkus Reviews*

"Readers curious about life in America a generation into the nineteenth century—during a crucial period when the last of the Founders were bequeathing their revolutionary handiwork to their children—will find a great deal of interest and value here." —*The News & Observer*

ANDREW BURSTEIN

America's Jubilee

Andrew Burstein is the author of two previous books on American political culture: *Sentimental Democracy: The Evolution of America's Romantic Self-Image* and *The Inner Jefferson: Portrait of a Grieving Optimist.* He has had a varied career, working as a China scholar and international trade consultant before earning his Ph.D. from the University of Virginia. At present he is a professor of history and coholder of the Mary Frances Barnard Chair at the University of Tulsa.

America's Jubilee

America's Jubilee

ANDREW BURSTEIN

Vintage Books

A Division of Random House, Inc.

New York

FIRST VINTAGE BOOKS EDITION, JANUARY 2002

The Library of Congress has cataloged the Knopf edition as follows:
Burstein, Andrew.
America's jubilee / by Andrew Burstein.—1st ed.
p.   cm.
Includes bibliographical references (p.) and index.
ISBN 0-375-41033-3 (alk. paper)
1. Eighteen twenty-six, A.D.   2. United States—Anniversaries, etc.
3. United States. Declaration of Independence—Anniversaries, etc.
E285.B88   2001
973.3'6—dc21   00-020302

Vintage ISBN: 0-375-70918-5

Author photograph © A. J. McCoy

www.vintagebooks.com

For Nancy

And all that Memory loves the most
Was once our only Hope to be,
And all that Hope adored and lost
Hath melted into Memory.

—Lord Byron

Contents

Illustrations and Maps

Chronology

1767	Mar. 15	Andrew Jackson born in Waxhaw, South Carolina
	July 11	John Quincy Adams born in Braintree, Massachusetts
1772	Nov. 8	William Wirt born in Bladensburg, Maryland
	Dec. 15	Ruth Henshaw (Bascom) born in Leicester, Massachusetts
1773	June 2	John Randolph born in Cawsons, Virginia
1775	Apr. 19	Battles of Lexington and Concord
	June 17	Battle of Bunker Hill
1776	July 4	Declaration of Independence adopted; Ethan Allen Brown born in Greenwich, Connecticut
1777	Apr. 12	Henry Clay born in Hanover County, Virginia
	Sept. 11	Battle of Brandywine; Lafayette wounded
1781	Oct. 19	Battle of Yorktown ends in British surrender
1789	Apr. 30	George Washington inaugurated as president
1797	Mar. 4	John Adams inaugurated as president
1801	Mar. 4	Thomas Jefferson inaugurated as president
1815	Jan. 15	Battle of New Orleans restores pride, as War of 1812 ends through diplomacy
1817	Sept. 20	John Quincy Adams arrives in Washington, becoming secretary of state after eight years in Europe

America's Jubilee

Introduction

On TUESDAY, July 4, 1826, cities and towns across America cele-brated the fiftieth anniversary of the Declaration of Independence. There were elaborate parades and speeches, and dignified Revolutionary War veterans on display for awestruck youth. It is a moment that American history has forgotten, a moment when two critical generations reaffirmed their connection. The rising generation, having come into its political inheritance, stopped to acknowledge what had silently occurred some time earlier: it had separated from its constituting predecessor, it had taken the place in society of those who had given birth to the United States.

In his inaugural address the year before, the president of the United States, intellectually gifted John Quincy Adams, hailed the sons and daughters of the Revolutionaries for their zeal in sustaining popular government during a period of unprecedented growth. Between Independence and the mid-1820s, America's population had tripled to twelve million, while its territory had more than doubled on the strength of Thomas Jefferson's Louisiana Purchase alone. The nation's newest flag—it was just being dubbed "Old Glory"—had twenty-four stars, aligned in four rows of six. And the federal Constitution, having stood the test of time, was, as the new president reminded his fellow citizens, put in place by the founders "to promote the general welfare and secure the blessings of liberty to the people of this Union, in their successive generations."[1]

Successive generations. Harking back, Adams used superlatives to

3

describe the nation's forefathers, his own father among them. They were "illustrious benefactors," "eminent men" with giant aspirations, who had seen the first four million inhabitants through "a most eventful period in the annals of the world." Now, momentously, it had fallen to their heirs to secure continued freedom and happiness for the twelve million and growing: "We now receive it as a precious inheritance from those to whom we are indebted . . . to transmit the same, unimpaired, to the succeeding generation." The first half-century constituted a lesson in legitimacy. The groundwork was complete. Posterity would judge the successors on how well they carried through the work of the founders.

July 4, 1826. Fifty years of independence. So significant a Fourth of July apparently merited a sanctification beyond what citizens' already rich collective imagination had conceived. This unspoken wish was granted as the long lives of patriots Thomas Jefferson and John Adams ended within hours of each other on that memorable day. The author of the Declaration, who had since achieved Olympian status as the Sage of Monticello, expired just before 1:00 p.m. in Virginia. His warm-blooded fellow committeeman in the Continental Congress of 1776, who was probably the boldest member of that body to cry out for Independence, died at approximately 5:00 p.m. in Massachusetts. Both passed from the world in the presence of watchful, doting family, a slender Jefferson at eighty-three, a stout Adams at a remarkable ninety. Could any more unearthly coincidence have been imagined?

In his March 1825 inaugural address, the public-spirited son of John Adams had been the first to sound the jubilee. The election year of 1824 was the fiftieth anniversary of the creation of the Continental Congress, America's first united governing body. And so, John Q. Adams fittingly remarked: "The year of Jubilee, since the first formation of Our Union, has just elapsed; that of the Declaration of our Independence, is at hand." In the western part of the Union, the *Kentucky Reporter* picked up on the president's allusion with a noticeable satisfaction. Think of all the associations we know of, its editor surmised. "Among the Jews [the word "jubilee"] denotes every fiftieth year . . . at which time all the slaves were made free, and all the lands reverted to their original owners. . . . Jubilee, in a more modern sense, denotes a grand church solemnity or ceremony." The *Reporter's* research revealed that Edward III of England had caused his fiftieth birthday in 1362 to be observed "in the manner of a Jubilee . . . , releasing prisoners, pardoning all offenses except treason, *making good laws*, and granting many privileges to the people." The application of the term to America in the 1820s, the editor explained, did not have to lead to an acceptance of the "minutiae of this ancient institution"—lest one forget, Kentucky was a slave state—"but simply reminds us of the general spirit of the Jubilee at a time of universal felicitation and good feeling."[2]

Only the audible was missing from this description of a jubilee. Although the *Reporter* did mention that the year of jubilee was traditionally introduced by music, it did not specify that among the early Hebrews a ram's horn was used as a trumpet, or that the Latin *jubilaeus* means "to shout, halloo, or huzza."[3] Nor could it quite predict that among American celebrants in 1826, there would be, even more powerfully than on previous Independence Days, colorful military bands; ceremonial cannon blasts; loud, hearty toasts; and earsplitting fireworks—preceding and succeeding much patriotic oratory—to mark the day. It was something acutely real and, at the same time, immeasurably more.

THIS BOOK is a portrayal of Americans in the year of national jubilee, when the country had reached a watershed in its history. In part it is a literary journey across a still largely unsettled expanse of territory, a story to challenge old myths as it picks through private diaries and long-lost publications, trying to uncover the soul of the successor generation. It is an intimate look at select men and women who are meant to represent on some level the collective life of the nation. Some of the main characters were unheralded even in their own time, though in their emotion-filled yearnings they marvelously exemplify the successors' state of mind; others are noteworthy members of an exclusive political cadre, national celebrities of the 1820s whose public personae and personal peculiarities have long since ceased to resonate in Americans' historical memory.

It was their negotiation between past and present that makes these cultural observers of the rising generation so interesting. Democratic expectations drew upon the language of 1776 but suddenly required more comprehensive application. What was a sound democracy? people inquired. They were putting eighteenth-century forms behind them, while paying a loving tribute to the old Revolutionaries. Though they thought themselves peace-loving, an agonizing struggle over definitions of political progress and moral security raged among them. All Americans agreed upon one thing, and, it seemed, one thing only: that homage should be paid to their Revolutionary origins. It was that universal devotion which promised to preserve a language of unity and harmony and pure motives in an era of widely divergent tastes and purposes. Behind them lay glory days, ahead lay civil war. For them, as for us, the past was a comfort.

The Americans of 1826 were, overall, a robust breed, a people of longings. Certainly, they were attuned to the disruptive potential of issues like slavery to divide them. But, approaching this moment of national celebration, they were also eager to acknowledge their collective commonness, that quality of "elegant simplicity" (to use a Revolutionary-era phrase) underlying a democratic concept just then in the process of being appropriated by the supporters of Andrew Jackson.

While this book is written both for general readers and professional historians, it is meant to humanize more than to intellectualize; at the same time, it is calculated to revise the popular myth that Jacksonian Democracy arose and flourished only with Andrew Jackson's election in 1828. The culture of the "common man" that became enshrined in 1835 in Alexis de Tocqueville's *Democracy in America* was already established in the years *before* the French observer sailed across the ocean, *before* Jackson had captured the presidency.

Historians have minimized the significance of what was happening in the mid-1820s. I intend to show the narrowness of that view, which too often directs the writers of U.S. survey textbooks. It is an all-too-neat consensus that divides political periods into such categories as "the Age of Federalism," "Jeffersonian Democracy," "the Era of Good Feelings" (marking James Monroe's first term and the rise of a "new nationalism"), and "the Age of Jackson." In representing a dramatic generational transition, *America's Jubilee* means to call into question these convenient categories, as it captures ordinary events in the life of America as much as symbolic performances of the jubilee year.

Drawing on personal diaries, public journals, and popular literature, this book sets the margins of daily life in 1826. It seeks to provide a palpable sense of emotional as well as political currents. This is a study of memories, of nineteenth-century ontologies. In the writing process it has also become an unplanned appreciation for a community of human beings whose wrinkled images have needed smoothing. That is what has made the research so enjoyable. As historical narrative, the book's purpose is to restore to our senses the once intense and lively feelings of past subjects, and importantly to do so without forfeiting the critical goal of separating the real from the ideal. The two-part question that I propose to answer is this: What were the American people trying to retrieve or restore as they celebrated on July 4, 1826? And what did the jubilee mean to them?

CHAPTER ONE

An Esteemed Friend Twice Touches Hearts

T HE GREAT EVENT staged in anticipation of the national jubilee was in fact spread out over two years, 1824–25, and touched all twenty-four of the United States. This was the heartening return of the Marquis de Lafayette, a celebrity on two continents whose name was associated with the language of liberty and rights and the republican spirit in both the American and French Revolutions. He was the last of a dying breed, having fought with the Continental Army, having led American forces at the rank of general—and all America knew that he had been like a son to George Washington. Lafayette was an integral part of the national creation story.

Embarking on his eighth and final year in office, James Monroe was the last Revolutionary War veteran to serve as president. In early February 1824, he wrote out an invitation to the now sixty-six-year-old hero, offering to send an American frigate, expressly equipped for the general's comfort, to the French port of Lafayette's choosing. "Since then," Monroe followed up a short time later, "Congress has passed a resolution on this subject, in which the sincere attachment of the whole nation to you is expressed, whose ardent desire is once more to see you amongst them."[1] For Americans who wished to revisit the season of their national birth, no experience could be richer than to catch a glimpse of the last surviving general from the War for Independence.

Nineteen-year-old Gilbert du Motier de La Fayette* was of high spirits, uncommon candor, and beautiful ideals when he met General Washington in 1777. The young marquis put himself at the disposal of the commander of the Continental Army and exhibited utter faithfulness to him throughout the war. What these two men shared, despite the twenty-five-year gap in their ages, was an enthusiasm for the battlefield. Both had a keen sense of themselves as vital actors in a drama with enduring possibilities.

There was something about the Frenchman that cried out for a cause. Educated to be a military gentleman, with a strong purse and noble lineage, Lafayette had resolved to aid the American insurgency sometime after scrutinizing the Declaration of Independence. Purchasing and outfitting a vessel called *La Victoire*, he sailed the Atlantic on an uncertain romantic enterprise. He saw America as he saw himself, resolute and humane. He was impressed that the distance between rich and poor was so much less than in France. The Revolutionary forces were in a sad state, but even this could not shatter Lafayette's ideals. When he was first presented to Washington, no American official knew what his role would be; in his first engagement, a miserable loss at Brandywine Creek, the French volunteer was shot in the leg. The wound healed while he was under Washington's roof, and that father-son relationship began to develop. Lafayette had hardly known his own father, who was killed a decade earlier in the Seven Years' War, and he had lost his mother when he was thirteen.

The implausibly young Major General Lafayette took command of a division of the Virginia militia, which he equipped largely at his own expense, serving also as an aide-de-camp to Washington. He traveled north to Albany and the Iroquois homeland in central New York State where, to assert his authority, he launched small raids against periodically hostile Indians, and smoked the long-stemmed pipe with those whom he sought to convince that America's cause was just. He harassed the British in the Pennsylvania countryside and proved himself an able tactician. He increasingly impressed Congress with his movements and his eager commitment.

---

* This was the Revolutionary-era spelling of the name. It was Lafayette himself who subsequently adopted the common modern spelling—that is, all as one word.

More than ever convinced that America was a sanctuary of liberty that needed to be protected, Lafayette sailed back to France to lobby his government for more direct aid. He returned in the spring of 1780, armed with his king's promise to send vessels of war and six thousand infantrymen. In the decisive year 1781, he chased after General Charles Cornwallis, whose army was having its way in Virginia. Sly and agile, the enthusiastic Frenchman made Cornwallis, hitherto a master at maneuver, reluctant to proceed; ultimately Cornwallis settled on the Yorktown peninsula, where he allowed himself to feel secure. That was when Lafayette wrote Washington of the opportunity to trap their enemy. Washington's forces marched south to join Lafayette, and the long-awaited French navy sailed past their confident foe and left the British cut off from escape. After a siege of three weeks, Cornwallis surrendered. Lafayette, who would give his second daughter the name Virginie, took a prominent role at the Yorktown ceremony. The disarmed British marched in embarrassment, as their shamed commander hid away, protesting illness. Two months later, triumphant, Lafayette went back to France.[2]

He had visited his adopted country only once more, in 1784. At that time he encountered the civilian Washington at home, a fifty-two-year-old planter in the process of rebuilding his life after having spent the war years more worried about an exhausted, underprovisioned army than actively conceiving victory and peace. Lafayette, doubtlessly calmed at the sight of this domestic routine, stayed at Mount Vernon two weeks.[3] Of his young friend's departure, Washington wrote: "In the moment of our separation upon the road as I travelled, & every hour since—I have felt all that love, respect & attachment for you, with which length of years, close connexion & your merits, have inspired me." With a tenderness uncharacteristic of the tenacious leader, he continued, "I often asked myself, as our Carriages distended, whether that was the last sight, I should ever have of you? And tho' I wished to say no—my fears answered yes."[4]

After this, Lafayette never again saw Washington alive, and would not see American shores until 1824. But he had ample occasion to strengthen his friendship with Americans in the meantime, beginning with Virginia's wartime governor, Thomas Jefferson, who spent 1784–89 as American minister to the court of Louis XVI. Jefferson resided in Paris just long enough to witness Lafayette rise to assert a vision of liberty for his native country, as the Bastille fell.

THAT WAS THEN. Lafayette did not call for the special frigate President Monroe had offered, but left Paris on July 11, 1824, with his son, the memorably named George Washington Lafayette, and his private secretary, retired French army officer Auguste Levasseur. The party waited at the port of Havre for the American merchant ship *Cadmus* to set sail. According to Greek mythology, Cadmus was the wise brother of the beautiful Europa; and here, the fraternity of an aging French soldier and a skillful American captain named Allyn made for a safe and sure ocean crossing. On August 14, they sighted New York.

The next day, Lafayette ceremoniously set foot near Manhattan's Battery before thousands of spectators. The doors of City Hall were left open and the hero made available to citizens for over two hours. "Public attention continues to be almost exclusively engrossed by our distinguished visitor," reported the *New-York American*. He was six feet tall, but not extraordinary in looks; a bit chubby now, he was by no means a stylish dresser either, conscious to appear "republican."[5] Outside City Hall, Broadway was active, "the bazaar of American industry," wrote Levasseur, "side-walks, solidly constructed and flagged with broad stones." If the main thoroughfare was "clean and regular," and surrounded by elegant buildings, the streets that led from Broadway to the wharves were far less agreeable. Exploring on his own, Levasseur found them dirty, with badly built frame houses and a large indigent population, drunks lounging, and prostitutes much in evidence—though, to the Frenchman, America's commercial hub was still a less degenerate place than London. Here were "not more than three thousand public women," less than 2 percent of the city's population, compared to London's 5 percent. New York had grown to six times its population of 1790, when George Washington had taken the oath of office a short distance from where Lafayette now sat greeting a diverse group.[6]

Mothers brought their children to Lafayette, to receive his blessing. "Feeble" veterans talked over the war with him. "Men of colour" reminded the liberal thinker of how much his trust in their commitment to America had meant to the still uncertain cause of human equality. Many people were prevented from speaking only because they could not find words beneath their tears of joy. Everywhere he went, General Lafayette was greeted and honored as "the Nation's Guest."[7]

From New York, Lafayette and his party traveled overland through Connecticut and Rhode Island, on roadways crowded with well-wishers, to the accompaniment of cannon salutes. He had promised to be at Harvard College for commencement ceremonies, grateful for the honorary degree that that institution had conferred on him back in 1784. After countless testimonials along the way, he arrived in Boston in the dead of night. Waking in the town where the Revolution had been sparked in the spring of 1775, he was treated to an unexpected scene outside his window: men in the very uniforms that his light infantry command had once worn strode before him again. "How much I loved them!" Levasseur heard Lafayette exclaim.

A reflective young man presented him with a sword, one of French manufacture. "My father received it from your hands," he explained with a forlorn look. "He religiously preserved it in memory of his general, and would have been happy to have presented it to you himself: the day before yesterday he still hoped to do so, and this hope softened his last moments." Lafayette examined the sword, and addressed the grieving son: "Take it, guard it carefully, in order that it may in your hands be used to preserve the rights it has so gloriously contributed to acquire in the hands of your father." It was this kind of poignancy that filled the pages of Levasseur's notebook, as he chronicled one vignette after another of the old hero's reception by two grateful generations of Americans.[8]

The day following Harvard's commencement, Lafayette listened as a thirty-year-old professor of Greek, Edward Everett, delivered the annual Phi Beta Kappa oration, titled "The Circumstances Favorable to the Progress of Literature in America." Everett might have been the most accomplished scholar of the successor generation. Lafayette had met him several times in France, impressed by the young Unitarian who had become pastor of the Brattle Street Church at the age of twenty, in 1814, and was the first American to receive a Ph.D. from the prestigious German university of Göttingen just three years later. Before the year was out, a convention held in the Revolutionary town of Lexington was to nominate Everett for a seat in the House of Representatives, where he would serve for the next ten years.

Everett's declamation before a packed meetinghouse that day was "his most spectacular triumph," according to an admiring biographer with the unambiguous name of Paul Revere Frothingham. At the end of the address, the Boston orator faced Lafayette directly and invoked the name of Washington: "On the banks of the Potomac," Everett pronounced solemnly, "he lies in glory and peace. . . . His voice of consolation, which reached you in the Austrian dungeons* cannot now break its silence to bid you welcome to his own roof. But the grateful children of America will bid you welcome, in his name." The salutation followed: "Welcome, thrice welcome to our shores." As Frothingham related the story, "a period of absolute silence followed," and when the spell finally lifted, loud cheers and waving handkerchiefs filled the hall.[9]

Josiah Quincy was the mayor of Boston, and the inheritor of a Revolutionary name. His father, who died young, at sea, just after Lexington and Concord, was an early associate of Samuel and John Adams. He had sat in councils that planned the actions which led to the American Revolution. Now it was the son and namesake, a congressman from 1805 to 1813 who had returned to state politics, who delivered official remarks that stood as a model for all those welcoming addresses Lafayette was to hear over the next thirteen months.

> General Lafayette:—The citizens of Boston welcome you on your
> return to the United States, mindful of your early zeal in the cause
> of American Independence, grateful for your distinguished share
> in the perils and glories of its achievement. . . . In your youth you
> joined the standard of three millions of people, raised in an
> unequal and uncertain conflict. In your advanced age you return
> and are met by ten millions of people, their descendents, whose
> hearts throng hither to greet your approach and to rejoice in it.

According to Levasseur, the mayor had a "fine countenance" that became animated in speech, while thousands sat in "solemn silence."

---

* During Washington's presidency, as the French Revolution turned on many of its early liberal supporters, Lafayette spent the years 1792 to 1797 in prison.

Solemn silence? A later account by Mayor Quincy's son Edmund offers a contrary image of the moment: he states that the city leader was "interrupted by the shouts of the multitude around." The lesson is, then, that as old texts are consulted, writing reliable history requires as much critical distance as sympathetic engagement.[10]

Proceeding slowly through the streets of Boston after the official welcome, Lafayette purportedly turned to Mayor Quincy: "Pray tell me, is the widow of John Hancock yet alive?" "Oh, yes," Quincy replied, "and I have no doubt that we shall see her at one of the windows as we pass by." Near Boston Common, the window came into view, as did the "venerable dame" whose late husband was not only the first signer of the Declaration of Independence, but the governor of Massachusetts at his death in 1793. Lafayette's coachman halted across from the door, and the general bowed to her. She returned the gesture from the balcony, and he entered the house where he had been entertained nearly a half-century before. The crowd witnessing this nostalgic drama cheered enthusiastically.[11]

Just south of Boston, in the town of Quincy—it had been settled by the mayor's direct ancestor in 1636—Lafayette paid a visit to eighty-nine-year-old John Adams. The ex-president could not leave his room and was barely able to raise himself from his chair. In Levasseur's words, he needed the "pious assistance" of his children and grandchildren to take his meals. Nevertheless, "his heart and head felt not less ardour for everything good. . . . We left him, filled with admiration at the courage with which he supported the pains and infirmities which the lapse of nearly a century had necessarily accumulated on him." With somewhat more animation than this account suggests, old Adams later wrote to his favorite correspondent, Thomas Jefferson: "You and I have been favored with a visit from our old friend General La Fayette. What a wonderful Man at his Age to undergo the fatigues of such long journeys and constant feasts. I was greatly delighted with the sight of him and the little conversation I had with him." Just as curious, Lafayette remarked to Mayor Quincy at dinner on the day of his meeting with Adams, "That was not the John Adams I remember!" and Adams independently conveyed to Quincy not long after, "That was not the Lafayette that I remember!"[12]

Already, newspaper readers around the country thrilled at the commotion caused by the general's visit. William Wirt, the attorney general of the United States, wrote from Washington to Virginia judge Dabney Carr in late August: "Did you ever see the like of the reception given to La Fayette at the North? There is, no doubt, a good deal of ostentation in it—and yet there is so much feeling, that reading it made me weep like a child." Something about Lafayette provoked a diverse people to celebrate vicariously, and to relate the festive appreciation of an aging hero to the joys conceivable in their own lives.[13]

Before heading for the South in September, the general's entourage returned to his port of entry, New York, for a longer visit. At the southern tip of Manhattan rose a pyramid-shaped tent, seventy-five feet high and illuminated with colored lamps. A bridge lined with evergreens guided the Lafayette party inside, where a triumphal arch topped with laurel and oak wreaths and a colossal bust of George Washington fed into an amphitheater. The celebrated novelist James Fenimore Cooper wrote for the *New-York American* of the city's redoubled effort to stage a suitable welcome: "At the first view," he wrote expansively, "the eye was satisfied, and the spectator felt willing to stand and gaze at the entrance of this fairy scene." Close to five thousand people had come, by carriage and steamboat alike. Dancers performed in this dreamlike setting, and the Nation's Guest walked past the galleries—in Cooper's words, "receiving the eager pressure of thousands of fair hands, and the fervent and affectionate wishes of thousands of hearts."[14]

After New York, Lafayette visited Revolutionary battle sites at Trenton and Princeton, New Jersey. En route, the returning hero stopped at Bergen, where he was presented with a cane carved from the apple tree under which he and General Washington had once sat for breakfast; it was, according to the press, richly mounted with gold, and its historic pedigree inscribed in it: "Shaded the hero and his friend Washington, in 1779." Lafayette passed from here to Newark, "a pretty small town," where choruses of boys and girls sang for him. The boys' tune opened:

> *Hail! the gallant Chief, whose fame*
> *Is pure as Heaven's ethereal flame!*
> *Who comes our peaceful fields to cheer,*
> *A father of ten millions dear!*

And the girls':

We wear the wreath, we pour the wine
Where smiles like sparkling sunbeams shine;
And hail the thousands fondly met
To greet the matchless La Fayette!

From Newark, he continued on to Philadelphia, shaking the "hardened hands" of many a mechanic, standing with the "plain clad farmer" and exalted magistrate alike, greeting clergy and, as always, listening to the recollections of veterans.[15]

The party then trekked to the bustling city of Baltimore and remained five days before arriving at the nation's capital. Lafayette was received at the President's House by its courtly and somewhat starched occupants, James and Elizabeth Monroe. Of Washington, D.C., itself, Levasseur noted that for the vast scale upon which it was designed, its thirteen thousand residents were hardly sufficient to give it the feel of a fully developed city, let alone a national metropolis; it was, he said charitably, "an infant colony struggling against difficulties." Streets were bad, the jail overcrowded with debtors and runaway slaves— approximately 30 percent of the population was nonwhite. A brisk trade in human beings persisted, men bound in ropes and iron chains at times being led past the Capitol itself. (The first protest from Congress would occur in 1826, when a sightseeing free Negro from New York was jailed as a runaway.) In addition to the visible scars, Washington was known for frequent outbreaks of bilious fever. Nonetheless, it would be Lafayette's base of operations through the unsteady national election season upcoming, and for the ensuing winter months as well.[16]

First, however, there were important pilgrimages to be made in Virginia: George Washington's Mount Vernon plantation on the opposite side of the Potomac; Yorktown, farther south, where Lafayette had played so pivotal a role in the British defeat; and Monticello, where his old friend Thomas Jefferson was enjoying a productive, if debt-ridden, retirement. The general was accompanied to the first by Monroe's secretary of war, John C. Calhoun of South Carolina. Soon after arriving, Lafayette went into Washington's vault, set amid "sombre cypresses." Behind a simple wooden door, the remains of his old commander and friend were entombed. After some minutes alone he reemerged, "his eyes overflowing with tears," and led his son to the hallowed spot. In fact, George Washington Lafayette had been the last of the Lafayettes to see Washington alive. When his father was a political prisoner in 1795, his mother had sent their fifteen-year-old to America for sanctuary; the first president had paid for the boy's schooling at Harvard, afterward allowing him to live at Mount Vernon for a year and a half. Now, as they reappeared from Washington's vault, the two Lafayettes each clutched a branch of cypress, cut from over the tomb. Together, silently, they marched from the great man's resting place to the Potomac shore.[17]

An overnight steamboat took them to Yorktown. The state's executive had early on invited Lafayette to rendezvous with Virginia's volunteer companies, and from New York in August the Frenchman had responded effusively to his invitation: "Happy would I be to have the inexpressible gratification to meet them at the place & on the anniversary of the day [October 19] which closed our labours." At Yorktown, Chief Justice John Marshall waited at the head of a welcoming committee and brought Lafayette to his "headquarters," the very same house that Lord Cornwallis had occupied during the siege forty-three years earlier.[18]

Yorktown had never really been rebuilt, appearing to Levasseur as he imagined it was when Lafayette last saw it: "houses in ruins, blackened by fire, or pierced by bullets; the ground covered with fragments of arms, the broken shells, and overturned gun-carriages; tents grouped or scattered according to the nature of the ground; small platoons of soldiers placed at various points, all in a word, conveyed the idea of a camp hastily formed." The guests' lodgings were suitably spartan to maintain that illusion of time standing still, and they lay that night on narrow straw mattresses, awakened at daylight by cannon fire "thundering from the plain." Led to the place that had once been Washington's battlefield headquarters, Lafayette received the officers assigned to him this day. Two of the old Revolutionaries who came to shake the general's hand fainted away.[19]

In 1781, Lafayette had charged a British redoubt while bullets whizzed overhead. In 1824, he maneuvered instead past "a double row of ladies whose vivid joy and elegant costume singularly contrasted" with the scarred soil that had changed little over the intervening years. After a round of speeches, all returned to "Cornwallis's" house for an evening ball, lit up by what still remained of the British general's blackened, but still usable, candles, newly discovered in the cellar of the house.[20]

On November 4, Lafayette approached Monticello, Jefferson's private mountain. His carriage was enveloped by an escort of mounted Virginia gentlemen, with Revolutionary banners held aloft, to the accompaniment of military tunes. The fanfare of trumpets ended as the general pulled up to the great lawn in front of the white-domed neoclassical structure. The Frenchman stepped from his carriage, as Jefferson, his tall frame only slightly bent, moved briskly to embrace him. As the two men held each other, eyewitnesses wept for the joy of that historic moment.[21] Too late to glimpse the encounter, Judge Dabney Carr, the son of Jefferson's sister, wrote preciously to a friend, "as to the Fayetting [surely a play on the verb "to fête"], I am child enough to be pleased with the whole shew. There may have been a bit too much of parade; but there is so much good feeling at bottom—the moral effect is so fine—so sublime." Carr held back nothing as he marveled at Lafayette's ability to move people: "What a noble character is the old general; so consistent, so true to principle—so modest—such excellent sense, as all his replies prove, & as every one testifies who has conversed with him—I would have given my best coat to have witnessed the meeting between him & Mr. Jefferson."[22]

At the Charlottesville banquet held for Lafayette the next day at the site of the new University of Virginia, Jefferson's words had to be read for him. "I am old," he explained, "long in the disuse of making speeches, and without voice to utter them." He had been dependent in 1781 as well, when in the months before Yorktown a beleaguered Jefferson ineffectually held the office of governor. The state was bankrupt, and the Virginia legislature had had little to do. General Washington wrote Jefferson of the impossibility of sending troops from New York to provide relief: "we should lose at least one-third of our force by desertion, sickness, and the heats of the approaching season, even if it could be done." More than four decades later, Jefferson recalled those frightful times as "a scene which his [Lafayette's] military manoeuvres covered from the robberies and ravages of an unsparing enemy." Lafayette's army had been the only force on hand to deflect the assaults of Banastre Tarleton, Cornwallis's most brutal commander, a man who went so far as to dispatch a party of soldiers to scale Monticello in an attempt to make the governor his prisoner. But in banqueting

Lafayette in 1824, the Sage of Monticello chose to praise his guest's peacetime aid over his military exploits. While Jefferson was minister to France in the late 1780s, he explained, Lafayette had been a "powerful auxiliary and advocate." Seeking international respect for the newly independent nation, Jefferson had merely "held the nail," while America's eternal benefactor, Lafayette, "drove it."[23]

Peace and the nation's well-being were helping to sustain Jefferson's celebrated mildness and affability. Though the frail ex-president could not project his voice, he bore up under the "exhausted powers of life," as he put it on this occasion. His Charlottesville neighbors well knew how he exerted himself to sit astride Eagle, his favorite horse, ride down his mountain, and cross over to the university that he had dedicated his late years to building. His final legacy to America's enrichment was this institution, set to open in March 1825. It was designed to add to Virginia's "virtue and prosperity," but also, as he put it now, in the presence of Lafayette, to add to an "indissoluable union."[24]

Levasseur was impressed with Jefferson's memory as well as his record as a humanist. The infirmities of age did not defeat the charm of this worldly provincial. The visitor delighted, too, in the lively, grandchildren-filled house, its irregular octagon shape and porticoed entrances, patriotic busts and paintings—and he politely made note of the "good appearance and gaiety" of the slaves who tended a generous acreage. Lafayette was well known for his impatience with the persistence of slavery in his adopted country, and Levasseur was every bit as critical as the general, though careful to generalize the problem rather than to isolate individual masters who were as constant as Jefferson appeared to be in the cause of bettering the human condition.[25]

James Madison, at seventy-four, had ridden much of the day from his plantation to take part in the Charlottesville banquet. Jefferson had sat on one side of Lafayette, Madison on the other, as the latter proposed a witty toast, "To liberty, with virtue for her guest, and gratitude for the feast." Before the Lafayette party left with Madison for a stay at his home, Montpelier, a university professor presented a live rattlesnake—venom removed—to George Lafayette. Then Lafayette accompanied Madison back, enjoying four days of promenades and provocative conversation.[26]

At Montpelier, too, Lafayette received explanations for the mild and tolerant form of slavery practiced by the "enlightened" Virginians who shared Madison's dinner table. To Levasseur, however, tolerable slavery was no preference so long as liberty loomed as the alternative. Other than to report on Madison's still "youthful soul of sensibility" and remarkably active mind, Levasseur left the profound ex-president's liberal views out of his ordinarily detailed account. This is a shame, because the pragmatic Madison had by now adopted a rather sophisticated posture for his time, regarding African Americans as a people equal in intellectual promise to those of European origin. He favored a gradual, methodical emancipation that included compensation to masters for their loss of "property."[27]

But Madison was also a firm supporter of the American Colonization Society, founded in 1816 and headed by Bushrod Washington, the first president's nephew. The organization sought to finance black Americans' return to Africa, where self-government was expected to restore a people's lost pride. The patronizing whites who waxed eloquent about colonization generally ignored the fact that the intended beneficiaries (especially free blacks) did not wish to be removed from American soil simply for the convenience of those whites who, perhaps inadvertently, were aiding a slave-owning class that feared the encouraging symbol that free black communities represented for those enslaved. On the subject of emancipation, little, it seems, was resolved at Montpelier. Slowly, then, Lafayette made his way back to Washington.

Though he had been in the country for four months, the Frenchman was officially welcomed by the federal government on December 10, 1824, in the Capitol. Ladies were invited, and "took possession of the sofas and seats, which were appropriated for their reception." George Lafayette and Levasseur were seated on a sofa beside Monroe's secretary of state, John Quincy Adams, as Lafayette entered the bustling chamber. Speaker of the House Henry Clay introduced the guest of honor, and pronounced America's gratitude for his earlier sacrifices and for his "uniform devotion to regulated liberty." In the middle of his address, Clay struck a nostalgic tone:

> The vain wish is sometimes indulged, that Providence would allow the patriot, after death, to return to his country, and to contemplate the intermediate changes which had taken place—

to view the forests felled, the cities built, the mountains levelled, the canals cut, the highways constructed, the progress of the arts, the advancement of learning, and the increase of population. General, your present visit to the United States is a realization of the consoling object of that wish. You are in the midst of that posterity.

Lafayette responded to Speaker Clay's encomium by saying that he was merely "one of the American veterans," honored to have been chosen to symbolize the common contribution of the many who had fought to realize a national triumph. He had, for the half-century since the end of the Revolution, enjoyed "constant affection and kindness" from Americans. Their "approbation" was as much as he could desire in life. "Posterity has not begun for me," he explained generously, "since, in the sons of my companions and friends, I find the same public feelings . . . which I have had the happiness to experience in their fathers." After Lafayette had finished, every member of Congress stayed on to shake his hand.[28]

In Washington, Lafayette was witnessing firsthand the most tangled presidential election contest since Jefferson had defeated Adams in 1800. At that time, Jefferson's running mate, the mercurial Aaron Burr of New York, had inadvertently received the same number of electoral votes as the Virginian under whom he was meant to serve. As the Constitution provided, the House of Representatives sorted out the matter, but only after weeks of tense politicking; in the end, the Federalist opposition unenthusiastically deferred to Jefferson as the lesser of two evils. As a result of the election of 1800, the Twelfth Amendment was adopted in 1804, to prevent competition between candidates for president and vice president, and for a time the system functioned more smoothly. In the fall of 1824, however, entering a crowded field late, Andrew Jackson of Tennessee secured more electoral votes than runner-up John Quincy Adams, though not enough to win a majority. The election was thrown into the House for the second time in the short history of the American republic, and on February 9, 1825, the House voted and Adams emerged as president-elect.

Beneath the surface of protocol and propriety, partisans seethed. And so, the Marquis de Lafayette, surrounded by presidents, expresidents, and presidential hopefuls, spent the long Washington interlude between parades and raucous celebrations in America's interior delicately expressing his sincere attachment to all the competing candidates. Indeed, he was mindful not to wear his military uniform, so as to avoid inadvertently influencing the electorate in favor of Jackson, the military candidate. He made it a point, as he told some Washington dinner guests when queried, to wear "my plain blue coat and round hat" when he reviewed American troops.[29]

The week after Adams's victory, Lafayette resumed his travels, moving south to continue his tour of the twenty-four states. He visited the Carolinas and Georgia, before sailing into the Gulf of Mexico and stopping at the hub of French culture in America—New Orleans. On his first day there, French-speaking citizens of the city woke him with cries of *"Vive la liberté, vive l'ami de l'Amérique!"* Lafayette disembarked to a thunderous artillery salute and toured the lines where General Jackson, outnumbered four to one, had bested the British in the climactic battle of the War of 1812. Tennessee and Kentucky musket shot were said to have been constant and deadly accurate during the foggy morning assault that resulted in scattering the headstrong English columns. Jackson, incredibly, lost only seven men in the three-hour battle for the strategic port, while the enemy suffered seven hundred dead, including their commanding general. With this stunning victory, the pride and optimism of the first stages of the American Revolution revived, and the "gallant" Andrew Jackson was credited in popular verse as Washington's spiritual successor.[30]

Despite a violent rain, the scheduled procession went forward, and Lafayette was honored at a triumphal arch specially erected in the public square. The monument was sixty feet high, decorated with symbolic statues of Justice and Liberty, and topped with the figure of Wisdom "resting her hand on a bust of the immortal Franklin." The names of all the signers of the Declaration of Independence, and select officers who had distinguished themselves in battles of the Revolution, were inscribed on various parts of the arch.[31]

After ceremonies, the general was conducted to his hotel, where he stood on a balcony and reviewed elegantly uniformed troops. Somewhat irregularly, at the rear of these troops marched a hundred Choctaws in single file. They were allies of the United States in a recently concluded war against the Florida Seminoles, where once again Jackson had been at the head of a determined American army.

The Choctaws had encamped in New Orleans for a full month just to catch a glimpse of the warrior from France who they understood had been "the brother of their great father Washington." Lafayette, wrote one observer, "appeared touched" by this display. Before he left the city, the compassionate French nobleman met with another under-acknowledged group—free blacks who had taken part in the city's defense in 1815. To cap off the portentous visit, a violent dispute broke out among officers of the militia, who competed for privilege in presenting themselves to Lafayette. There was a distinct air of self-aggrandizement and indifference in New Orleans: Choctaws, destined within a decade to be herded beyond the pale of white settlement, onto unfamiliar Western land, pathetically awaited their fate; free blacks who would know no real equality throughout their lives exhibited a quiet dignity; squabbling militia units clamored for recognition. These encounters, combined with the stormy weather, marked an uncivil interlude along an old idealist's journey.[32]

Lafayette traveled next on the steamboat *Natchez* up the Mississippi River to the area around St. Louis, where he had occasion to be moved once again by an encounter with Native Americans. A young Indian woman named Mary, who lived some distance away, in the forest beyond the small settlement of Kaskaskia, amazed Lafayette and his party by producing a letter of commendation written and signed by Lafayette himself in Albany, New York, in 1778. The letter had been given to her father, an Iroquois chief named Panisciowa, expressing gratitude for his honorable service in the American cause. The tale Mary related of her father's life—he was not long deceased—caused Lafayette to reflect on the tragic consequences that befell those Indians who had shown their commitment to the colonists' cause. Despite his courageous contribution to the war effort, Panisciowa had been driven west, leaving New York State and settling with the Great Lakes Kickapoo, before removing with his daughter to the less troubled reaches of St. Louis. There he had permitted her to live with well-meaning Christians while he went off to hunt, and she converted, afterward reconsidering the choice and returning to Indian ways because she found modesty and simplicity superior to the adornments of the white world. For many years, Mary's father had preserved Lafayette's letter, and when he died she took it into her own care. Dressed in her coarse clothing, Mary conveyed the holy relic that had survived so many winters and so many journeys. Lafayette "could not conceal his emotion," recounted Levasseur, as the Frenchman and the young Indian survivor together sensed how unlikely their meeting, in so remote a locale, ought to have been.[33]

From Kaskaskia, Lafayette retraced his river passage south as far as the mouth of the Ohio River, then east along the southern Illinois border with Kentucky, where the Ohio feeds into the Cumberland River. The Virginia-born governor of Illinois Edward Coles was with him; Levasseur called Coles "a man of agreeable conversation and extraordinary merit." With polite encouragement from Thomas Jefferson, but no real political support, Coles had emancipated his slaves, bringing them with him to the free state of Illinois, where he gave them all a decent start. "This act of justice and humanity considerably diminished his fortune," Levasseur explained, "but occasioned him no regrets." Coles had gone on to battle those who wanted to amend the state constitution to permit slavery; through his outspokenness, he found himself elected to Illinois's highest office. Ironically, however, Coles was now accompanying Lafayette down the Cumberland River to visit a prominent and unapologetic slaveholder of the frontier.[34]

It was May 4, 1825, three weeks after his departure from New Orleans, when Lafayette was received in Andrew Jackson's hometown of Nashville. He rode in a carriage next to America's most popular living model of valor, as the two formed a procession along the broad avenue that led into the city. The streets were lined with militia in brilliant uniforms, and yet another triumphal arch marked the site for speech making. In a well-orchestrated pageant, Governor William Carroll expressed affection and gratitude, and forty elderly Revolutionary veterans, having come from all parts of the state for the occasion, approached Lafayette at once from both sides of the arch. The assembled crowd applauded. One of the hoary veterans could not contain his joy, and threw himself into Lafayette's arms, sobbing, "I have enjoyed two happy days in my life, that when I landed with you in Charleston in 1777, and the present. . . ." He had nothing more to live for, he exclaimed; this was enough. The crowd listened to this outpouring, and stood silent. Later, Levasseur confirmed that the man had been born in Germany and saw American shores for the first time precisely when Lafayette did, aboard *La Victoire*.[35]

That day, Lafayette dined with Jackson in Nashville. Citizens

Fig. 1. Invitation to a ball held in honor of Lafayette during his visit to Nashville, 1825. *(Courtesy, Tennessee State Library and Archives, Tennessee Historical Society Collection.)*

selected to attend a welcoming ball received printed invitations that featured a triumphal arch highlighting the achievements of America's three greatest military heroes. The worldly importance of the event was stressed by placing the bust of a Romanesque Jackson atop one column and the bust of the plain, republican Lafayette on the other. A cloud-borne Washington, his wreath-halo suspended from the beak of the American eagle, floated above the two other generals. Thirteen stars represented the original thirteen states, and the year "76" was illuminated above.

Lafayette visited the Hermitage, Jackson's home, which lay a few miles upriver, receiving a tour of the appealing garden and lands, a tour marred, in Levasseur's words, only by the "spectacle" of slavery. Slave-owning had not affected George Washington's reputation, and indeed Washington's heirs lauded Jackson on February 22, 1825, Washington's birthday, when Lafayette was pressed into service on behalf of the first president's family. He was asked to convey a relic to the Tennessee hero, a ring containing a sample of George Washington's hair, of the color it was at the time of the Revolution.

Before Lafayette's visit to the Hermitage ended, his host showed off one more prized possession that associated him with Washington: a pair of pistols presented by Lafayette to his commander in 1778. The French visitor acknowledged these as genuine, and politely assured their new possessor that he was worthy of such tokens of esteem. Jackson blushed, then recovered, pressing the pistols and Lafayette's hands to his own breast. "Yes! I believe myself worthy of them," he exclaimed, "if not for what I have done, at least for what I wished to do for my country." Those present reflexively cheered Jackson's confident statement.[36]

The Lafayette party left Nashville and headed for Louisville, Kentucky, accompanied by Tennessee Governor Carroll, who had fought with Jackson at New Orleans. They were awakened from their sleep in the middle of the night of May 8, as the vessel on which they powered up the Ohio suddenly received an "extraordinary concussion." With their boat sinking and passengers nervously crying out names in the darkness, Lafayette's manservant, Bastien, dressed the aging aristocrat. Struggling onto the tilting deck from his cabin below, Lafayette resisted moving to the safety of a smaller batteau until the other passengers were all safe, but he was finally persuaded off the fated vessel.

According to Levasseur, the real hero that night was George Lafayette, who calmly remained with the sinking boat long enough to see that Bastien, who was desperately trying to save his personal effects, left before it was too late. They recovered what they could at daybreak, as the barefoot Governor Carroll helped row to the wreck; all were ferried on to Louisville, after which the indefatigable general agreed to cross the Ohio once again to satisfy the citizens of neighboring Jeffersonville, Indiana. From Louisville, the persevering troop moved overland to Lexington. Here the general paused to visit the Ashland estate of the charismatic Henry Clay, who had just been appointed secretary of state by President Adams. Clay was hard at work in Washington, but his amiable wife Lucretia, long cherished for her kindness in Washington circles, was present, and proved a gracious hostess in his absence.[37]

There was something else of significance during the brief Lexington stopover: as the chairman of the town's trustees reminded their distinguished guest, their county had been the first in the United States to be "called after your name." Fayette County had come into being, he said, because "the first settlers in this Western Wilderness" were impressed by "your memorable exertions in the glorious struggle, which resulted in the establishment of our Freedom and Independence as a nation." And so, Lexington endeavored to make the general's single day there a special one. He was given a suite of apartments, "fitted up," as the town's newspaper reported, "with great taste and elegance, and adorned with a profusion of fresh flowers." After a night's rest, the "amiable and gallant old Soldier" sat for a Masonic breakfast, where baskets of fresh oranges and lemons were placed before him, accented with roses and fragrant honeysuckle. At the end of a day of touring—at the university, an ode was spoken by one Thomas Jefferson Jennings, a senior—a ball was held in Lafayette's honor, in a room that accommodated fully eight hundred ladies and gentlemen, its walls decorated with pictures of Lafayette, Washington, Jefferson, Clay, "a beautiful transparency of Daniel Boon [sic]" (the prototypical Kentucky pioneer), and the "poets, orators, and heroes" of the ancient world.[38]

On May 19, Lafayette arrived in Cincinnati, "a handsome city," according to Levasseur, where the river flowed peaceably. Thirteen guns fired their salute, as cries of "Welcome Lafayette," echoed. In his prepared remarks, former Ohio congressman and future president William Henry Harrison boasted of the state's widespread prosperity. Levasseur was suitably impressed: "The simple progress of its population borders on the marvellous. In 1790 there were in it only 3000, whilst at present there are nearly 800,000. In 1820 the town of Cincinnati contained only 9642 inhabitants, now it has 18,000." This pivotal region formed the supple spine along a "great line of internal navigation" linking New York and New Orleans, and, as Levasseur was always quick to point out, "A slave becomes free as soon as he touches the happy soil of Ohio." He was anticipating Harriet Beecher Stowe, who would later dramatize this fact in the opening sequence of *Uncle Tom's Cabin;* in her novel the Ohio River serves as a moral divide and excites powerful consequences.[39]

Along his route from Ohio to Niagara Falls, Lafayette stopped in Pittsburgh, where some soldiers of the Revolution tested his memory. One who presented himself was the recruit who had been the first to offer to carry the wounded Lafayette from the Brandywine battlefield in 1777. "No, I have not forgotten Wilson," the general embraced him, as he recalled the man's name. Another was a clergyman, whom Lafayette still recognized, and who, despite his professional calling, had shouldered a musket to fight alongside the French volunteer.[40]

"Plunged in a reverie" of a different kind during their visit to Niagara Falls, the Lafayette party exchanged the awful roaring of electrified nature for the quiet constancy of the Erie Canal, which led 363 miles east to the Hudson River at Albany. This marvel of American engineering was in its very first year of complete operation, destined to accelerate the pace of industrial progress and social change. At Lockport, as the deafening sounds of new detonations and shattering rock tailed off, Levasseur noted: "No where have I seen the activity and industry of man conquering nature so completely as in this growing village. In every part may be heard the sound of the hatchet and hammer. Here trees are felled, fashioned under the hands of the carpenter, and raised on the same spot in the form of a house; there, on a large public square, which exists as yet only in project, an immense hotel already opens its doors to new settlers, who have not any other habitation." It was a picture of a people on the move, ambitious, undeviating, and unstoppable. Aided by steady horses along the towpath, the French party enjoyed "the comforts of life" in their canal boat, plodding east along the artificial waterway, almost to Albany. They picked up the journey on land and arrived back in Boston on schedule, a few days in advance of the fiftieth anniversary of the Battle of Bunker Hill.[41]

June 17, 1825, was a fine, sunny day, and the heat nowhere near as stifling as it had been on the day of the battle half a century before, when volunteer militiamen, short on ammunition but accurate with their muskets, had stood their ground against a succession of direct attacks by red-coated professional soldiers coming at them in close formation. It was one of the bloodiest encounters of the war. Fifty years later, leaders of the Masonic order conducted Lafayette, in an open carriage, along a processional march to the battle site, where he helped lay the cornerstone of a new monument. Even more than her view of Lafayette, Virginia traveler Anne Royall was deeply touched by the living history she beheld: A withered old man sat propped up in a moving carriage. Dressed in an old coat, bullet holes distinctly visible in it, he waved his old army shot-bag back and forth, so that people could see that it still contained the bullets he had relied upon at this place a half-century before. The future author and journalist was equally impressed by the incomparable patriotism and raw intelligence she sensed among Bostonians.[42]

The main speaker of the day was New England's dark-eyed oratorical talent, Congressman Daniel Webster. Fifteen thousand heard Webster's address in all its grandeur and display. "This uncounted multitude before me and around me proves the feeling which the occasion has excited," he began. "These thousands of human faces, glowing with sympathy and joy . . . proclaim that the day, the place, and the purpose of our assembling have made a deep impression on our hearts." To Webster, Bunker Hill symbolized national unity and national resolve. He spoke earnestly about the power of memory, how historical incidents always served as a guide for posterity. He predicted that the greatest of all memorable events on the international stage would long continue to be what he termed "the wonder and the blessing of the world"—the American Revolution. Its principles were bound to endure, he proclaimed, because "Human beings are composed, not of reason only, but of imagination also, and sentiment." With his faith in the power of knowledge, Webster hailed America's present pursuit of progress: "Our proper business is improvement," he said. "Let our age be the age of improvement."[43]

The celebrations continued. On the Fourth of July, 1825, the forty-ninth anniversary of American Independence, Lafayette witnessed the festivities in New York City. As the clock struck midnight, artillery announced that the day was at hand. From daylight, the streets of the city were lively and, as Levasseur put it, "the air resounded with thanksgiving." The French visitors heard the annual public reading of the Declaration of Independence, appreciative of the fact that the revered document was also being read in many homes, where it was hung on walls as a "splendidly framed" engraving, with facsimile signatures.[44]

Then, Lafayette and company moved on to Washington, D.C., to mark an official end to the long visit. When they had reposed there the previous summer, Monroe's presidency was winding down. Now Adams was in office. John Quincy Adams was no stranger; Lafayette had known him since 1785, when, as the eighteen-year-old son of a diplomat, Adams had accompanied his father to Parisian dinner parties (the younger Adams described the then four-year-old George Lafayette as "a very pretty child"). In the spring of 1815, after heading the delegation that negotiated an end to the War of 1812, John Quincy Adams lingered in Paris, and the genial Lafayette insisted on entertaining him at La Grange, his country estate. In his diary, Adams described the impressive setting: "The General took me out to see his flocks of merinos, of which he has a thousand, his cattle, and his horses. . . . His park was laid out by a painter, in the English style, and is beautifully picturesque. He has surrounded his house with trees— poplars, willows, pines, firs, locus, and the horse-chestnut and oak at further distance." There they spoke of the general's hope for a more representative system of government in France, causing Adams to reflect privately on Lafayette's demeanor—"always cheerful." It was precisely ten years later, and their roles were reversed: he was Adams's guest at the Executive Mansion.[45]

Before returning to France, Lafayette was determined to visit with Virginia ex-Presidents Jefferson, Madison, and Monroe one last time. On August 20, 1825, they all convened at Monticello. Lafayette found Jefferson, now less than a year from death, lacking the spirit he had shown in 1824: "enfeebled health kept him . . . in a state of painful inaction."[46] The moment was bittersweet; the parting that all four of these eighteenth-century men resisted was, inescapably, the final goodbye to their younger visions, which they all cast in a pure light.

Back in Washington, Lafayette's last gatherings with his American friends were all tinged with a comparable sorrow. The new frigate *Brandywine*, named after his first American battle, was being outfitted nearby to take the general home. The era of the Revolution had ended much earlier, but in the autumn of 1825, ten months before America was to celebrate the national jubilee, the war was being consecrated in doleful displays. At the center of every such scene stood a beloved French friend.

A final outpouring of the emotion that Lafayette's return had brought occurred on September 7, as President Adams, surrounded by his cabinet, paid homage at the President's House. Interested observers watched through the open doors. "General Lafayette," Adams spoke, "it has been the good fortune of many of my distinguished fellow-citizens . . . to greet you with the welcome of the nation." Recalling Lafayette's pivotal role in giving birth to the United States—what Adams termed a more amazing series of events than "the fairest fable of antiquity"—he noted that the Frenchman had consistently acted with unrivaled magnanimity. America had had five decades to take to heart this fact of one man's devotion.[47]

The president continued to press the issue of generational transition. Of the general officers who had served in the Revolution, who had fought to secure America's happiness, "You alone survive." Meanwhile, he said, a new generation had risen, a generation well taught by their elders in the practice of freedom. The reserved Adams was speaking with a kind of fervency that was unusual for him: "You have been received with rapture, by the survivors of your earliest comrades in arms: You have been hailed as a long-absent parent by their children, the men and women of the present age!"

The president's remarks stopped short of tedium or maudlin excess. The *Brandywine* awaited its passenger, to carry him back to "the land of brilliant genius, of generous sentiment, of heroic valor." Admittedly, Lafayette belonged to France, yet America, too, Adams said, would "claim you for our own . . . , ours by that tie of love, stronger than death, which has linked your name, for the endless ages of time, with the name of Washington." He then bade Lafayette "a reluctant and affectionate farewell."[48]

The general repaid this unusually warm address with his own words of gratitude and commitment: "God bless you, sir, and all who surround us. God bless the American people, each of their states, and the federal government. Accept this patriotic farewell of an overflowing heart; such will be its last throb when it ceases to beat." According to Levasseur, as he spoke these words Lafayette "threw himself into the arms of the president, who mingled his tears with those of the national guest." A vast crowd stood at the edge of the Potomac as the hero set sail, and a short while later, as he stared south, a pensive Lafayette took in a last view of Mount Vernon. The next morning, passing through the Chesapeake under full sail, all on board the *Brandywine* were witness to a brilliant rainbow, fulfilling for posterity every possible metaphor needed for the story of Lafayette's return to constitute a new and wondrous patriotic myth.[49]

IF LAFAYETTE'S commitment to the ideal of liberty had impelled him in 1776 to join Washington's "family," his emotional return in advance of the national jubilee enabled him to experience the poignancy of memory—his own and that of the Americans who clamored to see him and express renewed gratitude. Two generations, a fast-fading and a fast-rising one, came together to mark the meaning and character of the Revolution. It was a moment of self-conscious thanksgiving. It was an act of naming—and thereby moving past—a heroic age.

What distinguished the particular patriotism of the jubilee year, as we shall see, was a people's sense of their extended range. They felt growth. They charted a physical expansion that seemed to them never-ending. This is why a kind of wandering quality pervades their texts. As they thrilled to the activities of the touring French general, Americans were busier than ever before and, at the same time, willingly caught in their romantic reconception of the Revolutionary past. History contained both moral lessons and the seeds of promise.

The people of 1826 were practical enough in prescribing a brand of national development they called "internal improvements," the road and canal building and river traffic that brought their settlements closer. They were able to combine compassionate feeling with unadulterated profit seeking, science with experiments in spirituality. In this elastic universe of their creation they recognized themselves as a people engrossed in a heated kind of politics, while accommodating the dreamy state of things that their quasi-religious adoration of the Revolutionaries afforded. Political division was profound and injurious, but the spirit of '76 sustained the many who otherwise would have bemoaned the nation's fate.

This book's journey is undertaken in a similar mode to Lafayette's and Levasseur's. It revisits many of the people and places that we have just seen through the lens given us by Levasseur. But in relating the history of the same generation from a far greater distance, we inevitably contend with changing perspectives. As guests of a special character, the French entourage was obliged to honor certain patriotic presumptions; as inquisitors of a different kind in different times, we undertake our task more critically. We are not unsympathetic, but neither are we bound by convention. We serve our present by reporting on an unfamiliar state of mind, and by attempting to do so judiciously.

This is not to denigrate Levasseur's discussion of Americans' blemishes in addition to their cultivated features. Much of what he wrote was wise and worthy of our notice. Levasseur's account still conveys a personal engagement that is deeply moving. *America's Jubilee* could do worse than to treat its subject in the manner of the French traveler. We will be observing an expectant people, the Revolution's successors, as he did, and seeing them through the fiftieth anniversary of Independence, which he did not—through to its final utterances. We do so to capture, as Lord Byron put it, "all that Memory loves the most."

CHAPTER TWO

The Benevolently Disposed
Mr. Wirt Sends Kisses

I F THE AMERICANS of 1826 were a people of longings, underappreciated by later historians, no better symbol exists to warrant their resuscitation than William Wirt. A name known to very few by the twentieth century, he was once a nationally prominent figure—indeed a virtuoso. Author of fiction and biography, a famed trial attorney who argued several of the most significant Supreme Court cases of his era, he also holds a record for government service that remains unbroken, as U.S. attorney general for twelve successive years, through the administrations of James Monroe and John Quincy Adams.[1]

Wirt arguably did more than anyone else of his generation to link the Romantic movement in America with the Revolutionary spirit.* When all was said and done, it was Wirt whom the city of Washington selected to cap off the season of observances in 1826 with a masterful oration in the U.S. Capitol—Wirt, who had devoted his public career to furthering the work of the founders; Wirt, who admitted to having wept "like a child" on reading newspaper accounts of Lafayette's welcome in 1824; Wirt, whose serialized essays, *Letters of the British Spy*, had much earlier established for him a reputation as a patriot susceptible to outbursts of emotion in defense of the national heart. But it was his *Life of Patrick Henry*, first published in 1817 (the same year that he

* Nineteenth-century American Romanticism is best understood as an emotionalized form of the inherited political concepts of reason and virtue.

received his appointment to the cabinet), that delivered the pathos and poignancy which gave him the credentials for conveying the general spectacle of the nation's jubilee.

If the stirring orator Patrick Henry was the voice that announced the arrival of the Revolution, his biographer, then, would become the voice that sacralized the jubilee. Wirt had conceived an oratorical standard to suit the Romantic age: "The *hearts* of the audience," he wrote, "will refuse all commerce except with the *heart* of the speaker." Wirt was a man of legal sagacity who also lavished soulful words, who could perceive godliness in the natural world and in human contemplation of bettering it: "I cannot, for instance, look abroad on the landscape of spring, wander among blooming orchards and gardens, and respire the fragrance which they inhale, without feeling the existence of a God: my heart involuntarily dilates itself, and, before I am aware of it, gratitude and adoration burst from my lips." In 1826, a year when granite or marble monuments to Revolutionary greatness were being erected, thoughtful men readily (rhetorically) acknowledged that their "feeble" powers enabled them to do nothing more to commemorate heroic deeds than to offer up "cold and lifeless" objects of stone that would eventually turn to dust; and so they looked to Wirt for persuasive eloquence, in order, they said, to do better justice to the valued past, to express in precious words the successor generation's adoration for the wisdom of those they called "departed worthies."[2]

Wirt was a classic overachiever. His dual purpose in life was to be wealthy and to be well liked. Conceiving his *Life of Patrick Henry* as a means to both ends, he had embarked in 1805 on what became a twelve-year project. He called it an "intimate" portrayal of a model of Revolutionary integrity, whose greatest mark of fame was his humbleness, and who spoke a secular gospel that continued to define right and patriotic commitment for the next generation. The biographer wrote with a zeal that was barely distinguishable from ecstatic religious experience. Given that no reliable text of Patrick Henry's Revolutionary speeches existed, Wirt therapeutically confided to his favorite correspondent how the imagination interfered with his historical project: "the style of the narrative, fettered by a scrupulous regard to real facts, is to me the most difficult in the world. It is like attempting to run, tied up in a bag. My pen wants perpetually to career and frolic it away." And so, only a romantic truth has survived.[3]

His pose was that of the consummate American gentleman, purposeful, proud, and deferential to the cause of '76. He cites in the preface as his "pure" authorities a range of men who closely interacted with Patrick Henry in the Revolution. These encompassed Henry's childhood neighbors in Virginia, distinguished legislators and judges, and even Thomas Jefferson. Conventionally, Wirt apologized for any remaining "defects" in his book, but he relied at the same time on the indulgence of those he called his "benevolently disposed" readers, hoping that they might use his suggestive anthology to tap their own historical imaginations and, with a pleasure they themselves were meant to generate, recapture the outstanding character of his hero.[4]

Employing the same convention, then, proposing that the reader's fancy ultimately produces the most useful image of the subject, this chapter seeks to do for Wirt what Wirt did for Henry—to sketch the career of a bold patriot. In the present case, though, the benevolent disposition of the reader and the benevolent disposition of the subject are of equal measure.

Wirt had his own admiring nineteenth-century biographer, John Pendleton Kennedy, who described his subject at the opening of his two-volume work as a tall man with clear blue eyes and arching eyebrows, broad shoulders, and a massive chest, his facial expression alternately sober and "radiant with a rich, lurking, quiet humor."[5] Ultimately, Wirt is the centerpiece of the present chapter because he was a man whose great exertions make him a compelling example of masculine ambition in the year of national jubilee.

William Wirt was born, unpromisingly, to a tavern owner in Bladensburg, Maryland, a town just outside Washington, D.C., in 1772. His father was Swiss, his mother German, and William the youngest of their six children. Both parents died by the time he was eight, and his modest inheritance was exhausted by his fifteenth year. Thus he received an education only through the philanthropy of an early classmate's father, and as an adult, even as a successful attorney, he would always be plagued by the memory of these tenuous circumstances—no matter what he did he would never come to feel financially comfortable. In the prime of his life, while maintaining household slaves and supporting a large family, William Wirt employed himself in every way he could: he wrote from the heart, gave public speeches, peripatetically advertised his legal services, argued cases before the Supreme

Fig. 2. A Byronic likeness of Attorney General William Wirt, from the frontispiece of the 1850 Philadelphia edition of John P. Kennedy's *Memoirs of the Life of William Wirt.*

Court—and despite it all never felt that business was sufficient to meet expenses or fulfill his honorable ambition. The more he earned, and the more visible his public presence, the more an inner contentment seemed to elude him.

He was what a successful lawyer had to be in early America: a man with numerous acquaintances, an attractive character who found patrons and rose through the social ranks. Establishing a practice in Virginia in the 1790s, he romanced the daughter of Thomas Jefferson's friend and neighbor Dr. George Gilmer, a successful planter. This match enlarged Wirt's circle of friends to include some politically connected Virginia names, but the premature death of Mildred Gilmer Wirt in 1799 (the same year that Patrick Henry died) cast a dark cloud over her young husband that led him into a period of gambling and dissipation, from which he only emerged in 1802 with his successful suit of Elizabeth Gamble, eighteen-year-old daughter of a wealthy merchant, Robert Gamble of Richmond.[6]

From this point, Wirt's fortunes improved steadily. He specialized in criminal cases in Norfolk, Richmond, and Williamsburg, and, in spite of what he may have thought of the defendant, orchestrated the acquittal of the man (the victim's nephew) accused in the poisoning death of the much beloved George Wythe, a signer of the Declaration of Independence and law tutor to both Thomas Jefferson and Henry Clay. Most notably, though, in 1807 Wirt was given the lead role in the government's prosecution of visionary ex–Vice President Aaron Burr for treason against the United States in having purportedly conspired to sever areas of the Western frontier from the Union. Chief Justice John Marshall, President Jefferson's most inveterate detractor, presided at the Richmond trial, naming John Randolph of Roanoke, the president's principal critic within his own party, as foreman of the grand jury. As prosecutor, Wirt had an uphill battle.

The rising attorney made himself conspicuous when he advocated the doctrine by which a president could determine which documents were critical to national security and could thus legitimately be denied to the defense. Wirt battled obstructive motions with a flair and oratorical fervor that impressed the court and the country. Although it was clear that Burr had been concocting something, the defendant's physical presence at that place where the conspiracy was launched could not be proven—this being Chief Justice Marshall's overly demanding definition of treason. Wirt countered with a persuasive speech:

> If it require actual presence at the scene of assemblage to involve a man in the guilt of treason, how easy will it be for the principal traitor to avoid this guilt and escape punishment forever? He may go into distant states, from one state to another. He may secretly wander like a demon of darkness, from one end of the continent to the other.
>
> He may enter into the confidence of the simple and unsuspecting. He may pour his poison into the minds of those who were before innocent. He may seduce them into a love of his person, offer them advantages, pretend that his measures are honorable and beneficial, connect them in his plot and attach them to his glory. He may prepare the whole mechanism of the stupendous and destructive engine and put it in motion. Let the rest be done by his agents. He may then go a hundred miles from the scene of action. . . .[7]

Wirt loved allusions. In the course of the trial, he sought to expose the opposing counsel's deceptions by referring to certain remarks as "meteors of the brain which spring up with such exuberant abundance," "flying in the path of reason or sporting across it with fantastic motion" so as to "decoy the mind from the true point in debate." With feigned humility, he called his own argument "naked as a sleeping Venus, but certainly not half so beautiful." Employing theatrics to decry theatricality, the orator played to his audience.[8]

Though Wirt lost, the Burr prosecution made his name as both a model orator and an outstanding lawyer. Another of his speeches during the Burr trial became a text that nineteenth-century schoolchildren were asked to memorize; it rapturously defended the honor and integrity of a man named Harman Blennerhassett, whom Burr had duped. Many eminent individuals attended the trial and heard Wirt; they were as impressed with the thoroughness of his preparation as they were with his delivery. He was now a favorite of President Jefferson, who praised Wirt's "talents and correct views" and urged him in 1808 to seek a congressional seat. But the trial attorney politely refused, explaining that "I have a wife and children entirely unprovided for. They subsist on the running profits of my practice." He professed, too, that his temperament was not suited for the "cruel and diabolical insinuations" to which elected officials were subject. Only after he had achieved a comfortable fortune, he imagined—and so informed the president—could he even conceive of submitting himself to a life of public service; and then, he allowed, he would finally be able to do so with the requisite "spirit and ardor."[9]

It was with spirit and ardor that Wirt had been preparing his *Life of Patrick Henry* since 1805. In what the humbly born biographer termed "detached sketches," he was finally able to celebrate, at a high point in his own public career, the fairy-tale rise of the outwardly deficient Patrick Henry. This was the saga of a young man of no apparent promise, a failed Hanover County storekeeper who wished to practice law as a way to avoid poverty—a person with no great attachment to the principle of justice. Wirt confided to his friend Dabney Carr that his study of Henry revealed both "ugly traits" and "ugly blanks." But an altruistic strain in William Wirt carried into his prose, and he worked to translate homeliness into genius.[10]

Or perhaps it was more than simply an altruistic strain. Wirt's own flirtation with masculine indulgences before his second marriage continued to both unnerve and excite him. Henry was just a more immoderate example of what he himself had experienced. The future Revolutionary's reluctance to study was almost as pronounced as his passion for entertainment; indeed, the tavern had served as his first office. The best that could be said of him was that he possessed, according to Wirt, "cheerfulness of spirit" and, perhaps more important, "acuteness of feeling." Wirt admitted to Carr his own burning desire for literary fame, his own preference for the "lighter works of the imagination" over "grave history." If his letters are to be believed, Wirt had a dark side, a torment that fed his tenderness toward Henry; he and his subject shared, in his mind, an "acuteness of feeling."[11]

Wirt's consciousness of his own rise from obscurity never went away either. Henry's restlessness, for this reason, was something to which Wirt easily related. Contemplating his daughter's prospective choice of a husband, Wirt would write to his wife in 1826 that "many of the most illustrious men of England were the sons of mechanics—and so in our own country—Patrick Henry's father was a Scotch schoolmaster, Mr. Jefferson's the surveyor of a county—Old John Adams was himself a school master." He added that Edmund Pendleton, patriot, member of the Continental Congress, and celebrated presiding judge of the Virginia Court of Appeals from the Revolution until his death in 1803, "was himself in early life a shoe-black in a clerk's office."[12]

The right kind of modesty appealed to Wirt. Henry provided him with a supreme exemplar of that breed of Virginian who, like Chief Justice John Marshall, were known for their slovenly attire, jaunty nonchalance, and boisterous self-assurance—unconvincing traits, it would seem, but traits that, when combined with a perceptible intelligence, won the respect of a protective circle of important friends. "The only badge of nobility," Wirt told his wife, "is personal worth." Not surprisingly, they named a son, born in 1818, "Henry Wirt."[13]

It was "acuteness of feeling," then, that in biographer Wirt's mind was destined to connect America's greatest orator to popular causes. Nature had accorded to Patrick Henry a certain genius that needed years—and a great crisis—to awaken. What could be more democratic, more consistent with nineteenth-century aspirations, than this humble child of nature, who was ultimately equal to any task?

Before the reader makes what would seem an obvious association, an important exception must be drawn: William Wirt cared little for that other child of raw nature, Andrew Jackson. He was to disparage the Tennessee general as hot-tempered and petulant, a fraud even, and a dangerous demagogue lacking every talent that *his* Patrick Henry came by through his unique sensory strength. It was not a "Jacksonesque" phenomenon that Wirt sought to identify in his imaginative biography of the Revolutionary herald, but something that transcended the savage courage of the Hero of New Orleans. Wirt had never met Henry. He was not burdened by what many of the Revolutionary leaders understood, what Thomas Jefferson had observed and had strongly conveyed to the solicitous Wirt—that Henry's knowledge of the law was "not worth a copper," that Wirt's hero in fact was "avaritious & rotten hearted." Jefferson put it bluntly: "His two great passions were the love of money & of fame: but when these came into competition the former predominated."[14] Wirt registered Jefferson's comments, but chose to overlook them. He saw too much of his own complexity in Henry. He could not permit himself to make Henry as simple as a past mirror of the Jackson quality: rustic, unhewn, hearty, masculine, charismatic, a man whose mere presence excited. One day William Wirt himself would run for the office of president of the United States, solely to offer a thoughtful alternative to the reckless Tennessean. If the rude Patrick Henry, in all his splendor as an orator, with his thrilling message of hope for an independent United States, was not presidential material, then certainly Washington, D.C., was no place for the unfathomable, intellectually obtuse Jackson.

What, then, was Wirt attempting? In painting his subject as "naturally kind and obliging," he gradually fashioned a moral hero capable of sublime achievements. Henry's first court appearance, in 1758, gave Wirt his first opportunity to deliver drama. The untested attorney faced the most learned, most severely critical men of Virginia. The courthouse was packed, with an "immense and anxious throng" listening at the door. Henry rose "awkwardly," he "faltered much," and "people hung their heads at so unpromising a commencement." Then, all of a sudden, the failed storekeeper's "wonderful faculties" revealed themselves; "and now was first witnessed that mysterious and almost supernatural transformation of appearance, which the fire of his own eloquence never failed to work in him." He glowed, and stood erect, and "genius awakened." Wirt sought only superlatives: "nobleness and grandeur," "lightning in his eyes," "graceful, bold, and commanding" action, "magic"—the sum of it all "struck upon the ear and upon the heart, *in a manner which language cannot tell.*" Not enough? Wirt's Henry "painted to the heart with a force that almost petrified it." Those who were there recalled that "he made their blood run cold, and their hair to rise on end." Wirt's subject was immediately larger than life.

So astounded was the court at Henry's performance that it "lost the equipoise" of judgment. And so unwilling to resist his own romantic inclinations was Wirt that it did not trouble him to admit that in his research he had not even learned what the orator said on that day in 1758. Those he had interviewed who claimed to have been present at Henry's debut "seem to have been bereft of their senses. They can only tell you, in general, that they were taken captive." If Henry's strength lay in something other than substance, Wirt only cared that he performed effectively.[15]

His Henry was "made of good revolutionary materials." Being of the yeomanry, he belonged to the body of the people. He retained their manners, dressed in plain attire, ate "homely fare," and needed no contrivance to hold their "affections." In a "new theatre," the Virginia House of Burgesses, he acquired the character of a statesman without becoming intoxicated by his new respectability. The pithiness of his eloquence and imagination impressed his colleagues; he possessed an instinctive ability to condense long arguments into a single, persuasive line. Aristocrats were amazed by the "rugged might" of Henry, this "*phenomenon* from the plebian ranks." He stepped forward once again in May 1765, when the colonies first learned that they were to be taxed by Parliament and deprived of liberties they had formerly presumed. Seemingly alone in his wisdom, Henry spied imminent danger and introduced a bold set of resolves that were far less conciliatory than what his elders in the legislature had preferred.[16]

Self-government was not negotiable. Henry, at twenty-nine, took the lead in the Burgesses. With allusions to Samson and the Philistines, Wirt noted of his fiery hero's trenchant pose: "The fainthearted gathered courage from his countenance." Conservative elders cried out "Treason!" and Henry "faltered not for an instant." Recall that in his first court appearance, he did falter for an instant (to achieve Wirt's dramatic effect). Henceforth, Patrick Henry's course was irreversible; he could not be contained. The author's strategy had become to fashion his subject as a metaphor for the sublimity and awesome power of Nature, who unleashed "the most determined fire," "an incessant storm of lightning and thunder." Wirt's Henry was firmness itself; he was absolutely fearless. If Washington was the Revolution's voice of calm judgment and steady virtue for the second generation of American leaders, Henry was meant to be the embodiment of the Revolution's ardent spirit, its purging fire.[17]

The Revolution was unstoppable because Henry was unstoppable, in the literary conceit that Wirt adhered to. Henry was prescient: "His vision pierced deeply into futurity." His senses were keen and he "saw, with the eye and the rapture of a prophet." Before anyone else, it was he who portended, "She [Britain] *will* drive us to extremities—no accommodation *will* take place—hostilities will *soon* commence—and a desperate and bloody touch it will be." If one is to believe Wirt, the orator with the uncanny, perhaps extrasensory ability not only *spoke* with a purpose and effect that surpassed his peers, but *saw* beyond the norm as well. Before the Continental Congress had even met, he was said by one of Wirt's credible correspondents to have used the phrase "our Declaration of Independence" in speaking to the forlorn hope of reconciliation. Henry's audience at the time was astounded when these words were uttered, "for they had never heard any thing of the kind before even suggested." Wirt's Henry awakened possibilities.[18]

Wirt's purpose, of course, was to restore the Revolution to living memory for his generation, even if his book had to take on a quasi-mythical character. To make the patriotic past present, he would have to lift up oratorical culture, embellishing as necessary. Readers were meant to imagine that because clairvoyant Patrick Henry had let slip the words "Declaration of Independence," upstaging even Jefferson, the immortality of that document was insured. Patrick Henry had become, one-third of the way through the book, a mouthpiece for God's truth. When others were tongue-tied, or for some other reason stilled, he had to be present to initiate action, to make sure that the providentially ordained Revolution occurred.

The First Continental Congress convened in Philadelphia in September 1774. Henry was there, Wirt tells us, along with America's "most eminent men." These giants were strangers yet, and awed by each other's reputations. For a time they could not break from a "long and deep silence"—and a moment later Wirt repeats: "deep and death-like silence." Wirt rendered the solemnity of the scene overwhelming:

the assembled delegates were reluctant to proceed, knowing that their business was "fearfully momentous." It was then that the prophet Henry rose to speak, letting all of them know that he understood what was inside them. Wirt explained: "he merely echoed back the consciousness of every other heart."

Substantively, what did Henry contribute to the Continental Congress? Again, Wirt cannot transcribe his words; seemingly it is enough to know that the patriot-oracle was present to accelerate destiny: "There was no rant—no rhapsody—no labour of the understanding—no straining of the voice—no confusion of the utterance. His countenance was erect—his eye steady—his action noble—his enunciation, clear and firm—his mind poised on its centre—his views of his subject comprehensive and great—and his imagination coruscating with a magnificence and a variety, which struck down even that assembly with amazement and awe." Where Wirt was concerned, Henry's job in Philadelphia was done when he ignited minds and inspired communion. "He delighted to swim the flood, to breast the torrent, and to scale the mountain," but he would yield when it came to the "masters of the pen." The unlettered Henry would yield so that he could release his energies in less exalted settings, where common people could flock to their hero; he was formed to be "left at large, to revel in all the wildness and boldness of nature." Others wrote the Revolution; Henry enacted it.[19]

Wirt's dramatic exposition of Henry's prowess culminates in his treatment of the period preceding Lexington and Concord, when the man of action and inspiration displayed an unmatched courage in standing up to British might. The king's spokesmen were issuing mild addresses, all the while preparing to compel submission. Well-intentioned colonists were continuing to express their fond hopes that peace would return. Henry, however, "saw things with a steadier eye and a deeper insight. His judgment was too solid to be duped by appearances; and his heart too firm and manly to be amused by false and flattering hopes." In Richmond, on March 20, 1775, Virginia convened an assembly in which Henry directed the whirlwind. His "unerring prescience, that perfect command over the actions of men," led him to speak with a new kind of self-possession: "Let us not," he addressed the convention, "deceive ourselves any longer. . . . An appeal to arms and to the God of hosts, is all that is left us!" With this, Henry contrived his most famous words. As Wirt related it:

> "I know not what course others may take; but as for me," cried he, with both his arms extended aloft, his brows knit, every feature marked with the resolute purpose of his soul, and his voice swelled to its boldest note of exclamation—"give me liberty, or give me death!"

Henry's audience was cast into a trance. The orator was proven to possess a "supernatural voice." All that was left was for Patrick Henry himself to take the field, to lead men against that force, contrary to nature, which threatened to extinguish the future.[20]

The biblical cadences in Wirt's narrative intensify. And so it was, in April 1775, even before Virginians had learned of the fighting outside Boston, that the royal governor seized the gunpowder stored in a public magazine in the colonial capital. The British had been made oppressive for the same reason that God had "hardened Pharaoah's heart"—in order to redeem the chosen people. Now it was up to patriots to tramp through a sea of blood to their deliverance, to prove themselves worthy of this "divine interference." A volunteer company formed under Henry's command. Gathering thousands as he marched, Henry proceeded to the seat of colonial government to exact payment for the symbolic powder. The governor denounced him. He termed Henry's act "extortion," his aim "rebellious." As Wirt tells it, the incident fulfilled Henry's mission: "the same man, whose genius had in the year 1765 given the first political impulse to the revolution, had now the additional honour of heading the first military movement in Virginia, in support of the same cause." The Revolution ran its course only because stout, sturdy hearts refused to be deterred by conservative, reasoning heads. Thomas Jefferson would write similarly after the war was won: the Head had recoiled before Britain's superior "wealth and numbers," while the Heart had "saved our country." For Wirt, it was Henry who had caused that heart to beat.[21]

Yet at Monticello, in 1824, Jefferson commented to visitors from Boston, Congressman Daniel Webster and Professor George Ticknor, that Wirt's book was "written in bad taste, and gives an imperfect idea of Patrick Henry. It seems written less to show Mr. Henry than Mr. Wirt."[22] If Jefferson's observation is accurate—and he knew Wirt well—then it relates directly to Wirt's desire to justify his own emergence as a member of the national elite. The Marylander had become a Virginian through marriage, but he did not have the pedigree of the Virginia gentleman—neither the name nor the inherited lands. As the writer of romantic literature, he fretted over his own destiny, working to resolve long-held fears through his reconstruction of Patrick Henry. Concluding his romantic biography by restating the character of the hero in terms that mirror his own self-image, Wirt described Henry as "one of the kindest, gentlest, and most indulgent of human beings." Though Wirt himself was widely read and Henry, in this regard, indisputably lazy, the Revolutionary orator had read from "the great volume of human nature. In this, he was more deeply read than any of his countrymen." The basis of character, then, was *strong natural sense.*"[23]

Wirt the active lawyer, seeking a fortune and social acceptance, studied hard for each case. He wrote out long and thoughtful arguments—striving for what Henry seemed to effect effortlessly. Henry was his larger-than-life model of masculine performance. Glorifying the Revolution through his biographical subject, Wirt ignored the possibility that the real Patrick Henry could have been just what Jefferson considered him: vulgar and malicious.

For a true romantic, though, the facts ultimately are less true than the nostalgic vision. William Wirt reaped a long harvest from his lavish attachment to Patrick Henry. He protested often to correspondents his desire to write an accurate history, yet he did not respond directly when John Adams criticized Henry's source of power: "Oratory will always command admiration," the ex-president wrote the biographer. "But it deserves no great veneration." Adams in fact felt much as Jefferson did, that at the root of Wirt's project was the desire to feel good about the past rather than to know, in Adams's words, "the real origin" of the Revolution. Wirt revealed his total commitment to patriotic sentiment when he wrote Adams from Washington: "The present and future generations of our country can never be better employed than in studying the models set before them by the fathers of the Revolution."[24]

As a writer and as a public man Wirt wanted sorely to please. He especially fought to gain acceptance from the privileged old families of

Virginia. In an early newspaper essay, "The Old Bachelor" (1811), he wrote that the Virginians were of "a lofty and chivalrous spirit . . . , parent of the fairest virtues."[25] The closest Wirt would come to being a Virginia squire was, much later and only briefly, as a Florida slave-holder, investing in an estate called "Wirtlands." Influenced by the casual gallantry of Southern patricians, he became susceptible to all forms of masculine distinction and masculine competition that applied in their world—extending to the controversial practice of dueling.

He had first prepared to risk his life for honor by volunteering in the War of 1812, raising an artillery company to defend Richmond, though, as he put it to Dabney Carr, he fought mostly "in imagination," wherein "I have already beaten and captured four or five British detachments of two or three thousand each."[26] Five years later, just after *Patrick Henry* was published, Attorney General Wirt felt insulted by rival lawyer William Pinkney, and challenged him to a duel.

The two had tangled before the U.S. Supreme Court in 1816, and while he acquitted himself well in that encounter, Wirt displayed another side of himself—jealousy. He felt the need to disparage Pinkney in letters to his friends, telling Francis Walker Gilmer that the pleader put on an act, and lacked true substance, that his was "a dogmatizing absoluteness of manner" that had somehow fooled ordinary minds; "and he has acquired with those around him a sort of papal infallibility." Wirt nervously asserted to Dabney Carr, that "*with full preparation,* I should not be afraid of a comparison with Pinkney, *at any point,* before genuine judges of correct debate." Pinkney appeared overconfident, and Wirt wanted to put him in his place. But that would be difficult. Pinkney had preceded Wirt as U.S. attorney general, distinguishing himself in Madison's second administration, and had been wounded in battle during the War of 1812, in Wirt's birthplace of Bladensburg. An amateur hunter, the Maryland lawyer was considered a good shot besides.[27]

Wirt was a rising star if ever there was one in the young republic. Yet he could not stop feeling that his career was only precariously fixed. At this juncture in American history, the post of attorney general did not require constant attention—indeed, it assumed that the office-holder would continue to argue private cases. Just as being the government's top lawyer had helped Pinkney earlier, Wirt regarded the job as a station of honor that would attract more and wealthier clients to him.

Feeling vulnerable, however, he was moved to react to his rival's "rude remark" in a Maryland courtroom. Pinkney's language, he wrote, "was such as left me no alternative but resentment out of court."

Wirt described the unspecific insult as something that was bound to affect every aspect of his life. "I have a character to bear to my family," he explained, "the richest inheritance . . . that I can leave them." Dueling protocol understood that a man deprived of character would remain forever, as Wirt put it, "to wander, at large, a despised and contemptable *coward*, to be licked from the bar and to be kicked thro the earth, scorned by every eye." Challenged to a mortal encounter, Pinkney retracted what he had said, "a voluntary apology on the scene where the insult was given." By his own standard, Wirt had recovered his sense of honor and reputation. The erstwhile antagonists were able, then, to meet for breakfast a few days later, accompanied by the gentlemen who had earlier agreed to be their seconds.[28]

Unless he was certain that Pinkney would back down, Wirt could hardly have been thinking rationally when he issued his challenge. He was in Baltimore, his wife of sixteen years and their six daughters and three sons living in Richmond. Elizabeth Gamble Wirt was understandably perturbed that her husband had kept her in the dark about the duel—and would even think of risking the happiness of his large family: "Oh thought of horror and frenzy!" she moaned. "Have I been so near to being desolate[?]" Writing back, the overburdened attorney was unapologetic, admonishing her: "You are not a judge of these things, my love.—Your husband's honor should be left in his own hands."[29]

As a family man, William Wirt was both effusive and elusive. While away conducting his legal practice, he wrote home regularly (almost daily) and lovingly, but in his prime—including the dozen years that he served as attorney general—he spent little time with a wife who felt deserted and did not hesitate to tell him so. His public life always came first; domestic life for him was a pleasant distraction, and while in his letters he professed to yearn for it, he ever insisted on pursuing financial security first. Like many of his generation, he speculated, and not always wisely. The Wirts lived at the level of his greatest earning power, and the well-dressed children were either tutored or placed in expensive boarding schools, compelling him to maintain an eagle eye for clients.[30]

"Kiss [our] sweet ones for me," he wrote Elizabeth from the army in 1814. "Don't fail to write every mail." In letters home he termed his wife "my most beloved, most affectionate & most tenderly attentive." Recalling their closeness provided him, he said, "delicious moments," as he contrived: "My heart choaks me and my eyes are swimming: But these times will pass away and you will be again restored to my arms."[31] Though he indulged often in romantic hyperbole, he taxed his weary wife by adhering to a busy schedule. He continued to spend more time outside of Washington than in the capital, even after purchasing a spacious residence near the President's House in 1817, one fit for entertaining as well as for accommodating their large family.[32]

The Wirts' marriage was sustained by the regular mail coach that made a daily run between Washington and Baltimore. Elizabeth Wirt invariably responded to her husband's letters the day after he wrote them, and he answered hers in like fashion. During the mid-1820s hers were typically addressed to "My beloved Husband" and his to "My dearest love." Hers would end "Heaven bless you—ever & ever," and his "Love & kisses to all the dear children—Heaven bless you forever & ever." Both signed over the words "Your own," avowing their unbreakable commitment, even amid the strains caused by his insistent separations.

Serving President Adams, he continued to drum up business in Baltimore, and the gulf that separated him from domestic comforts widened. Wirt disappointed his family by staying away at Christmastime 1825, declaring on the twenty-fourth that "my heart sinks," and weakly wishing "Merry Xmass to you dearest love and to all our chickens" on the twenty-fifth. Neither his profession of anguish nor his lighthearted quip was of much cheer, however. On the twenty-sixth, as he was writing "I am surrounded by the documents in several cases that are pressing for trial," his wife was going through emotional chaos. Burdened by persistent headaches and sick young ones, Elizabeth wrote on that day that she attributed her condition to the cheesecake at Christmas dinner, rather than to the stress of another holiday spent without the children's father. This explanation, however, only partly concealed her deeper concern. Afflicted with sudden self-doubt, she wrote William: "Do you love me—or are you angry with me. I [dreamt] you had taken to yourself another wife." As is often the case with dreams, the object of her husband's affections appeared not as a young beauty but, inconceivably, "old Mrs. Turner . . . but somehow she did not live long to tease me ____ This was after hearing one of the children read a story of some Indian that had done the like—and the first wife killed herself by rowing to the falls of the Niagara." Then she abruptly closed the letter with a "Heaven bless you with health & peace."[33]

The next day, William wrote expansively to her from Baltimore, forgoing the usual salutation and opening with his ready passion:

> Do I love you? dearest—Ay, do I love you—and when I love you not, chaos is come again—angry with you? for what, my dearest, best of wives?—What a monster of sin and ingratitude should I be to be angry with you . . . sole partner of my heart, I am not angry with you—I know your worth—I give thanks to Heaven night and morning for having given me such a wife—and I love you with all the truth, all the holy fidelity, all the exclusive devotion that your own dear heart can ask or desire. What a dream was that? another wife!—I promise you that when I take another wife it shall be old Mrs. Turner of George Town—and now I think your heart may be at ease—another wife, another! Pray does your coach want a fifth wheel?[34]

Though his facility for language was unusually keen, the tension in their lives was most palpable. In 1823–24, he suffered from hemorrhoids. In 1825, pursuing private cases most of the time, the busy attorney general felt trapped in Baltimore and Annapolis and seemed desperately to want to extricate himself. "I am *very very* tired of these long separations," he complained that May, urging Elizabeth to take the Maryland stage around the Fourth of July and to bring their daughter Agnes with her. Not waiting for a reply, he optimistically met the incoming coach—"I felt a sort of lightening of the heart as if I should certainly see you and dear little Agnes"—but they had been forestalled by the illness of three of the other children. When will court recess? Elizabeth prodded him. "I doubt whether I shall be able to get home before the last of next week," he replied.[35]

Disappointments like these characterized their correspondence. His work represented to him "a painful sacrifice of the few pleasures of this fleeting life—but," he rationalized, "the object sanctifies it—I must get out of debt if possible before I die and leave you wherewithal to feed and clothe the dear children—This is the cause—and I must be content to suffer in it." And so, in November 1825, he wrote: "I shall hardly be settled at home 'til February. Work—work—work—money—money—money—wife and children—children—children." At least Elizabeth must have understood that his singular invocation of "wife" among his multiple concerns meant that she did not burden his mind to the degree of "work" and "money."[36]

Washington socialite Margaret Bayard Smith, whose pen never failed to depict people with all their blemishes, wrote of the two Wirt daughters she saw most, teenagers Catharine and Lizzy: "tho' they participate in the general amusements of society, it is with that moderation, which fulfills the precept of St. Paul, to use the world, but not abuse it." Catharine, though too often in "delicate health," was "one of the loveliest and most interesting creatures I have ever met with, and so tender, so carressing [sic], so delicate and soft in her manners." On one evening during the Adams years, in visiting the Wirts at home, Mrs. Smith encountered a scene that was, for her, domestic perfection. While Mrs. Wirt read by candlelight, her girls showed their guest their album of original poetry and painting, and later treated the company to music. Catharine sang "sweet songs" as she played the harp, then joined her sister Lizzy for a duet at the piano. Their father, in an uncharacteristic pose as a homebody, listened "in rapture," and interrupted several times to make certain that harp and piano were tuned within "half a hair's breadth" of each other.[37]

The eldest of the Wirts' children, Laura Henrietta, was twenty-three in 1826. When she was born, her father had chosen what he himself termed a "romantic" name, by combining the beloved "Laura" to whom the Renaissance poet Petrarch had dedicated his most affectionate verses, with the name of his own late mother, German-born Henrietta Wirt.[38] In the jubilee year, Laura was due to be married to Thomas Randall, an up-and-coming lawyer. Catharine and Lizzy were being readied for the marriage market—dressed in fine Parisian fashions as the Wirt house added new carpets and furniture to the room where gentleman callers were to be received. "If the room can be handsomely painted," the status-conscious William Wirt wrote his generally frugal wife, "it will be worth the carpet." Elizabeth expressed equal confidence that such measures would succeed in their object, that once Laura was "off," the two younger daughters would "come on." Hopeful about their daughters' prospects, the Wirts cultivated a fine, successful garden in the spring of 1826. Not only did the flowers look lovely, "the straw-berries are most abundant," as Catharine reported to her father. "We have had two days' feast of them, and it seems not to have made the least diminution, although we have had them for breakfast, dinner, & supper."[39]

Lizzy and Catharine boarded at Miss Garnett's school in Essex County, Virginia, not far from where Patrick Henry grew up. William Wirt consistently urged his daughters to apply themselves to their studies. He counseled them both in late 1825 that "the degree of improvement which is made depends more upon the scholar than the teacher. The best schools afford only the facilities for information; it rests with the scholar to make the most of these advantages." He felt only rebuke for those girls who returned from the best schools no better in "mind and manners" than when they arrived. "Learning is not *going* to *come* of its own accord," he wrote, accentuating the danger of passivity.[40]

Amid improvements of the nineteenth century, intellectual laziness on the order of Patrick Henry was less forgivable. "I am very desirous for you to become a good reader," Wirt wrote Lizzy. "I do not mean a rapid reader—that you are already—but a graceful and effective reader." Signing off as "Yr. affectionate father," the prolific, overworked attorney offered his "respectful accomplishments" to an acquaintance at the school, then crossed out his unintended slip of language, and laughed at his error: "(I am asleep—I mean compliments)." But it was, of course, "accomplishments," his *and* his daughters', that preyed on his mind.[41]

The dutiful Lizzy, back home for the Christmas holiday that William notoriously failed to partake in, wrote a long, discursive letter to her father in which—even with a mundane subject—she did her best to dramatize that erudition he clearly expected. "Mama has just returned from a day's bustling expedition of shopping," she began, "and is now seated by [seven-year-old] Henry's couch administering an emetic for his sore throat. She is so full o' care that she cannot sit down quietly to write. . . . All this preamble is to explain so unusual, surprising and unhoped for a happiness as a letter *from me*." Aping her father's satirical style, she defended herself against any deficiency he might find in her writing: if the letter lacked the spirit *"con amore"* of others, it was owing not to insufficient affection but to a miserable headache that had produced a "lassitude and aversion to all sorts of exertion."[42]

Writing again on Christmas Day, when her mother was so pained and disillusioned, Lizzy painted a portrait of domestic frolic: eggnog, comic songs, stockings, and "hearts full of joy and content." "We played at every game which has ever been in vogue since the tide of times as hide the thimble, magic music, criticism, &c." A hard rain prevented the family from attending church, but they made up for it at home by reading from a published Christmas sermon and singing a hymn. Their servants received gifts and shared in the family's joy, according to Lizzy, "and even the grumbling German baker has been so contagiously affected as to have sent in a *mammoth ginger cake*." Lizzy's plaint—her mother's persistent plaint—came at the end of the letter: "Oh my dear father how I wish you were here! Can't you be here on New Year's day? Ma & *all* the children send *best* love."[43]

The absent father met this one requirement, for on the morning of January 2, 1826, he paid a visit to President Adams at the Executive Mansion, which was situated only a short walk from the Wirt residence. Adams had urged Wirt to appear, to advise on an official matter, and Wirt proceeded to inform the president at their morning meeting that he was obliged to return promptly to Baltimore. Whether Lizzy's plea had had a weight comparable to the president's summons is not stated, but on January 4 the attorney general once again took the stage north.[44]

Lizzy remained a regular correspondent that season, although she, like the other Wirt women, routinely felt neglected by the busy breadwinner. On January 22, William wrote her:

> How are you, my beloved daughter? I suppose you think that because I haven't written to you I do not value your letters and care nothing for you—but if you think so—you are much mistaken—but you do not think so—knowing as you do that you have been your father's pet from your birth to this moment— Your letters afford me great gratification.

His gratification was meant to be shown in compliments on her letter writing, but these were trumped by his critical insistence that she do even better: "I like your off-hand way of writing," he affected, "collo-quial ease and sprightliness are the best characteristics of a letter—every thing stiff and formal and elaborately fine and sententious is revolting." But, he went on at length, she needed to do more to present fullness of thought without giving the product a belabored feel. His own letters were his model of agreeable writing:

> I pause too for expression—not for want of language—but to mend the expression to see whether it cannot be turned with more care and grace and spirit or stamped more impressively in the form of an aphorism. There is your racing letter—your gal-loping letter—and your cantering letter—Your rainy letters and such as sister Laura generally writes which are very good of their kind—but they give a sober man a vertigo to read them.

Employing wit was the way that letter writers of this period sought intimacy with their correspondents, and here Wirt clearly meant for his daughter to delight in sharing wordplay. Among his equine metaphors, the "cantering" letter was the one Wirt recommended to her most for friendly conversation, being "easy, sociable, and delightful . . . and your companion can keep up along side of you, too, without whipping, spurring, hard-trotting or any other inconve-nience." Finishing what he surely meant as a compassionate mode of instruction, Wirt assured his daughter that it was her innate talent and strong efforts—"the *materials*" she possessed—that compelled him to be so demanding of her. He feared, he said, that she might otherwise languish through "self neglect." Unknowingly, perhaps, the absent father was suggesting that he could distribute his love sufficiently by writing letters, and that daughter Lizzy, her mother's namesake, ought, as he had often begged of her besieged mother, to trust him, and to trouble him less about his absences. By making them all more self-sufficient, he could continue to rationalize his absences.[45]

Wirt had had a less than wholly sympathetic relationship with his sensitive eldest son Robert, who embarrassed the family with his rebel-lious antics while at the U.S. Military Academy at West Point in 1821, and who died in Europe (the journey at sea was meant to aid his health) of a lung ailment in late 1824. Wirt's last letter to his son, which arrived too late, grumbled: "I begin much to fear that we have acted imprudently in committing you to your own guidance, in the wayward state of your mind."[46]

But Wirt believed strongly in a rigorous female education, and in 1826 he permitted his name to be associated with the school of Mr. and Mrs. Bonfils, at F and Twelfth Streets in Washington (practically around the corner from his own home), that his ten-year-old, Agnes, attended. The school elaborately advertised itself as a place that conveyed what "young ladies" were meant to acquire: "all the scientific and ornamental branches, requisite to a useful and polite education." The French-speaking couple emphasized their native tongue in the home setting they established, with Spanish and Italian to round out "a finished English education." Yet theirs was an American school, offering lessons in penmanship, arithmetic, geography, rhetoric, grammar and conversation, poetry, astronomy, and moral philosophy. The tuition of $177 per quarter included instruction, dancing, drawing, room and board, fuel costs, and laundering service. Among the fifteen men of distinction who were listed as patrons of the school were Wirt and two other cabinet secretaries, James Barbour (Department of War) and Samuel Southard (Department of the Navy). Mr. and Mrs. Bonfils occasionally supped with the Wirts, enjoying their abundant strawberries that May.[47]

William Wirt's true favorite, it seemed, was young Agnes. He reveled in long letters to her that contained sweet stories, and dressed up his travels in language fit for the adoring child who he imagined was reading his every word in rapt attention. Thus, buying buttons for a dress became an adventure worthy of Lewis Carroll. Was it at Webb and Varnum's or Varnum and Webb's? Wirt playfully posed. He could not be certain:

> Nor am I perfectly sure that it was exactly a dozen buttons that was bought—very possibly it might have been only half a dozen or eight—your mother perhaps can remember this too, so that you can ask her; or if she should have forgotten, Varnum and Webb or Webb and Varnum (for as I have already said, I have really forgotten which name stands first) may possibly have made some entry on their books, that they may ascertain the precise

number. I say *possibly:* because it is by no means certain, the habits of different merchants being very different on such occasions.[48]

In December 1825, Mr. and Mrs. Bonfils's attentive pupil "Aggy," as Wirt sometimes called her, pronounced a problem for him to solve:

> What word would you use to express these words Sir stoop down and kiss me. there was a very tall gentleman and a low woman she asked him to stoop down and kiss her in one word what is the answer?

He replied in his next letter home: "Tell my dear Aggy that her question is 'a perfect conundrum' . . . I suppose her word is 'baizer' [in modern French, *baisser* and *baiser*]—because that word, at sea, signifies 'lower your flag' as well as 'kiss'—."[49]

In Baltimore, Wirt was often barraged with this kind of small request from home, and he left no child without his or her fair share of affectionate wit. He wrote an endearing P.S. on January 7, 1826, in which each mention of "kisses" was enclosed in a roughly shaped oval, meant to indicate the action of a kiss—and meant to be transferred from writer to recipient:

> My dear little Agnes—six kisses—because she always sends her bestest love to her dear father—and my blessed dear little monkey Hen [Henry] six more and then bless them all—for as my mind lights on each one, it thinks it most blessed—so kiss them all, *all to peices*—[50]

On January 21, he wrote of the influenza that was so prevalent across the country, and which Agnes had lately contracted. Assuring her that she was "a precious child and precious may you be in the sight of Heaven," he explained lightly that in Baltimore the flu was so common that "Even that dog just now under my window was manifestly hoarse with a cold and I dare say had something of a sore throat for he soon cut short his barking." Agnes recovered, and the kissing custom continued. To a newsy letter in May, she added a P.S., with the word

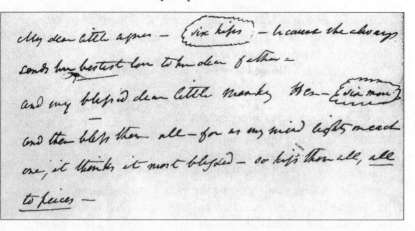

Fig. 3. Postscript from an affectionate letter of William Wirt to his ten-year-old daughter, Agnes, in 1826. *(Courtesy, Maryland Historical Society, Baltimore, Maryland.)*

"Kiss" circled and curled with her agile pen: "Kiss the word kiss for I have kissed it 4 times." Wirt responded immediately, and with the usual endearments, concluding his letter with a similarly adorned "18 kisses" and an explanation: "three a peice," to be delivered to the six of his children who were at home in Washington.[51]

William Wirt was in a rut. In April 1826, though, he was offered the presidency of the new University of Virginia by its founder, Thomas Jefferson. Wirt had visited Monticello the previous August, riding in the carriage of his old friend Judge Dabney Carr, who was Jefferson's nephew. At the time he was accompanied by his eldest, Laura, who was greeted by Jefferson's one surviving daughter, Martha Randolph, and given a tour of the Monticello art collection; but the ex-president had been feeling too ill to entertain company, "too unwell," Wirt wrote his wife, "even to be seen by me in his room." Thus, the April letter must have pleased Wirt, for it explained that he was so highly regarded in Virginia that if he did not accept Jefferson's offer, the position of president would be promptly eliminated by the Board of Visitors, which governed the university. And it was indeed, when Wirt refused to give up his itinerant life to settle in Charlottesville. Predictably, as an earnest purveyor of patriotic romance, a paragon of American ambition, a constant cavalier, and an inconstant lover, he preferred to press on as he had.[52]

He had acknowledged as early as 1805—only three years after his marriage to Elizabeth Gamble—that he aspired to a "patriarchal" presence, to be the father of a prospective twelve children. He quite nearly realized his plan: by 1826 Elizabeth had endured eleven pregnancies, and nine of their offspring still survived. Just as revealing, the careful attorney had also projected in 1805 his plan for an eventual release from the law, to be succeeded by the more fulfilling life of a landed gentleman. He knew, in a way, all along that he was just stargazing, modestly conceding: "I have seen too many luminaries, infinitely my superiors in magnitude and splendor, to believe myself a comet." He knew what most lawyers in early America could expect, that "independence, by my profession, is a great way off." And yet in 1805, at thirty-three, he felt the need to fantasize a future—the age of forty, he said—when he would begin to practice law "at my ease," and indulge more in "literary amusements."[53]

In 1826, he was in his fifty-fourth year. Dreams wavered and faltered, but they did not die. The occasional husband and father left his family to their own wits while he pursued, in their interest, he insisted, a life of determined toil. His benevolent disposition had already taken him far, but his wide-ranging activities amid an unending, Sisyphian drive for greater prosperity baffled and unsettled those he most loved. He was marveled at as an American virtuoso in 1826, but he was also a man of literary skill and profound sentiment who was pitifully unable to script his own happiness.

CHAPTER THREE

Eliza Foster Courts a
Chivalrous Spirit

A s the jubilee year approached, the American Revolution was, not surprisingly, a major theme in books. Joseph Sanderson's nine-volume *Biography of the Signers of the Declaration of Independence* came out gradually between 1823 and 1827. Just after Lafayette docked in New York harbor, William Wirt recommended that his Virginia friend Dabney Carr write a historical novel on the Revolution. It was New England, however, that led the field in embellishing American literature with Revolutionary themes.

In 1826, a thirty-two-year-old writer, Elisabeth Lanesford Foster of Brighton, Massachusetts, on the outskirts of Boston, idealized the commitment of Lafayette just as Wirt had zealously embraced his Patrick Henry. That year, the Boston printers Wells and Lilly published her two-volume novel of duty, glory, and threatened virtue in the closing days of the American Revolution: *Yorktown: An Historical Romance.* History has ignored this book and its author. Eliza, as she was known, was the unmarried daughter of John Foster, an outspoken Congregationalist Unitarian minister. We do not know what Eliza looked like, but we can easily surmise that she was enamored with Lafayette as a youthful hero.

She grew up in a respectable household. Reverend Foster was a graduate of Dartmouth College, ordained in 1784, who served in

Brighton for forty-three years. Yet it is Eliza's mother whose influence must appear the most pronounced; for while precious little is known about her, Hannah Webster Foster was a famous novelist, enjoying a literary reputation far greater than her daughter's. She found such success with one slender book as the more prolific Eliza would never attain—a success that was quite unusual for a woman of the Revolutionary generation. Eliza was only three when her mother's 1797 novel of seduction and tragedy, *The Coquette,* was published. By 1826, at least twenty editions had been issued; more would follow.

Yorktown was Eliza's second novel. The first, *Saratoga: Tale of the Revolution,* had appeared in 1824. A synopsis in the *North American Review,* a New England literary journal, labeled it old-fashioned, however crediting the author with a facility for characterization. The reviewer expressed mild astonishment that "this book does not appear to have received from the public, the notice that others [of its kind] have enjoyed." The *North American Review* did not choose to review *Yorktown,* in a sense *Saratoga's* sequel.[1]

Neither of Eliza Foster's melodramatic romances enjoyed a wide readership, nor received reprinting, in spite of the advantage one might imagine Eliza having as the offspring of a favored novelist. It is this curious genealogy, though, that makes *Yorktown* deserving of our attention. It links Lafayette's two American tours—the first in war, the second in commemoration—and it can be viewed as a book that sensationally relates the minds of a mother and daughter.

The central character in Hannah Foster's *Coquette* is also called Eliza—Eliza Wharton. This Eliza was a fictionalization of the real Elizabeth Whitman, whose hapless fate was revealed in New England newspapers in 1788: before dying, the unmarried Whitman anonymously gave birth at an inn some distance from her home, where a well-bred young woman might go unrecognized. Hers was a tale of woe befitting an age of restrictions.

Hannah Foster and her character Eliza Wharton clearly belong to the bloodless, pre-Romantic epoch. The fictional Eliza is missing the perspective that fifty years of republican government had instilled in the minds of a more active and democratic reading public by 1826. *The Coquette* lacks a prescience and interiority discernible in *Saratoga* and *Yorktown.* Eliza Foster clearly resolved to write about the Revolution to honor a stable republic—or perhaps we should say, to enable the past to "rescue" an endangered future.

The earlier book reflects unsettled times. Eliza Wharton is deficient as a human being, having little regard for anything greater than individual manners; she does not come by the level of patriotism that nostalgic feeling can arouse. Like a young heir just come into a fortune (this is how George Washington once fearfully described his countrymen in the 1780s), she rationalizes her selfishness, while her concerned friend Mrs. Richman warns against "fashionable dissipation." Nevertheless, the coquette responds to the pleasure-seeking Major Peter Sanford, a tasteless character of uncertain principles. All the fated heroine can think to profess to her friends is the expectation of more "fancied joys." Her dangerous imagination paints in "alluring colors." Major Sanford will eventually succeed in seducing her, because she lacks maturity, prudence, and foresight.[2]

Eliza Foster's novel differs from her mother's in form as well as plot. *The Coquette* is an epistolary novel, told entirely through a series of letters to and from the principal characters. *Yorktown* is a long, meandering, maudlin saga of family, battlefield courage, and the excruciatingly slow unraveling of impossible connections before two lovers can be joined. But both stories emphasize responsibility. Both attempt to expose moral truths, mete out justice, and reward generous emotion. We cannot know how much the mother was overseeing the progress of her daughter's work. What we do know is that the two remained close, living under the same roof until Hannah's death in 1840. Also, Eliza and her younger sister Harriet had already collaborated on a children's reader, *The Sunday School or Village Sketches,* published in 1820.[3] On the surface, all we can safely conclude about the Foster family from their fiction is that desire, transgression, sorrow, sympathy, and redemption were constant themes in their religiously inspired lives.

But there are ways of probing deeper. As a novel of sensibility driven by the power of sympathy, and one that undertakes to impart the virtue of self-suppression, *The Coquette* conforms to the moral standards set for literature during the Revolutionary generation. *Yorktown* profits from an emerging body of romantic literature that allows for greater mobility and action, but it, too, is highly sentimental. As we piece back together Eliza Foster's long buried world, and relate her fiction to Hannah Foster's more widely read morality tale, we have a legitimate means of undertaking to compare the sensibilities of the Revolutionary and successor generations.

The daughter's treatment of the Revolutionary consciousness in *Yorktown* is important for another reason. Like Wirt's *Patrick Henry*, it is a clear expression of the romantic nationalism of 1826, loyalty to the nation perfected through the careful creation of an historic parable. It is, moreover, ultimate proof of the value of Lafayette to Americans *for their own sake*. It is hard to imagine that the Fosters did not ride the five miles from Brighton along with innumerable "country people," as they were still called, to catch a glimpse of the Nation's Guest during one or both of his sojourns to Boston in 1824–25. He was the symbol of a great rejuvenation, whose rousing presence united two generations in their common devotion to the life-giving Revolution. And he was, in fact, the individual to whom Eliza Foster dedicated her novel *Yorktown*.

While Lafayette supplied her with a hero, no one captured the romantic mood of 1826 quite like the impassioned British poet George Gordon Byron, offspring of a rakish gambler and a graceless Scottish heiress. He achieved instant fame in the 1810s with the first two cantos of his epic poem *Childe Harold's Pilgrimage*. Success lured the young Lord Byron into sexual intrigues with notable women, a voluntary exile to Venice, and a romantic attachment to the Greek Revolution (equally the cause of the politically outspoken Lafayette). The poet died a premature death in Greece in 1824, at the age of thirty-six.

The New England critic who analyzed three works on the life of Byron in 1824–25 could not rid himself of an obsession with the poet's "lamentable defects" of character. Born to a mother who was "unfit," the neglected child had reputedly come to associate with the wrong kinds of people, "trifling and profligate men" and "fashionable and dissolute women." His vices had produced "discontent" and a permanent melancholy which soured—indeed "polluted"—his work. And yet the demanding moralist would not dispute the poet's mastery of language: "No one had more power than Byron, to utter that thrilling voice, which speaks a mind desolate, but unbroken." Rather than lose himself in sympathetic praise of the ill-starred poet, however, the critic counseled the rising generation to recognize Byron as one unsuited to an era of improvement: "The fashions of one age," he assured, "are the ridicule of the next."[4]

Eliza Foster was less reproachful. She responded as many of her generation did, with solemn intensity, to Byron's unearthly departure from the cold Age of Reason. Like the poet, she seemed eager to mix the structured sentiment and affecting eloquence of the late eighteenth century with the more demonstrative passion of the democratizing nineteenth. Thus the epigraph she selected for *Yorktown* consists of four lines from Canto III of *Childe Harold's Pilgrimage*, four lines that convey a seemingly desperate tone:

> *In a moment, we may plunge our years*
> *In fatal penitence, and in the blight*
> *Of our own soul, turn all our blood to tears,*
> *And colour things to come with hues of night.*

Time had turned the bloody Revolution past into the tears of the nostalgic successor generation. But what of things to come?

Here we must be careful not to jump to conclusions. While Byron's poem is the tale of a moody young man wandering alone in Europe, his message—and Eliza's message—is not at all reducible to a single emotion.[5] Byron's Harold is a lively, if fitful, pilgrim. He respects equally the enchantments of nature and the human potential. He is sensitive both to the achievements of heroes and to the sufferings of nations over time. The poet shifts back and forth from a veneration of the altogether beguiling, kinetic effects in the universe, to the virtuous ferocity of primitives, to an admiration of the high-aimed writings breathed onto paper by "gigantic minds," the historians, philosophers, bards, and wits whose literature has been preserved for his time—for Eliza's time.

History is meant to teach. And so, *Yorktown*'s epigraph is drawn from that part of the poem in which Byron is ruminating on both military conquest and the inescapable loneliness of the soul. (So is Eliza Foster in her novel, as we shall see shortly.) This is just after Harold has stood "upon this place of skulls" at Waterloo—Napoleon's Yorktown. Yet Byron is by no means all despair. He has nostalgic regard for rich, turbulent minds. He cherishes the eighteenth century's eloquent, contentious Jean-Jacques Rousseau, "whose dust was once all fire," who understood "how to make madness beautiful." The philosopher's contribution to the cause of love was his evocation of ideal beauty. Rousseau's fictional Julie from *La Nouvelle Héloïse* (1760) was, to Byron, "all that's wild and sweet." There was in love much more than vulgar pleasure and much more than tame security; and there ought to be in every life such stirring of appreciative feeling that would render all other pain endurable.

Such sentiment courses through the pages of Canto III. Immediately preceding the four lines that serve as *Yorktown's* epigraph, Byron's words are cautionary: "Midst a contentious world, striving where none are strong." He welcomes the susceptibility of being. So does Eliza Foster.

This section of *Childe Harold* was written during 1817–18. Eliza would have known while writing *Yorktown* that in 1823 Lord Byron made a romantic pilgrimage of his own, to Greece, offering his support to the revolutionaries who were at that time, and still in 1826, struggling against the oppressive regime of Ottoman rulers. It was there, in 1824, that the restless poet contracted his fatal fever. He was barely older than Eliza, and she clearly shared not just his generation and his love for the power of the written word, but his outstanding compassion, as they separately envisioned an upturn of destinies in a time of heightened affections.

As much as Lord Byron was on her mind, so, of course, was the Marquis de Lafayette. An entire page is given to Eliza's salutation to "the Venerated Hero of TWO GENERATIONS." (As it happens, less than a year separated the births of Lafayette and Eliza's mother.) The author contends in her dedication that the story to follow will describe events "supposed" to have occurred at that place where Lafayette conspicuously performed his fearless defense of America's right in 1781, and helped bring an end to the "Glorious Drama." He is honored in her work, not simply for his "Brave Arm," but for his "Chivalrous Spirit" as well.[6]

And so, the novel begins:

Towards the end of a sultry day, in the latter part of the eventful summer of 1781, a small detachment of American troops halted

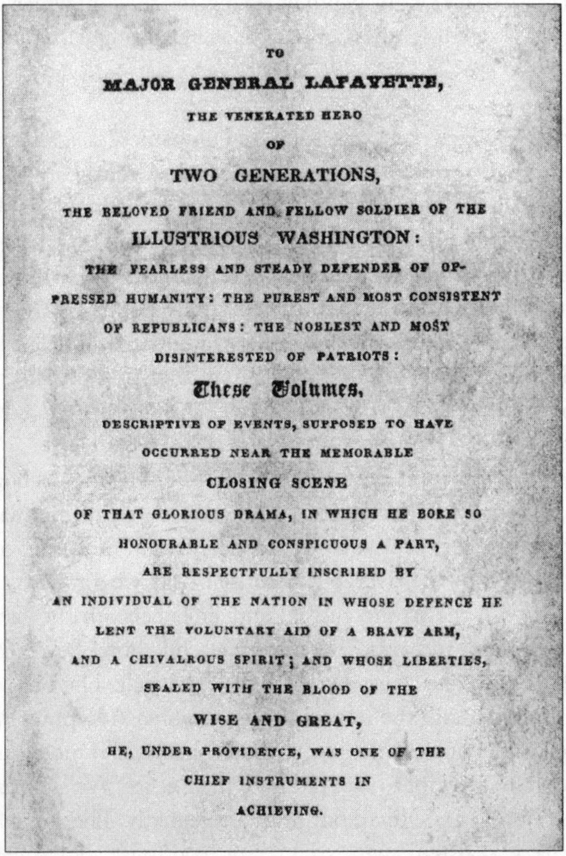

TO
MAJOR GENERAL LAFAYETTE,
THE VENERATED HERO
OF
TWO GENERATIONS,
THE BELOVED FRIEND AND FELLOW SOLDIER OF THE
ILLUSTRIOUS WASHINGTON:
THE FEARLESS AND STEADY DEFENDER OF OP-
PRESSED HUMANITY: THE PUREST AND MOST CONSISTENT
OF REPUBLICANS: THE NOBLEST AND MOST
DISINTERESTED OF PATRIOTS:
These Volumes,
DESCRIPTIVE OF EVENTS, SUPPOSED TO HAVE
OCCURRED NEAR THE MEMORABLE
CLOSING SCENE
OF THAT GLORIOUS DRAMA, IN WHICH HE BORE SO
HONOURABLE AND CONSPICUOUS A PART,
ARE RESPECTFULLY INSCRIBED BY
AN INDIVIDUAL OF THE NATION IN WHOSE DEFENCE HE
LENT THE VOLUNTARY AID OF A BRAVE ARM,
AND A CHIVALROUS SPIRIT; AND WHOSE LIBERTIES,
SEALED WITH THE BLOOD OF THE
WISE AND GREAT,
HE, UNDER PROVIDENCE, WAS ONE OF THE
CHIEF INSTRUMENTS IN
ACHIEVING.

Fig. 4. Dedication page of Eliza Foster's 1826 novel, *Yorktown: An Historical Romance. (Courtesy, American Antiquarian Society.)*

for the night on the northern bank of the James River, not many miles above Williamsburg, in Virginia.

The leader of this force is Major Louis St. Olmar, a young French officer as "ardent and chivalrous" as his commander Lafayette.

He was just at that period of life when youth is deepening into manhood, and the fine proportions of his noble figure, the for-

eign grace of his air, the depth of feeling and thought which softened the eagle brightness of his eye, were all singularly marked
and attractive.

Next the reader meets St. Olmar's companion, a "gallant" young
lieutenant, the Virginian Edward Leslie, "whose ruddy lip was not yet
shaded with the down of manhood." The Frenchman notices that
Edward is fallen into a melancholy reminiscence—something has
transformed him from a soldier into "a tearful girl." At first, St. Olmar
is unsympathetic. Edward then meaningfully points to the mansion
across the river: it is the estate of his late father and the scene of much
earlier happiness. But he will not say more, attesting that his tears are
"a transient weakness which should not have been indulged in your
presence."

Just at this moment, Edward spots his sister Helen on a boat in the
middle of the river. He rushes to the shore. As he calls her name, she
sees him, but in her surprise loses her balance and tumbles overboard.
Edward dives into the river, but because of the weight of his clothes
has trouble with the strong current and sinks beneath the "whelming
waves." When he recovers his senses back on shore, he realizes that
St. Olmar has rescued him—and his sister as well. The boat she had
been on pulls up, and the nasty Loyalist Colonel Adolphus Walstein,
Helen's guardian uncle, emerges. He had considered it more important
to steer than to attempt to save either of the Leslies. Walstein deigns to
thank the heroic St. Olmar, but only offhandedly. The Frenchman is
not deceived. Walstein snaps back: "And you must allow me to wish
you greater happiness and a fairer prospect of fame than you can have,
or hope to win, in the service of this rebellious country." When the
colonel refuses to allow Edward to accompany Helen home, Edward
murmurs a bitter farewell to the occupied Heathland, till "God shall
free my country, and reinstate me in my rights."

As the opening sequence shows, masculine stoicism was as much a
requirement of sentimental fiction as female vulnerability. The men in
Yorktown try to resist revelation of their feelings, to show how sturdy
resolution can overcome all momentary emotion. While they posture,
Helen enters as a beautiful victim (in a white dress, no less), and, so far,
without a will of her own. Yet St. Olmar's first impression of her is of a
"firm and cheerful" demeanor. Edward assures the major that he is

right: she has "a spirit which will not yield to lawless tyranny." And yet the machinations of Walstein, the false guardian, are so devious that they require a stronger defense than she alone can muster.

As the serpentine plot of *Yorktown* unfolds, Edward Leslie leads an attack on the combined British and Loyalist forces. He is taken prisoner by the Loyalist Colonel Clifford, a friend of Walstein. St. Olmar, meanwhile, regroups at a secluded house, whose occupant returns from an unknown mission of her own. She is a mysterious woman, wearing a scarlet cloak and hood. Drenched from a hard rain, she flings back the hood to reveal "a form, thin almost to emaciation, and a visage wrinkled as if with the blasts of eighty winters, though as yet it had not witnessed threescore. Her eyes alone might have appertained to a more youthful face—there was something supernatural. . . ." When St. Olmar identifies himself to the ageless woman, she shrieks, "so wild and piercing, that even the dying soldiers seemed startled by the sound." The reader has come face-to-face with Maude Mansel, whose exploits and sorcery will lend shock and surprise at every major juncture in the novel. She represents, in a sense, the penance that Hannah Foster's charming, fallen Eliza Wharton pays in a grotesque reincarnation.

Maude's first trick is to make Edward Leslie appear from her damp cellar. Somehow she had taken advantage of a moment of confusion and spirited him from under the nose of the British. Reunited with St. Olmar, Edward establishes how he knows Maude, with a preposterous ambiguity that sets up an equally preposterous subplot of seduction, bribery, and a host of consequences. She is, he says tediously, "a sort of hanger-on in our family, a kind of mysterious personage, who goes and comes when she pleases, says what she pleases, and oftentimes exerts a degree of influence over my uncle."

St. Olmar leads his troops on and they spot the enemy. In the engagement, attention is directed to a figure "whose habiliments, half feminine, and half warlike, gave a singular and grotesque air to the person of the wearer." Maude has joined the ranks, of course. Her "wasted form," her "haggard face," her "scorching eye," provoke "sounds of stifled laughter, as the withered amazon shouldered her musket and took her place amongst them." The mysterious Maude, patriot-hag, silences the men scornfully: "Peace, fools! Your idle mirth is like the cracking of thorns under a pot. Do you laugh because a woman stands among you!" A veteran growls knowingly, in the author's attempt to effect a yeoman's speech:

> Well said, my brave old goody! I guess now if this here State of Virginy could send out a whole rigiment of sich 'are she tigers, there would'n't long be sich a tarnal sight o'red coats swarming over their tobacco fields.

British steel meets American intrepidity. Through the dense smoke, St. Olmar and Leslie fight fearlessly, driving the enemy back. Eventually, Edward is carried too far by his "rash courage," and is captured a second time. St. Olmar, attempting to free him, is run through by the sharp point of a saber, and left for dead. Maude fights on with seeming recklessness, but comes to no harm: "her life seemed charmed,—all appeared to shun her, and to fly with a kind of superstitious terror from that uplifted weapon which never fell in vain." Maude is an Untouchable. Her shrill voice wails above the others, as St. Olmar's men surrender to Colonel Clifford. Maude knows who Clifford is: the hand of Helen Leslie has been promised to this ally of the evil Walstein. As she sizes him up, he harangues her: "Woman or fiend! Which am I to call you." Maude taunts back.

Clifford is dignified and honest, despite the pronounced flaw that is his choice of friends—the British invaders and Walstein. He paroles all the troops except for the two protagonists, Edward Leslie, who is to be tried as a spy, and the unconscious, dangerously wounded St. Olmar. Maude takes advantage of her conditional release to visit Helen and convey the fateful news. Helen expresses undue concern for St. Olmar: "And what is that Frenchman to you," Maude charges, "that you ask after him, as breathlessly as though it were your last gasp?"

> "He is my brother's friend," said Helen, calmly; "he saved his life and mine but yester-eve, and I have no wish to conceal my interest in one, to whom I owe such service."

Romance is in the air, as every reader of 1826 has by now guessed.

As Maude apprises her of the ominous details of her brother's plight, Helen exhibits weakness and indecision. Maude grows ever more hard-hearted, predicting misery and destruction. She reveals her own design: to persuade Helen to marry her son, Rupert, whom Helen has known since childhood and regards, at best, as a "brother."

Walstein arrives, and seeing Maude, he cowers. She has an unspoken hold over this man of depraved purposes—she is the only one who can make him afraid. He tries to regain control over the situation by proposing a deal to Helen: if he can succeed in convincing Clifford to spare Edward, then she must marry Clifford—or if not Clifford, Maude's Rupert. Either way, Walstein implies, his own position will be secured.

Helen struggles in her mind, and then, melodramatically speaks: "Yes, I will consent to all, any thing which may save him." But as we are to see, she is not beaten. She faces Walstein with steadfast eyes:

> The authority entrusted to you by my father, sir, extends not so far as this. He would not have swayed my inclinations in a choice, which so nearly concerns my happiness; nor will I permit any one else to assume such power over me. If I marry Colonel Clifford, it will only be to save my brother's life . . . !

Meanwhile, as the prisoner Edward sits on the bed where the insensible Major St. Olmar lies, "the torpor of despair chilled Edward's heart." The moment arrives when he thinks he hears his sister's voice; discovering that he is not imagining it, "every fibre of his heart" is "thrilled." He trembles with emotion, his cheek turns pale, "and like a terrified girl, he looks around for some secret recess, where he might remain hidden from observation." Again, as in the opening scene, he resists his own sentimental tendencies.

"I come to talk of life," said Helen quickly. . . .

From this moment on, her resolve is firm. She informs her helpless brother that she has obliged Colonel Clifford to let her visit, bargaining away her own happiness in order to spare Edward. Her logic is simple: "As the husband of your sister, his petition for your life must have a weight and influence, that—"

Of course, Edward will not hear of this. (Her sacrifice must not exceed his chivalry.) But Helen is more resourceful than she lets on. As Walstein's carriage comes for her, it is a disguised Edward who returns to Heathland, while she remains to be discovered by Clifford. As the Loyalist becomes aware of her trick, he is unsure whether to despise Helen or love her more for this noble display of devotion. He decides that honor is too great a thing to "sell," even for a woman's love. "I was led by passion," he openly admits to her, chastened by the superior heart of woman. Thus the jilted Loyalist proves himself capable of reform, giving truth to the patriots' assertion that, through sublime justice, they could reclaim most of those who initially opposed a righteous destiny for America.

Clifford brings new intelligence: French ships have come to the aid of General Lafayette and have the York River blocked. The British cannot disparage the American forces quite so easily as they had before:

> "And Lord Cornwallis resolves not to abandon his present encampment?" inquired Colonel Walstein, with a frown as dark as Erebus.*
>
> "Of course not," returned Clifford.

Adding new mystery to these fateful circumstances, Maude appears before Walstein and informs him that she has snatched a letter in French from a "secret pocket" in St. Olmar's coat, containing evidence that can sink Walstein. She vows to carry out "an act of justice," if Helen is not given to Rupert. At this juncture, the author intrudes to reveal to the reader that Rupert was fathered by Walstein. As Maude announces that she is rejoining the American army, Walstein explodes:

> "What, you go to join the rebels!" he exclaimed; "and I too must look to it that my good sword be sharp and bright; for should we meet, and my last breath be failing me, I will rouse myself to plunge it to your heart; yes, yours, tormenting demon, who through life have haunted and harassed me with your hated presence."

As Washington, the "gallant and invincible chief," marches south to join Lafayette's army and place Yorktown under siege, St. Olmar at

---

*In Greek mythology, Erebus is that place in the kingdom of the dead where the departed first pass.

last regains consciousness. Still under house arrest, he writes Lafayette, asking to be exchanged for a British prisoner of comparable rank, so that he may return to action. Edward writes Helen from the front lines, noting that Maude is "among the common soldiers," dressed as a man. Thus ends volume one.

EARLY IN volume two, Maude seeks out the upright Helen and confides the story of her past—as the "seduced woman" of convention:

> I was nursed in the arms of luxury and indulgence. My infant days were bright and happy, my youth joyous and unsullied. I grew up fair as the fairest flower of the parterre,—I was the pride of fond hearts, the delight of admiring eyes. But I loved, trusted, and was betrayed. My lover left me, and to hide my shame, I fled. . . .

She had been Maude Steinkirk, born on the banks of the Danube to a man of no rank but immense wealth. Like the coquette Eliza Wharton, she was "a creature of impulse." Her faithless lover, Adolphus Walstein, was pursued by Maude's chivalrous brother—the two dueled, and the brother fell. The murderous Walstein soon went into exile in America, where he fought alongside the Virginian Leslie in Quebec during the French and Indian War, and met and married his friend's sister. But Walstein, not surprisingly, proved "a stern and cold husband, to one, who had given him a heart, warm with the tenderest and purest love." His mind became more and more embittered; he shunned society. Maude, by now, had landed on American shores as well, marrying the man who accompanied her from Europe, a well-intentioned "menial" named Mansel, previously employed by her father.

The narrative returns to the present. As French and American forces begin to concentrate around the British position, Maude is back at her cottage. Something has happened, but we do not know what until she is found by a Heathland servant named Old Jenny Upton, groaning amid the briars, "a purple stream issuing from her breast." Jenny binds what is evidently a stab wound from the "sharp and bright sword" of Walstein.

The siege of Yorktown intensifies. Washington's and Lafayette's combined forces are "formidable." The British are "hemmed in." Major St. Olmar's heart "beat high with the hope of glory." He marches toward the British redoubt, just a step behind Lafayette himself, and with "an impetuosity which bore down all before them, they trampled over every thing which threatened to impede their progress, tore away the palisades and abatis, and, assaulting the works on every side at the same instant, forced their way into them."

For really the first time, Eliza Foster's story takes a page directly out of history: the storming of the redoubt. The author must have read in the newspapers, when Lafayette returned to Yorktown in 1824, how he once again marched up to the undisturbed earthen fortification that he had captured in 1781 at the head of American light infantry. The note-taking Levasseur encountered a farmer who still lived near the battle site and who had been a captain under Lafayette during the siege. The aide recorded their conversation: "Lafayette thought correctly," the farmer recalled for Levasseur, "that to carry entrenchments defended by experienced soldiers with young troops, he could only count on the audacity and rapidity of the attack; in consequence . . . he led it himself, sword in hand, at full speed across the abatis, and in spite of the enemy's fire entered the redoubt, of which he was soon master with the loss of but few men."[7]

In the fictional account of the siege, Edward Leslie maintains himself as a "youthful lion, amid the fury of the fight." He and St. Olmar are among the first to enter the redoubt. Edward watches as one particular soldier "rushed wherever peril beckoned"; "his human power, made those around him shrink and gaze." It was Maude's son Rupert. The excitement fades from Edward's heart as he sees Rupert fall. And then, at once, he hears an agonizing shriek; soldier Maude leans over the lifeless body. "Maude!" Edward calls to her. "Does he live?" She looks "wildly" at him, and continues wailing until an all-too-predictable vision strikes and Maude sings out:

> Edward, look! The white bird flutters over him, waiting to bear
> his soul where mine may never go!

The battle is won. Cornwallis surrenders. The wound inflicted on Maude by Walstein had begun to heal, until reopened during the final fight. She and Rupert both, behind the vine-covered walls of her cottage, are slowly dying. Helen and Edward and St. Olmar are all there. Maude appears to them "a living skeleton." Rupert, throughout the book more a shadow than a real character, momentously asks for Helen to come to his side and comfort his dying moments:

> "Helen, press your hand upon my eyes," resumed Rupert; "they will never open more upon the light of the world; but a brighter day is dawning on me . . . Mother—Edward—dearest Helen, farewell!"

In walks Walstein. An American general magnanimously permitted him to return to Heathland. Maude appeals to Helen: "Behold the author of my shame and misery!" Now she is ready to finish her tale and gives up the amazing secret that she pieced together from coincidence and circumstantial evidence: in Quebec during the prior war, the father of Edward and Helen Leslie had been captured, his life saved from an "uplifted tomahawk" by the "generous valour of a young French officer." That merciful officer, named de Stainville, by a reversal of fortunes, became an English prisoner, and Leslie repaid the kindness by bringing him—along with Walstein—home to Virginia at war's end. Neither of Leslie's friends, the Frenchman or the German, could resist the charms of Leslie's sister Isabelle, who was to receive a large inheritance, which, should she die unmarried, reverted to her sister Anna. Isabelle chose de Stainville, who was shortly thereafter summoned back to France. During his absence, the spurned Walstein "persecuted" Isabelle "with his lawless passion," but succeeded only in overturning her fragile mind. De Stainville later returned to Heathland, only to learn "dreadful tidings," while Walstein privately reveled in his rival's wretchedness: Isabelle Leslie was lost and presumed drowned, her veil found floating in a stream. De Stainville could not bear to remain in America any longer.

In fact, though, Maude had rescued Isabelle and nursed her. The dying Maude explains:

> Her disordered hair, her torn garments, her pale and touching beauty excited my compassion and surprise. . . . I saw she was a maniac; but my heart was not so hardened, as it has since become. . . . I led her to my home—I fed and soothed her.

Isabelle, having eluded Walstein's rabid pursuit at the cost of her reason, was pregnant with her husband's child. She gave birth to a son, but she herself never recovered. Maude's lowborn husband was returning to Europe and carried the infant with him, intent on reuniting father and son. Instead, Mansel's vessel shipwrecked, and the infant washed ashore in Bordeaux, to be found there—most implausibly—by none other than de Stainville.

De Stainville adopted the boy, not knowing his identity. In Virginia, the calculating Walstein married Anna Leslie, presuming that she would inherit her sister Isabelle's wealth. One day Maude told Walstein of Isabelle's true fate, and that there was in fact an heir—wherever that child might be. Her narration continues:

> But with the devilish arts, which he well knew to practice, he assailed my weakest side—he prated of my son and his, he promised largely, and spoke of future greatness and distinction, which my ambitious heart most fondly coveted. . . .

In short, he had promised her that their son Rupert would marry Helen and gain respectability, if only Maude would keep silent about what she knew.

As Maude's story concludes, the long absent de Stainville appears from out of nowhere at the cottage door. St. Olmar embraces his adopted father—his *real* father:

> "My father! my father! take to your heart the son of Isabelle Leslie!"
>
> "No they have mocked you, Louis; this cannot be; such happiness were more than I could bear!"

But of course it is true, and "the manly cheeks of both were bathed in tears of unmixed happiness." The elder Frenchman gazes next at Helen, his wife's niece, whose remarkable eyes bring back sweet memories of the misused woman he once fiercely loved.

Amid celebration, no one has noticed Walstein's disappearance or, for that matter, that Rupert has taken his last breath. Maude is found slumped over her son, an empty vial of the opiate laudanum beside her body. The author explains: "She died as she had lived, the miserable victim of passion."

Eventually, Heathland returns to calm and "exquisite enjoyment." The extended family receives word that Walstein has conveniently perished at sea. Louis St. Olmar marries his cousin, "the smiling" Helen Leslie, and they go off to France. Edward Leslie recovers his "paternal estate," and the reader is left to understand that he will one day marry "a fair Virginian."

YORKTOWN is melodrama. But if sensational agony defeats any attempt to probe human complexity, this is still commemorative literature. Like the newspaper reports of Lafayette's visit, it makes new associations with the Revolution, and it shows how the successor generation was daily contributing new emotion to the national creation story. Eliza Foster pays homage to republican sentiment while she seeks to recover Revolutionary consanguinity—the uniting of North and South, the selflessness of the French ally—all that which made 1776 a hopeful moment in the annals of politics.

But Foster reveals even more. Hers is a story about men and women—purportedly the men and women of the Revolution, but really the men and women of 1826. How she borrows from, and extends beyond, her mother's treatment of the politics of gender is revealing.

Hannah Foster's male characters in *The Coquette* range widely in their self-presentation: General Richman, Eliza Wharton's patient friend, is imperturbable and unfailingly decent, capable of providing his pleasing wife with protection and respectability. Another kind and considerate male, Reverend Boyer, is the upright but jilted suitor of the tragic heroine. He is rewarded with the love of a fine woman because he can admit his sensibility, or softness, in the "effeminate relief of tears" that Edward Leslie in *Yorktown* has so much trouble showing, and Louis St. Olmar, whose very name is an anagram for love (*l'amor*), does not openly exhibit until nearly the last page, when he and his father are reunited and "the manly cheeks of both were bathed in tears."

The rakish seducer of *The Coquette,* Major Peter Sanford (the Wal-

stein equivalent), is in all manner a false gallant and designing scoundrel. At one point he confides to a male friend, "I am a mere Proteus,
and can assume any shape that will best answer my purpose." Though
all of these characters seem one-dimensional, part of Hannah Foster's
literary success was due to her clarity in assigning recognizable traits to
her leading men.[8]

Eliza Foster's deserving men fly from one mishap to the next.
Though committed to right, they are uncertain of their course until
the climactic assault, alongside Lafayette, on the British redoubt at
Yorktown. Before that, events inevitably overtake them. They understand duty but, amid their hurried actions, are vague in defining the
responsibilities of their gender: Colonel Clifford needs Helen to help
him sort out his feelings; Edward is either slow to conceive action or
simply rash; St. Olmar begins by rescuing Helen and Edward from
drowning, but is literally unconscious when he ought to be doing the
most good.

Hannah Foster's characters, male and female, good and bad, readily offer their opinions. Eliza Wharton, the narrator states, "judiciously, yet modestly" takes a position on political subjects in mixed
company. Mrs. Richman, speaking in Eliza's defense, asserts that men
are wrong to fear the consequences when women "meddle" in politics.
"Why then," she asks, "should the love of our country be a masculine
passion only?" But Eliza Wharton is "volatile," and admits as much.
She craves independence, accepting no limits. This is her downfall. In
Yorktown, Helen Leslie prevails because she is firm in her judgment
while expressing the obligatory tenderness of American womanhood.
Her motives are clear. Her actions are both patriotically efficient and
personally responsible. Though consequences vary, both mother and
daughter fiction writers grant their heroines independence of mind.

And then there is Maude. Her cause is the American cause, yet she
is not an example of republican womanhood. Excepting her role as
nurse to Isabelle Leslie, there is no softness to Maude, no feminine
conscience. It has been stripped from her—Walstein spoiled her
chance to live life as a "real" woman. Her soldierly proficiency, her
nerve, shows that women can bear arms; but Maude's disagreeable
physical appearance renders her actions suspect. This again suggests
that female firmness had to be softened for men by exhibition of an
agreeable exterior.

The successor generation had internalized such models as these, even as heroic examples of female battlefield glory lived on in the Revolution's mythology. The most famous true account was that of Deborah Sampson, popularized in book form by New Englander Herman Mann, on the basis of private interviews, in 1797 (the same year that *The Coquette* was published). There can be little doubt that Eliza Foster knew the story of Deborah Sampson, a woman—in Mann's words—"born and educated in humble obscurity [who] voluntarily offered her services in the character of a *Continental Soldier*."[9]

The Sampson of Mann's parable conveyed "extreme modesty and trembling diffidence" in allowing her life story to be publicized. Consistent with the image of ideal womanhood that Hannah Foster promoted in her novel, Mann's subject was a "virtuous female" who inspired "manly thoughts." Under the darkened skies of April 1775, nature had reversed itself—something in the air as the Revolution began "seemed to lacerate the very vaults of nature," making a transgendered response to the American crisis almost excusable. Like her emotional antithesis Maude, the humble Deborah (before being transformed) reacted to male soldiers' vulgar taunts, and found an unusual kind of courage within herself, a voice capable of arresting abuse from men. Called a "Slut" by one soldier for being improperly dressed, she challenged the "arrogant coxcomb" by alluding to his "sartorial superiority" as something irrelevant to battlefield performance. This opened the possibility, or seemed to invite, her own exchange of female for male attire.[10]

Deborah enlisted as Robert Shurtlieff, mustering into the army in Worcester. As Mann explains, it was not that she did not find the prospect of love for a man desirable, but that "Her love extended to all," and was thus identical to the patriotism that young men felt who were impelled to fight for freedom. So how did she fool her comrades? "Her stature is perhaps more than the middle size. . . . She has a skin naturally clear, and flushed with a blooming carnation. But her aspect is rather masculine and serene, than effeminate and sillily jocose." She strapped a bandage around her chest, to disguise her breasts.[11]

According to this popular retelling, Deborah Sampson (like Maude) fought with Lafayette at Yorktown. Mann describes the moment much as Eliza Foster does: "Perpetual sheets of fire and smoke belched, as from a volcano, and towered the clouds. And whilst the eye was daz-

zled at this, the ear was satiated and stunned by the tremendous explo-
sion of artillery." Deborah, now deemed "the gallantress" and "our
Heroine" by her biographer, took part in storming the redoubt, escap-
ing harm though her battle coat was "torn apart . . . during the melee"
by a broadsword or musket.

What Americans of this period did not know was that Mann had
romanticized Sampson-Shurtlieff's exploits much as Parson Weems
in 1800 made famous the invented story of an honor-bound young
George Washington chopping down a cherry tree. Deborah Sampson
did not participate in the Battle of Yorktown, though Mann was correct in recording that she shortly thereafter received a bullet wound in
the thigh in a skirmish with Tory resisters, extracting the ball herself in
order to prevent discovery. His account ends with the revelation of her
true sex and, editorially, a discussion of her exemplary character. The
real Deborah Sampson married just after the war, and bore three children. Her husband, as it turned out, was unsuccessful at farming, so
that even with the veteran's pension she was awarded, she had to help
support her family by dressing up in a Continental Army uniform and
recounting her story to live audiences.[12]

The perverted "Deborah Sampson" and hellish "Eliza Wharton"
who are reincarnated by Eliza Foster as the unpredictable Maude bring
convulsions into the world of the novel. But it is an optimistic world
nonetheless—an unbanishable positive spirit needs to emerge and
assert itself over the forces of moral decay. The innate quality of generosity that would allow Maude to be a properly gendered "woman" is
only sporadically shown. She is, in short, a mutation rather than a
woman. The manifest difference between this seduced woman and the
seduced woman of Hannah Webster's day is that Maude is not sen-
tenced to die upon delivering a child out of wedlock. She lives on as a
freakish reconstitution of her former self, so as to make the life of her
seducer miserable.

Helen Leslie, Yorktown's scrupulous, sensible heroine, is present to
illustrate that woman is man's intellectual equal or superior. American
arms are feminized, too, in a way—virtuous, vulnerable, and ultimately
valiant—while the enemy relies only on a traditionally masculine sense
of power through numbers and unappealing bravado. Maude's presence further proves that the moral conduct of war is not an easily
definable, singularly masculine affair.

National independence is a prize to be won by relying on those positive qualities—virtue and valor—that either male or female can demonstrate. Helen and America both take part in an active contest against the harassment of the invader/usurper; Helen and America alike must outwit British and Tory machinations. But as strong and determined as she may be, and despite her declaration of independence from her false guardian (mirroring America's Declaration of Independence from the false political parent), Helen, in the end, remains a prize to be won. She will be wedded to the victor in battle. While womanhood triumphs, it does so without winning political equality.

In *The Coquette,* an obverse justice prevails, because the 1790s are too soon for an independent female to possess the adroitness of a Helen Leslie. Eliza Wharton's fate is sealed when she refuses to comply with her assigned role as the prize of a worthy man. Like Helen, she is attractive, "amiable and accomplished," but her declaration of independence is an expression of her whimsicality. What she imagines as happiness is in fact frivolity.

The more discerning Helen, as she cultivates herself, comprehends that her pursuit of happiness must ultimately accommodate marriage. Her acts are self-generated, but they are not self-centered. She establishes herself first as an agent of the Revolution's self-evident truth—that the pursuit of happiness is cumulative, active, conscious, and, above all, moral—before assisting the forces of good in winning choice back to her.

ELIZA FOSTER did not overtly challenge the rules, put in place in the decades after the Revolution, that concerned the way men and women were meant to understand how to extract moral lessons from America's history. Men continued to insist that they should censor young women's reading, fearing in most novels a dangerously imaginative picture of what "real life" could be for the susceptible, romantically inclined, and unmarried. History writing, in any event, had to be uplifting.[13]

The most celebrated writer of American historical fiction in 1826 was New Yorker James Fenimore Cooper, whose manly heroes were invariably symbols of protective arms and stern self-reliance, and whose female characters were resolutely pure and hopelessly vulnerable.[14] It was in the early months of 1826 that his classic *Last of the Mohicans: A Narrative of 1757* was published, widely advertised throughout the year in newspapers of the Northeast, the South, and the frontier West alike.

This dark novel about the French and Indian War features the Daniel Boone–like character Hawk-eye (so named for his quick and accurate sight) and his friend the Mohican chief Chingachgook, who together guide their less accomplished companions through a wilderness beset by enemies. The delicate Cora and Alice Munro are in constant danger. It is their sheltering father, the somewhat pessimistic commander of an outlying fort, who seems to disparage their strengths most: "The tender limbs of my daughters are unequal to these hardships," he says. "We shall find their fainting forms in this desert." These descriptions are meant to elicit sympathy, not respect.[15]

Like Louis St. Olmar and Edward Leslie, Cooper's young professional soldier Duncan Heyward wants to be a rescuer. He dozes off during guard duty and dreams he is "a knight of ancient chivalry, holding his midnight vigils before the tent of a recaptured princess." But the facts do not always bear out men's constructed fears for their women or even support Cooper's own stereotypes: Cora and Alice do not faint away at their first brush with danger. Thankful when men attempt to succor them, they must find ways to excuse themselves parenthetically with a "weak girls as we are . . . ," in affirming their ability to stand watch in the Indian-infested forest. And so it is that the men of Cooper's fiction, no matter how flawed, reassure themselves of female delicacy and passivity in order to be roused to their chivalrous obligations. Even the redoubtable Hawk-eye, the naturally superior frontier scout, finds Cora (like Helen Leslie) to be cool and level-headed in formulating a plan of escape when others of the party are prone to despair: "There is reason in her words!" he exclaims to his Indian partners. "Chingachgook! Uncas! hear you the talk of the dark-eyed woman!"[16]

It was expected for brave men to lose their lives in war. Their women were meant to weave garlands to ornament their tombs. The melodramatic author of an 1826 essay, "The Grave of a Female," broods over the special sorrow that attends a lost female life. "For myself," he begins, "I can pass by the tomb of a man with somewhat of a calm indifference; but when I survey the grave of a female, a sigh involuntarily escapes me. . . . I think of her as the young and bashful virgin, with eyes sparkling, and cheeks crimsoned with each impassioned feeling of her heart; of the kind and affectionate wife, absorbed in the exercise of her domestic duties." To this representative male, woman is formed "to adorn and humanize mankind, to soothe his cares and strew his path with flowers." He is "energy," while she is "softness." The modest female makes herself precious.[17]

In the pages of newspapers and popular magazines of 1826, unobtrusive American women, like the "pure" Helen Leslie, were accorded a quality of sturdy self-knowledge. They were unmistakably less vulnerable to seductive arguments than Hannah Foster's coquettish heroine. They knew how, when, and to whom they ought to commit themselves. In the memoir of his travels with Lafayette, Levasseur notes that it was not only the married women, but affianced young girls who early on in their social careers established such poise:

> The American ladies are not more remarkable for their severe conjugal fidelity, than the girls are for their constancy to their *engagements.* At parties I have often had pointed out to me young ladies of eighteen or nineteen, who had been *engaged.* . . . [They] hold the middle place in society between their still disengaged companions and the married ladies. They have already lost some of the thoughtless gaiety of the former, and assumed a slight tinge of the gravity of the other.

When a forward bachelor approaches such a young lady, Levasseur adds, he is met with the words "I am engaged," given sweetly enough, but also firmly, which "soon destroys all his illusions, without wounding his pride."[18]

A British tourist at Niagara Falls likewise marveled at American women. Words could hardly do justice to their "unaffected ease and elegance." Unassuming, unassailable, self-possessed, and socially adept, these "ladies" performed with greater confidence as they and the nation became more secure.[19] Yet to be so flattered, they were meant to conform to men's images of who they were. Their serenity was as studied as their self-policing inner reserve. They were permitted to change men's minds, but only passively, serving as moral examples but not as vocal critics.

In this environment of overprescribed social roles, Hannah Foster's flirtatious Eliza Wharton and Eliza Foster's passionate Helen Leslie offer compelling rejoinders. The first, despite her tragic failure to come to terms with social norms, is sympathetic and, we sense, an expression of the author's resistance to the political invisibility expected of females in the Revolutionary age. The second is of an independent mind, quintessentially American; she awaits an honorable mate, but remains, as her brother describes her early in the novel, in possession of a "spirit which will not yield to lawless tyranny." Worthy women had been cultivating strategies to stand up to the tyranny of men since the mid-eighteenth-century epistolary novel first introduced the scheming seducer. Helen represents the decided success of an alert and agile approach to the world that men made.

Yet there was more than one point of view in the year of America's jubilee. In an age when female delicacy was publicly matched by female assertiveness only in areas of moral improvement—temperance societies, religious life, and early childhood education—a telling quip made the rounds:

> A beautiful woman said to a general officer, "How is it, that having obtained so much glory, you should still seek for more?"
>
> "Ah! Madam," he replied, "how is it that you who have so much beauty, should still put on *rouge*?"[20]

There is really only one way to interpret this tepid example of humor. The very masculine soldier appears to be yielding a compliment to the woman while he is really dismissing her for having failed to appreciate what all men of the day were meant to internalize: proof of valor defined one's social worth. A man was nobody without persistent exhibition of his talents, as William Wirt has already shown us. Society was a competition for him, and his performance was being scrutinized. Though increased emphasis on female education was producing more and more intellectually gifted women, it was supposed to be enough for the average woman to warrant attention—she was meant be satisfied in having her physical charm appreciated. How she looked was still worth more to society than what she thought.

The women of Eliza Foster's generation were being reared to temper their desire for public self-expression. While increasingly able to pursue intellectual pleasures, even to publish, they had to reckon with the different expectations of men and women in society. Women felt profound pressure put upon them to yield eventually to domestic cares, no matter what their talents. Even as she wrote popularly—clearly apprenticed by her mother—Eliza Foster aspired to nothing more public. She might teach patriotic duty, or shape the public taste, but she would do so without naming herself.[21]

We do not have any description of the author Eliza Lanesford Foster, who shared the name of the tragic heroine in her mother's popular novel. But in 1826, as it happens, the *New-York Mirror, and Ladies' Literary Gazette* published an anonymous column that rhapsodized the meritorious traits of a generic Eliza, the feminine ideal:

> Eliza is really what writers have so often imagined. . . . In her person she is almost tall, and almost thin; graceful, commanding, and inspiring a kind of tender respect. . . . Possessed of almost every excellence, she is unconscious of any, and thus heightens them all. . . . She has neither pride, prejudice, nor precipitancy to misguide her: she is true, and therefore judges truly. . . .[22]

Surely Eliza Foster was more than this. If the romantic history she authored is sterile and formulaic, her feeling for Revolutionary American virtues, like her feeling for the power of commitment within a fanciful, fabulous love, allows us to appreciate the extravagance of memory. She tried to write of the higher powers that embraced American lives and, had she the skill, would have perfected the Byronic enterprise of making solitude of the mind the path to knowledge of a deeper nature.[23]

CHAPTER FOUR

Mrs. Bascom Takes the Late
Mr. Wallis's Profile

ASHBY IS a bucolic community set on high ground in north-central Massachusetts, forty-seven miles northwest of Boston, near the New Hampshire border. It contains about twelve thousand acres of mostly hilly, stone-ridden, but fertile country. Small streams flow east. Indian lore surrounding its Watatic Mountain (altitude 1,847 feet, west of town) says that unhappiness comes to any who ascend to the top without placing a stone on the stack of rocks that lies there. The imposing church in Ashby's common that still stands was built in 1809, and its pulpit continues to be called the "Bascom desk."[1]

Ruth Henshaw Bascom was born in 1772, the eldest of ten children. In 1826, in her mid-fifties, she was living in Ashby with her husband, the Reverend Ezekiel L. Bascom. Their lives have eluded most sub-stantive histories (just as Eliza Foster has eluded literary critics), but that does not mean the Bascoms are without historical significance. Indeed, it is their plainness that makes them representative, and Ruth's unadorned reactions that help us to better understand the ordinary range of private thoughts among unheralded Americans of 1826.

She had begun keeping a detailed daily journal at the age of seven-teen, the year George Washington took the oath of office. She gener-ally wrote on coarse paper, stitched together by hand into annuals. The most perceptible emotion one recognizes in reading Ruth's adult years' writing is her devout acceptance of the fragility of life. As a regular churchgoer her entire life and the wife of a minister, she marked in her rather undisciplined scrawl that "Mr Bascom," or "Mr B," as she alternately terms the man she married, is visiting the dying, or eulogizing the dead. He is called upon to share in the grief of neighbors near and far, picking up on a moment's notice and steering their one-horse chaise a day's distance, spending nights away from home. And Ruth, it seems, is constantly left to reflect on the inability of human beings to arrest nature's course.

Ruth, like Eliza Foster, grew up with a strong consciousness of the American Revolution. She was the daughter of Colonel William Henshaw (1735–1820), a conspicuous figure at a critical juncture in the Revolutionary movement. A veteran of the French and Indian War, he helped to organize the Massachusetts militia in the mid-1770s and is credited with having been the first to propose to the colonial legislature the formation of "Minutemen" to protect vulnerable American households from England's hostile professional soldiery. In 1775–76, Colonel Henshaw assisted General Horatio Gates during the long British siege of Boston, and fought with Washington at the nearly disastrous Battle of Long Island shortly after Independence was declared. In later years, serving as a justice of the peace, Ruth's father named his eighth child after his old commander (who went on to greater fame in 1777 as the hero of the Battle of Saratoga). Horatio Gates Henshaw, though sixteen years her junior, was a favorite, and perhaps the closest to Ruth of all her siblings in later years.

Colonel Henshaw, "Billy" to his family and friends, had married Phebe Swan in Leicester, the town immediately west of Worcester, in the autumn of 1771. Ruth was born one year later. In early 1775, as armed conflict impended, Leicester's confident colonel was in close touch with his brother Joseph, a colonel in the Concord militia, and was moved to write to his superiors: "It appears very probable Gentlemen that before the end of this year we may be called into the field in defence of our Rights & Privileges. I heartily wish we may be prepared for it, being forewarned. . . ." He called for training all militiamen in the use of the bayonet, "to strike a greater Terror in our Enemy." Away from home after Lexington and Concord, Colonel Henshaw and his wife Phebe exchanged letters, mingling loving sentiment with patriotic exclamations: "In the Cold Nights," he wrote in one from outside Boston in January 1776, "I am sensible of the want of a Bed fellow, &

not knowing how long it will be before I enjoy the satisfaction of having you by my side—This unhappy War seperates many Dear Friends—I pray it may be shortly that every Person in this once happy Land may again enjoy the sweets of Liberty." He urged his wife from New York: "Encourage the Children in Learning & every virtuous action." And Phebe Henshaw, a very religious woman, dealt with separation by being "thank full for all the many Mercys which God is besto[w]ing on me," in granting continued health to her family, despite hardship.[2]

Nothing is known about Ruth's first sixteen years, though the "Daddy" of her diary must have been a powerful presence. Early journal entries describe her domestic duties—"washed the kitchen," "washed floors baked"—and feature incongruous pairings—"I had a tooth ache very bad had a new pair of leather shoes"—but mostly center around her parents' comings and goings. These depict a naive, protected girl who only marginally comprehends events and motives. For instance, March 3, 1789: "Cloudy rainy night Daddy & maam went to Northb[o]ro[ugh] in a Slay. Mr Andrews had allmost all his things took away from him by Mr Salsbury for Debt."[3]

At twenty-eight and still living with her parents, Ruth noted grave transitions in her own and the national consciousness. The death of "the illustrious" Washington and public commemoration of his life in the winter of 1799–1800 preceded the Henshaws' participation in the first Fourth of July celebrations of a new century. On June 1, 1800, she recorded melodramatically, "I have begun a new leaf on my journal and a new one in the volume of time. . . . How very swift the seasons roll away! We are too apt to forget how fast we are 'gliding down the current of time'! and consider not that each revolving day is taken from the short span of life—"[4]

Over the fifty-seven years in which she maintained her daily journal, every entry opens with a weather report. Many of these foretell the day's mood: for instance, coming home after her father's death in February 1820, she begins, "a thunder shower early in morn, and a little hail a very little snow scattered thro the day. in forenoon prepared for the interment of our much beloved parent." Were it not for her absorption in the culture of bereavement, Ruth Bascom's journal would be largely a catalogue of the names of guests who came to her door and "tarried." The black ink of the diary, which she mixed with sugar and a copper solution, chronicled one death after another: "Mr. Rice came up from

Northborough and brought word that Grandmother Gleason was but just alive, in a sort of a Lethargy"; "my dear Aunt Joss who died 27 of last month in her 79 year. O may these repeated calls awaken us from our Lethargy. . . . Death may come to us as a thief in the night!!!"[5] Her exclamation marks most often followed expressions of anguish or affliction rather than joy.

In 1804, at the relatively advanced age of thirty-one, Ruth married Dr. Asa Miles of Westminster, a good distance above Leicester. He was forty-three and a widower.[6] They were married for little more than a year when Asa began to complain of violent headaches. In March 1805, the doting wife was obliged to confront her husband's rapidly deteriorating condition. After a week absent of entries, her diary explains:

> 6 April Saturday. a storm of snow from the North east, which added to the gloom which pervades this habitation. Last week, on Wednesday evening, 27th March, it pleased the great Arbiter of events to take from me, my best and dearest friend, Dr Asa Miles! And the Saturday following we followed his dear remains to the dark and silent grave—O may the God of mercy consider my affliction, and grant that this heartfelt trial, this day of adversity may be sanctified—and may I so improve it as to be able to say it is good for me that I have been afflicted!—may I be anxious, only that I may be prepared to follow my departed husband whenever it shall please my Creator to call me into the world of spirits.

Attentive to the mortal truth of which her religion constantly reminded her, Ruth jotted down the psalm selected by the preacher at the funeral: "As for man, his days are as grass, as a flower of the field, so he finisheth . . ." And, without attribution, she added in a clear hand:

> Death cannot make our souls afraid
> If God be with us there.

Year after year, her diary shows that February and March were months of particular human suffering in her New England surroundings. (In 1826, it would be the height of an influenza epidemic that was felt not only in central Massachusetts but all across the United States.) The widow did not have to wait for the next February, however, before burying another family member. Her younger sister Catherine, especially adored ever since she was a toddler, suddenly died in mid-January 1806, at the age of twenty-one: "Our dear sister Catherine left this world of sin and sorrow, without a groan or struggle! a pattern of patience, of calmness, of resignation!—Dear sister! We mourn her early and unexpected departure—we mourn our loss—but we cannot mourn without hope—without hope that our loss is her gain."

Catherine's funeral took place three days later. But by now Ruth had already attracted the young Congregationalist minister of nearby Phillipston, Ezekiel Lysander Bascom, a man six or seven years her junior. They would be married, with her father's certain approbation, nine days later.[7] Her entry for February 26 is oblique:

Daddy & Mr Bascom attended the funeral of Mr Jonathan Sergeant. . . . At night Mr Moore returned with Daddy and administered the "oath of Alegeince" to my friend in presence of our family & the before mentioned friend E. L. Bascom & myself. . . .

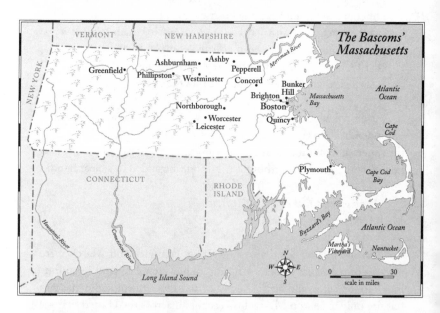

Map 1. The Bascoms' Massachusetts.

Three days after he and Ruth were married, Reverend Bascom preached at the behest of Reverend Moore: "No good thing will be withheld from them that walk uprightly."

Ezekiel Bascom knew suffering and deprivation as well as his wife did, and one wonders how he—indeed, how increasingly sentimental Americans in this still medically primitive age—steeled themselves to it. Words of resignation to the will of God, everywhere written and recited, seem like small ammunition. Though only in his mid-twenties, Ezekiel Bascom had already lost two wives. Five years before, his first, Priscilla Elvira, died—she was but nineteen. He remarried soon after to a woman named Sally, who bore a daughter, Priscilla Elvira, in 1803 (evidently named in honor of Bascom's late first wife). When their second child, a son named Lysander, was born in May 1805, Sally died. The infant was not strong either, and, poignantly, died three days before Reverend Bascom and the widow Ruth Henshaw Miles were joined together before family with an "oath of allegiance." His surviving daughter, who went by her middle name, Elvira, came to live with Ruth and him in 1807; though Ruth would remain childless, she grew attached to her stepdaughter.[8]

Shreds of a correspondence between the Bascoms and Ruth's brother Horatio Gates offer something beyond consolation—almost a sense of good fortune, of permanence—extending from the culture of bereavement. During the first decade of the marriage, Ezekiel Bascom presented himself as a sociable man who was often worn down by "fatigues & trials," but who persevered out of a belief in the value of Christian charity. "Ruthy," as she was termed in this series of letters, designated "Brother Horatio" as "a Sentinel" conveying the family news. In a rushed hand suggesting an agitated mind, she was nonetheless warm and beseeching: "It is a great source of happiness to me," she wrote, "to hear often from my friends." Much like Phebe Henshaw's wartime letters to her absent husband, her daughter Ruth humbly remonstrated with her own apparent happiness: "We enjoy a good share of health, and many other blessings that we do not deserve."[9]

From Phillipston, then, the Bascoms remained in close touch with "The Old Mansion" of the Henshaws. Ruth's record dwells mostly on external circumstances, until death, by custom, demands descriptive language from the diarist. In 1808 Phebe Henshaw "departed this life [after] a lingering decline." On the day after the funeral, the daughter claimed to have "heard a voice from heaven" instructing her that "blessed are the dead who die in the Lord." At the time of her octogenarian father's death of "lung fever" in 1820, Ruth was once again able to take solace, on the premise that this loved one, too, had departed with an "unshaken faith in the aliment of his Savior."[10]

THE BASCOMS resided in Phillipston until the end of 1820. Beginning in June of that year, and nearly every month thereafter, Ezekiel Bascom began making trips to Ashby, staying days at a time and always putting pen to paper so that his wife did not have to wait for his return to know of his activities. Ashby, an agricultural community with a population of just under 1,200, had experienced some turmoil when a minority in the Congregationalist Church (mainly women) combined with a majority of the town to resolve that they preferred a liberal Unitarian minister to an orthodox Calvinist one.

It was the same battle over doctrine that was taking place in more than a hundred congregations across the state. The liberals rejected the Trinity and believed instead in a Jesus who, if less than God, was nonetheless sinless and worthy of the highest love. While they stressed the freedom of human action, Unitarians still embraced the clergy as an elite corps who undertook moral responsibility for their communities, who served as guides to behavior while taking the lead in charitable activities. Meanwhile, in Phillipston, where he had been ordained twenty years earlier, Reverend Bascom was suffering a very perceptible, if unspecified, "disaffection" that made the prospect of a change desirable.[11]

Early in the process, as he was ingratiating himself with the people of Ashby, Bascom gave an address before the Freemasons of the town. The address was never recorded, but its content can be extrapolated from three earlier Masonic addresses that he gave, which were deemed worthy of publication. Indeed, Brother Ezekiel L. Bascom, as he was known in print, was reckoned a most zealous member of that fraternity.

Freemasonry, to those like Reverend Bascom who stood in awe of it, was a patriotic creed practiced by divinely inspired men, and linked to ingenious moral leaders of the past. To others—and this would become dramatically manifest after the events of the national jubilee were played out—the brotherhood had turned into something mysterious, alien, and suspect, an exclusionary cult up to no good, or pursuing a privileged interest for its members.

Masonic lodges had proliferated in England in the early eighteenth century, before finding their way to the American colonies. In the middle of the Revolution, young Lafayette became an American Freemason in a ceremony supervised by Brother George Washington during the Valley Forge winter.[12] Through most of his triumphal visit, in such cities as Boston, Baltimore, and New Orleans in 1824–25, Lafayette was in the company of Masons, or viewing Masons on parade. In Richmond, Levasseur wrote of one such parade, which included Chief Justice John Marshall: "A detachment of brethren with drawn swords, preceded the march." Levasseur emphasized the gravity of the ceremony by noting the silence of the spectators who crowded the route. A clergyman belonging to the fraternal order gave a discourse, reminding all that "true masonry reposed on *truth, equality,* and *charity,*" discharging duties to God and the human race at once. Lafayette's toast at that day's banquet was: "Liberty, Equality, Philanthropy, the true masonic symbol."[13]

After Independence was won, national dedications partook of the symbols of Freemasonry. The reverse of the Great Seal of the United States, adopted in 1786, features Masonic elements; Washington wore a Masonic apron and performed Masonic rituals in laying the cornerstone of the U.S. Capitol in 1793; in his role as grand master, Paul Revere laid the cornerstone of the Massachusetts State House on July 4, 1795. The considerable relationship of Masonry to political power in the early republic is suggested by historian Steven Bullock's statistic that at least seven of the thirteen men who served in President (and non-Mason) James Madison's cabinet over the course of the War of 1812 were known to be Masonic brethren.[14]

At the core of its system of belief, the Revolutionary brotherhood claimed a connection to ancient workmanship and ancient knowledge, to a profound and illuminating wisdom that modern practice was meant to revive. Freemasonry made the case that its primary mission was to spread benevolence, thus regarding itself entirely compatible with modern Christianity; Jesus was recognized in Masonic imagery as the "architect" of the church. With their secret signs, initiation rites, and mystical speculations, the Masons combined gentility and good fellowship with faith in a primal truth. According to Brother DeWitt Clinton, enterprising governor of New York during 1817–23 and 1825–28, their "signs, addressed to the *eye*, the *ear*, and the *touch*," were what enabled Masonry to "impress" its lessons "with greater force upon the mind" than other forms of moral persuasion.[15]

Freemasonry did not seek to undo science. The American order in particular revered this branch of knowledge. But it held that receptivity to a superior wisdom traceable to ancient builders, a wisdom unsullied by the intervening twists and turns of human history, made Masons better people and the progenitors of an enlightened society. As one newspaper report put it in 1826, Masonic principles had by this time already "extended across the states" with subtle strength, "a powerful influence, tho' it has been silent as the law."[16]

Masons like Bascom avidly associated their creed with religiosity, community stability, and national union. An 1826 poem published in an Ohio newspaper struck the tone of Masonic pride:

> *Empires and kings have passed away*
> *Into oblivion's mine:*
> *And towering domes have felt decay,*
> *Sin auld lang syne.*

> *But Masonry, the glorious art,*
> *With level square and line,*
> *Has lived its mystic light t'impart,*
> *Sin auld lang syne.*[17]

In 1826, "mystic light" meant nothing more mystical than if it had said "integrity and judgment," qualities of mind and culture understood to arise not spontaneously but through active cultivation. The "glorious art" of the Masons was their trust in an inheritance, which through civic consciousness and celebratory practices committed them to sociability and moral progress. This is why they organized so effectively to welcome Brother Lafayette, and why they eagerly anticipated the national jubilee. As another pro-Mason piece in the same Ohio newspaper explained, "The celebration of important events, and the solemnization of particular festivals, has been sanctioned by the wisdom of the ages. It has been the means of keeping in remembrance the most exalted virtues of human nature." Freemasons were convinced that they were agents of national honor, diffusing a Revolutionary public virtue that was consistent with good government.[18]

Reverend Ezekiel L. Bascom's 1800 "Masonic Discourse ... before the Officers and Brethren of the Republican Lodge" in Greenfield, Massachusetts, was delivered prior to his ordination in Phillipston. On this occasion Bascom mourned "our Father, our Brother" George Washington, who had died just two weeks earlier, identifying "benevolence" as the late president's highest excellence. "Real and undissembled benevolence," Bascom avowed, was the most morally comprehensive of obligations, the mark of elevated minds: "We shall extend our charity beyond the narrow limits of our own society." Using Masonic symbolism, he went on: "Let the *square* of wisdom and integrity; the *plumbline* of benevolence and charity; and the *compass* of piety and justice ever direct us."[19]

In subsequent addresses of 1815 and 1817, Bascom invoked benevolence and charity no less, but he woke to the controversy—the charges of unnecessary secrecy—already besetting the fraternity. He acknowledged that Masonry had its doubters and its enemies, and he acknowledged that one reason for this was that some Masons, "void of a Mason's heart," had failed to live up to the moral teachings of the order. Its members practiced the religion of Jesus, he assured, and that was how Masonry sustained itself. Here he sought to make Masonry and Christian piety one, appealing to his listeners: "I hope, while I have endeavored to speak the language of a *Christian*, none has taken offence at my views ... so I would continue to hope, that, while I attempt the language of a *Mason*, the Christian may not suppose me thinking *more highly* of the Order, *than I ought to think*."[20]

Association and mutual commitment (formative principles of Freemasonry) were, he reminded, "most powerful in ameliorating the condition of man, by softening his heart, smoothing his passions." "Fidelity, compassion, and charity," he repeated, the minister's cadence detectable in his prose, "and the virtues which endear us to each other, add to the sum of rational felicity and throw some sunny tints on the sombre picture of human life." Finally, almost as a catechism, Bascom tied the conscience of his generation to its predecessor: "The sage ... who rendered harmless the lightning and the thunder— *Franklin was a Mason*." "The orator ... whose mind was an assemblage of virtues—*Hamilton was a Mason.*" "The man in whose praises all unite . . . *Washington was a Mason.*"

From here, however, his defensiveness resurfaced. He tried to explain to his mixed audience—men and women—that the brotherhood was not undemocratic, though it met in secret conclaves rather than submitting to public debate. It had to be trusted—*he* had to be trusted—with moral agency: "To the indiscrete advocates of female Masonry I have little to say," he charged severely. "The duties of Masonry, like the affairs of state, are unsuitable to their tenderer sex. . . . The delicacy of their sex would shudder at the idea of joining in those secret assemblies, which are indispensably necessary to the honor and advancement of our institution." Bascom rested Freemasonry's case on the perverse presumption that his argument logically proved that the brotherhood was not engaged in any compact with the devil. Some secrecy was required, he said, if "real men," devout, trustworthy community leaders, were to forge progress.[21]

By mid-November of 1820, Ashby—or as Ruth Bascom referred to it, "the Committee of that Town"—decided by "a unanimous call" to invite Reverend Bascom, now in his forties, "to settle with them as a gospel minister." He would be paid an annual salary of $475. On December 22, 1820, a day on which Ruth noted the two hundredth anniversary of the landing at Plymouth Rock, the Bascoms began preparing for a transition. And on the last day of the year, having officiated during his twenty-year residence at 127 marriages and 247 deaths, Reverend Bascom preached a farewell sermon to his Phillipston congregation. As a text it proceeds rather dispiritedly:

> The hour of separation is a most interesting hour. It calls up the finer feelings of the heart; and when the word "FAREWELL" trembles on the tongue, a thousand tender images assemble around us. We see pictures of "departed joys"—
> "Departed—never to return!"

Such mournful tones could have come as well from Ruth's diary. Bascom, though he was to be but a day's drive from his remaining Phillipston friends, could not find any analogy but death to convey his appreciative sentiments:

Desponding clouds surround us, darken the view of brighter scenes, and leave us to feel how much wo[e] may be crowded into this little span of our existence!

He repeatedly invoked the one image—"the brevity of human life"—to a congregation no doubt long accustomed to his funeral sermons. "We come into this world in tears," he went on, "as though instinctive nature prepared her pupils for discipline in the school of adversity." The Masonic brother who regularly acclaimed acts of benevolence appears, at least in print, a condescending man who made his living reminding people of the inevitability of suffering.[22]

Or perhaps the emotion he most felt was bitterness. "Look to the example of your Saviour," he pled vaguely, "And O, be entreated to be much in prayer for the future Union of your Society. Pray for the peace of Jerusalem." Imagining the congregation crumbling after his exit, the preacher bade his people to find other places of worship that suited their individual tastes. His muddled speech never rose from doubt and veiled cynicism, as he urgently explained away any suggestion of selfishness on his part: "I am fully confirmed in the belief that *it is expedient for you that I go away* [citing John 16:7, according to Ruth's diary]. . . . I have not been seduced from my duty and the Church by the glare of *profitable offers.*" Rationalizing uncomfortably, Bascom could only enshroud the true cause of his departure in mystery: "The separation, now it has taken place, seems rather like a dream—like an illusion of the imagination, than a reality; and, O happy should I be, could I awake and find it so!" Conjuring images of death and remorse, masking his real feelings, Ezekiel Bascom left Phillipston in darkness.[23]

His forbearing wife, meanwhile, was unwell, "confined to the house & till lately, to my room." She wrote unpropitiously, "This is the close of the last year we are to spend in Phillipston and perhaps on earth!" It was an awkward moment in her life. She had been under the same roof for nearly fifteen years, finding peace amid "my little loved house and shrubbery & tall surrounding popplers, and pleasant gardens." A "beam of joy and gratitude" had greeted her every time she arrived "from excursion" at her own door. Still, she accepted the move to Ashby, anticipating that the new community would be "equally pleasant & equally friendly—but they are not 'Old friends.' "[24] Two days after she penned these remarks, her husband was off to preach his first sermon as Ashby's pastor, returning to Ruth the next day at dusk, and repeating this demanding commute for a full month.

Reverend Bascom's installation at the Ashby Church took place on January 2–3, 1821. Ministers from thirteen churches were present. They came from greater distances than the new pastor himself—from Concord, Lancaster, and New Salem, from Wilton, in New Hampshire. Indeed, the clergyman selected to deliver the sermon in Ashby on that day was Eliza Foster's father, the Reverend John Foster from Brighton, at the edge of Boston. His address was solemn and focused on clerical duty. Foster cautioned that Bascom's work would be "arduous," that "publick teachers" were often "assailed," yet, he acknowledged, Ashby's new minister had already proven in Phillipston an "unconquered attachment" to service. The assembled council concurred, and the Reverend Jonathan Osgood of nearby Gardner charged Bascom to "commend thyself to every man's conscience in the sight of God," at the same time cautioning: "You will, no doubt, meet with opposition from wicked and unreasonable men; but remember you are set for the defence of the gospel."[25]

On February 16, the Bascoms, accompanied by a few friends, finally loaded their belongings onto carriages and braved a "stormy ride" up to Ashby. We have to contrive to hear as well as see this fragile world in motion, to imagine through the diarist's words these, the most common sounds to reach the ears of early American travelers: the snapping of the whip, a clattering of horses' hoofs, the creaking of the wheels over hard earth and the expected bumps and mudholes, rocks and stumps and breakdowns. Saying goodbye was a mixed moment for the Bascoms; personal quarrels among the church membership in Phillipston had given them, as Ruth acknowledged, "many unpleasant weeks & months."

Believing that there was "no happiness without its alloy, & no affliction destitute of its consolation," Ruth adapted quickly to her new neighborhood. In spite of high snowdrifts and "poor sleighing," the nineteenth of February was "a monumental day with us—as we this day commenced housekeeping." Her husband had already purchased a new home, one-third of a mile north of the meetinghouse; he sometimes walked, sometimes rode to services. The Bascoms' "good neighbors" had assisted in the wintry move, and Ruth soon found the hospitality of Ashby's residents to be more than surface cordiality.

Her days consisted largely of conversations with young and old, attending church services, encouraging the Sabbath singers, dining and taking tea with neighbors, and worrying along with them when loved ones took ill. "Mr B" himself occasionally suffered stomach pain, headaches, and "spasms." In the main, her journals contain the somber repetition of his official duties, and deaths which came in clusters: "15 [March 1823] Mr Bascom to Ashburnham [the next town over, to the west] to see Revd Cushing, and attend the funeral of Capt Cushing's wife, who died on Thursday aged 63." "30 [March] Sabbath . . . Mr Bascom on horseback to the funeral of Mr Hartwell's infant, whose mother was buried on Thursday last." "28 [April] . . . Mr Bascom to Ashburnham (at 9) by request to see the bereaved family of Dr Cushing . . . Mr Willard evening with Mr Bascom who heard of the death of George Cushing, only child of the late Mr George Cushing, a fine youth of 17, the only earthly hope of his widowed mother! died in W. Indies."

The Cushing tragedy continued to unfold: "30 [April] All the company returned to their homes, except the family connexions, Mr Bascom & myself, who tarried over night; about 5 after much preparatory conversation, Mrs George Cushing was informed of the death of her only Child (at Havana) . . . the family having kept the knowledge of the distressing event from her several days in compassion to her & the already bereaved family." Reverend Bascom prayed with the survivors. It was, of course, all that he could do.

The year 1826 opened for Ruth with a conventional lament, common to the bound diaries of previous years: "A new year! O the flight of time." Her husband was feeling under the weather for the first half of January, though he managed to preach "all day" on the eighth, a day of calm and sunshine. Applying pressure, salt, and vinegar helped his headaches to a degree, and Ruth prepared hot baths as well. Neighbors' regular visits continued, and the "singing committee" met over tea and stayed several hours. On the first of February, fourteen men took supper with the Bascoms after chopping wood for them for three hours; on the thirteenth, another gang (this time twenty-four men) appeared and "cut sawed & piled wood for us & a part supped here."

The minister, feeling somewhat improved, was out and about in accordance with his habitual ministering schedule, though he and everyone else were proceeding with caution in their sleighs on the icy, rough roads. The Bascoms' entertaining gradually increased, as the reverend found strength to preach "all day" for the first time in five weeks. When her husband made late calls and Ruth did not accompany him, she wrote, only half-persuasively: "I tarried at home in evening, *alone* but not *lonesome*."[26]

Toward the end of February, Ruth and Ezekiel Bascom were confined to their house with coughs and colds, "though mine," she wrote, "not severe enough to be called influenza." As the couple struggled, Ruth recorded parenthetically on the twenty-sixth, between accounts of yet more deaths nearby, what seemed to be a breath of thanksgiving: "(is it possible? Twenty years this day, since my name became Bascom!)."

Also during the month of her twentieth wedding anniversary, Ruth paid especially close attention to the Worcester-based newspaper that the people of Ashby read, the *Massachusetts Spy*. The four-page weekly had begun 1826 with cautionary references to the winter ills all knew to expect. A page-one story "On Death" conjured images of a welcome end to earthly life: "The Poet has lent his fictions, the Painter his colours, the Orator his tropes to portray Death as the grand destroyer." But it was life, the writer insisted, that brought the only misery. "Life is the gaoler [jailer] of the soul in this filthy prison, and its only deliverer is Death. What we call life is a journey to death, and what we call death is a passport to life." On page two, a different article intensified this fixation, with the headline "Burning of Widows." It reported on the Hindu practice, reprinting an English observer's letter: "I stood gazing at the still blazing pile, lost in reflections on the scene I had witnessed."[27]

On March 1, over a foot of snow lay on the ground, and a damp snow fell the whole day. Ruth complained that she had not breathed the air for "some days past." Another of Ashby's residents had just buried an infant, who had only survived two days. On the fourth, she read the latest issue of the *Spy* and remarked on the death of a twenty-year-old woman from her hometown of Leicester. Widening her perspective without changing the subject, she noted that "the Influenza prevails in every corner of this country." In Boston, thirty thousand were in the throes of it, or had successfully weathered it over the previous three weeks. A New York weekly had called it "the barking disease," prescribing barley water, taken in large doses, sweetened with brown sugar and "impregnated with acid." Ruth copied down the *Spy*'s recommended treatment, though it was perhaps even less inviting: an ounce of castor oil added to "spirits of Turpentine mixed & swallowed at one draught at the beginning of the disease, affords the most relief." In Philadelphia, where "scarce an individual has escaped," forty-five people died of influenza in a single week, causing the columnist to take solace that the number was so low.[28]

As the perilous month of March wore on, the *Spy* published melancholy verse:

> *The tear which falls upon thy tomb,*
> *It would not win thee back to earth,*
> *Nor bind thee to the darker doom*
> *Of one of mortal birth:—*[29]

At the end of that month, one more funereal exclamation pops from the pages of Ruth's diary: it was a cool and windy day, as the Bascoms attended the interment of "Mrs Farr's two children, who were both buried in one coffin!" Ruth stayed after most others had left to view the uncommon sight, as the coffin was opened to reveal the "remains of the little sufferers."[30]

However, March went out quietly. Inclement weather and reports of deaths seemed to dissipate at once. Ruth was taken by a story in the *Spy* on the success of a medical operation in the western part of the state: a team of doctors in Southampton had opened a child's windpipe and removed a fragment of coal that had lodged there, saving the young life. She doubtless was recalling from a few winters past the Phillipston neighbor who had died when a piece of meat had lodged in his windpipe. But it was an ironic article in the same issue of the *Spy* that captivated her more than any other that season. In Paris, France, a "miserable looking wretch, who fed on bread and water" (she quoted the story directly) was found frozen to death in an obscure shed, in possession of 30,000 francs in gold that were hidden inside his belt. Back in his garret, another 100,000 francs were discovered inside a mattress. The man's family had "sent a cart to carry him to Potter's Field," but on finding his wealth, recalled the cart and hired a hearse.

"His only friend," Ruth noted, "was a dog, who slept in his closet." Extraordinary stories always piqued her interest.[31]

The spring of 1826 was filled once again with happy visits to and from neighbors. Ruth made certain that the widow Gates was occupied, showed off her new sofa to Captain Goodhue and daughter, and watched nervously as her husband wore himself out working hours on end in the garden. Fruit trees began "putting forth leaves" in early May. Good neighbor Almira Gobson came for tea and then "washed our pew, pulpit, and stairs &c." The State of Massachusetts enacted a law abolishing whipping and one "for the punishment of Fornication and for the maintenance of Bastard Children."[32] It was at this time, too, that Ruth took out her art supplies.

Ruth Henshaw Bascom was already widely known as an amateur artist. She had begun cutting paper profiles in 1801 and would compile a portfolio of as many as a thousand such creations by the end of her years. She had been influenced in some way by the itinerant Ethan Allen Greenwood (1779–1856), whom she had first met at the Leicester Academy in 1800 and who had spent several days with the Bascoms in 1807, painting Ruth, Ezekiel, and little Elvira. While he opted for oils, Ruth specialized in the silhouette, perhaps because it was easy and inexpensive to acquire the necessary materials—all she had to do was to place a candle beside her subject and draw on paper from the shadow cast. Then she could cut out the image and either render it black on white or white on black paper, the latter method enabling her to touch up the profile with color highlights.[33]

Beyond keeping a fairly prosaic diary, then, the minister's wife found inspiration in producing portraits of the people she knew. When Almira Gobson performed her service for the church in May 1826, Ruth obliged her to stay and "took her profile." On the eleventh of that month, after Reverend Bascom paid a call at the home of the ailing Mr. Wallis, Ruth noted in her diary that "the sick man continued to take little or no notice of passing objects thro' this day, and at 10, evening slept the sleep of death (without moving a limb or a feature) aged 78 years." On the day following, the late Mr. Wallis's two daughters prevailed on Ruth to take a profile of their father, and so she did. Unlike Greenwood, who grumbled that "to paint a likeness of a dead person . . . is such a job I wish to never undertake," Ruth apparently found such occupation less disagreeable. She sat patiently with her

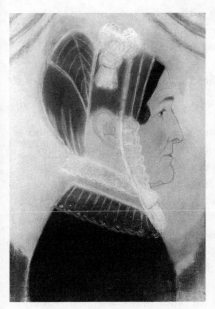 

Fig. 5 (a & b). Ruth Henshaw Bascom, self-portrait, and Ezekiel L. Bascom, by Ruth Henshaw Bascom, pastel on paper, c. 1829. Her diary captured the everyday life of a minister's wife, while the production of profile portraits widened her role in a small New England community. *(Courtesy, Historic Deerfield, Inc.)*

deceased subject and did not arrive home until after sunset. Two more days passed, and Reverend Bascom preached a funeral sermon for Mr. Wallis, expanding on a line from Job 30:23: "For I know that thou will bring me to Death."[34]

The rituals surrounding death invited artistic expression for a variety of American Romantics. In *The Sketch Book,* the work published during this period that introduced Rip Van Winkle and made him a celebrity, Washington Irving wrote bewitchingly of the shared experience of burying loved ones, and of the culture of consolation. In "The Widow and Her Son," he depicts a sunny country scene in which two laborers stand digging a grave in that corner of the church property where "the indigent and friendless were huddled into the earth." Irving, as narrator, continues to loiter as a hapless young man is laid to rest. As the men with cords lower the plain coffin into the grave, the dead man's glazed-eyed mother, amid her "wretched reverie," is comforted by a single soul whose whispers elicit only a helpless shake of the head. The "creaking of the cords" cruelly antagonizes the bereft woman, and upon "a jostling of the coffin, all the tenderness of the mother burst forth; as if any harm could come to him who was far beyond the reach of worldly suffering."

To chronicle this humble life amid death, Irving resolves to see the story through to its natural conclusion. He explains how, lost in lonely grief, the impoverished woman appears in church the next Sunday, "offering up the prayers and praises of a pious, though broken heart." She goes through the motions of honoring the recently departed by wearing signs of mourning: "a black ribbon or so—a faded black handkerchief." All this serves but to hasten her own passage to the grave, and, concludes the author, "in the course of a Sunday or two after she was missed from her usual seat at church, and before I left the neighborhood, I heard, with a feeling of satisfaction, that she had quietly breathed her last. . . ." "The grave is the ordeal of true affection," wrote Irving elsewhere. "The sorrow for the dead is the only sorrow from which we refuse to be divorced."[35]

So, Ruth and Ezekiel Bascom's desperate immersion in the lives and deaths of neighbors was by no means their singular lot. A romance with the power of death was as nationally "popular" at this time as Americans' consummate fascination with the splendor of the Revolution past. Jan Lewis has shown in her study of early nineteenth-century Virginia that personal dramas surrounding suffering, consolation, and bereavement enhanced the meaning of relationships. A good death, she writes, was a great consolation.[36]

Here is where the two generations distinctly differed: in the Revolutionary era, people did not ordinarily register the last days of loved ones. The accustomed process of death, like conjugal love, was made public as dispassionately as possible, stated matter-of-factly and not disclosed in its torture and torment. When his wife died in 1782, for example, Thomas Jefferson described his condition as a "stupor," as though it were dulling rather than a profoundly disruptive interior event. In his time, death could be called a "melancholy episode," but unraveling melancholy into its sensational components was thought disagreeable. Only the death of Washington in December 1799 was permitted to evoke an outpouring of public tears; yet even then, citizens mourned through chaste, external symbols, such as the purifying painting, put on wide display, which showed the late president in the care of heavenly forces, serenely bathed in a divine light, lifted to paradise by angels.[37]

The new century and a new generation gradually allowed the natural passion of mourning lost loves to be extravagantly exhibited. Diarists recorded the course of vanishing lives with a sentimental engagement: Virginian John Cocke witnessed his wife Nancy's slow demise in 1816, noting how she sought to arrest his fears by a display of her own fortitude, how she "would not murmur against" God's decree. Husband and wife spoke of her impending death without code words: one night Nancy said that she had "heard Mrs. Coalter died as easily as I am now going to sleep." Again she assured John, "I feel not the least alarm and never had at contemplating death." She considered the parting gifts she wanted to bestow upon her family, removing her wedding ring for the very first time and giving it over to her husband. She named the dead whom she said she looked forward to meeting after being separated from her body, and, in her husband's words, "an angelic smile lighted up her emaciated features."[38]

Waking to another day, Nancy Cocke began to be concerned that her thorough preparations might be for nought: "It will be a pity if I am not to die now, for perhaps, I shall never again be as well prepared." A few more days passed before her final moment approached, when her feeble hands gently pressed those of each member of her family, and John Cocke inscribed in his diary: "such was the calm and peaceful rest of her blessed spirit, that it left her mortal remains without the slightest tremour of a nerve or the agitation of a muscle."[39]

Washington Irving and the Cockes of Virginia found, with Ruth and Ezekiel Bascom, a dark communion. Nature in a multitude of ways excited the human spirit, and when Adams and Jefferson both died on the day of jubilee, their deaths enriched the life of the nation. If people were to contrive it as such, death could be a perfect reconception of the life of the mind for those whom it snatched from earthly existence. This was all they had to temper the grim reality of human loss. In vibrant imagery, Lord Byron as well alluded to the course of human events when he wrote of the heart's endurance amid visceral convulsions:

The hull drives on, though mast and sail be torn;
The roof-tree sinks, but moulders on the hall
In massy hoariness; the ruin'd wall
Stands when its wind-worn battlements are gone;
The bars survive the captive they enthral;
The day drags through, though storms keep out the sun;
And thus the heart will break, yet brokenly live on.[40]

In the unquiet of American life, the people of 1826 knew that they only temporarily occupied their certain space. Yet they steadfastly pursued their ownership of that space, conscious that the passing generation had generously bequeathed it to them. Expressing at once the vigor and anxiety of their times, they ruminated publicly on what they might do with the possibilities of the present. If there was a "cause" in 1826, it was this, to seize the opportunity to improve their world.

CHAPTER FIVE

Old Cheese Goes up for
Sale in Chillicothe

E THAN ALLEN BROWN had the glorious distinction of being born
on the same day as his country: July 4, 1776. His father was a
Connecticut farmer of means, a militia officer since 1769. The record is
fragmentary, but it shows that Ethan was the youngest of seven in a
decidedly patriot family. In 1775, before Ethan was born, his oldest
brother, David, at age eighteen, joined the rebel cause and rose to lieutenant under the restive Connecticut farmer-general Israel Putnam, a
celebrated participant in the Battle of Bunker Hill.[1]

Ethan was named for another local hero. The robust adventurer
Ethan Allen was a scrappy speculator who had earlier migrated north
from Connecticut and just weeks after the Battles of Lexington and
Concord led his rustic Vermont band, the Green Mountain Boys, to
the gates of Fort Ticonderoga on Lake Champlain. In a surprise
attack, Allen took the strategic fort and denied the British a decisive
water route from Canada to New York's Hudson River Valley. On the
auspicious day when Brown was born, the daring Ethan Allen was a
British prisoner of war, having erroneously believed after his first
momentous act of patriotism that he could as successfully invade
British Canada. Colonel Allen's 1780 account of his four-year captivity
became an instant Revolutionary bestseller.[2]

His namesake matured, meanwhile, studying French, Latin, and
Greek, and dividing his time between farming and the law. In 1798,

twenty-two-year-old Ethan Allen Brown went to New York to further his education, and ended up working in the law office of Alexander Hamilton. By the time he was admitted to the bar four years later, Brown had found ample companionship among the curious young intellects of the fast-growing city, the men of his generation who practiced self-improvement in the manner of Benjamin Franklin, by forming literary clubs. Judging his professional opportunities in New York to be limited, however, Ethan decided to strike out for the West. He rode on horseback across rural Pennsylvania, still a patchwork of old Indian paths and military roads, some dating to the French and Indian War. Investing in two flatboats loaded with flour, he floated down the Ohio River to the Mississippi, and on to New Orleans. Unable to find a buyer for his product, he transferred it to a vessel bound for England, where it was successfully sold. Encouraged by his western travel, the young man purchased several thousand acres of Ohio River land in what would become Rising Sun, Indiana. It lay thirty-five miles below the rough-and-tumble frontier town of Cincinnati, the population of which was barely one thousand at the time Brown set up his law practice there.[3]

It did not take long for Ethan Allen Brown to rise to prominence in Ohio. Despite his former association with the Federalist leader

Fig. 6. Popular Ohio governor and canal promoter Ethan Allen Brown, born on the Fourth of July, 1776. *(Courtesy, Ohio Historical Society.)*

Hamilton, Brown switched party allegiance after his removal west. He must have attracted a following among Cincinnati Jeffersonians by 1806, because he was engaged at that time by President Jefferson's treasury secretary, Albert Gallatin, to examine the books of the Cincinnati land office. He went on to serve as prosecuting attorney for Hamilton County, until being rewarded with an appointment to the Ohio Supreme Court, where he sat until his election as governor in 1818.

He was a man on the move in a state on the rise. During the campaign, a supportive newspaperman editorialized that the enthusiastic Brown had never once deviated from "the principles of republican rectitude." A less overwhelmed Ohioan wrote that the office seeker was known to fall asleep on his horse, slumping for miles at a time as he rode, owing to a mysterious dysfunction of the brain. In either case, at the age of forty-two, the incoming governor was notably euphoric about Ohio's prospects as a trading dynamo within the Union. He particularly counted on an economic alliance with the state of New York, which, having embarked on construction of the Erie Canal, would benefit coal and iron ore mining interests in the northeast part of his state, as well as the dairy and wheat lands of central Ohio.[4]

Riding out the devastating Panic of 1819, when farmers' mortgages were called as a result of a nationwide tightening of credit, Governor Brown aimed to protect his state from an economic slowdown. As part of his strategy, he decided to tax the two Ohio branches of the Bank of the United States. This brought on an eventual U.S. Supreme Court battle, in which Ohio's case of its right to tax a congressionally constituted bank lost to the superior arguments of Attorney General William Wirt, and two other government attorneys, Henry Clay and Daniel Webster. That was in 1824, the year Lafayette and Levasseur gazed at the peaceably flowing Ohio River and remarked on the free soil of a burgeoning Cincinnati. By then, however, Ethan Allen Brown had given up the governorship to accept the seat of a deceased U.S. Senator.[5]

He retired at the end of his Senate term in 1825, to labor full-time soliciting Eastern loans on behalf of canal building. Since 1818, he had staked his reputation on a canal system for Ohio—"Brown's Folly," it was at first called, to match its forerunner, the much praised Erie Canal, once disparaged as governor of New York DeWitt Clinton's "Big Ditch." To Brown, who had guided a flatboat all the way to the

Gulf of Mexico, his adopted state's future rested on its ability to transport its products.

While Brown held its top elective offices, Ohio, more than any other place in America, symbolized the road west. It was a model of human and commercial growth, its people of the pioneering mold, self-sufficient yet social, and, like Brown, explicitly risk-takers. During the first quarter of the nineteenth century, Ohio's population had miraculously jumped from forty-two thousand to eight hundred thousand. It had become the fourth most populous state in the Union, after attaining statehood only in 1803, the year Brown arrived there.

Place names manifest Ohioans' patriotism. Of the earliest counties formed (even before statehood), one east of Cincinnati on the Ohio River was named Adams and another near the Pennsylvania line, just above Wheeling, was named Jefferson. Public-spirited citizens were rather free with their naming, as a reviewer of John Kilbourn's *Ohio Gazetteer* wryly noted in 1826. Each of the fifty-nine counties seemed to have either a town of Jefferson (there were eighteen in all), a Madison (nineteen), a Monroe (twenty), or a Washington (twenty-two). "A more deplorable confusion of names could hardly be imagined," the reviewer observed. "[T]he legislature of Ohio could not do a wiser thing, than to appoint a committee of ingenious men to devise as many distinct names as there are separate towns in the state, and then let them be assigned by lot."[6] The frontier condition exasperated the early organizers of Ohio: in the 1790s Virginia Republicans had poured in, overturning the orderly designs of elite New England Federalists who had aimed for a restrictive kind of settlement. Yeoman energy prevailed until, by the mid-1820s, systematic minds were ready to redesign the maturing state.[7]

Ohio politics could not be easily characterized. In the unwieldy presidential election of 1824, when John Quincy Adams squeaked past Andrew Jackson, Ohio's Adams and Jefferson Counties both went for Jackson, while the most popular candidate statewide was, in fact, neighboring Kentucky's Henry Clay. Indeed, to make matters seem even more confused, Jackson County, organized in 1816 (the year after the Tennessee general's great victory at New Orleans), cast its majority for Clay as well. Of course, Adams finally won the presidency in the controversial House runoff election, and in doing so received the votes of the Ohio congressional delegation. Clay, Ohio's favorite in 1824, was

Map 2. Ohio Canals, 1826.

excluded from the runoff, because, according to the Twelfth Amendment, only the three leading vote-getters could participate, and Clay had placed fourth in electoral votes behind Jackson, Adams, and Georgia's William Crawford, in the general election.

If Ohio was a political hodgepodge, nothing quite explains the fact that all of those congressmen who chose Adams over the more popular Jackson in the House runoff were subsequently reelected. The bitterness that persisted among Jackson supporters elsewhere in 1825–26 was less pronounced in Ohio. Although Jackson would capture the state's popular vote in 1828, local issues still remained of greater concern to commercially oriented Ohioans than the noisy distractions of national politics.[8]

This was equally a time of movement and consolidation. Centrally situated, Columbus did not become the state capital until 1816, shortly before Governor Brown's tenure began. At the time of statehood in 1803, the capital had been Chillicothe, lying along the Scioto River in the south-central part of the state. It was still Ohio's third largest town in 1826, after Cincinnati and Steubenville, and had a population of 2,426, according to the 1820 national census. Wagon roads, built by state-approved turnpike companies, connected the principal towns and collected twenty-five cents each ten miles from four-wheeled, horse-drawn vehicles, and two cents each ten miles for cattle. There were exceptions: folks driving to church or militia muster and ordinary pedestrians traveled free.[9]

Ohio's citizens in general lived at wide distances from one another. The vast majority lived on farms in outlying areas and in villages containing fewer than five hundred persons. Chillicothe's inland situation put it some fifty miles at the closest point (Portsmouth) from the commercial lifeline of the Ohio River, along a stump-ridden, pockmarked passage, and even farther from the state's undisputed principal city of Cincinnati. This made communications of the utmost importance to the former capital if it wished to remain integrated. The persevering town newspaper maintained postal links with other journals around the country, reported Eastern news, and kept townspeople alert to changes and opportunities to prosper.

Newspapers were important in the developing West, no less than in the older states. A musing Bostonian's inquiry, reprinted in Ohio, denied as "vulgar and untrue" the common conception that newspapers were "chaff, suited only to the capacity of inferior minds," or a respite from boredom. This particular press advocate applauded their probity and overall coverage: "There is a subject fitted to the condition, the character, the feelings and the taste of every individual.—the merchant reads the advertisements; the lawyer the report of trials; the divine, the enlightening news of missionary efforts; the husbandman reads of fine crops—the stock-jobber of a rise in the funds; the doctor of epidemics; and old maids of marriages, in cases more hopeless than their own."[10]

The Supporter, and Scioto Gazette, Chillicothe's weekly paper, was four pages in length. A typical issue in 1826 contained an original essay on historical, moral, or current political topics, plus poetry, agricultural hints, and extensive foreign news. Town leaders appeared quite anxious that their young people receive a proper education, and no segment of society escaped their attentive gaze. An essay "FOR THE LADIES" cautioned: "Never make *money* the object of marriage, for if you do, depend upon it as a balance to the good you will get a bad husband." It was a safer bet, the essayist concluded, to settle on a husband who was unashamed to be seen walking alongside his mother, "supporting her weak and tottering frame upon his arm."[11]

Chivalry marched alongside ads for chewing tobacco in the Chillicothe press. The ads themselves ranged from "piano for sale" to "good, clean HEMP," to "Found: two bunches of keys."[12] A local merchant, a Mr. Atkinson, ran one from February 15, 1826, to the end of July that went as follows:

OLD CHEESE, &c.
Just received and for sale, next door to
Mr. B. Eaton's Store, a fine lot of OLD
CHEESE, of a superior quality; and a large
assortment of NEW BOOTS, of good
workmanship.

To experience the ways of these people more closely, let us take up Mr. Atkinson's offer, and pause for an historic look at his product. American cheese in 1826 was mainly cheddar. It had been so for quite some time already. From England the Puritans had brought their cows and the know-how to make cheddar. Milk was set over a fire to warm and curdle, placed in a basket and pressed, drained, turned, and rubbed. Next the curd was placed in a cloth to dry and turned again. Then the soft product was left to ripen. This Puritan method continued to be employed in the eighteenth century, and frontier Ohioans probably did similarly.[13]

The quality of cheese, then as now, was affected by the quality of the milk, which in turn was conditioned by the grasses on which the cows fed and, more generally, the climate in which the cows were bred. Conditions of temperature and humidity determined smell and flavor, as did, of course, the aging of the cheese. In early America, a soft, mild cheddar was aged, or cured, two to three months; a mellow or medium-aged cheese was cured up to six months; and a sharp or aged cheese—and this is the meaning of Mr. Atkinson's "OLD CHEESE"—was cured longer than half a year. Such a cheese would have been hard, pungent, and stimulating.

In a time and an economy where little remained fresh for very long, a tasty food that could satisfy hunger and bolster social occasions was much prized. On January 1, 1802, the Baptist minister John Leland presented President Thomas Jefferson with a widely publicized "mammoth cheese." The members of Leland's congregation in the town of Cheshire, in western Massachusetts, had produced it from the milk of nine hundred cows—at one mass milking. The cheese left Cheshire by wagon in the autumn of 1801, was transported by boat down the Hudson River to New York and by boat again to Baltimore, before a wagon took it right up to the executive mansion. Crowds assembled along the route to view this dairy treasure, which then resided with the president until 1805. Newspapers proclaimed it "The Greatest Cheese in America, for the Greatest Man in America." By the end of the first year, some sixty pounds had been cut from the middle of the slowly decomposing gift, until it was either gobbled up at state events or dumped into the Potomac (the fate of this consummate cheese in fact remains uncertain). When Andrew Jackson came into office in 1829, an admirer would honor the new chief executive with another huge cheddar, set in the main hall of the President's House for the enjoyment of official and unofficial guests.[14]

In the 1820s, while Ohio remained economically diverse, the land of upstate New York was reconceived. Dairying began to replace arable farming in the central counties of Oneida and Herkimer, and west to Lake Erie, where the Erie Canal was under construction. In portions of western Pennsylvania, too, ordinary lives were changing. Topography and climate interacted in these hilly northern areas to provide the cow with—in the advocates' words—"pure water" and "sweet pasture." Their milk and, ultimately, their cheese were expected to profit from the salutary environment.[15]

The Puritans, of course, were not the only people to lead their cows aboard North American–bound vessels. The ancestors of American cows were from places as varied as the original European inhabitants themselves—from England's many parts, from Scotland, the Netherlands, and Scandinavia. During the middle decades of the nineteenth century, drovers frequently led dairy herds in both directions between central New York and Ohio.[16] Cheese producers became expert in spotting good dairy cattle. They looked for small- and thin-headed, broad-backed, large-uddered, long-teated animals, and though unattractive as far as cows went, these were the most desirable for milking. Part of an old English verse, still circulating in America, described the ideal docile milking cow (in words that also seem a bawdy allusion to female sexuality):

> *She's wide in her hips, and calm in her eyes;*
> *She's fine in her shoulders, and thin in her thighs . . .*

Cheese was being sold through country stores, but it was also being organized more and more through determined middlemen, who traveled far and wide, especially as the Erie Canal became operational.[17]

The dairy districts were bustling with commercial activity. In sum, whether Chillicothe's "OLD CHEESE" was a product of the cheese dairy farmers of central New York, as is very possible, or of an early Ohio entrepreneur, it was no doubt regarded as a special commodity.

On the Western frontier of this age—in Ohio, Kentucky, Tennessee, Indiana, and Illinois—families knew few luxuries. They raised corn to feed their hogs and to distill into affordable whiskey, which around this time replaced rum as the most favored alcoholic beverage. Indeed, whiskey formed an essential part of neighborhoods. In one revealing account, a Jefferson County, Ohio, pioneer recalled the custom of the 1820s: "It was used as an invigorator and a sign of hospitality; and the manner of taking it was from the neck of the jug, each man swallowing as much as he wanted." At every social gathering, all drank and none refused; even the women were given to whiskey, sweetened in the form of a toddy. An 1826 advertisement for "A first rate Farm to Rent," five miles outside Cincinnati, listed as its first attribute: "It has a fine distillery," only then touting its "commodious barn," "extensive orchard," and the land's suitability for dairy and other livestock.[18]

Eating habits reflected the real problems of transportation and lack of refrigeration. Westerners were big meat-eaters. Hogs were valuable because their weight increased 150-fold in the first eight months of life, and the flavor of the meat improved over time when preserved—that is, smoked and hung out to dry. Healthier foods were too perishable to form a major part of the diet. Fruits were eaten in summer only, and the high cost of sugar made it too expensive to preserve them. Peaches rotted and were fed to hogs. The pert English observer Frances Trollope asserted that in the two summers she spent in Cincinnati, 1828 and 1829, she had "never tasted a peach worth eating." This was another reason why cheese made sense. Many homes contained churns and cheese presses, and milk was immediately converted into butter or cheese, which could be kept a long time.[19]

So Ohio was not only being described as an inviting garden landscape. An unimpressed traveler wrote from Cincinnati in the winter of 1818–19 (the year Cincinnati was incorporated as a city) that the residents were too "indolent" to raise many crops. They survived, he wrote, on "hog, homminy, and hoe cake." Life was arduous and none too safe. "Poisoned milk," "sick wheat," and copperhead snakes caused him to doubt that the land was conducive to cattle, or human settlement. While a few apple and peach orchards appeared to hold out the promise of greater abundance, Ohio settlers from New York and New England, were, as this one traveler reported, "disappointed in their expectations, and dissatisfied with the country."[20]

Then why were such an immense number of Americans going west? Emigrants usually did not have much to begin with. New England farmers took breakfasts of weak tea or coffee, hot bread or "toast soaked in butter," and "cheese of the fattest kind"; dinner, the midday meal, was pasty, a pudding of turnips or potatoes that "swim in hog's lard." Life in the 1820s for the majority of white folks—let alone blacks, free or enslaved—offered little pageantry, but rather an ordinariness that could provoke resentment toward ease. It sounds perverse today, but raising green vegetables for home consumption would be seen by some in the political age of Jackson as excessively self-indulgent, undemocratic "elegance," and evidence of "foreign" taste. Few expressed their concern over the rotting teeth that unquestionably resulted from the average American's diet. Yet Thomas Jefferson, the man who had, perhaps more than any other of his generation, romanticized the way west for ordinary farmers, maintained a semivegetarian diet for most of his adult life. He imported seeds, experimented with thirty-nine varieties of peas, and tended his Monticello garden lovingly—with an unpaid labor force, of course, to work the fields and maintain his kitchen. Enjoying the mild Southern climate in his retirement years,

Jefferson continued to consider meat merely as a side dish, and when he died at eighty-three, still had a good set of his own teeth.[21]

For most Americans of 1826, however, meals were demanding and long in preparation, especially when it meant getting a large log burning in the fireplace. Vigorous outdoor lives made frontier folk physically strong—even the peevish traveler of 1819 had to acknowledge that the "beautifully undulating," "excellent" land occupied by backcountry Ohioans could be a stimulating sight. But before they acquired the wood-fired iron stove, these obliging people made do on a greasy fare that must have been, particularly in cold weather, quite monotonous.

As to Mr. Atkinson's "large assortment of NEW BOOTS, of good workmanship," a less elaborate account will suffice. In the 1820s, shoemaking was still a handicraft, and was not to be reshaped by the Industrial Revolution until mid-century. Many American shoes were made at home during the winter months: on a "forest-farm" outside Cincinnati, an independent-spirited farmer's wife told Mrs. Trollope that she made soap and candles for home use, knitted socks, and spun cotton and wool for clothes, while her husband, "though not a shoemaker by trade, made all the shoes." Where there was a gender division of labor, mothers and daughters did the "binding" (sewing the uppers together) and fathers and sons attached sole and heels to the bound uppers.[22]

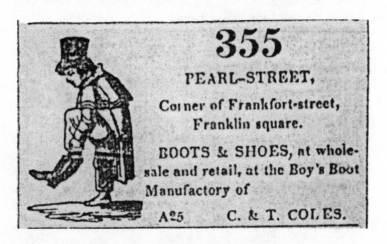

Fig. 7. Advertisement for boys' boots, in the *New-York American*, 1826.

Boots, the most basic of male footwear, were worn by people of all classes. At this time, the fashionable gentleman's walking boot of English origin came almost to a point at the toe; the black leather Wellington boot, so-called, was tall, and had a heel of about an inch. The square-toed hessian boot, which preceded the Wellington, remained popular in America after it went out of style in England. Metal tips were not unknown. All of these boots were tucked under trousers, succeeding the buckled shoe, which had lost its popularity with the aging of the Revolutionary generation. Style varied considerably, then, if color did not: it was predictably black. After quality of workmanship, shoe buyers of the nineteenth century were mainly concerned about finish: in 1822 in Newark, New Jersey, smooth, glossy patent leather was first introduced to the United States, and was an instant hit. There were boots for women, too, though women wore boots less commonly than men. And so, given shifting tastes and the local nature of most shoemaking, it is difficult to determine what kind of "NEW BOOTS" Mr. Atkinson had on hand in 1826, other than to say that they were black.[23]

It is possible to describe, in general, the homes in which the Ohioans of 1826 lived, though here, too, there was no single standard. Arriving on a plot of land, the majority of farmers got settled in log cabins, about twenty feet square, and then hurriedly cut down trees, cleared land, plowed, and planted, as pioneers before and since. Outside the principal towns, most houses were built of crude logs; the exceptions were merely made of hewn logs, flattened and then plastered over with a mortar of lime and sand. A good house withstood the winter cold, with the aid of a brick chimney. In the larger towns, some houses were frame and some brick. Well-to-do citizens of commerce, living along the Ohio River, built architecturally sophisticated homes, tending to reflect Southerners' fondness for neoclassical columns and long porches. Northern Ohio farmhouses, on the other hand, bore New England influences. The demanding Mrs. Trollope was entertained once at a "large and handsome mansion" two miles below Cincinnati's generously forested hills, on the Kentucky side of the river. She was enthralled as much by the nobility of the house as by the vista it afforded.[24]

Nevertheless, this well-bred Englishwoman found herself consistently ridiculing the Ohio River boomtown for its provinciality. People spat incessantly and, to her, lacked all understanding of the fine arts. At the same time, she complained that she could hardly cross any street without odorous hogs sniffing at her. And yet, she could not deny the activeness of Cincinnati's commerce. She reckoned the marketplace in general a place of "excellence, abundance, and cheapness," in spite of the "miserable" fresh fruit. Others held out more hope: Nicholas Longworth, a Cincinnati friend of Ethan Allen Brown, traded in his law practice for viniculture in 1825. He would taste his first wine in 1827, and go on to produce the nation's first champagne, so that, on the eve of the Civil War, Ohio ranked first among the states in winemaking.[25]

By 1826, the young city of Cincinnati was already more populous than Washington, D.C. If Mrs. Trollope thought it a rude and tentative scene, and felt at times that it represented a barbarous captivity for her and her English family, there were approximately twenty thousand Americans who would dispute her. Of the white population, 51.4 percent were male, indicating a healthy social balance. The region boasted its freedom from the "desolating epidemics" afflicting New Orleans and most other Mississippi and Ohio River towns. This fact alone was bound to encourage Eastern emigrants to remain.

There were jobs, too: twenty-nine boot and shoe shops, employing 257 workers; thirteen furniture shops; eight carriage and wagon factories; seven hatter shops; six chair factories; six book binderies; and two wallpaper factories. Thirty-five tailoring and clothing shops employed 132 men and 467 women. The largest of these establishments advertised the "latest fashions" imported from New York—"Olive, brown, and drab Cloths" for the men's large overcoat known as a "surtout," "Webb's Patent Suspenders," and "Silk Vestings" available in "Washington," "Lafayette," "Adams," "Clay," and "Jackson" patterns.

The nine printers in the city produced not only newspapers but almanacs, spelling books, and hymn and music books. Cincinnati's Western Museum, open since 1820, exhibited natural history specimens, including mammoth, reptile, and fish skeletons, thousands of fossils, and "the Tatooed head of a New Zealand chief." Admission was twenty-five cents. The city also had a privately endowed college, chartered by the Ohio legislature in 1818, and a Female Academy that offered instruction in French, music, penmanship, and needlework. There were twenty-eight clergymen in the city, and more than a dozen places of worship, including Presbyterian, Episcopal, Methodist, Baptist, German Lutheran, Roman Catholic, Jewish, and Quaker Friends, with a Universalist Church just being organized in 1826.[26]

Cincinnati had been advertised in London as the "wonder of the West," and a "metropolis" that thirty years earlier had been "aboriginal forest." That is why Mrs. Trollope had ventured across the Atlantic—as the vanguard in her detained husband's plan to establish a major emporium. Advertising tends to overstate, of course, and Cincinnati was not at all what she had expected. Only Main Street was completely paved, and the city routinely suffered from poor drainage. It did, however, have a modest equivalent of the high society she hungered for, hard as it was to identify such people within a large population of grim, calculating businessmen and their apprentices, and the men in dirty shirtsleeves who were introduced to her as "gentlemen."

Cincinnati was becoming an attractive haven for blacks from other parts of the Union. Approximately 3 percent of the city's population in 1826 was black, one-third of whom were among the 1,300 Sunday school children who paraded the streets on the Fourth of July, 1824. For twenty years, free blacks had been required on arrival there to provide proof that they were not fugitives, and obliged to put up a $500 bond to assure "good behavior." They were termed "good-humoured, garrulous, and profligate," in one representative travelogue, laboring in humble trades, doing "light and menial drudgery." There was an "African Church" to provide religious community.

The historical record contains little to reveal white Cincinnati's response to the migration of 280 blacks to their city between 1819 and 1826. As a mix of Northern and Southern emigrants, Ohioans were largely antislavery in temperament, though they acquiesced as slaves moved in and out of the state in the company of their masters. Ohio newspapers periodically ran advertisements calling for the return of fugitive slaves. Open-mindedness and forbearance were not to last much longer, however, as the Ohio River became an ever more distinct boundary between slave and free, and the state became a principal site for the resettlement of freed slaves.[27]

For the most part plain and unpretentious, comparing themselves only to what they had emerged from, Frances Trollope's clumsy, expectorating Ohioans continued to convey a confident sense of their progress in the pages of their newspapers.[28] In the town of Wooster, in the northeastern part of the state, the weekly *Ohio Oracle* ran an ad throughout the spring of 1826 for an improved cast-iron plow that could be guided over half an acre "and not molest its course"; the farmer did not even have to "touch hand to it." "PLOUGH, Against the World," the supplier roared across the front page. A resident of Steubenville, "the seat of the great woolen manufactory of the west," proposed that Ohioans come together in Baltimore to exhibit their finest merino sheep so that people from around the United States could gather and inspect the superior quality of Ohio's flocks. He was confident that no other state could effectively compete.[29]

Surpassing these and other ads, the constant story of 1826 in the

Fig. 8. "Plough Against the World." Advertisement in the *Ohio Oracle*, 1826.

pages of Ohio's newspapers was the recent completion of the Erie Canal and the thrilling first year of excavation toward creating an elaborate network of canals across the state of Ohio. New York's 363-mile man-made waterway, extending from Buffalo to the Hudson River, momentously united the nation's largest port city with the inland Great Lakes of the Northwest. Ohio, the next link, was only a few steps behind. A verse of early 1826 went:

> *The union of water, and Erie's bright daughter,*
> *Since Neptune has caught her they'll sever no more. . . .*[30]

Americans had never before seen so remarkable an example of human intervention to transform their physical world.

Thanks in part to the advocacy of Ethan Allen Brown, a colorful culture was just getting under way in Ohio: the felling of trees; carts and barrows; axes and shovels; hammers and saws; immigrant Irish accents; and deep pits that would shortly become the watery locks, where canal barges would glide slowly along a shallow, forty-foot-wide channel, and horses would drag the weight on towpaths. Here, too, fragrant wheat and the rich aroma emanating from tubs of cheese would waft through the air, as music blared from canal barge cabin roofs, delighting travelers in top hats or bonnets, some forty at a time, who paid a few cents per mile on kitchen-equipped packets that never exceeded a few miles per hour. As in New York State, new towns would spring up along the busy main canals—the Ohio-Erie, which eventually ran from Cleveland southwest through Columbus and Chillicothe to the Ohio River; and the Miami-Erie, linking Toledo to Cincinnati. Already in the spring of 1826, a presumably impartial Bostonian marveled at the pace of progress: "The magnificent project of canals, now in operation in Ohio, is second only to the undertaking of the great Erie Canal in New York. And, indeed . . . the people of Ohio have, in enterprise and energy, if possible, outdone their neighbors."[31]

Before the railroad was to propel the nation to the modern industrial age, canals were considered America's greatest engineering achievement and economic boon. A network of canals would mean timely access for farmers and manufacturers to both the Atlantic and the Gulf of Mexico. It was the canals, in fact, that would transport the rails and ties that were bound to make the placid waterways obsolete after the Civil War era. But in 1825–26, the novelty of the canal system and the combined zeal of state commissioners and the local farmers who worked part-time on canal construction led the weekly news in Ohio—finally taking the place of tracking Lafayette along each stage of his American tour.[32]

As governor, Ethan Allen Brown had initiated a canal policy with his call for legislative action in 1819: "Roads and canals are veins and arteries to the body politics that diffuse supplies, health, vigor and animation to the whole system." Three years later, the state legislature set up a canal commission comprised of seven members, all distinguished political figures. They engaged engineers and contractors and devised the two main routes. Financing efforts began with the essential encouragement of New York's Governor DeWitt Clinton, whose genius had made the Erie Canal profitable even before completion of the route, when tolls exceeded interest on the loans taken out by the state for construction. In 1826, the mastermind of the Erie Canal had his bust added to those of Washington, Lafayette, and Jackson at Cincinnati's Western Museum.[33]

The reason why the idea of canals was so popular was that the lucrative steamboat industry had lately preceded it. Robert Fulton's 160-ton *Clermont* had steamed up the Hudson River in 1807, and by 1811 a Pittsburgh-built steamboat became the first to dock in Cincinnati. The first steamboat built in Cincinnati itself was the one-hundred-ton *Vesta*, launched five years later. Quickly seeing the possibilities, citizens invested $500,000 in steamboat construction. It was a risky business: save for the *Paragon*, all of the vessels built prior to 1820 had either "worn out," "struck a snag," or burned by 1826. During that one year alone, however, Cincinnati completed seventeen new steamers, ranging from 50 to 325 tons. The busy river city now contained three steamboat yards, with two hundred employees. Among the more impressive vessels in service was the 280-ton *Andrew Jackson* (with Tennessee owners), active since 1823. Another Cincinnati-built steamboat with a Tennessee affiliation, the *Nashville,* had been launched before an audience of "a great number of ladies," only to be consumed in flames when a load of two hundred bales of cotton ignited. But failures deterred no one. The *George Washington,* 152 feet long, 30 feet wide, and weighing 355 tons, featured a promenade for passengers on its upper deck. And, according to Cincinnati promoters, "the Ohio and Mississippi have become the great highway, upon which all who live upon their borders, seek the business, or the pleasures of the North." Their city was the principal transfer point in travel between New Orleans and Baltimore, and the means by which many in the South were to tour Niagara Falls or experience the new Erie Canal. By carrying Ohio flour south, Cincinnati steamboats sought to enter the profitable Cuba trade.[34]

In less dramatic ways, too, Cincinnati and the rest of Ohio were connected to the wider hubs of commerce. The horse-drawn stage traveled routinely to Lexington (82 miles), Wheeling (242 miles), Buffalo (310 miles), and New Orleans (1,462 miles), as well as intrastate destinations. Throughout 1826, the Cincinnati post office ran twenty "mails" per week: by stage eastward via Chillicothe, Dayton, and Columbus; south via Georgetown, Kentucky; and to all other destinations by horseback.[35]

The Fourth of July was deemed a promising day for the beginning of new national enterprises. Under Governor Clinton's watchful eye, construction of the Erie Canal had begun on July 4, 1817, and groundbreaking on Ohio's ambitious canal network took place precisely eight years later, on July 4, 1825. On that day, after having traveled by steamer across Lake Erie to Cleveland (before the canal, this largest Ohio city of the future had a population of under a thousand), Clinton arrived at an elevated farm in Licking Summit, in central Ohio, where the "deafening cheers of thousands" accompanied his simple act of thrusting a spade into the earth. Encountering him in Albany not long before, maverick journalist Anne Royall described the soft gray-eyed canal advocate as "straight and well made," "robust and a little inclined to corpulency," calling him "the greatest man at this time in the world." Roaring artillery and volleys of musketry closed the Licking Summit ceremony, as Clinton spoke, recalling having thought at the time of Ohio's admission to the Union in 1803 "that she contained in her bosom the elements of greatness and prosperity."[36]

Internal improvements, as roads and canals were popularly known, were a subject of sometimes stormy constitutional debate. Inspired by the 1808 "Report on the Subject of Roads and Canals" of President Jefferson's treasury secretary, Albert Gallatin, New York legislators initially thought that Washington would finance economically feasible canals as it was financing the National Road, which extended from

Cumberland, Maryland, to Wheeling by 1818, and was progressing across central Ohio toward Indiana by 1826. Did the law of the land permit Washington to manage intrastate development? President James Madison thought it did not and vetoed an internal improvement bill passed by Congress that would have funded the Erie Canal—it was his last act before leaving office in 1817. But the question would not die. As one Delaware editor put it, "If *Uncle Sam* cannot help us, we must help ourselves." (The familiar symbol had acquired his national identity during the War of 1812.) And so state initiative succeeded, for as long as federal policy remained mired.[37]

Thus Clinton's Big Ditch eventually became the first proud, state-funded Western Canal. With enterprising solutions to real issues, New York lured westward-bound travelers onto the canal by exempting emigrants' personal articles and furnishings from tolls, compassionately assisting the multitudes who were uprooting themselves in order to seek economic well-being in western New York and Ohio. In both states, then, canals were seen advancing not just commerce but egalitarian beliefs: more Americans were taking the words of the preamble of the Declaration of Independence—life, liberty, and the pursuit of happiness—literally. In their newspapers, Ohio canal supporters repeatedly expressed the conviction that their prosperity was not theirs alone, but an expression of the national prosperity. The canal was an avenue of "the people," making its political parent, DeWitt Clinton, a popular innovator and superior statesman, whom some began to tout as a presidential possibility. Safe waterways meant many things in 1826: improvement over nature, the memorable association of the past and the future by bringing "civilization" to new places, encouragement of a flourishing marketplace, and a union of sentiment East and West.[38]

On an individual level, the canal phenomenon invited belief in the compatibility of moral instruction and financial gain. This was a notion that the Revolutionary generation had never been able to accept, assuming that acquisitiveness produced corruption. The canal changed hearts, seeming to guarantee that Americans would remain "one people," sharing values wherever they went. The canal, in short, was more than a ditch—it was democratic progress. Extending the canal network was so crucial to Ohioans' self-regard that the state seal was eventually reworked to feature a canal boat as its centerpiece.

In the spring of 1826, immortalizing "improvement" was on the

Fig. 9a. Original 1803 Ohio state seal, featuring a rising sun, a sheaf of wheat, and a bundle of seventeen arrows to signify Ohio's admission as the seventeenth state. *(Courtesy, Ohio Historical Society.)*

Fig. 9b. A print of the later seal, with a canal barge as the central motif (reputedly along the Ohio-Erie route, near Chillicothe). *(Courtesy, Ohio Historical Society.)*

minds of canal enthusiasts. When the first cornerstone of Lock No. 9 was set in place in Reading, just north of Cincinnati, the Lafayette lodge performed an intricate Masonic ceremony to sanctify the elaborate construction process. According to the *National Crisis* of May 18, "Every thing was arranged with perfect masonic regularity"—a procession led by men carrying their drawn swords brought master masons, junior deacons, secretaries, treasurers, royal arch masons, knights templar, and others to the site, where the canal engineers waited. One brother offered up a prayer, "impressively and solemnly," and a scroll was read and deposited in a bottle, corked and sealed, and placed beneath the cornerstone. The principal architect presented the "working tools" to the deputy grand master, who then "applied the *plumb, square,* and *level* to the work, and pronounced it to be *well-formed, true, and trusty.*"[39]

Feeling left behind, Virginians regarded the New York and Ohio projects and feared for their own commercial future. In the winter of

1825–26, the *Richmond Enquirer* ran a series on river transportation, in support of canal building. Part 7 began with the exhortation: "Go and do likewise," and a definition of the ideal civilization: "agriculture is conducted skillfully; manufactures and internal improvements exist in every variety of perfection; commerce is carried on with every part of the world, and science and literature, with the fine arts, propinquate [approach] to perfection." Looking to the progress of American canals, the writer reminded readers of the importance of canals to older civilizations: ancient Babylon's hanging gardens were "watered by hydrons, and aqueducts"; unsurpassed, China's canals reached twelve thousand miles; Sweden, France, Prussia, Denmark, all moved goods and people on artificial waterways. "Can WE stand here," the columnist posed, "all the day idle?" Before signing the piece as "A citizen of the West," he sounded an alarm: "Slumbering Virginia, awake! . . . Hurl away those rocks and hills, which endanger and impede the intercourse of your citizens."[40]

As Americans marveled at such improvement upon nature—making water flow uphill—they expressed at the same time as great a bewilderment as ever about the awesome power of nature itself. It was in May 1826, while in New York to attract investment as Ohio's canal fund commissioner, that former Governor Ethan Allen Brown toasted America's premier novelist, James Fenimore Cooper, before the Bread and Cheese Club on the eve of that gentleman's departure for Europe. Brown, once an avid, youthful member of a New York literary club, raised his glass to: "The spirit of literary adventure, that has dared to explore the American forest for character and manners still new to romance."[41] To a man like Brown, with his roots in the East, Ohio had not ceased to be the stuff of Americans' pioneering dreams. And to Cooper, peaceful, prosperous Ohio villages sprouting along a smooth-flowing canal would not have been offensive to the pastoral conscience, nor seemed to him too disruptive of pristine nature.

American readers were keen on entering Cooper's very visual fictional world, and modernizing Ohioans felt a particular spiritual kinship with the author's mid-eighteenth-century Hudson vistas. Cooper deposits his adventure-bound colonists in places where they are to be tested as conscientious representatives of civilization stepping alertly into a dazzling wilderness. His hero Hawk-eye in *The Last of the Mohicans* equally exhibits an aggressive kind of masculinity and an outstanding compassion. Versatile and resolute as he plies the active waters, he is justifiably proud of his mastery over nature. On those waters—here smooth, there rumbling—Cooper's character holds sway. The Ohio settlers, bound to their rivers and canals, metaphorically mimic the hero's experiences. He and they, at different times, both flow with and resist the current.

In the Byronic sense of relating soulful human behavior to encounters with visible nature, Cooper wrote with mysterious charm. His Hawk-eye is a combination of the plain, good-hearted settler and the nature-fed, noble Indian. Both personae understand the boundless American forest. Both have sprung from an admirable self-sufficiency. As the instinctive child of romantic nature, Hawk-eye does not require "class" in order to be seen as deserving, nor does he need official rank to be chivalrous. Thus the book is a deliberate commentary on history. It cherishes the human family. Hawk-eye, Indian-like, does not entirely escape his white identity; his Indian friends, rejecting the complexities and moral ambiguities of civilization, are shown as outmoded, destined to be rubbed from the present and removed to the pages of romantic history.[42]

The Last of the Mohicans found a ready readership in the West, where Ohio pioneers continued to feel the rawness of nature. They could not but have appreciated that in Cooper's tale, freedom and a generous spirit led to inner contentment; and the democratic hero could always be easily identified with the common good. How much Western readers elevated the tragedy of the Mohicans Chingachgook and Uncas is harder to gauge. The Shawnees and other Indians whose legitimate claims had stood in the way of white settlement in the 1790s now resided well west of Ohio's borders, but the frontier mind-set held strong.

All the same, modernity beckoned: witness the city of Cincinnati. It had reputation already; it was striving for refinement and taste. Ohio's governor in 1826, as much as his predecessor Ethan Allen Brown, was a booster of the state economy. Jeremiah Morrow was born near Gettysburg, Pennsylvania, in 1771. He was a sober Presbyterian who had trekked west in 1794, cleared land, built a log cabin, and brought his Pennsylvania bride (a cousin) to reside with him on the farm. After serving in the territorial legislature, he was elected Ohio's first congressman after statehood. In fact, he ran virtually unopposed from 1803 to 1813, the period during which the new state's population allowed it only one member of the House. From here, Morrow moved to the U.S. Senate, where he remained until 1819. Taking the lead in both national bodies in drafting federal land-sale legislation, he made it possible for emigrants to Ohio to purchase small tracts of land (as few as eighty acres at $1.25 an acre); nothing, perhaps, did so much to encourage that rapid population growth which produced Ohio's economic "miracle."

Morrow was a tireless public servant. Returning from the national capital for good, he put his mind to internal improvements as a canal commissioner from 1820 to 1822, resigning only to assume the governorship. On May 15, 1825, he greeted Lafayette in Cincinnati, and accompanied him by steamboat along the Ohio River to Wheeling; then, on July 4, 1825, he was present to welcome DeWitt Clinton to the Ohio-Erie Canal groundbreaking ceremony. It was to Ethan Allen Brown, who was no longer in elective office, that Clinton wrote in 1825, "Whatever may occur, my friend, in these political . . . battles, let us stick closely to the great cause of internal improvements and build our fame not on the miserable squabbles of personal ambition but in aiding the prosperity of our Country." Officially, though, it was on Jeremiah Morrow's watch that improvements in Ohio witnessed their greatest boost.[43]

The unstoppable canal-building spirit among the citizens of Ohio in 1826 can be summed up in the words of a simple cook, a man who had just put together a feast at Licking Summit, near the town of Newark, where some of the first work on an extensive "deep cut" had begun. With democratic sarcasm, the cook lifted his glass to detractors of the project: "The enemies of the Ohio canal—May their bread be sad and their beans half boiled, their butter stale, their pork too salt, and dress'd over a smoking fire."[44] Ohioans lacked a history, or at least a history of manners. That is how Frances Trollope found them, to be sure. They had a way of dressing up the ordinary, and a way of defining themselves with a single word: improvement.

As for Ethan Allen Brown, who shared America's birthday, he was one of the state's most public and most productive citizens, but he was privately enigmatic. Considered handsome and gregarious, Cincinnati's most eligible bachelor, he refused to take a wife. One literary friend from his New York days wrote encouragingly, back when he had first settled in the West, "That which inspires your Muse may influence your heart & will perhaps in a short time lead you to another sort of tribunal than a Court of Law. If it does be sure you let us know that we may meet & revel together." The next year another friend pursued: "When may I congratulate you on receiving to your bosom some dear little—Sweet—red lipped—black Eyed girl?" They would have a long wait. In 1824, the Cincinnati lawyer–turned–wine producer, Nicholas Longworth, gently pressed U.S. Senator Brown to take an interest in marrying while he was in the captivating social circle of Washington. He had delayed too long for the once eligible Mary Taylor, wrote Longworth, counseling: "Can you say . . . 'I might have had her.' "[45]

Brown seemed unwilling to pique interest in his life as a single man. For one, he could have capitalized on the moral questions surrounding his chief political rival, William Henry Harrison, when the former Ohio congressman and hero of Tippecanoe made known his intention of running for Brown's Senate seat during the winter of 1824–25. The fifty-one-year-old Harrison, married since 1795, was rumored to have seduced the daughter of a Cincinnati doctor. As Longworth explained the situation to Brown, the young woman was infatuated with the general, and her father "let him couch with her." Brown, for reasons either political or personal, refused to encourage a showdown with his morally suspect rival. Longworth, for his part, rationalized: "I should rejoice at your change [yielding his seat to Harrison], for I think your aid of vital importance as a Canal Commissioner."[46]

Not all of Brown's male friends were so undemanding. As the year 1826 began, his close confidant DeWitt Clinton wrote uninhibitedly from Albany: "You have done great good [to stimulate] the cause of internal improvements. . . . Have you not lived in the unhallowed state of Celibacy—Have you not violated the great command increase and multiply? Have you not bedewed the pillows of love-sick damsels with tears . . . !" Brown's reply is lost, as is any certain knowledge of his sexual preference. But another warm letter from Clinton in February suggests the tone of Brown's rejoinder. The letter opens: "I have received your able defence, if such a cause is susceptible of defence and admire your ingenuity in all respects and your candor in some respects. By a liberal use of the Metonymy and the Synechdoche and an artful confounding of cause and consequence you have escaped from most of my insinuations."[47]

What candor had Brown shown his intrusive ally? The "artful confounding," of course, is more easily imaginable in the case of this accomplished lawyer. Decrying Brown's "sophistry," Clinton goes on to deduce from Brown's tortured prose ("the intrepidity with which you endeavor to evade the accusation of discouraging the progress of Ohio's population") that his unattached friend was not inactive; that he claimed to be "scattering" instead of "concentrating" his seed. Clinton had reached the conclusion he imagined the evasive Brown wished him to draw: his friend was a man who "labored" unconventionally, but still successfully, "in the vineyard of population." The New Yorker remained undaunted, however. It was his certain hope that Brown would settle on "some charming widow of N.Y. in a state of languishment for you. One of them asked me to send her your profile. I told her that I should not amuse her with shadows and resemblances, but that the original would soon make his appearance." This was a subject that Clinton would not dismiss in 1826, signing off another business letter in April with "my respects to the fair widows," and adding a persistent P.S.: "Are the widows in a succumbing mood!"[48]

Ex-Governor Brown, like the nation, approached his fiftieth birthday in vigorous good health. He chose to remain slippery, though, when asked to justify his determination to live the bachelor life.

CHAPTER SIX

President J. Q. Adams Swims against the Current

WHEN JOHN DAVIS, a new congressman from Northborough, Massachusetts, rode by way of Philadelphia and Baltimore to the nation's capital in late November 1825, he left behind his wife of three years, Elvira, and their small son, whom he called "Young Master John." He missed them terribly, and wrote home nearly every day during that first month. Davis was thirty-eight, a graduate of Yale College, class of 1812. He would continue as a member of the House of Representatives for nine years before resigning to become governor of Massachusetts.

He arrived on a rainy December 3rd, two days before the Nineteenth Congress was set to convene. The final leg of his journey had taken him over roads of "coarse gravel mixed with a kind of earth resembling brick dust and miserably poor." Becoming familiarized with his boardinghouse adjacent to Capitol Hill, he immediately conveyed the contradiction he beheld: Washington was a combination of noble structures and dilapidated streets. The Capitol, put to the torch during the British invasion of 1814, had been so completely destroyed that it could not be reoccupied for more than five years; but it was, now, he told Elvira, "decidedly the most beautiful structure I ever saw." The new Rotunda rose 140 feet; the House chamber measured ninety-five feet across at its greatest length, and sixty feet high. And yet, he added, "after 25 years of labor they are just beginning to think of setting out a little shrubbery." The Capitol grounds, more than twenty acres enclosed by an iron railing, contained temporary sheds, "the rubbish of stones," and other remnant building materials.[1]

Washington had a deserted feel about it. The roads were dusty when dry, and a soggy ooze after a good rain. Until 1820, hogs freely roamed the streets, poking through fetid trash, for lack of a sanitary disposal method. A slightly later visitor wrote of a city "straggling out hither and thither," where one had to "strike across a field to reach a street." There were few structures on Pennsylvania Avenue between the President's House and the Capitol, as most of the city's population lived on the Georgetown side of the Executive Mansion. The desolation of most of the District made the cluster of congressional boardinghouses on the high ground the closest there was to a real community during the several months each year when government sat here. One could anticipate a bright social future for Washington, but it was still very much a dreary, unfinished, disconnected town offering little in the way of diversion. As Davis put it, the same rough appearance manifest in

Fig. 10. The U.S. Capitol in the 1820s. *(Courtesy, American Antiquarian Society.)*

the view from Capitol Hill "pertains to every part of the city (if city it can be called)."[2]

On his second day, Davis wrote his wife again, this time to describe his spartan quarters: "you would be much surprised if you could look in upon me and see the accommodations furnished to a member of Congress for the extravagant price he pays." He shared the house with five colleagues. "The walls are not papered but clean—I have two windows looking into Pennsylvania Avenue (which is a principal street in Washington) ornamented with coarse cotton curtains—an old fashioned plain bureau, an old pine table and a wash stand of like material with a white earthen bowl and pitcher—an old bed that with a queer sort of hanging or curtains amid cotton sheets—the bed I have not tried—two plain winsor [sic] chairs and about carpet sufficient to cover two thirds of the floor." His landlady was a "sentimental spruce little widow with one child—She is quite kind and attentive." Breakfast was served at eight-thirty, dinner at three, tea at seven in the evening. And then, he added, "Go to bed just when you have a will to."[3]

His first purchases included the materials of letter writing: a bottle of ink, a pencil, "a bundle of pens," sealing wax, and sufficient paper— "all at the charge and expense of Uncle Sam." Finding his way around after "the bustle crowd and elbowing of a week," Davis began venturing from boardinghouse culture out into the streets. As he located Washington's shops, the representative undoubtedly saw examples of what were called at this time "fancy goods." To judge from printed ads, there was a marked emphasis on accessories meant to enhance one's appearance: William Prentiss's "Jewelry and general fancy store" boasted an extensive variety of "superior goods"—selling for cash only. He advertised necklaces and gold rings, "Gold Hearts and Medallions," "Chrystal and Turquoise Ear-rings, with Bracelets to correspond," "Gentlemen's Musical Watches, which contains in addition to an elegant time piece, figures that play on the guitar, waltz, &c. &c." Silver coffeepots, teapots, milk pots, and "Slop Bowls" comprised kitchenware, and went along with miscellaneous items like tortoiseshell snuff boxes and ivory teething rings with whistles. For game enthusiasts, Prentiss stocked billiard balls, dice, backgammon boards, playing cards, and dominoes. A gentleman with exotic taste might favor the use of one of Prentiss's imported canes of Asian bamboo (available with or without a sword hidden inside). For daily hygiene concerns, there was "Aromatic Tooth Paste," plus perfumes with seemingly mystical properties—Eau de Vie, Eau des Alpes, and Eau Regeneratrice. Other oils were reckoned to both scent the hair and promote its growth.

Prentiss led with quantity, but others, like perfumer and hairdresser John Scotti, were on the lookout for a self-selected clientele. A number of satisfied customers already swore by his Oil of Naples, which claimed to preserve hair and made the head feel "truly comfortable." Scotti was cultivating the nickname "knight of the curling tongs," but as it was somewhat unsavory to tout one's own abilities, a rhetorical instrument had to be found. And so a patron took the lead in commending Scotti's styling services to the public: "Mr. Editor— Yesterday I called in on JOHN SCOTTI'S . . . and I was truly astounded. . . ." Contriving that "beauty has always stood pre-eminent in the United States," the patron went on to list the tradesman's extensive services. Thereupon, this master of the nineteenth-century makeover saw no choice but to insert an ad a week later to assure "the Ladies and Gentlemen of Washington" that his reliable scissors and tempting essences awaited them at his exclusive Pennsylvania Avenue location. His promoter put it most succinctly: "he will make the old young."[4]

Fig. 11. Advertisement placed by Pennsylvania Avenue hairstylist John Scotti in the *United States Telegraph*, Washington, D.C., 1826.

Congressman Davis went to work. After two weeks at his desk in the Capitol, still stimulated by the newness of each experience, he addressed a letter to his toddler: "I see here a great many things that please both little boys and great ones . . . by the door of the hall is a woman who has a table and wine and brandy and little cakes that she sells to any body that will give her money for them. Down below is another man who keeps all sorts of good things to eat and drink and has a table ready set all clean and nice." Beyond sustenance, the Capitol had "more rooms and alleys and passages in that great house than your little legs would carry you to in a day." For a patriotic education, one could inspect the freshly painted murals in the Rotunda, Revolutionary scenes that President Madison had commissioned of the artist John Trumbull after the War of 1812 ended: "four great pictures full of soldiers," as Davis explained. "One the capture of Burgoyne—one the capture of Cornwallis—one the signing of the Declaration of Independence & one the Resignation of Genl. Washington."[5]

Even past New Year, the congressman's tone expressed his wide-eyed amusement. He jotted down everything unusual: "The fog in the Capitol was so dense this morning that you could scarcely see across the Rotunda and the water literally ran down the walls and stairs so as to stand in puddles upon the pavement."[6] Most noteworthy, though, was Davis's reaction to his first state dinner, a lavish banquet hosted by the British ambassador. The New Englander felt entirely out of his league. He declared to his wife that he considered himself "wholly incompetent" before the sophistication of the diplomat he spoke of only as "Mr. John Bull." The affair opened with a display of conversational prowess: "Bull in a very fine and pleasant way took us by the hand and commenced a conversation with as much familiarity as if we had been old acquaintances." The British ambassador was small, and dressed plainly, but he carried on with dramatic effect for the first hour.

The thirty men who had been invited to dinner—there were no ladies—moved to the table when called, and Davis ended up seated directly across from the host. "Now here it is," he wrote, "that I feel myself wholly inadequate to give you any intelligible account of the entertainment." He was unable to count the courses with precision. Silver and mirrors and glass glittered before him, "plates were the richest porcelain gilt and the paintings very beautiful—beside each plate was a very large fork and spoon." It took him three pages just to describe the table layout. "In each plate was a small loaf of bread done up quite fancifully. . . . The first thing offered was soup—this over there came little pastry dishes and rolls. . . . Then a variety of dishes in rapid succession . . . my plate I believe was changed twenty times for the instant you stop eating way goes your plate and in an instant comes a new dish. Suffice it to say there was beef[,] turkey, fowls, ducks, pheasants, quails, ham, tongue and a thousand things I know nothing about. . . . when a dish was brought to you . . . a servant would tell you in french what it was. . . . I did not know what a piece of a plain honest turkey was it came to me in such a novel dress." These were confessions one could easily make to a wife, though the provincial congressman had pretended to be perfectly unshaken by the newness of it all.[7]

He was by no means alone. Four out of every ten members of the Nineteenth Congress were beginning their first terms in office. Davis and his freshman colleagues were learning the rudiments of Washington society, but they had a lot to learn about Washington politics. John Quincy Adams, on the other hand, was arguably the most accomplished man in America. He had been president for ten months, his expansive program formally sent to Capitol Hill on December 6, in the form of the annual message to Congress. The fifty-eight-year-old chief executive knew all five of his distinguished predecessors personally. He was secretary of state for the eight years leading up to his presidency, minister to England and Russia, a U.S. Senator, and a Harvard professor before that. He knew just about everything there was to know about governing procedures and political precedent, and what the laws stipulated. But the way things were in 1826, all his vaunted knowledge was to do him little good.

JOHN QUINCY ADAMS was born in 1767, three years after the intellectually penetrating, self-scrutinizing lawyer John Adams married the equally erudite Abigail Smith. Their son was not yet three in March 1770, when his patriot father took on the controversial case of the British soldiers who had fired into a crowd of protesting Bostonians, killing five in what was immediately termed a "massacre." John Quincy would grow up knowing what it was to be controversial.

It was a combination of John Adams's outstanding integrity and his canny ambition that impelled him to defend the soldiers, who

claimed to have been acting under orders and responding to a dangerous assault by an angry mob. While he sympathized with the radical
cause of his uncompromising cousin Samuel, there is every reason to
believe that both John Adams and cross-eyed relative Josiah Quincy
took up the defense case with genuine enthusiasm. After all, their radical friends were so sure of a guilty verdict that they wanted to supply
the enemy with lawyers who could not be accused of being second-
rate.[8]

But the team of Adams and Quincy did better than anticipated.
Successful in gaining the acquittal of some of his clients, leniency for
the others, John Adams saw his reputation build. He was esteemed as a
man of unequivocal principles, a very public man of intellectual energy,
earnest and fair. These distinctly "Adams" traits would prove sturdy,
but so would their correlative: hardheadedness. As a demanding
moralist, John Adams became obnoxious to many of his colleagues as
his fame grew, and yet he remained an essential force in the drama to
conceive a nation. The son would acquire the same willfulness and
overall pragmatism as the father, and achieve the same irksome unpre-
dictability in the minds of his presumed allies. What had once worked
to the detriment of the father's career would do the same for the son's.

On June 17, 1775, while his father was in Philadelphia attending the
Second Continental Congress, John Quincy Adams, almost eight,
accompanied his mother to the heights of their Braintree farm to hear
the booming of British cannon and see smoke rising from another
prominence, Bunker Hill. This indelible memory made the outbreak
of the Revolution a very personal event in the formative years of John
Quincy, who no doubt was informed by his mother (if he did not himself read) of a letter his father wrote home during the first week of July
1776. It forecast that the anniversary of American Independence would
be celebrated "by succeeding generations . . . as the day of deliverance . . . with pomp and parade, with shows, games, sports, guns, bells,
bonfires and illuminations from one end of this continent to the other,
from this time forward forevermore." Though hardly known for his
pithiness, as the quieter Thomas Jefferson was, John Adams put his
distinctive mark on the Fourth of July narrative with this simple, tune-
ful cadence, stringing together his hopes in the midst of war.[9]

In 1778, father and dutiful son journeyed to Europe. While the
elder Adams joined Benjamin Franklin as a commissioner empowered

to negotiate on behalf of the war-torn former colonies, the eleven-year-old John Quincy observed Old World society and made the acquaintance of important officials. They stayed one year, then made a more extensive trip to Europe at the end of the next year. The boy who had glimpsed the Battle of Bunker Hill was nearly halfway around the world in St. Petersburg, Russia, when the Battle of Yorktown was being fought. Incredibly, he was just fourteen when he was hired on as private secretary and French interpreter to the new U.S. minister to imperial Russia. En route to this distant post, he rode past the distressed peoples who wandered the difficult roads of Germany and Poland. Once in Russia, he found life fairly dull and without proper educational opportunities, enjoying more interesting encounters in Sweden, Denmark, and the Netherlands.

He followed his father's example by maintaining a regular and thoughtful journal of his daily activities. Its pages show how extraordinary his experience was for an American of his time. In August 1783, still sixteen, he wrote: "This forenoon I went to see the Pictures which are exposed to view in the Gallery of the Louvre; there are some good paintings there amongst a great number of indifferent ones. After dinner I went to see the experiment, of the flying globe. A Mr. Montgolfier of late has discovered that, if one fills a ball with inflammable air, much lighter than common air, the ball of itself will go up to an immense height of itself. This was the first publick experiment of it, at Paris." Young John Quincy Adams, underimpressed by the best examples of Parisian art and mildly curious about the new science of ballooning, was merely grown accustomed to worldly conversation. Two months later he was in London, attending *Hamlet* at the Drury Lane Theatre and witnessing Parliament in session; as to the tragedians, "They lay an emphasis upon almost every word; yet in some places they speak, both too low and too slow." The young critic, however, found the purple velvet robes of King George III and the Prince of Wales notably appealing. In mid-1784, after Abigail Adams sailed the Atlantic to join her husband and son, this well-bred youth took Thomas Jefferson as a frequent companion and dined with the likes of the Marquis and Marquise de Lafayette.[10]

The younger Adams was not simply a brittle mirror image of his father, though their stern New England values may have given such an appearance. He would be an Adams, but in his own way. After six years in Europe, John Quincy left his parents and returned to Boston to attend Harvard. His patriotic (if fairly unoriginal) commencement oration in July 1787 was his first published tract. "Survey the faithful page of history," he lectured, and follow "the paths of rectitude and justice," for the nation's sake.[11]

John and Abigail Adams arrived back from London and were reunited with their son in the spring of 1788. After two years as America's first ambassador to the former mother country, John Adams was to become the first vice president of the United States. John Quincy's ever-growing seriousness was reflected in his diary that summer: "My Time flies from me with the rapidity of a whirlwind. Every hour is precious, and every moment unemployed becomes a subject of regret."[12] In New York, the first national capital, John Quincy attended debates in the First Congress. Not surprisingly, after a European immersion, he found that he was more impressed with the imperious reserve of President Washington than the oratorical efforts of the people's representatives.

In the 1790s, the vice president's son proved himself every bit as dogged, moralistic, intense, and compulsive as his father. He notoriously began his political career by criticizing in print his and his father's old companion Jefferson. Despite their previous familiarity, John Quincy pseudonymously authored the 1791 "Publicola" essays, which denounced Secretary of State Jefferson for embracing the uncontrolled, if well-intended, French Revolution. Most readers regarded the style and assumed the essays to have been written by the vice president. They did not guess them to be the work of his son.

The political rupture between John Adams and Thomas Jefferson began thus, fed by the pen of the younger Adams. That rift widened and became more heated over the course of the 1790s. Without losing affection for the man, Jefferson saw his former colleague in the Continental Congress as an "apostate," willing now to espouse the same imperious British principles that they had struggled against together in the 1770s. The older Adams, less impulsively perhaps, thought Jefferson to be overreacting to what were merely subtle changes in his political temperament. The two men were pitted against each other twice: Adams defeated Jefferson in the first contested presidential election, in 1796, and Jefferson swept past the incumbent four years later.

As president, the pure and persevering John Adams found himself alone, scorned and slighted. His cranky mistrust of others was justified: the Jeffersonian Republicans had blatantly branded the astute but alienating chief executive a "monarchist." Meanwhile, in his own Federalist party, Adams was subverted by the charismatic Alexander Hamilton. Hamilton no longer held any office in the government, but he was such a magnet that Adams's cabinet would sooner rely on the New Yorker's advice than keep its faith with the president. The abuse Adams took from both sides palpably affected him, and when candidate (and vice president) Jefferson appeared complicit in published attacks on the incumbent, Adams reacted angrily, and skulked away to Massachusetts without attending the inauguration of his successor.[13]

Thirty-seven-year-old John Quincy Adams was elected to Congress in 1803, during Jefferson's first term. On July 4th of that year, his wife, Louisa Catherine, gave birth to a son, also named John Adams. (Their first, born as the new century dawned, had been named George Washington Adams.) The Massachusetts senator shortly proved as unmanageable for the Federalists as his father was, a deliberative independent rather than a party loyalist, and, most unacceptably, willing to cooperate with Jefferson's administration.

Here lies the key to understanding John Quincy Adams: though he had fired more than one rhetorical salvo against Jefferson, and scurrilously lampooned the president in verse after a liaison between Jefferson and his biracial house servant Sally Hemings was alleged and widely publicized in 1802, Adams reversed himself—as always, on principle. In 1807–08, the nation was divided after British aggression on the high seas moved President Jefferson to prevail upon Congress to pass his plan for "peaceable coercion." This meant a massive embargo of American commerce in order to deny America's principal trading partner the fruits of the land and thus "coerce" the British into acknowledging America's importance while respecting America's sovereignty. Adams was the only Federalist to vote for the measure. In his thinking, it was essential to defend the national interest against the parochial interests of maritime New England. The embargo failed miserably in its purpose, and America, of course, eventually went to war with England again in 1812.

What conditioned Adams's responses? In short, it was his comprehensive reading of law and history. He did not permit personal feelings to blot out a patriotic principle. Though he dined at the President's

House, drank Jefferson's fine wine, and occasionally opposed Secretary of State Madison across a chessboard, Adams generally mistrusted the Federalist-hating Jefferson, who was still estranged from his father. He thought Jefferson sly and power hungry beneath a cover of calm and cordiality; but as senator he maintained his sturdy self-sufficiency as he arrived at every judgment. Lecturing in rhetoric at Harvard at times when Congress was not in session, Senator Adams reasoned that his own state's heavy reliance on trade with England should not be used to rationalize American subservience. The critical importance of union demanded New England's forbearance.

By behaving with what he saw as integrity and what hard-core Federalists saw as a betrayal, Adams promptly lost the confidence of his party leadership. It was a mere decade since his father had been displaced, when John Quincy Adams was obliged to return to private life. Was he self-conscious of the ironies of politics? One thing is plain: the idiosyncratic Adams character was the very antithesis of the Jefferson quality. While the charming Virginian feigned conciliation toward his political opponents in the hope of softening their stands and eventually winning them over, the hard-nosed, self-respecting Adamses made little effort to court popularity and pointed themselves toward political self-destruction.

Amid the turmoil in foreign policy and his provisional embrace of the Jefferson administration, John Quincy Adams welcomed a third son. He was Charles Francis Adams, destined to be a congressman, minister to Great Britain during the Civil War, and the skilled editor of his father's and grandparents' papers. In 1809, with their toddler in tow, John Quincy and Louisa Catherine Adams went to Russia at the behest of the incoming Madison Administration; he had once before endured privations in St. Petersburg as a youthful secretary, and now he himself would serve honorably as U.S. minister.

In the rude, forbidding vastness of imperial Russia, Adams represented the ideals of the American republic as he saw them—a people actuated by a well-designed constitution, striving to overcome long-nurtured regional jealousies. Magnanimous as his words were, Adams, ironically again, would be branded by later partisans for having absorbed the "habits, opinions, and associations of the royal courts," admiring "the strongly concentrated and despotic governments of an hereditary aristocracy." His critics deemed him "illy fitted" to appreciate real republican sentiment, and he was cruelly imagined to have changed his allegiance from Federalist to Republican not out of conviction but simply to exchange "a broken and divided party for one in the ascendant."[14]

In Russia, however, he served his country equitably. As he cultivated Tsar Alexander I, that liberal autocrat consistently expressed a friendly attachment to the young republic. The U.S. Congress declared war on England, and Adams was present in St. Petersburg as Napoleon commenced his massive eastward invasion. Having many times since Bunker Hill marked the storms and stirrings of nations in flux, Adams again found himself witness to history.

Geographically, of course, he was isolated. He learned of events connected with the prosecution of the War of 1812 usually two or more months after they had occurred. As important, Madison's envoy was at a great distance from New England, where embittered Federalists, now a grumbling minority, spoke of secession. They wanted no part of the war. The pacific Madison did not want it to go on any longer than necessary either. After the tsar volunteered to act as mediator, Adams was called upon to lead the United States delegation in peace talks at Ghent, in present-day Belgium, to meet with British counterparts and put an end to the mutually unprofitable conflict.

Though London summarily declined the tsar's offer, Adams was joined by Speaker of the House Henry Clay and Treasury Secretary Albert Gallatin, forming an American negotiating team that consisted, respectively, of two strong-willed political minds and a nonconfrontational one—much like the personal experience of John Adams when he joined diplomats Benjamin Franklin and the milder John Jay to secure American Independence in Paris thirty years before. The difference this time was that there was no victory at Yorktown to influence the proceedings. The two sides were stalemated.

The Swiss-born Gallatin was not noticeably affected by Adams's disposition. Though as a Pennsylvania Republican Gallatin had roundly criticized President John Adams in the 1790s, John Quincy acquired a grudging respect for this cosmopolitan, and they operated well together. But the faultfinding Adams and the all-American Clay, a wise if irritable, Virginia-born Kentuckian, fell to quarreling with each other as much as with the British. Adams was frequently annoyed with the braggadocio of the hard-drinking, poker-playing frontier lawyer and legislator. Adams felt persecuted, confiding to his diary that "every line I write passes a gauntlet of objections."[15]

At the same time, though, Adams was self-critical enough to see in Clay a similar kind of overbearing dogmatism, "the same forgetfulness of the courtesies of society" that he recognized in himself.[16] Then, as the treaty was nearly fixed, Adams quibbled about fishing rights and positioning the words "Great Britain" before "United States of America" in the finished documents. Gallatin's son, who served as his father's secretary, wrote: "Mr. Adams is really a thorn. He is so absolutely 'Yankee' and of a common type. . . . Of course Mr. Adams is retarding matters with his pigheadedness."[17] Yet somehow, the Treaty of Ghent was signed on Christmas Eve 1814, retaining honor for America.

Adams had left his wife in St. Petersburg, and now, after a five-week carriage ride, she rejoined him in Paris. Here he also reencountered the Marquis de Lafayette. The Adamses accepted the general's invitation to relax some days at his country seat, the turreted granite castle La Grange. Soon they were off to London, where, as the new U.S. minister, Adams had to contend with the distasteful combination of British envy and disdain toward America.

Across the Atlantic, Federalism withered, and the patriotic upsurge occasioned by Andrew Jackson's victory at New Orleans strengthened a sense of nationhood. Adams needed to witness the new postwar spirit of American union up close, to see how his old politics of accommodation now predominated. A golden opportunity arrived, as incoming President James Monroe offered Adams the job of secretary of state that he himself had held under Madison. Adams noted to himself: "On my return to my native country, a new and, for some time at least, a busy and laborious scene threatens to open before me—a scene so laborious and so full of perils and perplexities that a stouter heart than mine would be appalled at the prospect of it."[18] Translated: he was ready to come home, to exchange contexts.

America in 1817 was vastly transformed from 1809, when Adams had sailed. Monroe had been a Jeffersonian ideologue who now felt not the least concern for the political differences he and Adams might have had under earlier political circumstances. Jefferson, while suspicious of Adams, understood Monroe's choice. "They were made for each other," he told friends at this time. "Monroe always saw his [own] point, but could not always *express* very well how he got there. Give Adams a conclusion, and he could always assign the best reasons for it." Jefferson was damning with faint praise, quick to disparage Monroe's intellectual acuity and not really appreciating Adams's critical detachment and discernment. Perhaps Jefferson saw his longtime protégé, Monroe, accurately; but he never could sound the depths of the precocious lad he knew in Paris, who shared his father's irascibility.[19]

The last of the presidents associated with the Revolutionary generation, and the last of the "Virginia Dynasty," Monroe was dull but viewed as meritorious. His postinaugural visit to New England went so well that a Federalist newspaper editor announced the "era of Good Feelings." Despite his awkwardness, Monroe was the first president since Washington (and arguably the last in history) to enjoy the preference of his nation without any real political opposition. Two terms later, he would make his own preference for a successor clear to all: it was John Quincy Adams. Also in the cabinet was South Carolina's John C. Calhoun, in 1817 a rather young (thirty-five-year-old) secretary of war, destined to be Adams's vice president, whose intellect as well as judgment Adams, now fifty, greatly respected at this time. Incoming Attorney General William Wirt also began to cross Adams's path more regularly.

As he returned to an American style of life, Adams shortly found himself at the center of a crisis involving England, Spain, and the three ambitious men with whom his own political future would be most intimately connected: Jackson, Calhoun, and Clay. During the War of 1812, the British had incited unassimilated Seminole Indians and ex-slaves in Spanish Florida to assail frontier Georgians. After the Treaty of Ghent, border disturbances continued. In 1818, General Jackson interpreted instructions he received from Secretary of War Calhoun to warrant a punitive campaign, including an incursion into Spanish territory if in hot pursuit. But Jackson not only caught and killed Indians and captured two Spanish forts, he executed two British abettors of the Indians. In the confused explanations that followed, Speaker Clay loudly urged Jackson's censure for having taken foreign policy matters into his own hands; Calhoun privately undermined Jackson; and only Adams among the cabinet supported the controversial general, in acknowledging that "retributive justice" was to be expected under the unique rules of frontier warfare. It was another irony to punctuate

Adams's career: at the moment when Jackson's political fate hung in the balance, the one man he presumed bore him no goodwill, Adams, came solidly to his defense; and another, his future vice president, Calhoun, whom he was led to believe spoke well of him, in fact refused to back him. To be misunderstood and underappreciated was nothing new for Adams.

The secretary of state went on to negotiate a treaty with the tottering Spanish Empire. The Adams-Onís Treaty of 1819 ceded Florida and established a long border between American and Spanish possessions, running along Southwestern rivers and across the Continental Divide to the Pacific. This treaty primed the increasingly confident, rising nation to lunge for more of the West. But in his 1821 Fourth of July oration in Washington, Adams did anything but gloat. He recited a sweeping history of British political thought, detailed the peopling of early America, and made such sense of the way in which civil society had advanced in the colonies, that the Revolution appeared to be a natural result of the laws of nature rather than a precipitous event.[20]

While explaining that the parent state had, at a critical time, treated the child with "neglect, harshness, and injustice," Adams downplayed any need to condemn England. "The resentments of that age may be buried in oblivion," he assured. It was more important in his mind to identify "sympathies" in life, cherishing the relationships that began at home and gradually extended from neighborhood to nation—the "moral ligatures of friendship," he called them, that constituted an "instinctive and mysterious connexion" between people and places. It was a brilliant reconception of the meaning of the American Revolution, well suited to the romantic spirit of the successor generation. Because an ocean had come between the colonists and their identification with England, new attachments had formed.

Midway through his address, Adams ritually read the text of the living parchment he held in his hand. It was forty-five years old now and unfaded—the original Declaration of Independence, which was then stored at the State Department. Its words had made history, he explained, in signifying "the first act of sovereignty by right," the first time any people had announced their own birth as a nation by the right of "transcendent truth." Other governments were founded by conquest; America, he said, by a people asserting the right to rule itself: *"A nation was born in a day."* As Adams spoke in pacific terms of his people's mission to enjoy the quiet pursuit of prosperity and continued freedom, he covertly employed a military metaphor to conclude of America: "Her march is the march of the mind."

Yet, after this time, it would become increasingly difficult for anyone to believe that public oratory could convincingly foster national harmony. With Monroe's impending retirement, the nationalist interlude was over. Ardent, anxious, *regional* champions of the post-Revolutionary generation were separately poised to take over the highest executive office for the first time. Adams of Massachusetts was opposed by a brash military hero from Tennessee with charisma that far exceeded his administrative insight; by a Kentucky gambler and artful political dealer who wielded power as Speaker of the House; and by Monroe's secretary of the treasury, the one old-fashioned states-rights Jeffersonian among them, the generally convivial, once sharp but now quite infirm William Crawford of Georgia.[21]

While each tried, none of the four candidates for the presidency in 1824 could claim to possess a truly national following. Each was readily identified with the culture and spirit of a particular section. Though Clay could spellbind when he appeared before an audience, this was not an age in which politicians made wide public appearances, and so the name of Jackson alone among them exuded an energetic and immediate power, a larger patriotic identity, a sense of something astir, of things to come. Everyone had read or heard about, and every patriot reveled in, the immense victory of General Jackson and his rough-hewn men over the British at New Orleans in 1815. What Adams and Clay had worked out in Ghent seemed flat and profitless; the document that brought the War of 1812 to a diplomatic close paled before the spectacle of New Orleans. Adams was the least popular of the candidates, if popularity is measured by an ability to appeal to the multitude. Sound capitalists and Eastern intellectuals—and, not insignificantly, the incumbent president—found his presence reassuring. He was thoughtful and deserving, but certainly not beloved.

The candidates were nominated in their respective state legislatures, and their candidacies promoted, town by town, across the regions where they were best known. While these state political caucuses lacked any strict party identity, the agitated atmosphere in which the contest was waged foreshadowed party antagonisms to come in the decade following, when a new, relatively conservative party of Whigs would organize to challenge rambunctious Jacksonian Democrats. Calhoun began the campaign season as a presidential hopeful but, as the youngest, and betting on the future, he dropped out in order to place himself in contention for the vice presidency, which he then—with none of the presidential candidates declaring a ticket—easily won. The remaining four aspirants were presented by their supporters as sober, dignified, and politically responsible. And, as of 1824 anyway, none was being called undemocratic.

A key change, an irreversible change, took place in the election of 1824. In eighteen of the twenty-four states in the Union popular votes were tallied and translated into electoral votes for the first time. In the other six states,[22] the state legislatures continued to appoint electors as they had for the first nine elections (and five presidents). While the tenth presidential election thus reflected a democratizing trend, it is important to point out that in an important state like Virginia, which turned to the popular method of electing the president, only 14,955 votes were cast from a white population of 625,000.[23] So it is difficult to assess the real impact of this wrenching shift in voting practice, other than to know that it reflected the growing pains of democracy.

Moreover, the election outcome was exceedingly complex and controversial. Because in six states no popular votes were cast, precise numbers from the general election are still disputed. Jackson clearly received the most popular votes (approximately 43 percent) and ninety-nine electoral votes, winning in Pennsylvania, New Jersey, and several Southern states. Adams ran second with 30 percent of the popular vote and eighty-four electoral votes, winning New England and little else. Crawford was fourth in popular votes but third in electoral votes, with forty-one—largely from Virginia and his native Georgia. Clay received thirty-seven electoral votes, most from Ohio, Missouri, and his native Kentucky.

Despite his strong showing, Jackson fell short of the majority needed for victory, and so, according to the Constitution, the decision passed to the House of Representatives. The House would decide among Jackson, Adams, and Crawford. Here the influential Clay, fourth-place finisher and excluded from the running, became king-maker. The longtime Speaker thought little of the bold, ungoverned general whose policies had never been articulated. And as a dedicated defender of economic growth for the new West, he felt a certain comfort with Adams. Thus Clay convinced his backers to support Adams, giving the New Englander twelve of the twenty-four states (each state bearing an equal vote, as determined by the majority vote of its combined Representatives). The thirteenth and deciding vote allegedly came when sixty-year-old Stephen Van Rensselaer of the deadlocked New York delegation made up his mind for Adams.

In the case of Clay's friend Henry Warfield of Frederick, Maryland, the elector resisted pressure put upon him by Maryland notables to vote for Jackson and sought assurance directly from Adams that as president he would not revert to a Federalist mind. Adams, according to his diary, asserted his independence: "I had been discarded by the federal party upon differences of principle, and I had not separated from one party to make myself slave of another." Thus, without guaranteeing anything, he merely had to demonstrate his lack of loyalty to any faction in order to convince Warfield.[24]

The election could hardly have been closer, and this meant that vengeful Jacksonians would not forget that the popular choice had been overturned by what seemed an unwholesome kind of politics. To make matters far worse, Adams selected Clay as his secretary of state, leaving many to assume that a deal had been made prior to the House vote—what became known as the "Corrupt Bargain." There is no evidence that the staunch and righteous Adams had done as his enemies claimed, but there can be no doubt that the move looked unseemly. And that is how John Quincy Adams entered office.

ON THE DAY of the House vote, February 9, 1825, a heavy snow fell on the nation's capital. It happened to be the sermonic voice of Daniel Webster of Massachusetts that announced the decision in the closed chamber. For months, Webster was to keep his thoughts about Adams to himself, but he finally revealed his quiet affinity in May 1826 when he addressed an old Federalist friend from North Carolina: "I believe Mr. Adams' feelings & purposes are extremely good," he wrote then. "Be assured there is nothing in him of narrowness or illiberality, or local prejudice."[25] Crawford supporter and Washington socialite Margaret Bayard Smith held other views, and wrote of how the president-elect, half-expecting Jackson to win, took the news of his narrow victory: "the sweat rolled down his face—he shook from head to foot and was so agitated that he could scarcely stand or speak. . . . If success, thus discomposed him, how would he have supported defeat?" If any celebration was ordered after the vote, it must have taken place quietly in private parlors. As Mrs. Smith explained, the snowstorm kept crowds of protesters among "the lower citizens" from forming. Only the black Americans present "expressed their joy by Hurrahs."[26]

From Monticello, Thomas Jefferson had affected neutrality. But the stubborn partisan persisted in him, the highly sensitive, wary Old Republican who remained afraid that Federalism would somehow rise again. He advised Albert Gallatin to be alert, and even wrote to Lafayette that while it might appear that "the wolf now dwells with the lamb, and the leopard lies down with the kid," there were still two

Fig. 12. The uneasy countenance of a controversial president: John Quincy Adams, ca. 1826, from a picture by Chester Harding. *(Courtesy, American Antiquarian Society.)*

identifiable political parties. Consolidationists, even if they called themselves Republicans, would use the presidency to submerge the states in an all-powerful national government, and this as "a *premier pas* to monarchy." Whether or not he really feared John Quincy Adams—and who else could he have been speaking of?—Jefferson insisted that the Federalist party was "now as strong as it has ever been since 1800." The threat was subtle, but, as he put it to Gallatin, "you will soon see into the disguise."[27] Writing to Samuel Harrison Smith, former newspaper editor and Margaret's husband, the suspicious sage coyly protested that his "age and last stage of debility" led him to prefer a quiet retirement to anything that threatened to "kindle new enemies, and lose old friends." Lest there be doubt about his concern, however, he alluded to Adams (though, again, not by name) as the candidate with whom he had had a "long acquaintance, but little intimate because little in political unison." It was clear enough.[28]

Politics was a "stormy ocean" for Jefferson, tranquillity, as he rhetorically put it, the avocation he was "moored" to in old age. Nothing better illustrated this disposition than the tenor of his conversation with the father of John Quincy Adams, his onetime adversary and predecessor as president. While Jefferson grumbled in letters to certain of his following, between themselves the two founders tried to keep politics subordinate to their literary restoration of the ancient world.

Jefferson and Adams had reconciled in 1812. With care and consideration, the Virginian sent only cool breezes north to Quincy in the early months of 1825. Masking what he truly felt—or perhaps representing that he harbored fears no longer—he offered "sincere" congratulations as soon as the results of the House runoff arrived, and he forecast a smooth administration: "So deeply are the principles of order, and of obedience to law impressed on the minds of our citizens generally that I am persuaded there will be an immediate acquiescence in the will of the majority as if Mr. Adams had been the choice of every man." Three weeks earlier, generous old John Adams had written an expansive letter to Jefferson, referring to his son as "our John"; this was meant to reflect on the halcyon days in Paris in 1785 when a teenage John Quincy "appeared to me to be almost as much your boy as mine." In Paris Jefferson had even imagined making a Virginian out of the young Adams, proposing that he attend his own alma mater, the College of William and Mary.[29]

John Quincy Adams was inaugurated on March 4, 1825. That morning, according to the Washington newspaper the *National Intelligencer,* "the avenues of the capitol presented a lively and animated scene." Some men had to fight their way through the Capitol doors, just to see the ladies to their envied seats. The incoming and outgoing presidents came together by carriage from the President's House, accompanied by a military escort and military music. Adams, dressed in black, was the first president to wear democratic pantaloons rather than Revolutionary-era knee breeches and hose. He was sworn in by Chief Justice John Marshall, who had given the oath to every president since Jefferson. His inaugural address lasted forty minutes and was read, according to the newspaper, "with a clear and deliberate articulation."[30]

The address contained no surprises, but bore a distinct historical flavor. With his consciousness plainly fixed on the generational shift that was occurring, Adams proclaimed the "perfect union" enshrined in the Constitution: "It is a source of gratification and of encouragement to me that the great result of this experiment, upon the theory of human rights, has, at the close of that generation by which it was formed, been crowned with success equal to the most sanguine expectations of its founders." Taking up issues that Thomas Jefferson still could not completely relegate to the past, he addressed the tenor of a half-century of politics head-on: the first two parties, Federalist and Republican, had both contributed "splendid talents" and "infirmity and error." The complexity of the world scene in the 1790s made this understandable: European conflict had divided Americans into pro-British and pro-French factions, resulting in a "collision of sentiments and sympathies." Federalists had acted out of a general fear of the anarchic influence of the French Revolution, approving of English social stability. Jeffersonian Republicans saw England as the home of aristocratic privilege—America's past, not its future.

With the War of 1812, Adams proceeded to explain, "the Union was shaken to its centre." But as the tumult of the French Revolution died, and America finally found practical peace with its former parent, "party strife was uprooted," and the gentler aims of the Constitution reestablished. "From the experience of the past," he could say, "we derive instructive lessons for the future." And so he termed America—and was the first U.S. president to do so in any public speech—a representative democracy. The word "democracy" had meant "anarchy" when applied to Jefferson's politics by Federalists of the first Adams era. For an Adams to apply this term to his country now signaled a real modification in the general understanding of a concept.

Adams had made sense out of the past. The one uncertainty that he raised, the first hint of the discord to come, was his vow "to proceed in the great system of Internal Improvements, within the limits of the constitutional power of the Union." Monroe, as a Southerner, could inch ahead with Washington's limited involvement in state transportation projects, but not so a Northern nationalist, a onetime Federalist. Any hint of an aggressive central government invited trouble.

In the discharge of his public trust, with a few decisive words, and a few more implications, Adams was about to go too far. After the speech, the *National Intelligencer* optimistically reported on the state of political peace: "General *Jackson*, we were pleased to observe, was among the earliest of those who took the hand of the president." Nevertheless, even on this inaugural day, less hopeful opinions were heard. *Niles' Weekly Register* reported that Adams was "visibly and considerably agitated" in his delivery. But Adams himself took comfort in the purity of his resolve. At a banquet in Baltimore honoring him, glasses were lifted, and the first toast hailed the new president as "a hero without ambition," a perfect democrat of the new age. "Yankee Doodle" was the accompanying tune. Next came cheers for the Constitution, and the song "Hail Columbia." The Congress earned a toast, as did General Jackson, William Crawford, and Henry Clay in turn—all this in a state where the electoral vote had been split, and Adams had bested Jackson by a mere 109 popular votes.[31]

As president, Adams was anything but showy. Because he was generally at his desk attending to affairs of state, acting with deliberation but without much flair, his political opponents were able to turn diligence into inertia. In fact, though, the president exercised vigorously. He regularly swam in the Potomac, taking on its occasionally formidable current. The Jacksonians—and not without effect—labeled him "sedentary" and "effeminate." As one who did not understand how to render his public image friendlier, he was never given a chance. Even as she learned grudgingly to appreciate the president's executive skills, the impression that Margaret Bayard Smith gained of the Adamses' public style—that is, John Quincy and First Lady Louisa Catherine alike—was a "silent, repulsive, haughty reserve."[32]

According to his own diary, as the year 1826 began, the president was leading a life "more regular" than ever before. He rose between five and six o'clock, well before the sun, and took a four-mile walk "by the light of the moon or stars," returned to the President's House, built a fire, and read from the Bible before perusing official papers. After breakfast he received visitors in succession until five in the afternoon, "sometimes without intermission." He reserved diary writing and reflection on public business for his private hours, after dinner. Normal bedtime was between eleven o'clock and midnight.[33]

Adams was by no means oblivious to the way others perceived him. His healthy routine did not relieve him of feeling that his accession to the highest office did not please most Americans. As the Nineteenth Congress assembled, Adams assumed that two-thirds of his countrymen remained "averse to the actual result" of the election of 1824. "Nearly one year of this service has already passed," the hardworking executive noted, "with little change in the public opinions or feelings," though, he added, "without disaster to the country" either.[34]

It was under such conditions, then, on December 6, 1825, that Adams presented his first Annual Message to Congress, the equivalent of the modern State of the Union address. (In the manner of the day it was printed out and physically delivered, not read by the president.) Though he had been in office nine months, this was the first official enunciation of his program and the first wide expression of the tone of his administration. Adams had discussed the contents of the Annual Message with his cabinet during the prior two weeks. Most of his advisers expected the assertive tone to annoy Congress, long accustomed to the patriotic pleasantries of Monroe. But Adams could not oblige. "The perilous experiment must be made," he wrote in his diary. "Let me make it with full deliberation, and be prepared for the consequences."[35]

Wirt had argued with the president for at least two hours. He said that he approved of the message, every line in it, but he calculated that Adams would lose Virginia's support, crucial to a New England president seeking confidence from around the nation. The mere appearance of what Patrick Henry had prophetically dreaded—"a great, magnificent Government," as opposed to an unintimidated collection of dynamic states—would be the charge against Adams if he called for a national university, a national astronomical observatory, national funding of scientific research and exploration, and an increased pace of national improvement through support of roads and canals. Not only were the states wary of Washington's power, systems of uniformity were unpopular, even outlandish. Why give Congress fodder when so many in that body already imagined Adams, as the number-two vote-getter behind Jackson, to be a usurper? Secretary of State Clay, the beneficiary of Adams's most controversial appointment, urged restraint of language as well.[36]

"Fellow Citizens of the Senate and of the House of Representatives," the message began with formal earnestness. God had blessed the nation. Its financial outlook was more promising than ever before. The navy was strong, with vessels stationed in the Mediterranean to secure commerce; in the Caribbean to suppress the outlawed African slave trade; and off the western coast of South America to monitor the "irregular and convulsive character" of politics in emerging governments that had been Spanish dominions not long before. Nothing had more favorably reflected on the attainments of the young, peaceable empire than the visit of General Lafayette, "a pleasing incident in the annals of our Union, giving to real history the intense interest of romance."[37]

From here, the president launched into the substance of his program, that "improvement" in communications—roads and canals—meant to shorten distances and strengthen union: "The spirit of improvement is abroad upon the earth," Adams proclaimed. Conceiving improvement in terms of intellectual as well as commercial projects, he went out of his way to celebrate the opening of the University of Virginia, Thomas Jefferson's brainchild. No doubt referencing Francis Bacon's heralded statement, "Knowledge is power," Adams marked sharply: "let us not be unmindful that Liberty is Power; that the nation blessed with the largest portion of liberty, must, in proportion to its numbers, be the most powerful nation upon earth."

The newly opened Erie Canal was a bright beginning, he said, as the waters of "our Western Lakes [the Great Lakes] mingled with those of the Ocean." Who could not see the potential? "If undertakings like these have been accomplished in the compass of a few years"—by state authorities—"can we, the Representative Authorities of the whole Union, fall behind . . . ?" Right issue, wrong president, a shrewd observer might have murmured. But it was in the Adams character to persist when a principle was made clear: Were the people not bound "by obligation of a high and honorable character" to support whatever added knowledge and strength to the nation? The improvement-oriented *Liberty Hall & Cincinnati Gazette* thought so, as its editor assessed the annual message: "It embraces every prominent subject of interest to the nation, and is written in a style suited to the comprehension of all classes of the community. We are glad to find that Mr. Adams has unfolded the principles of his administration with so much candour and boldness." Indeed, Adams's exhortation to the Nineteenth Congress was a stunning call to national purpose—*and it was dead on arrival in Congress.*[38]

The reasons for Adams's failure as president are systemic as much as they are related to his personality. It hardly mattered that this ingenious, dedicated individual was better trained in affairs of state than any man who preceded him. He had a deserved confidence in his ability to govern, discovering, in fact, that he had more time on his hands as president than he had had as Monroe's secretary of state. Rather, much of his predicament in 1826 was created by the Constitution.

After Jefferson, and until Jackson would revitalize the power of the office in 1829, presidents were dependent on and beholden to their cabinet officers, who in turn were responsive to the power of Congress. Under Jefferson, harmony (or at least consensus) prevailed in the executive branch. The president's longtime alter ego, James Madison, headed the State Department; steadfast Albert Gallatin, an exceptionally adept economist, ran the Treasury Department; and none of the other four cabinet members possessed the kind of personal ambition that might have tested their loyalty to the chief. The Republicans in Congress, despite a few fussing defectors, owed their stature to Jefferson, who had given their party its name. The president himself understood how to combine personal and political friendships, how to twist arms politely, how to get his agenda through the legislature by quietly pressing friendly congressmen to lobby his programs. Madison, for all his legislative experience, and Monroe, despite the absence of a serious opponent in two elections, were less adept at these things. John Quincy Adams, as well, lacked the ability to persuade at which Jefferson excelled.[39]

The diminishing power of the executive occurred in slow but sure steps. The unpopular War of 1812 might have begun in Jefferson's second term in reaction to British insults to American vessels, had not the president opted for the temporizing embargo of the nation's foreign trade in the final year before his retirement. This act of self-denial hurt the American economy as much as it hurt the British, and it encouraged smuggling. Jefferson lost his influence in Congress with the failure of his policy, the dismal end to what had been an otherwise successful presidency.

The sober Madison inherited an unstable world in 1809, and passively endured the political rise of the successor generation. The proud War Hawks, led by Clay and Calhoun, outpaced him—they were men with strong convictions and the burning desire to redeem the nation's honor. With its new, young face, Congress took advantage of a cabinet torn by personal battles and clashing ambitions, to strengthen its position vis-à-vis the executive. This was a case in which going to war did not bring unity—far from it.

Gallatin had remained in Treasury, but found himself at odds with Secretary of State Robert Smith, who resorted to the press to attack his colleague for an alleged misuse of public funds. Even their wives weighed in with unpleasant name-calling. After President Madison sided with Gallatin, Smith leaked cabinet confidences to his supporters in Congress and actively worked against the president's legislative recommendations. When an incensed Gallatin threatened to resign, Madison finally fired Smith. In the meantime, Secretary of War William Eustis had been opposing preparation for the coming war with England.

During two difficult terms, Madison had constant trouble keeping his cabinet loyal. Jefferson had held eleven individuals in cabinet positions over eight years (most of the turnover concerned the politically less sensitive post of attorney general), while Madison juggled eighteen appointees, including four secretaries of war and four secretaries of the treasury. Monroe, through his two terms, found similar obstacles to overcome. Peevish and contentious department heads indirectly fought each other for the front-runner position as future presidential contenders: Secretary of State Adams, Secretary of the Treasury Crawford, and Secretary of War Calhoun each had allies in Congress who helped scatter accusations about the others. It was rumored, for example, that Crawford was mentally unbalanced as he secretly investigated the finances of his rivals. Adams, though Monroe's choice as a successor, brooded that the administration was "at war with itself, both in the Executive, and between the Executive and the Legislature." It is indeed ironic that Monroe's stewardship of the Union was popularly referred to as the "Era of Good Feelings."

The Washington political community was quite conscious of the waning power of the executive relative to the Congress. Heads of departments were not expected to be an extension of the president's policies to anywhere near the degree that they are today; autonomous cabinet members transmitted reports to congressional committees without notifying the president of their contents. Monroe found in his second term that his cabinet was circumventing his requests, while responding far more readily to demands from Congress for information pertaining to legislative initiatives. As a cabinet member under Monroe, Adams was well acquainted with this state of affairs. He could not have expected his own cabinet to behave much more faithfully. He was fortunate, in fact, because it did. From 1825 to 1828 there would be no turnover in personnel, no rival factions within the executive. But not even this would strengthen the president's position.

Factionalism in Congress was aggravated by the long, bitter presidential campaign. The House reversal of the general election results of 1824, coinciding with the infirmity of Georgia's Crawford, caused the various anti-Adams elements to come together behind the likeliest alternative, General Andrew Jackson. Suspicious of a "Corrupt Bargain" between Adams and Clay, and ready to label the president imperious and overbearing without attempting to assess the economic benefits of his platform, the loudest voices in Congress were intent on being uncooperative toward all of the president's men. Little would get done, because Congress, from 1825, was simply looking ahead to 1828.

While the president's first Annual Message to the Nineteenth Congress went unheeded because of this distribution of power within the government, John Quincy Adams is not to be excused entirely either. He indeed seemed out of step. He reflected the masculine sensibility of the prior century, adding the appearance of disdain, the defiant directness, that he had inherited from his often isolated father. He did not wheel and deal politics, certainly not well. As vigorous in intellectual performance as he might be, he was not a popular man. And so, no one on Capitol Hill was prepared for his full-speed-ahead directive on the subject of internal improvements. He did nothing to assuage the states' fears of an all-powerful central authority dictating the course of national expansion. Nor did he give cabinet members the means to enable them to push his program with enthusiasm.

The Nineteenth Congress was an uncommonly disputatious body, and in the process of hardening along sectional lines. Other than men sympathetic to Adams's program, like ultranationalists Daniel Webster and Edward Everett, both of Massachusetts, there were strong-willed individuals like George McDuffie of South Carolina and John Randolph of Virginia who grabbed the public's attention with long perorations dismissive of the president's authority. These great stage-stealers were unsparing in their attacks, building steam toward 1828 while boosting newspaper circulation around the country. Supporters of the Adams Administration, speaking in terms of "frankness," "judgment," and other intuitive qualities, were hard-pressed to answer their highly motivated critics effectively.

Adams's political ideal got lost. That ideal was union. It was aptly summed up in a book review of *The Duties of an American Citizen*, published in the *North American Review:* "A moral and intellectual elevation of national character is the main thing to be gained [by citizens' devotion to political union]. As the power of the people is increased, in the same proportion must the intelligence of the people be enlarged, that they may know how to wield this power with discretion, and . . . direct it in a channel, where it shall produce the greatest amount of public benefit." The president understood his duty to the people, but he did not know how even to begin to reach the people's representatives; if the Annual Message had lyrical force, Congress was tone-deaf.[40]

Perhaps John Quincy Adams was meant, like his father, to be misunderstood. Still, there is something endearing about his perseverance. An incident described by Auguste Levasseur in his journal, near the end of Lafayette's tour, provides an appropriate, and rather visual, profile of this president. In the early autumn of 1825, as Lafayette, his son George, and Levasseur were about to leave Washington for a visit to ex-President Monroe's northern Virginia estate, Adams graciously accompanied them across the Potomac toll bridge. As they crossed over, the gatekeeper ran after them, shouting to Adams that he had underpaid. Seeing his miscalculation, the president took out his purse. As he was doing so, the gatekeeper recognized Lafayette and changed his mind directly, proclaiming that the toll was free for the Nation's Guest. Adams explained that on this day the general was traveling as a private citizen—as the president's friend—and as such was not entitled to an exemption. The gatekeeper accepted the explanation and received the president's money.

Levasseur took note. This was the only time in his travels that the general was ever subject to a toll—and it was the one day on which he was accompanied by the president of the United States! The French officer reflected that this most assuredly said something about the nature of a democratic republic.[41]

CHAPTER SEVEN

Congressman McDuffie Proposes an Amendment

O N FRIDAY, December 9, 1825, during the first week of the first session of the Nineteenth Congress, and three days after the president's message was delivered and read, Representative George McDuffie of South Carolina proposed what he believed a democratic remedy for the resentment and confusion that surrounded the most recent presidential election:

> *Resolved,* That, for the purpose of electing the President and Vice President of the United States, the Constitution ought to be so amended that a uniform system of voting by Districts shall be established in all the States; and that the Constitution ought to be further amended in such manner as will prevent the election of the aforesaid officers from devolving upon the respective Houses of Congress.[1]

The key to McDuffie's amendment was the phrase "voting by Districts," which was meant to localize the assignment of electoral votes (rather than deliver all the votes of a state to one candidate). This would restructure that convoluted form, the electoral college. Secondarily, when an election resulted in no candidate possessing a majority of electoral votes, the decision (pitting the top two vote-getters, not three, as in 1824–25) would ultimately revert to the states once again, rather than to the House of Representatives.

McDuffie spoke powerfully about the dangers and opportunities that faced his congressional colleagues. The present system, he charged, arrayed state against state "in the consolidated energy of their power." The district system of voting promised to reduce the sting of sectionalism by dividing loyalties within states and displaying the votes of local favorites alongside respected national candidates. Pluralism was a good thing, and the district system would encourage it, adding to "the strength and harmony of the Union."[2]

Fig. 13. South Carolina's Congressman George McDuffie, described as a graceless and unimposing legislator, whose oratory yet somehow unleashed a "convulsive power." From Edwin L. Green, *George McDuffie* (Columbia, S.C., 1936).

Once each state was divided into separate districts (roughly equal in population) for the purpose of casting electoral votes,[3] that state's votes could be shared among different candidates rather than assigning all of the votes to the single candidate receiving the greatest number of votes—the so-called general ticket plurality system that was established by the framers of the Constitution and which still prevails.[4] It is the general ticket system that made it possible in 1984 for Democrat

Walter Mondale to receive 40.8 percent of the popular vote and only 2.4 percent of the electoral votes (13 of a possible 538), and in 1992 for independent candidate Ross Perot to receive 20 million popular votes (nearly half of what the victorious Bill Clinton received) and yet not a single vote in the electoral college. The district system would have altered this picture.

To amend the federal Constitution was as daunting an object in 1826 as it is today. But in the agitated atmosphere of Washington after the controversial election of 1824, this was an alluring prospect for frustrated lawmakers, away from the seat of government many months between sessions. Upon their return in December 1825, the emotionalism surrounding the House runoff had still not receded, making debate over the McDuffie resolution animated and coverage very public and very intense. Election reform presented a means for eager partisans to inspect President Adams's character and redefine the national character at once.

Most Americans understood the basic workings of their government. Article One of the Constitution specified that members of the House of Representatives were directly elected by all persons eligible to vote. Since 1788, this has always been the case. The two members of the U.S. Senate from each state were to be "chosen by the Legislature" of their state. Not elected by the people. This is because the Senate was originally envisioned as a body of highborn landed gentry. McDuffie and his colleagues were not disputing the character of the Senate; it never occurred to them to "democratize" that body. In fact, senators would not come into office by popular vote until the Seventeenth Amendment became law in 1913.

Here is what McDuffie saw that appeared undemocratic:

Article Two. Section 1. Election of the President and Vice President: "Each State shall appoint, in such Manner as the Legislature thereof may direct, a Number of Electors, equal to the whole Number of Senators and Representatives to which the State may be entitled in the Congress." Thus the Constitution made it clear that the state legislature determined every four years who the presidential electors (the individuals who comprised the electoral college and voted for president) would be. The people simply did not elect their president. It was not only a question, then, of whether a state's electoral vote total was to be divided; it was also a question of allowing the people to determine

who their presidential electors were, rather than have their state legislators arbitrarily name them.[5]

The problem with the electoral system in the first fifty years of the
republic was that in granting states the power to choose the manner of
naming electors, the Constitution could not prevent the various legislatures from using different means to direct the process. Massachusetts, for example, altered its method from one presidential contest to
the next, up to 1824; in 1792 it used the district system in part so that
the people, in their districts, chose five of the sixteen electors, while the
state legislature picked the other eleven. In February 1826, a fired-up
Representative Henry Storrs of New York reviewed this provision of
the Constitution and, somewhat stupefied, proclaimed before the
House: "Nay, sir, there can be nothing to prevent them [state legisla-
tures] from vesting that power, if they have it, in a Board of Bank
directors—a turnpike corporation—or a synagogue." This is why, prior
to the election of 1824, no popular vote had been recorded in any presidential contest. Ordinary voters were electing no higher national official than their local congressman.[6]

The electoral college was created by the framers as a means of
securing elections that were efficient and tamper-proof. In 1787, the
people themselves were considered a potentially combustible force
when mixed together, and so they were intentionally denied the power
to execute a direct election of the president; but neither, theoretically,
was a self-anointed elite meant to have a free hand to interpose itself
and supplant the people in the electoral process. The Constitution's
original supporters in fact left notably uncertain how much active
power the people were supposed to exert over the process.

In *The Federalist Papers,* James Madison contended that state legislatures ought to have "a great share" in the outcome. But, as Representative John H. Bryan of North Carolina pointed out in 1826, it had to
be as much for logistical reasons that Madison consented to the
removal of the people by one step in choosing their president: America
was different, with settlements dispersed across an extent of loosely
connected territory, making direct election "impracticable." Alexander
Hamilton, Madison's coauthor of *The Federalist Papers,* had conceived
of the chosen electors as men of "information and discernment," ordinarily less subject to prejudicial influence than the people at large; but
he also explicitly wrote (again, as Representative Bryan explained it)

that these electors ought to be "chosen by the People." The judicious Madison confirmed, from his retirement, that the framers really had had a feasible district system in mind, envisioning a more popularly considered choice of presidential electors than what had evolved. Admittedly, the framers had not thought of every contingency.[7]

Thus encouraged to act, McDuffie and his supporters examined all the options. The district system certainly sounded more democratic than the general ticket system, but in fact the most democratic option of all would have been to allow the people of all the states to elect the president and vice president on a general ticket. Under such circumstances, the electoral college and electoral votes would be eliminated altogether, all popular votes being weighed equally. "The people" would have spoken. This possibility had been raised more than once in the early years of the republic, but it did not find much support because it could not be reconciled with the fact that different states had significantly different qualifications for the vote.

Democracy was having no easy time asserting itself. The drawn-out election of 1824 was the first national election in which most of the state legislatures had allowed the voting public to name their presidential electors—a partial popular vote was tallied. And look at the unwieldy results! The stage had been set for renewed debate, and nothing Adams could do would arrest the course of that debate, or place him in a dignified position while charges of a "Corrupt Bargain" loomed. When the Nineteenth Congress met for the first time, the many members who had not supported Adams would be eager to revisit Article Two, to update and standardize presidential voting practice, and what better way than by using his name as a symbol for injustice?

Politicians of the early republic had already shown that they were willing to debate the electoral system. The Twelfth Amendment, passed in 1804, provided for "distinct ballots" so that president and vice president no longer had to compete directly. But it was not until the beginning of 1826 that enough momentum had built and the motivation to act was most sudden and striking for a sustained constitutional struggle to be mounted.

It did not take long at all for the Nineteenth Congress to find a lightning rod for the considerable tension that Adams's election had generated. As debate proceeded in the House, McDuffie's was the name that was constantly invoked. It was his initiative that stimulated the most discussion, his stridency that prompted newspaper editorials. When on February 16 he said, "I am far from regarding power as, in itself, an evil," he was capitalizing on his new notoriety, staging a diversion to quiet those who saw him as a Southern states' rights partisan, unreasonably protesting some imagined New England Federalist conspiracy of consolidated power. "In fact," McDuffie shrewdly announced, "the sentiment contained in the Message of the President at the opening of the session, that 'liberty is power,' is strictly and philosophically true."

Though not generally thought of as an outstanding figure among the politicians of the early republic, George McDuffie was a curious breed of lawmaker who conformed quite well to the unsteady atmosphere of Washington in the 1820s. With a small turn here, a minor adjustment there, in the shape of national events, McDuffie could have been another Patrick Henry.

In fact, this popular South Carolina orator's childhood does read a lot like that of Virginia's legendary Henry. The fathers of the two men were born in Scotland, and both, from the most ordinary of backgrounds, were first employed as storekeepers before they trained in the law. McDuffie had the benefit of more formal education than Henry, excelling during his brief time at South Carolina College. There he delivered a valedictory on the permanence of the American Union. In the early years of his law practice, like Patrick Henry, McDuffie attracted a lot of attention. He soon sat in the state assembly, where he first fell upon a method for amending the way in which presidential electors were chosen. He was elected to Congress in 1820, at the age of thirty.[8]

Again like the disorderly Henry, George McDuffie was by no means physically impressive. His hair was raven black, his blue eyes deep-set, his hooked nose considered prominent. His natural countenance was rather severe and intense, his voice distinct and high-pitched. People did not congregate around him, nor did they shun him. Indeed, observers remarked that there was nothing impressive at all about the man—that is, until he was moved to address his fellow legislators, and then, all at once, "his eye flashed, his face would be lighted up," and his unsocial manner would be instantly transmuted into an exhibition of uncommon eloquence.[9]

A friendly newspaper went to great lengths to appraise McDuffie's oratorical skill. It reported in the spring of 1826, after a noteworthy speech on his amendment resolution: "We think that Mr. McDuffie deserves to be ranked among the first men on the floor of the House. . . . With an appearance not very imposing—with a voice which is deficient in compass, melody, and the power of modulation—with none of the graces of manner or attitude, which we are wont to associate with our ideas of an orator, there is that in what he says which will command attention from the most inattentive hearer. His gestures are made with a vehemence of manner, and rapidity of repetition." A complete study of American orators published in McDuffie's late years referred to his voice as "the harsh terrific blast of the trumpet." His was a "convulsive power." He was even able to step outside himself and satirize the orator's skill, replying once to Daniel Webster that "the gentleman should take care, lest, in soaring above the documents under the idea of statesman-like comprehensiveness, he should chance to soar above the subject." Clever wordplay garnered headlines in 1826, and "convulsive power," too, electrified the democratic masses who were eager for greater elective responsibility.[10]

As a first-term congressman, McDuffie aligned himself with the most prominent South Carolinian on the national scene, Secretary of War John C. Calhoun. He spoke in favor of military appropriations, then tangled with the vitriol of hypercritical Virginia congressman John Randolph—and, notably, emerged intact. But an opinion piece McDuffie authored for a Georgia newspaper in 1822, opposing the candidacy of William Crawford, elicited a challenge from the offended Colonel William Cumming of that state, who followed McDuffie to Washington intent on a showdown. Calhoun cautioned his friend against dueling, expressing the view that Cumming was insane; President Monroe did what he could to put a stop to it, but the savage interview finally did take place after the congressional session ended in June.

On the South Carolina side of the Savannah River, opposite Augusta, Georgia, Cumming's fire struck a rib and lodged in McDuffie's spinal column. The bullet remained where it had settled, because surgeons feared to operate. Cumming was not satisfied, however, nor McDuffie quiet about his opinions, and further challenges arose. North Carolina authorities stopped a second duel, scheduled to take place just over the state line, and Cumming protested in a published pamphlet. Accusing McDuffie of "crocodile hardness" and "habitual, prevaricating meanness," he insisted that his opponent lacked masculine courage. In their first encounter, Cumming charged, "His cadaverous looks, his feeble whine, his humble crawling over the field reminded me of some unhappy culprit, whose soul was swooning within him, at the approach of the fatal cord." Cumming even cast doubt that McDuffie's wound was serious: "he imitated a certain politic little animal of our woods, which falls and lies at the slightest blow, wisely considering it more expedient to *seem* dead, than run the risk of being so in fact." McDuffie reacted as expected. In their subsequent outing, the battered congressman declined his fire when his wily opponent assumed a stooping position and refused to stand. A final meeting five months after the first led to an exchange in which Cumming's bullet broke McDuffie's left arm. Those in Congress who spoke of the incidents reported that McDuffie was visibly altered by these confrontations, though the duelist himself claimed not to suffer too badly.[11]

The mutilated McDuffie missed one session of Congress, but he returned at the end of 1823 to take up the matter of making uniform among the states the means of choosing electors of the president and vice president. This was *his* issue. The session ended without any action being taken on the bill, and in the meantime, McDuffie promoted the presidential aspirations of Calhoun, whose brother had long ago employed him in his Augusta store. When Calhoun, seeing that his chances were slim, opted for the vice presidency, the loyal McDuffie transferred his support to Jackson—an alternative "people's choice." After the House runoff, McDuffie was among those in Congress who strongly criticized the "Corrupt Bargain," creatively terming Adams's cabinet "a feeble phalanx to stand against the people."[12]

There was no question as the Nineteenth Congress met that this persistent South Carolinian would once again raise the issue of amending the Constitution to make the presidential election process more democratic. In one of his more moving perorations, McDuffie revived a Jeffersonian interpretation of American patriotism, presupposing that the people's gut feelings could not be wrong. Democratic elections, he said, were "the renovating, self-sustaining principle of our liberties." By "laws of moral necessity," the people could not but "will their own happiness." He sought to explain why governments in the past had not permitted the people to elect their chief magistrates directly: it was that "the art of printing had not yet been perfected." By 1826, the proliferation of newspapers, pamphlets, and books—democratic access to the written word—had "given a new impulse to the energies of the human mind." The inhabitants of the most remote frontier town were, he pronounced, now equal in wisdom to the population of any coastal city. "Distance is overcome." To McDuffie's way of thinking, patriotism, "a cold and inefficient principle . . . unless it is an active passion," had greatly enlarged.[13]

His House colleagues rose, day after day, to apply their own active passions in this debate. Henry Storrs, from New York's dairy-rich Oneida County, a Yale graduate and judge, was one who took issue. Because of its "symmetry and harmony," the Constitution was a work of genius, he said. It was not to be tampered with on a whim. Storrs acknowledged that what happened in 1824 had "deeply agitated" the country, but he insisted that momentary feelings did not give sufficient cause to amend what was already a "just instrument." McDuffie's proposition, if well-intentioned, had failed to take the long view, to see that liberty had withstood a controversial election, a fact that offered "abundant consolation for our fears."[14]

William Archer of Virginia remarked that Storrs was dead wrong about one thing: the Constitution was made to be amended. The framers themselves would never have suggested that they were infallible, or that their document contained "more than mortal perfection." He agreed with McDuffie that election of the president should be taken out of the House; but he did not accept the superiority of the district system over the general ticket. Why change the balance within states "for the sake of a political abstraction?"

Archer took a moment to assess the tenor of the debate. Aware that he probably had not changed many opinions, he did what he figured was the next best thing and heralded the Union that made such deliberation possible. Columbus had gained immortality by discovering the New World, he said, and the United States had discovered a new method of governing it. Its free institutions stood to inspire others around the world. Even "benighted Africa," he said, was destined to "break through her cloud of centuries, to grow bright in the light of our radiating example." There would be no "future sun," no freedom on the earth, he assured, if America's light were ever extinguished. And so the country should not despair if the people's representatives argued extensively about their Constitution; it merely proved that Americans were morally secure enough to withstand honest controversy.[15]

One congressman after another took aim, chipping away at parts of McDuffie's resolution and tacking on new clauses, to form new resolutions. New York–born Edward Livingston of Louisiana, the younger brother of Robert Livingston (a signer of the Declaration of Independence) was one such outspoken voice. This former mayor of New York City and aide to Andrew Jackson during the Battle of New Orleans thought something obvious was missing from the mix. Of all the resolutions growing from McDuffie's, none had proposed "to carry the Presidential election directly to the People, and let them do that for themselves, which they are now compelled to do by attorney." So he advocated abolishing the electoral college altogether in favor of a simple, nationwide popular vote. As the debate wore on into March, Ebenezer Herrick of Maine grew so tired of the amendment spin-offs that he introduced his own resolution to allow constitutional amendments of any kind to be introduced only every ten years, beginning in 1830.[16]

One of the most memorable responses to McDuffie was the witty, if punctilious, diatribe of first-term congressman Edward Everett of Massachusetts. The night before his scheduled address Everett was unable to sleep, and asked McDuffie if he might rest up a day more. The South Carolinian was entirely unsympathetic, and so Everett went on.[17] Though new in Congress, he was a known commodity as a speaker. The Harvard-trained orator and Greek scholar had already spoken before Lafayette. He edited a celebrated literary journal, the *North American Review.* He was married to a woman whose sister would later marry the president's son Charles Francis Adams. In 1863, as an elder statesman, he would give the less memorable of two addresses pronounced on the battlefield of Gettysburg—his lasting two hours, Lincoln's two minutes. Here in Congress in 1826, his antique style of address was not yet thought out of fashion. When a speech went on for three hours, as this did, it was an event; during this high tide of congressional oratory, such bombast did not necessarily cease to sound fresh and pertinent to its auditors. Four-page newspapers sometimes devoted one-quarter of an issue to such orations.

Everett warmed up to McDuffie's subject by using a common ploy, taking seemingly minor issue with the Southerner's argument concerning the democratic implications of advances in printing. It was not printing that made democracy permanent, Everett insisted, but rather a "grand electoral and representative system"; that was what distinguished America from all other cultures, past and present. Ancient Athens had been the marvel of the world, and still reflected its buried glory. If McDuffie's logic was correct, culturally ascendant Greece, with its refinement, its rapturous arts and improvements, its republican political structure, should have survived to the present. It was a small point, indeed, and Everett was being deceptively coy in his address.

McDuffie, though he was no Harvard man, had woven into his oratory some severe lessons pertaining to both the grandeur of Greece and the catastrophic fall of Rome. Any ruler, he said, who was beloved by the people, would serve them well, even if lacking in character; he would be bent to the people's will because "the idea of being loved . . . would convert even a tyrant into the father of his country." And yet, McDuffie had continued, one who was brought to power not by the people but by some other "factious combination" and "the arts of political courtship"—and here he was clearly pointing the finger straight at John Quincy Adams—could easily be transformed into a tyrant, "however amiable his disposition."

From this critical point, the inspired Southerner had extended his imagery to the edge of apocalypse: the impure in Congress that elected such a disdainful chief executive could be said to have created a monster; corruption arising from the bribery of office "steals upon us in a thousand insidious forms." He spoke hotly, repeating the word "corruption." Corruption approached as invisibly but as surely as a pestilence. Vice assumed the form of virtue, coming not as "the naked deformity of the Fiend of Hell," but the devil disguised as a serpent, offering a delicious fruit. Somehow, to the excitable McDuffie, the electoral system put in place by the founders had become a fatal allurement to the final corruption of government, the death of what he called "our political Eden." He railed hyperbolically to each gentleman before him in the House chamber: *"Sir, the Angels fell from Heaven with less temptation."*[18]

Everett was not about to let all of this stand uncorrected. His decision to respond to McDuffie at length was no doubt prompted to a large degree by these passages. He countered in gently mocking tones:

> I listened to [Mr. McDuffie] with alternate delight and thrilling horror, as with such touching eloquence he expounded to us the apologue of our first frail parents in the garden of Eden. When I found him going back to the primitive records of our race, and searching the pages of inspiration, to find the key to our political situation here; and when I saw him returning with the discovery, that the President of the United States was the Devil . . . I was almost ready to exclaim, under the excitement to which the honorable gentleman had wrought us all—"Oh star-eyed science, has thou wandered there,/To bring us back the tidings of despair?"

After this flamboyance, Everett proceeded with more composure to explain the genesis, as it were, of McDuffie's confusion. It came in two bursts. The Bostonian's first linguistic counterpunch fell on the word "district," the key to McDuffie's system: Satan, declared Everett, had drawn Eve to "a solitary spot, to a lonely *District*, in the garden," and there "flattered her wisdom, her vanity, her love of power." Only an obscene kind of flattery, then, an appeal to the people's vanity and lust for power, could convince voters to eat the apple of constitutional revision. But Everett did not stop with a single allusion. He reworded his parable, stating that the "ambitious tempter" had prevailed over the "united strength" of Adam and Eve through "artful words." The linguistic device had been altered just slightly, but just enough to show how ambition threatened union. The clever Everett meant to demean more than McDuffie's resolution: he was implying that McDuffie's seductive art of speech had twisted a sober and sane administration, constitutionally elected, into something horrific, for the obnoxious purpose of spreading *disunion*.[19]

The magisterial style of Edward Everett was hard to match, and no doubt hard for some less sophisticated House members to relate to at all. North Carolina's John H. Bryan apologized to Everett in what amounted to the only possible insult a McDuffie supporter could muster: "I cannot spread before the committee the rich classical repast with which they have been so sumptuously regaled by the honorable gentleman from Massachusetts. It has not been my lot, like him, to breath the inspiring zephyrs of the land of Homer; I have not had my imagination fired, and my heart exhilarated and enobled by treading the plains of Marathon and Platea; I have not mused amid the ruins of Athens. . . ." It took but a moment to carry his point: "I come not here, Sir, from the Lyceum or the Portico; I come, Sir, from the Court-yards and cotton fields of North Carolina. . . . My life, Sir, has been spent among the People of my native State. . . . I know their wants, and I *feel* them too; I know, Sir, that they wish to participate in the election of the Chief Magistrate of this Union, and that they are dissatisfied with the present mode." Whatever the gallery might have thought of all the exhibitionism, this was indeed democracy in action.[20]

In the Senate, meanwhile, on December 14, 1825, Thomas Hart Benton of Missouri had undertaken the McDuffie position, proposing election of the president and vice president "by a direct vote of the People, in districts." South Carolina's Robert Hayne added to Benton's resolution—as McDuffie had already done on his own—that however the amendment was finally construed, it should make certain that there would be no repeat of 1824, that there would be no contingency that allowed the "intervention" of the House of Representatives in an election. A select committee, chaired by Benton, met and recommended a district voting plan. The Senate debated the issue from time to time during the winter and spring of 1826, but far less extensively and in less lively language than the clamorous House was employing. By May, the subject was dropped altogether.

Less contestable, though, was the notion of Senator Mahlon Dickerson of New Jersey. Doubtful that the district system would be an improvement on the existing general ticket system, he introduced an amendment resolution on December 19, 1825, to limit the president to two terms in office, in order, as he put it, to avoid the prospect of "an elective monarchy." A graduate of Princeton, former state supreme court justice, former governor, and U.S. senator since 1817, Dickerson was a moderate. His amendment had been proposed once before, in 1823, but was not acted upon. This time, except for the automatic opposition of the colorful and curious John Randolph of Roanoke, Virginia, it would not warrant extensive debate before passage.

Randolph was certainly one of the most entertaining figures of the early nineteenth century. By 1826, his antics were known by every citizen who read a newspaper, and his name was on everyone's lips. He was too outrageous to be hated, too lively to be dismissed. Born in 1773 into one of the most prominent old families of Virginia, he lost his father as an infant. Eight years old at the time of Yorktown, he matured into a votary of literature who at first sight was physically odd—tall, slight, and beardless—but, just the same, intellectually acute. The tormented, sexually ambiguous Virginian, with a grand, meandering pattern of speech, wore his Southern honor haughtily.

He grew into a life of privilege, sent to New York in 1789 to be educated at Columbia College. He stood in the crowd outside Federal Hall as George Washington was sworn in as president. But rather than cause the young Virginian to stand in awe of government, Randolph's presence at the first seat of national authority predisposed him to distrust centralized power of any kind. He was put into a frenzy of sorts as his older brother was "spurned" by the whip-wielding coachman bearing Vice President John Adams along a New York street. This insult to his family honor stayed with John Randolph; he spoke of it in Congress in 1826, in what may have been his most rational attempt to explain why he nurtured so profound a prejudice against all symbols of executive privilege.[21]

In his early twenties Randolph was described by a bookseller as a "gawky-looking, flaxen-haired stripling, [with] as much assumed self-confidence as any two-footed animal I ever saw."[22] He never married, and an apparently undiagnosed chromosomal aberration may have contributed to the various ills he complained of during his adult life, although this did not make him soft, pliant, or deferential. He overcompensated for his distinctive appearance, tending to initiate verbal attacks rather than wait to be challenged.

He first came to Congress in 1799. Except for two short hiatuses, he was a member of the House through 1825, when he entered the Senate to fill the seat of James Barbour, who had assumed the post of secretary of war in the Adams Administration. Year after year, all knew to expect Randolph's vituperative attacks to spare few who rose to speak in the national legislature. At first a Jefferson partisan, by 1805 Randolph charged that Jefferson had turned on his own popular principles and had become a too-powerful chief executive. The brash legislator anointed himself the people's protector, opponent of all unreasonable power. A most unsympathetic biographer, John Quincy Adams's grandson Henry Adams, described Randolph's tactics: "His method of attack was always the same: to spring suddenly, violently, straight in the face of an opponent. . . . In the white heat of passionate rhetoric he could gouge and kick, bite off an ear or a nose, or hit below the waist."[23]

Just after the War of 1812 had ended and before he embarked on his long career as a Harvard professor, George Ticknor of Boston had occasion to meet John Randolph in Philadelphia. "My eye fell on his lean and sallow physiognomy," he wrote, describing the congressman's head as "hardly larger than that of a well-grown boy." Randolph's hands and feet appeared malformed, disproportionate to his frame: "To his short and meagre body are attached long legs which, instead of diminishing, grow larger as they approach the floor, until they end in a pair of feet, broad and large, giving his whole person the appearance of a sort of pyramid." His face seemed to be a fusion of European and Indian: "In his physiognomy there is little to please or satisfy, except an eye which glances at all and rests on none. . . . His voice is shrill and effeminate, and occasionally broken by those tones which you some-times hear from dwarfs and deformed people." Ticknor was surprised on this occasion that, given his reputation, Randolph "talked little, but ate and smoked a great deal."[24]

Hugh Garland, an adoring antebellum Randolph biographer, pro-vides the opposite extreme. First glimpsing the congressman in 1825 at a friendly gathering in his home state, Garland fixed his eye on the "animated countenance" of the "swarthy" figure, and immediately pronounced Randolph his *"beau ideal"* of the orator: "the solemn glance, that passed leisurely over the audience . . . the graceful bend and easy motion of the person, as he turned from side to side; the rapid, lightning-like sweep of the hand when something powerful was uttered; the earnest, fixed gaze that followed, as if searching into the hearts of his auditors, while his words were telling upon them; then, the ominous pause, and the twinkling of that long, slender forefinger, that accompanied the keen, cutting sarcasm of his words—all these I can never forget."[25]

Washington Irving wrote from London in 1822 of encounters with Randolph, who had made the voyage for his health: "John Randolph is here and has attracted much attention. He has been sought after by people of the first distinction. I have met him repeatedly in company and his excentricity of appearance & manners makes him the more current and interesting. For in high life here, they are always eager after everything strange and peculiar." As a commentator on social trends whose fiction traded on the power of nostalgia, Irving took particular note of the Virginian's embodiment of Revolutionary-era deportment: "There is a vast deal too of the old school in Randolph's manners, the turn of his thoughts and the style of his conversation which seems to please very much."[26]

Randolph despised John and John Quincy Adams both, but he pursued an unusual affinity with the Adamses' neighbor and close kin, Boston's Mayor Josiah Quincy. The two had served together in the House of Representatives during Jefferson's second term. There, in 1807–08, arch-Republican Randolph found arch-Federalist Quincy a necessary ally in their common design to thwart the president. Randolph construed that upon donning his executive garb, Jefferson had turned his back on the principle that local government was to be at all costs protected from intrusive big government—what was then known as "national consolidation"; Quincy felt that, unlike honest, manly John Adams, it was impossible to know precisely where Jefferson stood, that he was an incorrigible climber, a dishonorable, devious, and entirely untrustworthy human being.

Quincy and his cousin John Quincy Adams had tramped together through a New England swamp as youths. Politics was yet another slimy bog for them. Not long before Josiah Quincy's political career began, John Quincy Adams had written him that in his opinion Jefferson had blundered his way into success as president and was in fact weakening America. But by the middle of Jefferson's second term, Adams was coming to be critical of fellow Federalists as well, knowing that his party was sinking. His acceptance of Jefferson's foreign policy finally estranged him from the Federalists. Quincy, on the other hand, never abandoned the hard-line stance that New Englanders had automatically expected from John Adams's son. Yet Quincy showed greater understanding than most toward the independent younger Adams. "He is, I fully believe," Quincy wrote to his wife in 1808, "as perfectly my friend as ever he was. He has just as good a right to his sentiments as I have to mine. He differs from his political friends, and is abused. Let us not join in the contumely."[27]

If Quincy was accepting of his errant cousin, he continued to see Jefferson's history as one of slyness and demagoguery—a "snake in the grass" in the 1790s who had pretended to maintain cordial feelings toward the first Adams while plotting to unseat him. The mild-mannered third president, insisted Quincy, was "the more dangerous from the oily, wily language with which he lubricated his victims and applied his venom,—the more seductive and influential from the hollow pretenses of respect." Protectively writing the senior Adams in 1808, Quincy further called Jefferson "a dish of skim milk" who stood "curdling at the head of our nation."[28]

John Randolph opposed Jefferson for entirely different reasons. He feared the transformation of the United States into an aggressive commercial power and wished for a dreamy isolation instead. From this stance he would never waver. Quincy and Randolph, unlikely allies, awkwardly appreciated each other, the parochial Southerner at one point commenting, "I never intend to set my foot on the farther bank of the Hudson. But if I ever should, your house shall be the first that I will enter." The Puritan-descended Quincy himself bore something of a New Englander's prejudice against Randolph, and he informed posterity that he had allowed only so much "intimacy as was practicable between me and a Southern man, haughty and wedded to Southern supremacy." Randolph, he said, was "a creature of whim and momentary impulse." There was something comical, if not crazed, in the soprano-voiced Virginian's ordinary costume, "his skeleton legs cased in tight-fitting leather breeches and top-boots, with a blue riding-coat, and the thick buckskin gloves from which he was never parted." Randolph's contempt for most everyone who served in Congress isolated him. But for reasons the New Englander did not quite comprehend, Randolph not only put up with Quincy's staunch Federalism but was unfailingly polite toward him. He entrusted the care of a beloved nephew to Quincy, when he sent the youth to Harvard.[29]

The two crusty politicians exchanged books as well as letters. It was in February 1826, while serving as mayor of Boston, that Quincy received from Washington what proved to be his last correspondence from the Virginia aristocrat. It was wildly discursive, in Randolph's familiar mode, and it dealt with literature more than politics. Still, the letter writer finally got around to the matter of their different social perspectives, a key motive behind the letter. Randolph meant no discourtesy to Quincy—that, a disentangling of his prose would reveal. To understand and be understood by another was a long and necessarily circuitous process for the irritable Southerner, lifelong even. He tried with excruciating goodwill to shorten the process: "What we are made of, to take sides in the factions of the circus (green or blue), and to doat upon the professions of 'feeling' and 'sentiment' and 'broken-heartedness' from the lips or pen of a fellow whose vocation it is to deal in those commodities. . . ." Randolph pronounced his opinion of the human character by quoting Lord Byron, "One wide den of thieves, or—what you will!" Quincy no doubt understood the attempt.

A long P.S. followed, because Randolph did not find it easy to put his pen away once he had commenced writing—just as he found it difficult to end a speech. Here the self-conscious man of infirmities, purposefully, poetically out of sync and madly advertising himself, wrote with plain nostalgia for Quincy's years in Congress. As he saw it, the two self-acknowledged ideologues had sought to insure that American politics would not find too comfortable a consensus, such that would make them irrelevant. While others rolled on toward the political muddle of imagined harmony and Monroe's "Era of Good Feelings," they had, to Randolph's mind, struck a necessary balance between two opposing "self-evident truths." But Quincy had been long absent from the national political scene in 1826, and Randolph now stood pretty much alone in defense of extremes. As he wrote his postscript, telling Quincy that he was literally singing "Auld Lang Syne" to himself as the pen moved, Randolph maintained "a perfect recollection" of old times: "I can see you now just as you were when a certain great man that now is was beginning to be,—but why revive what is better forgot?" As cool and deliberative as Randolph was warm and impulsive, Mayor Quincy appeared stupefied by the Virginian's perverse nostalgia for their former conflict: "Upon the whole," said Quincy, "he is a man who will always have more enemies than friends."[30]

Randolph repressed no thought. On March 2, 1826, with Mahlon Dickerson's amendment motion under consideration, he rose to harangue his Senate colleagues. This time he found himself dwelling on his own tendencies: "I know, sir," he began, "that this is a body, above all others, in which they 'shall not be heard for their much speaking.' " He was, in his own way, appealing for sympathy:

> . . . and yet, sir, circumstanced as I am, I am compelled. . . . May I hope to be pardoned for this, not only in consideration of the

peculiarity of my situation—of my condition—but in consideration of a defect—whether of nature or of education, it is perfectly
immaterial—perhaps proceeding from both—a defect which has
disabled me, from my first entrance into public life, to the present
day, to make what is called a *regular speech.*

As he attempted to get back on track, to address the Constitution,
Randolph traveled in his mind yet a greater distance:

Sir, in respect to these regular arguments, it has often struck me
that they resemble, in more regards than one, the modern invention of a chain bridge—which, provided the abutments and fix-
tures are perfectly strong, and provided there is no defective link
in the whole chain—are amongst the finest and most useful specimens of human ingenuity. . . .

An enemy of federally funded internal improvements, he was however
fixed on the metaphorical value of the latest engineering technology:

. . . but, sir, when we reverse the proposition—when the abutments are not sufficient—and there is one single link which is
defective—one is as good—as bad, rather, as a thousand—that
one is fatal to the whole structure, and souse down in the water
comes the unwary passenger. . . .[31]

The *Massachusetts Spy* that Ruth Bascom was reading extracted
Randolph's speeches of that week and, by way of an unidentified letter
from Washington, freely editorialized: "He spoke about one hour and a
half. It was a speech of a madman; a tale told by—. I won't say an idiot,
for he is the very antipode of an idiocy; but it signified nothing. . . .
Mr. Randolph's health is unusually good. His voice and nerves are as
strong as ever, and his eye has lost none of its fire. . . . His appearance
is as grotesque as formerly, except that he does not wear his hair so
long. . . . He wears and sometimes speaks in white gloves." There was
something about his trademark white gloves that seemed always to
warrant remark. It was as if Randolph wanted this kind of publicity,
and worked hard at soliciting it, all the while pleading to be given
credit for his humanity.[32]

The following week, the *Spy* again expressed astonishment at the senator's outbursts. How could he get away with attacking not only the current administration, but so much else—the political character of John Adams, the accomplishments of Thomas Jefferson, and the efforts of their successors, Madison and Monroe? Randolph "lashed reporters; talked Greek; spoke of all the Grecian heroes; admitted that he was descended from one . . . , contended that in times of peace the General Government had nothing to do, but attend to the concerns of the Post Office."[33] The *Supporter* in Chillicothe transcribed, in Virginia vernacular, some of the abusive senator's more unreasoning digressions. Here, between gulps of a malt liquor, was how Randolph had explained the manner in which John Quincy Adams abandoned his Federalist friends in order to embrace Jefferson's policies:

> The Royal George! Yes! I've a story to tell you about the Royal George! You remember the Royal George, sir?—But no!—It was before your time, sir. (Tims, give me some porter.)—1807 . . . I say January, yes, January. I remember it as well as if it was yesterday—I did not baptize it, sir,—no! though I was reputed Godfather, sir—as [Jefferson ally William Branch] Giles was the real Godfather to J. Q. Adams—the Royal George, sir,—was a huge unwieldy stage [carriage], in which Crawford used to send the members that boarded at his house to the Capitol. We used to meet Adams, sir, trudging through the mud, with his umbrella over his head—he would not ride with us, sir—But Giles at last coaxed him into the carriage, sir.—Aye, there it was, sir, that the "billing and cooing" began.

Next, Randolph read from a letter in his possession:

> Giles said that Mr. Adams was at first reluctant to call on Mr. Jefferson.—Coy—aye, a little coy, sir, reluctant to call on Mr. Jefferson! My life for it, sir, he did no [*sic*] go in the open day. . . . he went, like Nicodemus, in the dark—*in the dark*, sir—villainy always seeks the dark, sir.[34]

Randolph was a synonym for mischief. To those who appreciated his effect, who thought that his methods were wounding the administration, he was a knight errant, a comic genius. He was the one who was being abused, "so much talked of and so little understood."[35] To those who objected, he was a lunatic who had "a propensity to snarl and bark at every thing and every body."[36] A pseudonymous letter addressed to Randolph in the *Cape Fear* (North Carolina) *Recorder* from an ashamed Southerner found its way into the Northern press: "The inheritor of a name already consecrated to genius and patriotism," it pronounced, "a name inscribed by your ancestors on the first page of our history . . . , few men have set out, in public life, under happier auspices; or with more flattering prospects than yourself. . . ." But what had this Randolph done with his noble lineage? He produced nothing but an uncontrollable "spirit of invective." One could only conclude "that you were deficient in that strength of mind; that firmness of principle, and that steadiness of purpose" by which a public servant conveyed honor to the people. "The suddenness of your mutations of opinion; and the quickness of your transitions, from dogma to dogma, and from party to party, have scarcely left room in the public mind for the exercise of charity." Randolph raged, and citizens raged back.[37]

On March 30, Dickerson's amendment resolution, proposing to make the president ineligible for a third term, was brought up again for discussion. Randolph rose to declare that he opposed *all* amendments to the Constitution, "of every sort and kind." He wanted that sacred document left alone, because, as he put it (with unusual pithiness), "in stopping up one hole we made two." He urged, at the very least, postponement of discussion. Dickerson wanted to know why. "I will tell the gentleman at once," said Randolph. "It is unreasonable. . . . I will tell him at once, in my plain, old-fashioned, outright, downright, and I hope upright manner, that I am against all amendments of the Constitution that are nugatory." It was a moment of clarity for Randolph. "I put up no fences against usurpation, made up of paper or parchment. Power is the only thing that limits power." He would not have the Constitution become the exclusive tool of "quibbling" lawyers or "quibbling" planters; if there was a time to amend it, that time had been 1787: "I am for *ne quid nimis*—for the old doctrine of doing nothing—for a wise and masterly inactivity about the Constitution."

The next day, dismissive of all suggestions that an ambitious national government could effect positive progress in the states, Randolph spoke again, this time for three hours. Nevertheless, Dickerson's resolution passed the Senate on April 3 by a vote of thirty-two to seven, and was sent to the House for consideration. There it failed, however, and was not to become law until the presidency of Harry Truman 125 years later—though it was, in fact, the only Constitutional amendment among those proposed in 1826 eventually to be ratified.[38]

In May, when the first session of the Nineteenth Congress ended, George McDuffie went south. The House did not vote on his resolution, or on any of the other related amendment proposals. His official report stated that the select committee on amendments "had the said resolutions under consideration, but have not been able to agree upon any specific plan for carrying into effect the leading resolution, under which they have been appointed."[39] Congress was adjourned until December.

On May 3, from Washington, Congressman Daniel Webster wrote to a member of the British Parliament. He spelled out, as he perceived it, the less than impressive debate of the Congressional session just past:

Another long topic, has been a plan for amending the Constitution, in the manner of electing the President. This grew out of the events of the late Election. After much tedious discussion, we leave the matter as we found it. Our other subjects have not been of particular interest.

Mr Randolph was elected last fall a Senator, from Va. It was unexpected; but his great devotion to certain political opinions cherished in that State gave him the Election. He is a violent opposer of the present Gov't; & has conducted his part in the discussions in the Senate in a way hitherto unknown. The Vice President [as President of the Senate] has found out that he has no authority to call him to order, or restrain his wanderings: so he talks on, for two, four, & sometimes *six* hours at a time. . . . It is now said he will sail for England in a few days, to pass the Summer.[40]

On the subject of Randolph, Webster only failed to mention that the senator had just settled a score with an old rival, Henry Clay.

CHAPTER EIGHT

The Secretary of State Fires Twice

THE MOST CONTROVERSIAL figure in the Adams Administration was not President John Quincy Adams but Secretary of State Henry Clay. Long effective in the House, and known in Washington society for his good nature, charming manners, and enchanting tones, Clay was suddenly the most conspicuous symbol of a suspect administration. It almost did not matter to him. He was an artful man who brought drama with him wherever he traveled, a man of unusual intensity and highly effective self-presentation. He had acquired his winning style when young, migrating to Lexington, Kentucky, from Virginia in 1797, at the age of twenty, and rising to prominence almost overnight in that enterprising frontier town.[1]

Clay could not foresee the problems that would torment him into 1826 and beyond. Sending a copy of Lord Byron's posthumously published "conversations" to Frankfort, Kentucky, editor Francis Preston Blair, on the eve of the February 1825 House vote that certified Adams's election, Clay was supremely confident in his own position. Though he had come in fourth in the recent presidential election, he marveled at how he could toy with the sycophants who fawningly addressed him: the Jackson men cooed, "you know our partiality was for you next to the Hero; and how much we want a western president"; an Adams supporter approached "with tears in his eyes."[2]

Clay the power broker, with a few whispers to friends in the

House, had engineered Adams's victory—and more important, per-haps, Jackson's defeat. Not sensing any danger, he magisterially pro-nounced his opinion to his correspondent: "The principal difference between them is that in the election of Mr Adams we shall not by the example inflict any wound upon the character of our institutions; but . . . the election of the General would give to the Military Spirit a Stimulus and a confidence that might lead to the most pernicious results." Clay's role in the House runoff was indeed decisive, but his confidence was misplaced. By New Year's Day, 1826, Blair, who cam-paigned for Clay in 1824, gave up on him and enthusiastically joined with the Jacksonians. It was, unmistakably, a harbinger of things to come.[3]

After Adams had delivered his Annual Message to the Nineteenth Congress, Clay was still pronouncing his confidence. To Lafayette, he wrote: "The Session of Congress has commenced, under auspices as favorable to the administration as could be expected. Among the ele-ments disposed to opposition, there is a great want of cohesion. I do not apprehend that we shall have more than a salutary opposition." Events of the intervening months should already have chipped away at his optimism, but if he felt distress he was trying, as a seasoned politi-cian, not to show it.[4]

He was dogged by charges of a corrupt bargain even before he accepted the incoming president's offer of the very cabinet position Adams had held under Monroe. On January 28, 1825, twelve days before the House awarded Adams the presidency, a Philadelphia newspaper printed an unsigned letter (which was reprinted in Wash-ington), claiming that Clay was engaged in securing the presidency for Adams in return for a cabinet job. Clay responded by demanding that the "base and infamous calumniator" identify himself and meet Clay according to "the laws which govern and regulate the conduct of men of honor." The challenge to a duel appeared ludicrous when the only individual to step forward was a meek Pennsylvania congressman named George Kremer. In fact, though, Clay would shortly receive evidence that George McDuffie was in some way implicated in the Kremer letter. The South Carolina congressman made no admission; otherwise the twice-wounded duelist might have been obliged to sat-isfy yet another challenge.[5]

Clay soon regretted his impulsive suggestion, though he continued to project that he was a man of good conscience outraged by an inde-cent slur. Then, just days after the February 9 House vote, Adams ten-dered the offer and Clay entertained it—without much difficulty, it seemed—arguing to a close Virginia friend of many years that "I ought not to give the weight of a feather to Mr. Kremer's affair." He officially accepted on February 17. To the faithful editor of the *Liberty Hall & Cincinnati Gazette,* Charles Hammond, he wrote more precisely in April: "I could not refuse the Dept. of State. The Conspirators would have abused me much more if I had declined it. Then how could I have refused the first office under a President whom I had contributed to elect?" As he assumed office, Clay may have wished it otherwise, but he was very much on his guard.[6]

It is ironic that some were acerbically referring to Adams at this time as a malleable man, "our Clay President." For the Adams-Clay relationship had only recently grown congenial, and Adams at all trusting of the Kentuckian. In 1821, he had recorded his most complete characterization of Henry Clay:

> Clay is an eloquent man, with very popular manners and great political management. He is, like almost all the eminent men of this country, only half educated. His school has been the world, and in that he is proficient. His morals, public and private, are loose, but he has all the virtues indispensable to a popular man.[7]

The proud, scrupulous Adams never doubted that he himself was morally deserving of public honors, but at the same time he recognized that he was dour and unapproachable—or, as he might have imagined it, unapproachable because he was without peer. He knew that no others could be like him, and so he did not expect them to be. One has the sense that Adams's envy of Clay's ability to reach his audience was at best an abstract thing—Adams did not envy much. Rather, he grew comfortable with Clay because he saw that Clay knew himself, just as Adams knew himself—that there was surefootedness to go along with the gambler's reputation. The fact that their souls were far apart did not constitute a permanent fault line. They were two men of honor who understood each other's ambition, one reserved and the other uninhibited. The elements of an unimaginable harmony were becom-ing imaginable.

Adams continued his characterization, still trying to determine for himself what made his competitor tick:

> Clay's temper is impetuous, and his ambition impatient. He has long since marked me as the principal rival in his way, and has taken no more pains to disguise his hostility than was necessary for decorum and to avoid shocking the public opinion. His future fortune, and mine, are in wiser hands than ours. . . .

As he concentrated on their antagonism, assigning himself the morally superior station, Adams desired to be, if not quite sympathetic, at least humane:

> I have never, even defensively, repelled his attacks. Clay has large and liberal views of public affairs, and that sort of generosity which attaches individuals to his person. As President of the Union, his administration would be a perpetual succession of intrigue and management with the legislature.[8]

As things turned out, it was precisely that "intrigue and management" on Clay's part that would make *Adams* president. Adams in 1821 was loath to trust the canny Clay, and he was certainly right to harbor doubts. He could see easily how Clay's mystique threatened his own political ascent, but not how they might effect a lasting political alliance. That they managed to do so is simply another phenomenon of the many that marked 1826—a succession of unexpected combinations and irregular events that added sparks to an eventful Fourth of July.

Of the two members of the House chosen to count the ballots that elected Adams, one was John Randolph (not yet diverted to the Senate), who remarked afterward that "the cards were stacked."[9] Clay would become fair game, as Randolph saw things, by dint of his association with Adams, who was already the particular target of the trouble-seeking Southern gadfly.[10] Adams was not the sort to do more than shake his head disdainfully. But that was not Clay's temperament—his behavior in the Kremer affair suggested more. And he knew Randolph only too well. During his long tenure as Speaker of the House (from 1811), Clay had repeatedly scuffled—verbally, and rather gingerly—with the Virginian, one time ordering the removal of Randolph's dog

Fig. 14b. Henry Clay of Kentucky, portrait accompanying the 1852 obituary address. The statesman-like pose belies his reputation as a gambler.

Fig. 14a. John Randolph of Roanoke, from Henry Adams's unfriendly biography. The portrait captures his ambiguous sexuality.

These two nationally renowned men of honor faced each other in a celebrated duel in 1826.

from the House floor. He was certainly under no illusions about what to expect from his erstwhile colleague.

In Clay's new role as secretary of state, his relationship to Congress was nothing like before. His professional posture was different, his paperwork demanding and, most important, he could not find a means to escape the ghostly corrupt bargain talk, which followed him everywhere. Under these changed circumstances, Randolph's denunciations of the administration (this time directed from the Senate), as outlandish as they were bound to be, were fated to evoke an intemperate response from the sensitive Clay. Despite his odd appearance, Randolph was not George Kremer, a timid Northerner allergic to the field of honor. He was a son of the South, and reputedly a good shot.

Henry Clay was even more complex than many of his contemporaries understood. Though best known for his bravado, his occasional arrogance, and his all-night poker playing, he had adjusted his roguish image somewhat when in 1820 he determinedly patched together a bleeding Union and became the Great Compromiser. In 1819, Missouri had applied for statehood. New York's Congressman James Tallmadge kindled a bitter sectional controversy by introducing a resolution that would have made statehood contingent on the emancipation of the territory's slave population. As impassioned language flew, members of Congress recognized that a heightened struggle for power between Northern and Southern interests was at hand, and the integrity of the Union was called into question. It was imperative that action be taken to defuse the crisis.

At first, Clay rationalized that it would be a good thing to allow slavery to disperse across the West, that somehow this would advance the day when the hated system could be eradicated. He and other apologists imagined that the general increase in white population would drive down the price of labor until slavery could no longer compete. Such logic swayed few. So Congress resorted to a trade-off, whereby Maine would enter the Union as a free state at the same time as Missouri entered as a slave state; future "free" and "slave" states would then be added on the basis of latitude—those north of 36° 30' (other than Missouri) would prohibit slavery. Clay worked hard to garner the necessary votes, expressing generous concern for both Northern and Southern interests. The two sides reluctantly accepted compromise, owing largely to Clay's measured tones and his refusal to give up.

This was his greatest moment. In binding the states together again, he had achieved much greater stature than he already owned. Thomas Hart Benton, shortly to become U.S. senator from the new state of Missouri, called him "the *Pacificator* of ten millions of Brothers." Those embroiled in the Missouri controversy came to appreciate that Clay's standard for national conciliation was what America's founders had desired to effect: a harmonious union that recognized a variety of interests. All were happy—that is, save for the uncompromising John Randolph who, throughout the process, put roadblocks in Clay's path wherever he could. While Clay made his name as a compromiser, Randolph made his name as a spoiler.[11]

The national solution to the Missouri crisis had the ancillary effect of returning attention to local prejudices, exposing white Americans' discomfort with free blacks. Even James Fenimore Cooper made it a point to devise as his heroine in *The Last of the Mohicans* the alluring Cora Munro, whose dark skin partook of an African connection. Her father, the cultivated Colonel Munro, had loved and married a woman during his tour in the West Indies. And so, as Cooper paints Cora: "Her complexion was not brown, but it rather appeared charged with the color of the rich blood, that seemed ready to burst its bounds. And yet there was neither coarseness nor want of shadowing in a countenance that was exquisitely regular and dignified, and surpassingly beautiful." A brash critic in the Boston-based *North American Review* saw no constructive reason to make Cora other than lily-white. Professing that he meant "no offence whatever to the colored population of the United States," he enjoined: "but still we have (and we cannot help it) a particular dislike to the richness of the negro blood in a heroine."[12] Clearly, America's race problem was never just about slavery.

Uneasy interactions between whites and free blacks in both North and South proved that (excepting a small minority of activists) white America's self-image of generosity and public-spiritedness did not extend to a "modern" conception of racial equality, or anything close. The largest free black community flourished in Philadelphia, and represented 10 percent of the city's total population. Quaker abolition efforts had first spurred interest in the welfare of blacks there, and Revolutionaries like Benjamin Franklin and Dr. Benjamin Rush urged compassion and decency till the end of their lives, arguing blacks' capacity for autonomous development. When colonization of American blacks to the west coast of Africa was first proposed prior to 1800, most free blacks were unmoved, identifying with Enlightenment ideals about self-government but not with an African homeland.

White benevolence was most productive on a small scale, national solutions only distantly conceived. In 1816, however, the American Colonization Society was founded on the presumption that a dignified return to Africa represented the kindest way to carry out the emancipation of a people unlikely to thrive in a racially prejudiced society. The colonizationists were enthusiastically supported by prominent Southerners such as Presidents Madison and Monroe, Speaker Clay, and Bushrod Washington, a justice of the Supreme Court and nephew of America's "First of Men." For these optimists, colonization appeared a lofty solution; to less liberal-minded white Southerners, however, the organization was a means of ridding the country of dark-skinned people. And so, it was less the dream of a triumphant return to Africa, than the persistence of white hostility, that caused a few prominent blacks to reconsider the colonization experiment at this time.[13]

Negrophobia swelled in the 1820s, as free black craftsmen became ever more visible on city streets, and Irish immigrants saw themselves competing with skilled African Americans. Reformers could not dissuade the majority of whites from embracing the "science" of racial inferiority. Others who decried the free black "nuisance" responded to popular cartoons that exaggerated black physical features and poked fun at the caricatures' ignorant use of the English language. The message was that blacks, free or enslaved, could never "rise" to the level of being assimilable or even respectable. Even those whites who acknowledged that free blacks were arbitrarily caught in a hopeless netherworld between slavery and citizenship presumed that the problem was exacerbated by an "unwillingness of the coloured people to leave their habits of idleness."[14]

The paternalistic enterprise of the American Colonization Society was boosted by white enthusiasts around the country whose prose shed tears of sympathy. An 1825 piece published in New York burst forth plaintively: "Oh, unhappy Africa, how long must thy soil be washed with the tears of those who weep for their nearest and dearest relatives, who have been torn away from them, and dragged into bondage." The colonizationists were idealists who were loath to compromise their objectives. New England merchant and sea captain Paul Cuffe, of mixed African and Native American heritage, was a Quaker who had used his own funds to settle a group of free blacks in Africa in 1816. Could the pioneering spirit that white Americans exhibited be transferred to blacks? In 1824–25, hundreds of Boston, New York, Baltimore, and Philadelphia blacks, primarily members of the African Methodist Church in those cities, left for new lives in Haiti. By late 1825, however, most of the emigrants had returned to the United

States, rejecting the Caribbean climate and lamenting the plunder of their property by Haitians. They preferred to make their homes in the United States, even though they knew they had no choice but to struggle against hatred and violence there.[15]

These facts did not deter the well-meaning colonizationists. In 1826 they were unwilling to entertain any other destiny for free blacks: "Remaining *here,* they must continue ignorant, degraded, and depraved. The only alternative is *emigration to some other country.*" The Reverend Philip Hay was only stating what seemed an irreversible fact of life in America, when he observed sadly, "Until human nature is radically changed, they will never attain or participate in the privileges of American freemen." No town, he charged, would ever employ a black physician, no lawyer would ever take on a black assistant. And so, the humane minister was recommending what seemed most hopeful and broad-minded, when he praised the fledgling settlement of recolonized American blacks in Liberia: "O, what a spot is this, for the eye of charity to rest upon. In the midst of pagan darkness and savage rudeness, are seen the neat habitations of emancipated Africans. . . . They have as much health, and as large a share of animation, as they ever possessed in America."[16]

Charles Caldwell was a student of Dr. Benjamin Rush who had abandoned the egalitarian presumptions of his teacher for racial "science." Born in North Carolina, he later moved from Philadelphia to Clay's hometown of Lexington, where he taught medicine at Transylvania University. In his 1825 *Introductory Address on Independence of Intellect,* Caldwell confidently declared that "the Caucasian race is superior to the African not only in knowledge, but in the capacity to acquire and the talents to employ it." He justified this theory on the basis of nature's ordering system, assuming "subordination, the higher powers governing, the lower submitting to direction and rule." In human society, he said, "the more highly gifted give laws to those whose endowments are humble." According to his dictum "Follow nature," he underscored his belief that blacks would never possess the level of knowledge necessary to govern with fairness. But even knowledge, the doctor admitted, did not insure justice, for despotism and corruption among those wielding power was a fact of human history. His point, nevertheless, was that the knowledgeable ought to govern, because knowledge always supported democratization and threatened the arbitrariness of power—a point he was unwilling to relate to the intolerance suggested by his own racist presumptions.[17]

As unpalatable as Caldwell's theories may sound, they were not that unusual, nor regarded as particularly vindictive. Like the American Colonization Society itself, they are a fair barometer for measuring the atmosphere in which the Clay-Randolph conversation on slavery must have taken place. Both men, as individuals, had feelings of concern for the plight of blacks, and they were notably decent in dealings with their black body servants. But their politics, their prescriptions for managing the South's socioeconomic predicament, did not necessarily flow from their private sentiments.

Clay wanted to find a way of negotiating the gradual dismemberment of the system of American slavery. At twenty-one, a Jeffersonian Democrat, he had expressed noble and compassionate sentiments: "Can any humane man be happy and contented when he sees near thirty thousand of his fellow beings around him, deprived of all the rights which make life desirable, transferred like cattle from the possession of one to another?"[18] Born into a slave society, he, like Jefferson, did not entirely object to being the owner of humans; he could have risked his personal fortune if his feelings were so outraged. The famous example of Virginia-born Edward Coles, the Illinois governor whom Lafayette had met on the Ohio River, shows that this was possible. Coles brought his slaves with him to a free state, and started them on new lives. Rather, Clay was one of the many Southerners who were able to rationalize that their slaves were better off under responsible care than set free (especially in large numbers) in a society that did not welcome them. Much as he was genuinely uneasy with the fact that slavery existed and that he was a part of it, he rested his public career on moderate approaches to emotion-filled issues. Indeed, the enigma of Clay is that the private and public seemed incompatible, yet co-existed easily within him: he was unguarded, often indelicate, at times reckless, but he distinguished himself in the House of Representatives as an engaging speechmaker, reasonable yet emphatic, and intent on forging lasting compromises.

His avid participation in the American Colonization Society from its founding clearly helped to pacify his mind—the organization seemed to care, whether or not it was in fact moving toward a fair solution. But as a practical political matter, Clay believed, just as Randolph did, that the way slavery was to be eliminated in the states where it had long existed was a state problem, not a matter for the U.S. Congress to decide. Clay might have been a famous gambler, but he knew that extreme positions did not produce effective legislation. At times he did drop his statesmanlike pose and lapse into peevishness, as when a colleague like George Kremer criticized him. But on the whole, Clay was anything but erratic during his career in the House.

Erratic is precisely what Randolph was, of course. On slavery, he adopted an approach that was as ambiguous and unpredictable—and as sassy—as his pronouncements were on every other matter he addressed. He had inherited his slaves, felt bound to provide well for them, but he relished his rank and enjoyed command. He wrote smugly in February 1826 that "true humanity to the slave was to make him do a fair day's work, and to treat him with all the kindness compatible with due subordination." That was his public position. Curiously, in a codicil to his will prepared in 1826, he specified that his slaves were to be freed upon his death, and he begged his beloved Virginia to be "humane" and allow his human property to remain in the state rather than sent to Africa or the West Indies. He appreciated his slaves' humanity and, arguably, regarded them as Americans in spite of their condition of servitude.[19]

He had no patience with the American Colonization Society. That organization, Randolph argued bitterly, was mischievous, fanatical, and vain, uselessly pandering to the "morbid sentimentalist" who did not have to feed and clothe the slave, as the planter daily did. The colonizationists, at best, he said, would increase the number of free blacks whom they could do little to help, while through their self-serving "love of display," they would accomplish nothing but producing further disturbances in the lives of slaves.[20]

Clay wanted to find a permanent solution to slavery, one that was launched at the state level but could be regarded nationally as fair to all parties. Randolph resented easily, and in this case resented Northern snobbery above all, and the rough treatment Southerners received from those who did not understand their way of life. For Randolph, home was a retreat from the competitive style of Northern society in the 1820s, a retreat to the charms of unregimented pastoral comforts, a retreat to an undisturbed picturesque community. Plantation society evoked his nostalgia for eighteenth-century simplicity. Indeed, if Northerners could not appreciate the South, it was owing to their lack of an identification with the final glimmering consciousness of the Revolutionary era.[21]

Southerners feared what sudden change could produce in their section—the anarchic scenes and bloody possibilities that a race war would summon. This was not a new fear, but one that had been long incubating. Jefferson himself, "suspecting" the natural inferiority of Africans to Caucasians, initially encouraged justice for slaves in his draft of the Declaration of Independence. He viewed black America as a captive nation deserving self-government, but a captive nation that could not coexist with white America. Either a vast exodus would lead American blacks to a peaceful new life elsewhere, or they would eventually revolt against their oppressors.[22]

Clay was Virginia-born, Randolph of a respected Virginia lineage. Both were Southerners, both slave holders. Randolph insisted on making slavery and states' rights inseparable issues, an insistence, of course, that had fatal consequences for the ongoing North-South debate. The South could have chosen Clay's road, distinguishing the economic and political components of states' rights doctrine from the spiritually potent, viscerally felt slavery issue. Compromisers could have coordinated a policy with sympathetic Northerners (of whom there were many). But the South, led by John C. Calhoun, opted over the next quarter-century to see external pressure much as John Randolph had, as a total assault on the Southern way of life.

Calhoun eventually becomes the central figure here. In 1826, his resentment was slowly brewing. South Carolina–born, Yale-trained, he was a man of great distinction. As the youngest appointee to Monroe's cabinet, he had served as secretary of war for eight years before becoming Adams's vice president. Building a national following, Calhoun seemed to be acquiring presidential character, the oratorical spark, perseverance, and political effectiveness of the ambitious Clay—but without the same volatility. If a severe-looking version of Clay, he was a brilliant conversationalist. All believed that he possessed a bright future.

But in the first two years of the Adams presidency, Clay's manipulations proved decisive. There was not room for two "lieutenants." The vice president and secretary of state each had thought that he could influence the new president and place himself in line to succeed. Somehow, Clay gained an edge. In Calhoun's imagination, he had been squeezed out. His resort, just as it would be Randolph's resort somewhat later, was to aspire to a place within the Jackson coalition.[23]

But first, Randolph needed to expose more of his private pain— that was his apparent mission as he regaled the Senate with irregular language and historical recollections in the spring of 1826. In a truly pathetic way, he reveled in his loneliness. He invited scorn and ridicule. It kept him focused, even inspired creativity. He saw himself as a Byronic figure, moody and romantic, and "flung upon the world."[24] As a response, perhaps, to the imperfection in his physical nature, he had acquired a need to assert his difference. He chose anachronistic dress, outfitted as a comical Revolutionary-era gentleman among a modish bunch of nineteenth-century congressmen. And he disdained them all. It was a measure of purity for him to affect the Revolutionary garb. Dress-up was a game to make his life interesting and a strategy to make politics profitable for him. If he was redrawn in caricature, it was in opposition to the "realist" that Henry Clay assumed himself to be. John Randolph had poetically crafted himself into a metaphor.

As they represented two alternatives for a Southern posture toward management of the slavery issue—a consensus-building, nationalist solution vs. estrangement and alienation—one might expect that if Clay and Randolph came to blows, slavery would be in some way involved. But as meaningful as that debate already was, it was largely of rhetorical value in the congressional quarrels of 1826. What in fact led Clay and Randolph to a dramatic duel on the banks of the Potomac in early April was the latter's oblique reference to the corrupt bargain. It arose, of all things, in the context of a foreign policy debate: whether the United States, at the invitation of Mexico and Colombia, should send envoys to an upcoming conference in Panama whose principal design was to adopt a common hemispheric policy toward the former master of that region, Spain.

The matter of the Panama Congress was a non-issue that became a cause célèbre in the Nineteenth Congress only because it enabled the administration's noisy opponents to target Adams and Clay as ostensible power mongers. To counter British influence in Latin America, consistent with the Monroe Doctrine, and to strengthen ties with the newly independent republics of the Southern Hemisphere, Clay lobbied the president to send a U.S. delegation to the 1826 meeting. Some Southerners looked askance at the comingling of representatives of white and nonwhite cultures, but what was politically of more significance at the time, budding Jacksonians and self-anointed censors like John Randolph raised the specter of abuse of executive power. Before they confirmed the nominated envoys, the assembled critics in Congress nitpicked interminably on constitutional grounds and denounced the administration for its alleged failure to provide sufficient information about the Panama Congress.[25]

And thus it was during Senate debate on the Panama Congress on March 30 that the irrepressible senator went too far for Clay. It was the same speech in which Randolph offered his cranky discourse on the incident in New York in which the coachman who was driving the "Vice-Regal carriage" of John Adams "spurned" Randolph's brother. Rambling on thoughtlessly about ancient and near events all at once, Randolph alluded to the Adams-Clay combination with the sense of its being almost a monstrous political birth, at any rate an abnormal blending of opposites. He described "the coalition of Blifil and Black George," the previously unheard-of association of "the puritan and the black-leg."[26] Blifil and Black George were characters in Henry Fielding's novel *Tom Jones*. The Puritan was obviously Adams; the blackleg, or cheating gambler (with the connotation of a corrupt heart) was as obviously Clay.

The following day, Clay penned a note to Randolph:

Sir
Your unprovoked attack of my character, in the Senate of the U. States, on yesterday, allows me no other alternative than that of demanding personal satisfaction. The necessity of any preliminary discussions or explanations being superseded by the notoriety and the indisputable existence of the injury to which I refer, my friend General Jessup, who will present you this note, is fully authorized by me forthwith to agree to the arrangements suited to the interview proposed. I am, Your obedient Servant
H. Clay[27]

A host of biographers have, over the years, reported on the Clay-Randolph duel, but no one tells the story quite so well as Senator

Thomas Hart Benton of Missouri, who was there. He began a chapter in his memoir with that first-person confidence and conviction that one must heed, even if the storyteller's objectivity is to be questioned:

> It was Saturday, the first day of April, towards noon, the Senate not being that day in session, that Mr. Randolph came to my room at Brown's Hotel, and (without explaining the reason of the question) asked me if I was a blood relation of Mrs. Clay? I answered that I was. . . .[28]

Benton was Lucretia Clay's cousin: he was Thomas Hart Benton, and she was Lucretia Hart Clay. Because of the connection, Randolph resolved at once that he could not in good faith ask Benton to serve as his second in the duel he was to fight with Henry Clay. His next choice was Colonel Edward F. Tattnall of Georgia, who consented.

Benton was no stranger to the culture of the duel. In 1799, as a seventeen-year-old student at the University of North Carolina, he drew a pistol on the older brother of a grammar-school brat in Chapel Hill. Expelled from the university for theft a short time later, this morally unsteady young man emigrated to Nashville, Tennessee, where roughness was in vogue. In 1801, he first came to the attention of then Judge Andrew Jackson.

The hearty, blue-eyed Benton eventually established himself as a lawyer in Nashville. Like so many others, he looked up to Jackson, his elder by almost a generation. When the War of 1812 erupted, Benton volunteered, just to serve under Jackson. Appointed a colonel, he got on well with his charismatic commander. But during a lull in the fighting, something occurred to redirect Benton's path. Back in Nashville from preparatory actions in the deep South, Jackson involved himself in a quarrel between Benton's younger brother Jesse and Jackson's second in command, William Carroll. The principals came to blows in a most undistinguished interview: Carroll received a bullet in the hand, and Jesse Benton turned his back to his opponent and was struck by the return fire—in his exposed bottom.

Thomas Hart Benton was in Washington at the time of this incident. He had taken the long journey in part to appeal for funds to compensate Jackson for his movements in the South. So he returned to Nashville only to feel betrayed by the man in whom he had placed so much confidence. Relations soured, and an impatient Jackson lost his temper with his colonel one day and threatened to horsewhip him. Rather than shy from confrontation, Thomas Benton presented himself. An undignified brawl ensued at a hotel next to Nashville's public square. There are conflicting reports about what happened. Benton supporters claimed that Jackson drew a pistol and fired through Benton's coat sleeve. The Benton brothers both discharged their weapons—that much is agreed—and one of them wounded Jackson in the left arm. According to Thomas Benton, the great general bled profusely as doctors worked hard to save him, while the seemingly vindicated colonel was able to stride into the square and, finding Jackson's sword, symbolically snap it in two. Years later (after reconciling with Thomas but not Jesse), Jackson claimed that it was a "cowardly assassin" Jesse who had shot him from a concealed position, and that Jackson himself never fired his weapon.[29]

This murky incident spelled the end of Benton's hopes for political glory in the state of Tennessee. Having dealt rudely with his famous mentor, he removed to St. Louis. There, in 1817, new troubles arose. He was insulted at the polling place by a political rival, Charles Lucas, a young attorney and son of a prominent judge. Once again, Benton stood up to power. He called Lucas a "puppy," and Lucas, in writing, demanded satisfaction for the indignity. The two met on an island in the Mississippi, and as they exchanged fire, Benton emerged with a scratch below the knee, while Lucas took a ball through the neck. Asked whether he was satisfied, an ill-tempered Benton said no, and Lucas agreed to a second interview, meant to take place after his wound healed.

It was said to have been the willful Judge Lucas who made sure that his son took action to avenge himself and reclaim the family's honor. Benton was willing to follow the advice of his coolheaded friends, and agreed to call off the second duel, but new rumors spoke to his old Tennessee reputation, and ultimately provoked a fateful reencounter. From an absurd but agreed-upon distance of only ten feet, the two men fired simultaneously. This time Benton's pistol was the only one that found its mark. Lucas was struck through the heart and died within minutes, professedly forgiving his murderer as the scene closed.[30]

After this, the impassioned Judge Lucas never rested. He wrote first to William Carroll in Nashville, soliciting damning information about Benton's past. He explained to then Secretary of State John Quincy Adams how the savage Benton had single-mindedly pursued his son. Lucas also used the pages of the *Missouri Gazette* to remind readers that Colonel Benton was "crimsoned" with the blood of a promising citizen. As for Benton, it is said that he spoke little of the duel, burning what papers he possessed that pertained to the challenge and its resolution.[31] He did not seem proud of what had taken place. Perhaps, then, his lofty treatment of the Clay-Randolph duel contained allusions to his own regret, hard though these are to fix in a reading of his later memoir. Were the noble utterances and fascinating details he cites for posterity in the 1826 matter meant somehow to compensate for what he was denying to the curious on his own account?

Technically, Randolph could have refused the interview with Clay, because the code of the duel allowed him immunity. It affirmed that an elected official was not to be held personally accountable for what he said before Congress. According to Benton, Senator Randolph waived this privilege by reflex, saying that he would not avail himself of any excuse that some might construe as a "subterfuge." He promptly acknowledged his accountability to General Thomas Jessup, the bearer of Clay's challenge. Jessup in turn cautioned Randolph that he ought, as convention dictated, to consult with friends before replying. Randolph suddenly "seized" the messenger by the hand—a cavalier gesture one can easily visualize him acting out—and said, "You are right, sir. I thank you for the suggestion." Upon which—again, as Benton reviewed the chain of events—Randolph decided to seek him out.[32]

The Missouri senator assumed from the start that Randolph would not fire at Clay, because the challenged man himself had told him so. In forbidding Lucretia Clay's cousin from assisting him, Randolph had felt at the same time that he needed to "make my bosom the repository" of his secret. The childless Randolph insisted that Benton bear witness to his humane purpose: he would sooner forfeit his own life, he said, than make Mrs. Clay a widow or the Clay children orphans.

Randolph requested that the duel be fought on the Virginia side of the Potomac, across from Georgetown. If he fell, he wanted it to be on his native soil, in the state he loved. It was illegal to duel in Virginia, but Randolph rationalized that if he crossed the river to receive fire but not to issue any, he was not actually dueling. While the seconds for the two parties established the rules of engagement, Benton called on the secretary of state. "There had been some alienation between us since the time of the presidential election in the House of Representatives," he explained to readers years later, "and I wished to give evidence that there was nothing personal in it." Benton encountered his cousin Lucretia, "calm, conversable," and seemingly unaware of what impended. When she left the two alone, Benton and Clay talked until midnight, Benton offering his "best wishes" and departing gratified that the air had been cleared between them.

Precisely twelve hours later, Benton paid a visit to Clay's antagonist. He repeated his conversation with Clay of the night before, alluding to the "unconscious tranquillity" of Mrs. Clay, and how the youngest of the children looked as he slept on a sofa in the parlor. This was Benton's way to hear Randolph repeat his determination not to fire on Clay. Randolph understood perfectly, "and immediately said, with a quietude of look and expression which seemed to rebuke an unworthy doubt, 'I shall do nothing to disturb the sleep of the child or the repose of the mother.'" This moment of fabulous drama was silently enhanced as Randolph turned and continued doing what he had been doing—making out his will.[33]

The site of the duel was a small depression in the thick of a forest. The principals arrived and "saluted each other courteously," taking their places. A small stump jutted from the ground behind Clay; a gravel bank rose behind Randolph. Before Clay even had taken hold of his pistol, Randolph's went off, and a bullet shot into the dirt. "I protested against that hair trigger," the senator complained to Colonel Tattnall, his second. Clay stopped the mumbles of his own assistants by declaring the fire an accident. Randolph was handed another pistol. The order to fire was issued, and both duelists shot and missed.[34]

Clay erupted. "This is child's play!" he cried, demanding another fire. Randolph concurred. It is hard to imagine what had seized upon Clay at that moment, why he was so eager to have another brush with death. He had been tormented by illness and death for some time. Bedridden by fevers sporadically since the previous fall, he had told President Adams not long before the Nineteenth Congress convened that his health might very well oblige him to resign his office. He missed cabinet meetings. Two of his daughters died within a month of one another during this same interlude, placing him in—according to President Adams—"deep affliction."[35] A sense of catastrophe, ill-defined but no less real, had beset Henry Clay.

Benton, as he narrates the drama, took Randolph aside at this point and pressed him to come to an accommodation with Clay. But the Virginian's determination was strong, stronger than Benton had ever seen in him before. Randolph expressed his annoyance with Benton for unnerving him. As Benton later reconstructed it, "The accidental fire of his pistol preyed upon his feelings." Randolph was suddenly unsure of how that fire might be interpreted. His honor remained in question—or so he thought.

There was something else preying on his feelings. At a crucial moment during preparations, Colonel Tattnall had hinted to him that Clay wanted a slow count to allow himself more time to aim. Amid the distraction preceding the second fire, Randolph said something to Benton about "disabling" his opponent: Why would Clay need more time, if not for a better chance to *kill* him? Should Randolph, then, despite his vow to Benton, shoot to maim, that is, to "spoil his aim"? Randolph was unaware, as it would not be made clear until later, that Clay had actually sought a slower count because he was not practiced and feared he would be unable to fire within the specified time; he was only trying to operate according to the rules.[36]

As his thoughts flew, Randolph considered the misfire again. Something convinced him not to fire at Clay regardless of the consequence. He turned back to Benton, and with much feeling stated, as only Randolph could, that he "would not have seen him fall mortally, or even doubtfully wounded, for all the land that is watered by the King of Floods." Yet as a man of Southern honor, he would do nothing to avert the second exchange of fire. Benton retreated to his position, and the combatants readied themselves again. After the count, Clay fired, and the bullet tore through Randolph's loose-flowing coat, near his hip. Randolph fired into the air, saying as he did, "I do not fire at you Mr. Clay!"[37]

It was done. Randolph advanced to the man who might have ended his life, and offered his hand. As Clay gave his own in the same spirit, Randolph moved, "You owe me a coat, Mr. Clay," and Clay was happy to reply, "I am glad the debt is no greater." Benton rushed up, conveyed the "secret" that Randolph had never intended to shoot at him, and, as Benton concludes the parable, "we immediately left, with lighter hearts than we brought." Clay never shared his reason for insisting on the second exchange of fire.

Two days later, the duelists exchanged calling cards, signifying the restoration of social relations between them. For Benton, "it was the last high-toned duel that I have witnessed." In retirement, he added a commentary in his memoir of the event, reassessing that violent practice associated with American manhood, which he himself had so easily warmed to when young: "Certainly duelling is bad," an older Benton bemoaned, "and has been put down, but [it is] not quite so bad as its substitute—revolvers, bowie-knives, blackguarding, and street assassinations under the pretext of self-defence."[38] To appreciate Benton's statement, we have to understand that the precepts of nineteenth-century manhood did not necessarily forbid an armed display, where personal reputation was to be upheld. Retributive justice or the right of self-defense was a commonly accepted moral resolve in the 1820s. The duel also persisted at this time, because there was no war to function as an outlet for men who needed to exhibit their chivalrous attributes, who felt bound to do something comparable to protecting the nation's weakest citizens from an external enemy. The Clay-Randolph interview may seem an unattractive option for men of substance to resort to, but to Benton, its rules of civility were preferable to the wantonness that entrapped the next generation of intemperate American men.[39]

It must appear absurd from our vantage point, the image of these two unapologetic attention-getters, who had known one another for many years, staging a preventable, deadly (and illegal) confrontation to satisfy a superficial understanding of fame and honor. Yet not everyone in 1826 took the requirements of manhood as gravely as Benton did. Judging from accounts in hometown newspapers, their incredulity was not grossly at odds with ours. Under the heading "Another Duel," the *New-York Mirror, and Ladies' Literary Gazette* noted tersely that shots were exchanged "without effect, and, we are happy to state, the affair ended in *smoke*." While "considerable sensation" arose in Washington, D.C., as news of the encounter spread, the *National Intelligencer* reported the event in a tone that suggested a sporting event; and its rival, the *United States Telegraph*, reflecting an antiadministration position, asserted that Clay had been "electrified with spontaneous admiration" for his adversary's "heroic" conduct on the field of honor.[40]

In similarly florid language, Clay's friend Christopher Hughes wrote him of "the joy of my heart, at your safety, after the *rencontre* with Randolph!" In Baltimore, where Hughes lived, "There is but *one opinion*! The only regret is that you had not bled him copiously. . . . My blood thrilled through me when I heard of the meeting." A diplomat, recently returned from Europe, Hughes was most undiplomatic with his pen. He was filled with tough talk: Randolph having been properly dispatched, how now to deal with the "miscreant" McDuffie? That man's "despicable slanders," Hughes submitted, unlike Randolph's, were better off ignored. After all, a gentleman did not "condescend" to engage in a duel with a person who was not of equal station. Praising Clay's "gallant & honest & affectionate heart," Hughes added of the duel, "thank God it is over; and I think your mind will be, & must be, completely composed, by your having given so severe a lesson to Randolph, and shewn the world your readiness to chastise such insolence."[41]

As for Clay himself, he appears to have gone back to work and put the matter out of his mind. He wrote to editor Charles Hammond in Cincinnati ten days after the incident as matter-of-factly as possible: "You will see that I have had an affair with Mr. R. His assaults were so gross repeated and unprovoked that I could not longer bear them. I rejoice that no injury happened him." Considering only the criticism he might suffer on moral grounds for engaging in a duel, Clay added the neat (and conventional) rationale: "Submission, on my part, to the unmerited injury, I can only say, would have rendered existence intolerable."[42] There is every reason to believe that the antagonists both felt, just as their friends continued to assure them, that the affair had concluded with each having successfully defended his honor as a man.[43]

In that vein, however, the impression made on John Randolph is less easily apprehended. New York's Governor DeWitt Clinton suggested to his friend Ethan Allen Brown, "I think that Randolph was fairly a non-combatant," while he called Clay (not Randolph, as more generally supposed) a self-destructive madman.[44] The *Richmond Enquirer* informed expectant readers that the Virginia senator returned to his seat on Capitol Hill as if nothing had happened, proving himself once again a "champion of the people." Had he refused Clay's challenge, the report continued, his censorial power would have dissipated all at once, "his very person the subject of scorn and future outrage." Now, having defended his honor, he could go on "presenting the administration in the most odious colors to the community"—though not out of any particular spite, for he had opposed all administrations equally.[45]

Randolph's adoring biographer and contemporary, Hugh Garland, insisted that Randolph was the best shot in Virginia and could have killed Clay if he chose. But, he added ambiguously, this man of many words for a time sank into speechlessness, claiming for himself the "*hysterio passio* of poor old Lear." Perhaps this is what is to be gleaned from Randolph's complaint to his favorite correspondent, Dr. John Brockenbrough: "I am all but friendless." Clay's antagonist was a doomsayer. He roared in the public arena, always knowing that he was far outnumbered. "The least mental fatigue, above all, the jabber of Congress, fatigues me," he had penned a few months before. In March 1826, as his antics in Congress were reaching their height of intensity, he had quite nearly begged for a mortal confrontation: "I cannot sleep. Death shakes his dart at me; but I do not, cannot fear him."[46]

There was much speculation in his lifetime to the effect that John Randolph was, in physiological terms, less than a man. In the decades after his death, too, Virginia neighbors held to the firm conviction that a doctor who examined Randolph's remains found his sex organs to be underdeveloped, his testicles "mere rudiments." On the other hand, while vouching for this intelligence, his well-respected early-twentieth-century biographer William Cabell Bruce offered that Randolph had had romantic encounters as a young man of a kind that suggested he had at least at some point in his adult life expressed conventional male ardor. Bruce speculated that a "wasting" disease like the mumps may have been responsible for what the doctor at the postmortem inspection observed.[47]

Most probably, John Randolph had the genetic condition known as Klinefelter's syndrome. In approximately one in every eight hundred live male births, the individual will have two X and one Y chromosomes. These individuals are often tall, with narrow shoulders and disproportionately long limbs. Randolph was fully six feet tall (far more unusual in his time than now) and only thirteen inches across the shoulders. George Ticknor's description of his physical appearance in 1815—"small shoulders" and "extremities . . . unnaturally protracted," "long legs which . . . grow larger as they approach the floor"—are all consistent with Klinefelter's. Such individuals are infertile, their testes small and firm. While symptoms vary, they also are known, like Randolph, to have light facial hair, and are predisposed to hyperactivity.[48]

On those occasions when his virility was crudely questioned in the course of public debate by men who felt injured by his satiric reproaches, Randolph merely amplified his rhetoric in response. Once in Congress when he was bluntly called unmanly (the precise language was never recorded), Randolph countered by claiming that his attacker evidently lacked an understanding of the "ennobling passion" of love. Surely, he pursued, no one would want to suggest that a man's passing familiarity with animal urges was equal to "generous sentiment of the heart." The droll Randolph warranted that boasting of superiority in "those parts of our nature which we partake in common with the brutes," was not true superiority. Rather it was the possession of large *feelings* that made a man.[49]

How do we assess his inner life? This gangling, lifelong bachelor, with a dark countenance and fair hair, was sickly and emaciated from the late 1810s onward. If we take him at his word, he had a difficult time believing that he ever had trustworthy friends—or, that they were fewer and fewer as the years went on. In his correspondence he embraced his disappointments. A sympathetic nineteenth-century biographer, Powhatan Bouldin, wrote that Randolph "frequently talked about shooting people," yet he was not "dangerous," as modern criminologists understand that term.[50]

The duel with Clay appears to be a distinct, but not an exceptional, attempt on Randolph's part to call attention to his struggle for honor, that he believed attainable by proving purity of commitment. He was always trying to upstage himself, to improve on the last performance. It hardly needs to be said that as he poured out his tortured soul, the brilliant if clownish Virginian was viewed by many of his colleagues to be deranged. Benton thought he had "temporary aberrations of mind." Bouldin insisted that Randolph was never insane, though "his nerves were strained to the highest pitch." Looking back at the record, Randolph can be best described as an eccentric, a habitual attention-getter and stage-stealer, wallowing in and relishing his loneliness. It was said by some who felt they understood his plaint that the gloomy romantic could have written Byron's *Childe Harold's Pilgrimage*. Suffice it to say that Randolph of Roanoke was relentless.[51]

WASHINGTON politics appeared more deadly than ever before. An editorial writer in Lexington had announced just after Adams's inauguration that "a new epoch is commencing." The writer did not see this as an encouraging sign. He was assessing what the incoming president had pretended not to notice in his inaugural address—that political parties no longer arose from principles but from the lure that was cast by popular men. The personalities of party "chieftains" somehow meant enough to voters, while ideas had become of secondary importance. The Kentucky editor's evident fear, of course, was the Jackson phenomenon. Jackson stood for little beyond the heroic constitution of Andrew Jackson. With Clay as a loyal secretary of state, and out of the running, "We now have the Adams party, the Jackson party, the Crawford party, and the Calhoun party. Of the three latter it is much to be lamented that a leading object seems to be the destruction of Mr. Clay."[52]

Henry Clay was not destroyed by slander, nor by bullet, in the year 1826. But it may be justly said that his accommodation with John Quincy Adams, bargain or not, did much to undo the national reputation that the Great Compromiser had attained a few years earlier. Meanwhile, the "three latter" parties whose threat to principled government the Kentucky editor fearfully conjured in 1825—Jacksonians, Crawfordites, and Calhounites—had unmistakably converged by the middle of 1826, if not before. They were now the "Jackson party."

CHAPTER NINE

General Jackson Leisurely Views the Passing Scenes

FROM THE HERMITAGE, his plantation home just outside Nashville, General Andrew Jackson wrote on May 3, 1826, to his staunch Tennessee ally, first-term congressman James K. Polk, who was then in Washington. The letter was marked "Private" and concerned delicate political subjects. Polk, another future president (1845–49, and before that Speaker of the House, 1835–39), had just delivered his first speech in Congress. Jackson had read it. It was in support of the McDuffie amendment.

"I have been leisurely viewing the passing scenes at Washington," wrote Jackson, "and your speech on the amendment of the constitution I have read with much pleasure." The general agreed with McDuffie and Polk that the district system for electing the president was "the true meaning of the constitution," but his chief point was that the House of Representatives should never again be allowed to determine the election of any president. Jackson feared that such a proceeding would bring on "the destruction of our happy republican system." Clearly, expressing concern for such a system was a means to avoid personalizing the problem, but words could not mask his visceral response to something he obviously regarded as a personal injustice.[1]

Although he was spending a good deal of his time within Tennessee, Jackson was attuned—and one wonders how "leisurely"—to events in Washington. He preferred, as he told Polk, for "conciliation and compromise" to animate the national legislature, rather than the unwelcome "warmth" that was prevailing in the Nineteenth Congress. "In that august body," he averred, "nothing but decorum ought to exist." Jackson was trying to carve out an image of reserve and statesmanship, while allowing his supporters to emote.[2]

It was Polk whose pen most particularly smacked of derision toward the Adams Administration, with foremost attention to Secretary of State Clay, whom he discourteously referred to as "prime minister." One month before, Polk sounded downright excited in conveying to Jackson what he then termed "sharp shooting" in the House—bitter comments directed by Clay supporters toward McDuffie. In response to them, McDuffie issued an indirect challenge. The South Carolina congressman well understood "the game," as Polk had put it, and reported to Clay that it was not necessary to send "his tools & understrappers" (in this case Congressmen Joseph Vance of Ohio and David Trimble of Kentucky) to issue insults on his behalf. When he wrote to apprise Jackson of developments, just five days before the Clay-Randolph duel (and unaware of it), Polk seemed a bit disappointed that the incident enveloping Clay and McDuffie appeared destined to be resolved without an armed encounter. Nonetheless, he was expectant. Something was bound to happen, if not at this time than at some future date. His letter contained the predictable pre-duel vocabulary of gentlemanly honor, noting the exchange of "abusive words," the utterance of certain "allusions," the poses of "champions," and the series of justifications that proceeded from one side to the other.[3]

Jackson understood this vocabulary better than most. Like Southerners McDuffie, Clay, Randolph, Benton, and even Wirt, he had experience in affairs of honor. He had challenged more than one man, and taken the life of Nashville lawyer Charles Dickinson in a grisly 1806 duel that arose, in part, out of a horse race in which both men had a betting interest. As with most early-nineteenth-century duels, the final interview was the result of a complex series of instructions and interactions. While inebriated, Dickinson had allegedly insulted the honor of Jackson's wife Rachel. As the unforgiving protector of female virtue, Jackson immediately demanded satisfaction. The charming, confident Dickinson, at this point, easily apologized for what he had said, and the matter might have disappeared. But a while later, Dickinson was rumored by a Jackson friend to have dealt dishonorably with the details of the payment due Jackson over the horse race. Transmitted messages spun out of control and into newspaper attacks, and the two men of honor, now equally offended, ended up a day's ride north of Nashville along the Red River, just across the border in Kentucky. They faced one another from a distance of twenty-four feet at a quiet clearing in a poplar forest.

The cocky Dickinson was reputed to be the best shot in Tennessee at this time, and he stood unafraid. At the call to fire, he aimed his pistol quickly, pulled the trigger, and struck Jackson in the chest. Jackson, it is said, clenched his teeth, as Dickinson looked astonished when his target did not fall. The future hero of many battles shot straight through the lawyer's midsection, and waited while his adversary bled to death. Dickinson's bullet had hit. It was too close to Jackson's heart for the surgeon to remove it. The pain of fractured ribs eventually subsided, and the bullet remained permanently where the dead man had delivered it.[4]

It was not only the culture of the duel that Andrew Jackson shared with McDuffie, Clay, Randolph, Benton, and Wirt. Like those other men (excepting, perhaps, Randolph, who was orphaned but never lost gentry status), he grew up on shaky social ground, craved financial success, and vigorously sought land and the life of a gentleman. Born in the South Carolina hill country in 1767, Jackson was orphaned at fifteen after having seen a bit of action as a young teen in the Revolution. He and his older brother, who would not survive the war, had banded together with patriot neighbors. The boys were captured by the British and briefly imprisoned. From this adventure, young Andrew Jackson acquired a scar and, one might speculate, his vengeful disposition as well. He and John Quincy Adams were the same age, old enough to have retained images of the War for Independence. Adams had seen the smoke rising from Bunker Hill; Jackson had been slashed by a British officer.

Jackson made it a habit to follow trouble. Not long after his deadly duel with Dickinson, he was an interested observer at the Richmond trial of Aaron Burr. During Burr's flight after having killed Alexander Hamilton in the most famous duel in American history, Jackson had twice entertained Jefferson's controversial vice president at the Hermitage, and even sponsored a ball in his honor.[5] When Burr and Jackson, already a major general in the state militia, discussed doing something about Spain's American possessions, Jackson was led to understand that Burr was operating with authorization from Secretary of War Henry Dearborn. Only much later did Jackson see the possibility that Burr was conspiring to engage in a foreign adventure on his own accord and not as an agent of the government; but even then, the evidence shows, he did not fully share President Jefferson's conviction that Burr was engaging in treason.

Jackson's temperament becomes clearer in his subsequent public performance. When Dearborn intimated that Jackson might himself be a conspirator along with Burr, the enraged Tennessean lashed out at him for giving credit to "stories" instead of character. In Richmond, Jackson testified in defense of Burr, whom he believed more patriotic and less culpable than the commander of U.S. armed forces in the Louisiana Territory, General James Wilkinson. That corrupt manipulator had been on the Spanish payroll while seducing Jefferson with his purported proof of Burr's plot.[6] Thus when he perceived a miscarriage of justice, Jackson seethed; a decade later he himself used Indian raids into Georgia as a pretext to lead U.S. troops into Spanish-held Florida, reaping a unique revenge, if not for Burr, then for himself. And when accused of exceeding his orders in the 1819 adventure, he had occasion to write: "What I have done was for my country; had I erred in the discharge of my official duty, that error would have originated in the warmth of my devotion to her interest." Jackson's most marked quality was his boldness and determination. To sit idly by was exceedingly difficult for a man of action.[7]

But in 1826, approaching sixty, he was not as easy to label. It is said that men grow steadier and more cautious in temperament with age—in the case of Jackson, this adage is not entirely free from ambiguity. The combative frontiersman in him did not easily convert to the gracious, tactful candidate he sought to portray in the mid-1820s. In this vein, his relationship with one-time protégé William Carroll is instructive.

Carroll had come to Nashville from Pittsburgh at twenty-two, in 1810, to establish a nail business. After Jackson was enlisted as a second in Carroll's ungraceful duel with Jesse Benton in 1813, Carroll went on to serve as Jackson's trusted second in command at the Battle of New Orleans. He drummed up support for a Jackson candidacy in the presidential election of 1820, and all seemed to be going well, until Jackson reversed himself and lent his prestige to Carroll's opponent in the gubernatorial election of 1821. Their falling out may have related to Carroll's compounding bitterness after Jackson assumed Tennessee's pride all to himself in what ought to have been a shared victory, for General Carroll and his troops displayed particular heroism on the receiving end of Britain's greatest fire at New Orleans.[8]

It is hard to figure the Jackson-Carroll dynamic. Born to a business partner of Republican mainstay Albert Gallatin, and married to a cousin of Dolley Madison, Carroll had Jeffersonian credentials and might have ridden Jackson's coattails but for their imperfectly matched egos. Still, Carroll somehow held his own against his former commander. The younger man must have thought himself shrewd in 1823, as he warmed up to Henry Clay after being snubbed by Jackson. Altogether, Carroll won the governorship of Tennessee a remarkable six times.[9] In 1826, he was in his third term, noted for having engineered a sound fiscal policy and lent support to internal improvements.

Jackson had a knack for making staunch friends and staunch enemies. Benton's removal to Missouri and Carroll's unplanned exile from the Jackson camp were not the only illustrations of Jackson's petulant desire to have things go his way and people fall into line—behind him. Curiously, his early Washington experience did not foretell this at all. He served obscurely in both houses of Congress during the presidency of John Adams. He never proposed bold programs as his main competition of later years, Henry Clay and John Quincy Adams, did when they first came into the national legislature. Ordinarily thought ill-educated and a poor speller, Jackson was not a skillful orator either, as McDuffie, Randolph, Webster, Clay, Calhoun, and Wirt were. Unless he felt his honor at stake, others spoke for him more convincingly than he spoke for himself. In other words, his admirers spoke for him once his manly actions spoke first. His similar response to personal and national injury, and his comfort with authority, would make Jackson president.

After his near conquest of the presidency in the election of 1824, the hero-general was without a serious rival. Anti-Adams men, including Adams's own vice president, John C. Calhoun, scrambled to serve him, and the consternation among Adams-Clay supporters was palpable. Clay's friend Charles Hammond, editor of the *Liberty Hall*

Fig. 15. A martial Andrew Jackson, engraving by J. B. Longacre, after Thomas Sully, 1820, conveys the pose of the peerless Hero of New Orleans that his backers sought to preserve during Jackson's bid for the presidency. *(Print collection, Miriam and Ira D. Wallach Division of Art, Prints, and Photographs, New York Public Library; Astor, Lenox, and Tilden Foundations.)*

& *Cincinnati Gazette,* fulminated: "We must conclude that the President and Secretary of State are mortally hated by every body: and that every body is prepared to bow to the knee and pay divine honors to Gen. Jackson." Hammond expressed his disgust with what he termed "the coarse vituperation" shown toward Adams and Clay and "the clumsy and fulsome flattery" shown toward Jackson. It was hard to know where Jackson was vulnerable, given the vagueness of his politics. Frustrated by the phenomenon, Hammond would ultimately resort to crude attacks on the candidate's morals, charging Andrew and Rachel Jackson with bigamy—just as onetime Jackson nemesis Charles Dickinson had done, with fateful consequences, in 1806.[10]

Jackson's political strength was almost magical. His supporters designated him simply as "The Hero" in their public statements. They were feeling confident in pitting their candidate against the popular Governor Carroll in 1823, but chose ultimately to send Jackson to the U.S. Senate, to better facilitate his run for the presidency. After unseating the incumbent, Senator John Williams (yet another former subordinate during the War of 1812, who had become his enemy), Jackson went to Washington to make a brief but respectable showing prior to the election of 1824.

The retailored general needed to be visible and better acquainted with the rising generation of leaders, as the twenty-four-year dynasty of Virginia presidents moved to a close. That is why Jackson had to appear in Congress and demonstrate his emotional steadiness, that demeanor which continued to come through in his 1826 correspondence with Representative Polk. As a matter of expedience, he patched up his old differences with Thomas Hart Benton, now a vocal senator, and he attended social gatherings with his presidential competition, becoming nearly as adroit as the gifted Clay at the political art of amiability. He pretended to forget the past.

Toward people he trusted, the Tennessean did allow himself to slip into a self-satisfied tone in his letters from Washington. John Coffee, who had been at Jackson's side when he tangled with the Bentons in 1813, was perhaps the most constant of his friends. In February 1824, Jackson wrote coyly to him that while he easily "wearied" of life as a member of the Senate, he had found himself "become a perfect philosopher," remote from intrigue and backroom politics. To another old soldier, he feigned modesty: "I am content rather to be a listener, than an actor," grateful for every honor and the attention he was receiving, "without any covert solicitation on my part." And to his wife, he noted that he had a "cavalcade" about him whenever he went out.[11]

When Congress was not in session, Jackson was back at the Hermitage. From here, he freely reflected to Coffee—one of the few he was not trying to fool—on the outward transformation in his personality. His smugness was even more pronounced as he narrated what had happened during his months in Washington, how he cleverly swayed colleagues who had at first assumed that his former reputation remained unchanged: "Great pains had been taken to represent me as a savage disposition; who allways carried a scalping knife in one hand, and a tomahawk in the other, allways ready to knock down, and scalp any and every person who differed with me in opinion." The surprised legislators had then discovered, at least in Jackson's idealized self-conception, a new and highly persuasive political achiever: "instead of this . . . [they] found a man of even temper, firm in his opinions advanced, and allways allowing others to enjoy theirs, untill reason convinced them that they were in error." He proudly reiterated how he had studiously crafted this mild political character, taking "the high ground," even giving his "enemies" room to "lye" without his taking objection—just so long as they did not cross the line into character assassination. Recognizing the presence of "enemies," the new Jackson affected statesmanlike diction and presidential-style dignity, in conclusively pronouncing to his friend: "I have pursued the dictates of my matured opinion with the sole view to the independence, prosperity, and happiness of my country." He had voted with his "conscience" during the Senate session, he said, and in one short season had come to regard himself practiced in the ways of Washington.[12]

Writing to others during the tense period between the inconclusive 1824 presidential election and the decisive February 1825 House vote, Jackson professed that he would remain happy, even in losing to Adams or Crawford, because the loss would enable him to "enjoy the sweets of domestic quiet." When he sensed intrigue on the part of those who were combining to defeat him, he maintained his public calm and composure. Yet, once again, he could not help but confide to Coffee from Washington that "hypocrisy and hollow heartedness predominated in this great city." Then, upon Adams's victory, he affected that his loss was really the country's loss: "I weep for the liberty of my country when I see . . . the rights of the people have been bartered for promises of office." And so, before he went home, he sniped at Clay, whom he insisted "never yet has risked himself for his country, sacrificed his repose, or made an effort to repel an invading foe." He shook his head, too, at the pomp and pretense of Adams's inaugural, contrasting it with the suitably simple way in which Thomas Jefferson strode alone from his modest boardinghouse on Capitol Hill in March 1801 to his new home on Pennsylvania Avenue. "But it seems that times are changeing," Jackson grumbled. The aging soldier was surely more resentful than he let on.[13]

After Jackson had returned to Tennessee, others in Washington and around the country took up their pens in a continuing campaign on his behalf, vilifying Adams and Clay. Placing the general above contention, they vindicated his character, portraying the Hero as one who "breathes the language of the purest patriotism," and who combined the uttermost manliness with a generous, temperate disposition.[14] They wrote to Jackson at the Hermitage, as Polk did, to reassure him that every "devoted Friend of our political Faith," as yet another congressman put it, was maintaining a bold and energetic posture on his behalf. He could sit pretty while others forcefully molded the Jackson image into a new masculine ideal for the self-conscious age of assertive, enlightened democracy.[15]

In 1826, Jackson could not but see the writing on the wall. The "corrupt bargain" was a surefire campaign issue, and his calculated display of restraint much to his advantage. He was cocksure, primed to win the presidency in two years. He was proving to voters that he could be entrusted with executive power—all he needed to do was to continue to exhibit a controlled intensity under political pressure to match the hardiness (a distinctly democratic virtue) that his promoters were claiming he had demonstrated as a military man. Despite the unprecedented loss of a presidential contest after winning the popular vote, he had not made a public scene. The message was plainly drawn: only a man of extraordinary rectitude could remain so composed. In sum, his softened public manner effectively offset the reputation of rude manliness that he had acquired in and out of uniform prior to the 1820s.

As he wrote letters to a variety of well-wishers, Jackson continued to reply warmly, humbly, in cautious and nonspecific terms, indicating that he was remaining keenly focused on upholding the public good. That seemed to be all he had to do. Like the mild-mannered Jefferson before him, he floated above, allowing others to sling the necessary political mud. Subtly, chastely, he conjured the language of the Declaration of Independence, counseling all patriots to continue "opposing with manly firmness where injury is to result to the country." (The Declaration asserted that the king had maliciously dissolved the colonial legislatures for their "opposing with manly firmness his invasions on the rights of the people.") He directed his "heartfelt gratitude" to his fellow citizens, repeating that he was dedicated to their interests alone; they, "the people," were sovereign.[16] And thus he legitimated his claim on the presidency that had been denied in the last election by an undemocratic theft.

Meanwhile, in the politically turbulent spring of 1826, Jackson supporters in Congress and the press were putting the idea in people's minds that a high and mighty President Adams had countenanced a fraud against the American people. He had been swayed by Clay (by far the greater scoundrel in this affair), and now sat remote from "the people." A born aristocrat, subverted by his devious, designing minister, Adams, if left unchecked, would arrogate powers to himself that were kinglike and injurious to democracy.

When relaxing, Andrew Jackson smoked a long-stemmed pipe. One who claimed to see through the smoke screen was, not surprisingly, his Western antagonist, Henry Clay. Clay had been in Europe in 1815 after participating in the Ghent negotiations, when he learned the results of the Battle of New Orleans and the victorious general's criticism of the Kentucky militia for having exhibited insufficient battlefield courage. Perhaps his dislike of Jackson began then. On hearing of Jackson's election to the Senate in the fall of 1823, Clay was incredulous about the reported abatement of a well-known impetuosity: "I understand that the General has altered essentially his course of personal conduct," he wrote at the time, "and has become extremely gentle, affable & conciliatory. . . . What would *you* think of receiving from him a sincere and cordial shake of the hand?"[17]

After Adams had put together his cabinet, a defensive Clay unreservedly branded Jackson a "military chieftain," temperamentally unqualified for the presidency. To discharge the duties of president of the United States, he said in defense of his role in electing Adams, one had to be a statesman, not a mere military commander. Speaking publicly to his constituents in Lexington, Clay assured them that if Jackson had ever behaved in a statesmanlike way, "the evidence of the fact has escaped my observation." George Washington was a military commander, too, Clay noted, but in his "extraordinary person, united a serenity of mind, a cool and collected wisdom, a cautious and deliberate judgment, a perfect command of the passions." Jackson stood in stark contrast, a would-be Caesar who was, in the end, of questionable "competency," and "unfit" for the office he sought.[18]

Those who personally encountered him in the mid-1820s invariably described Jackson in terms of his sickly complexion. Because of his physical appearance, a rumor circulated in 1826 that his health would prevent him from seeking the presidency in 1828. According to Cincinnati's *National Crisis,* reporting on information received from the *Carlisle* (Pennsylvania) *Gazette:*

> Gen. Jackson WILL NOT *stand a candidate for the Presidency at the next election!* Of this fact you may rest assured. . . . Neither the General nor his friends, desire to enter into the heat of another electioneering campaign. *Old age is creeping fast on him in the shape of a shattered constitution,* and he courts retirement, quiet, and tranquillity of mind.[19]

But if the candidate bore unremarkable features, there was still a fire in his eyes. He stood an inch above six feet. As a young U.S. senator in 1797, he had received this curious characterization from Pennsylvania Republican Albert Gallatin: "a tall lank, uncouth-looking personage, with long locks of hair hanging over his face, and a cue down his back tied in an eel-skin; his dress singular, his manners and deportment that of a backwoodsman." When the son and namesake of Boston's Mayor Josiah Quincy encountered Andrew Jackson as a mature politician, he expected to find him much as Gallatin had painted him, boorish and socially objectionable. Instead, the old warrior presented "a knightly personage,—prejudiced, narrow, mistaken upon many points, it might be, but vigorously a gentleman in his high sense of honor and in the natural straightforward courtesies."[20]

This modification in Jackson's conduct may not have been accomplished with earnestness, but its impact was meaningful nonetheless. For so long routinely labeled by his political enemies as rough and inelegant, dangerous and unpredictable, he could be portrayed by his friends as the voice of good sense now—it was a performance he seemed to enjoy staging. In his measured reply to the devoted new Tennessee congressman James K. Polk, in May of 1826, it was "alarming schemes," "Visionary politicians," and "disagreeable colision & dispute" that Jackson decried like a cautious statesman. He professed not to relish a Clay-McDuffie duel. With unconventional orthography, he asked Polk finally to excuse his "hasty scrall," as he determinedly pronounced the mildness of his political faith.[21]

In mid-1826, the now "knightly" Hero of New Orleans loomed as the embodiment of the democratizing conscience. There is a better way to put it: the democratic conscience prevailed in America already, and only lacked a president who would resurrect Jefferson's convincing call for the restriction of privilege. If President Adams was a scion of the old school, a living reminder of a more socially rigid time, Jackson, despite his comfortable plantation life at the Hermitage, appeared to embody the chances of the ordinary white male citizen. He represented continued growth for middle-class economic individualists— small business operators, farmers, and mechanics (that is, those citizens who labored with their hands). Furthermore, as a national military hero, he would prove able to transcend his sectional identity and appeal to a variety of interests in the North, South, and West.

Awaiting his turn in the spring and summer of 1826, the "new" Jackson was in Nashville, answering his correspondence from comfortable quarters. He had helped put the town on the map. Named after General Francis Nash, the place was first settled by Revolutionary War veterans from North Carolina; because that state had no better means to compensate them for military service, its hardy fighters were paid in land along the navigable rivers of what was at that time the Atlantic state's ambiguous western frontier. Nash himself never saw the region, having died in action as he led a North Carolina brigade against the British at Germantown, Pennsylvania, in 1777. The cannonball that lacerated his horse's neck and tore open Nash's thigh also killed Major James Witherspoon, son of a signer of the Declaration of Independence. Germantown was a disastrous battle, fought in an autumn morning fog; the weather caused Americans to fire on their own men, giving the red-coated infantry, after an initial beating, a chance to regroup and turn the tide of battle. That day, Washington's army suffered over a thousand casualties. Thirty-seven years later, General Andrew Jackson and his Tennessee sharpshooters faced a different, if equally confident, British force on a deadly, foggy morning. This time, of course, the results were quite the opposite: destruction of the enemy at New Orleans, which yielded a satisfying conclusion to the otherwise unproductive War of 1812, and with it a resurgence in American morale. The beneficiary of that victory, Nashville's favorite son, was an instant hero.[22]

ANDREW JACKSON had arrived in Nashville in 1788, as a combative twenty-one-year-old who enjoyed horse racing and cockfighting. He was a North Carolina–trained country lawyer with little formal education. He went on to acquire his fortune by planting, horse breeding, and land speculation, while serving as frontier lawyer and judge. After trying his hand briefly in government, as a congressman and a U.S. senator, he acquired his better-known reputation as an Indian fighter. The year before he made history at New Orleans, he made headlines by vanquishing the Creeks below the Tennessee River in Alabama and northwest Georgia.

Like the rest of America, Tennessee's history cannot be completely told without explaining the displacement of its first inhabitants. The region was first opened to white settlement after the Revolution, when the "parent" North Carolina state government neatly assumed that for having sided with the British, the Cherokees had in effect relinquished their title to the land. Overmatched, the Indians fought to avert cultural ruin, but eventually sued for a peace that they were led to hope would protect the integrity of their remaining territory. Watching helplessly as more and more whites descended on Cherokee ground, one elderly chief remarked, "Your people settle much Faster on our Lands after a Treaty than Before." A bellicose Thomas Jefferson, as a member of the Continental Congress, had wished for the North Carolina–Tennessee tribe to be "driven beyond the Mississippi" for their active resistance to white Southerners' land hunger—an irritability that had led them to make incursions into isolated parts of Virginia. In defending their towns in a rapidly changing world, the numerically reduced Indians were far too easily lumped together by white frontiersmen as savages, brutal and expendable.[23]

Tennessee became a U.S. territory in 1788. Nashville belonged to a part of Tennessee that the Cherokees had largely ceded, but unfriendly bands continued to traverse the outlying countryside for some years. Almost immediately upon settling there, Jackson, as a mere private, took part in a punitive expedition to drive away an attacking party. In treaties of 1805–06, significant land cessions in the southern and eastern parts of the state further reduced the Cherokee presence. By then, President Jefferson was speaking with sympathy toward the Indians' condition[24] while acting aggressively in support of white land claims. Without federal protection, removal of the Indians was inevitable.

The naturally aggressive Jackson grew up seeing the Cherokees as most Southern whites did—as people who stood in the way. He did not feel for the Indians, he did not trust them, and he did not have the patience to reason with them. He would, however, eagerly employ large numbers of friendly Cherokees against other Indian opponents.

After the outbreak of the War of 1812, a branch of the Creek tribe known as the Red Sticks allied with the British, attacking Fort Mims on the Alabama River and killing some four hundred American settlers who had huddled together within the walls of the fort. Though the wound he had recently received from one of the Benton brothers had not yet healed, General Jackson, under authority of the Tennessee legislature, marched south with a 3,500-man army. With his Cherokee and other Indian auxiliaries, he moved against the main Creek force at Horseshoe Bend, killing 750 of the 900 warriors who remained after a season of skirmishes. The victor dictated severe terms at the surrender—the cession of more than 20 million acres in Georgia and Alabama.[25]

He had spilled much blood, but Jackson was applauded by President Madison for his effectiveness at a time of war. Indian policy continued on the same path. The Monroe Administration, following precedent, preached "magnanimity" and "justice" toward Indians, while practicing wholesale absorption of Indian lands.[26] And through 1826, the Adams Administration, too, was proving as ineffective as any other regime, before or after, in averting disaster for Indian policy.

On February 7 of that year, alarmed by resistance from the remaining Creeks, the president's cabinet convened in order to discuss the subject. Secretary of War Barbour proposed a "great territorial Government west of the Mississippi," within which to organize all displaced Eastern tribes. Adams was well-intentioned but ineffective here, judging Barbour's proposal "full of benevolence and humanity." Yet he could not imagine a "practicable plan" that stood any hope of reconstituting the Indians as "one civilized, or half-civilized Government." Treasury Secretary Rush, Navy Secretary Southard, and Attorney General Wirt all concurred: there was little to hope for, and little to be done. Clay, not present at the meeting owing to a relapse of the flu, had made an impatient assertion to the president the previous December, saying that "there was never a full-blooded Indian that took to civilization." Adams was shocked when Clay next blurted out that "he did not think them, as a race, worth preserving." While refusing to condone any act of inhumanity toward the Indians, Clay insisted that "their disappearance from the human family will be no great loss to the world." The uncharacteristically coldhearted secretary of state added on this occasion that he did not expect any full-blooded Indian to survive another fifty years in America.[27]

Cherokees and Creeks had learned to face the U.S. threat collectively. They exchanged ambassadors and participated in each other's tribal councils. But year by year, factionalism within the tribes intensified over the impact that land cessions were having on political independence. With the Indians divided among themselves, the Adams Administration was unable to prevent further deterioration of the tribes' position. At one point, the president feared meeting a Creek delegation, lest the Indians "set forth their distress, and throw themselves upon my mercy and compassion. If I should answer them inflexibly, it would only increase their distress. If I indulged any sympathy for them, it would imply censure upon the treaty, which we must yet maintain." Adams was too moral to intimidate the beleaguered Indians, but he had no solution to their problems either.[28]

Jackson had for some time past contended openly that there was no point for the United States to make treaties with Indians, so long as it had the power to enforce its "benevolence" upon these increasingly dependent peoples. Persuaded that degradation and poverty were inevitable if Indians remained east of the Mississippi, he was convinced that removal west was in their best interest. On an individual level Jackson had shown that he could care for particular Indians—he had adopted a Creek orphan, and spared certain of those who had taken up arms against him—but on a national political level he was firm in his conviction. To the Tennessean known to his Indian foes as "Sharp Knife," Indians were too easily corrupted by those whites who would manipulate them.

In the popular fiction of James Fenimore Cooper, Indians possessed judgment, and uncommon insights. Just as Mohicans Chingachgook and Uncas read impressions in the forest earth, Indians in general were thought to have a prodigious knowledge of nature that made their poverty and relative simplicity the benign attributes of a wholesome people. Stoical when facing death, Cooper's Indian was also capable of familial affection, as when Chingachgook turns to Uncas, his son, and speaks in "soft and playful tones." The colonizers in Cooper's work inevitably lack sufficient imagination to appreciate cultural alternatives to the single-minded march of Protestant "civilization." And so, at the end of the narrative, just before the pure-blooded Uncas and the biracial beauty Cora are thoughtlessly executed at the feet of the merciless Magua, Uncas, "the last of the Mohicans," reaches out to his partner in fate: " 'Cora, Cora!' echoed Uncas, bending forward like a deer." The moment of his crying out is the more shocking, because the reader has only encountered Uncas's quiet ingenuity and stiff determination over the preceding thirty-two chapters. When she insists to her captor, "I will go no further," the courageous Cora is unconsciously disclosing that her bloodline will go no further. The tortured consciences of the deserving Indians and the deserving whites are intertwined in this final scene.[29]

This sense of loss was widely shared in literature. Distant from the generation when New Englanders warred on Pequots, Nipmucks, and Wampanoags, Northerners increasingly romanticized the "noble savage." Lydia Maria Child's 1824 tale *Hobomok* depicted a loving relationship between an Indian man and a white woman.[30] But no literary treatment was to alter the treatment that Indians would receive once Andrew Jackson became president. Sharp Knife was unbending. He would let nothing stand in the way of the Indians' expulsion.

IN 1826, the haggard general was more concerned with personally urgent matters. While public men beyond the bounds of Tennessee labored to make him president, his wife's health was steadily worsening, and his own teeth began to rot away. Jackson partisans took over the *United States Telegraph* in February, making certain that there was an antiadministration press in Washington, so that men like Polk, McDuffie, and the canny New York senator Martin Van Buren could lead the charge on behalf of their knight. In Nashville itself, rival weeklies acted primarily as civic boosters, only gradually coming to face up to the political fight that would center on the character of the white-haired consumptive who was their most famous resident.

These two lively newspapers, the *Nashville Republican* and *Nashville Whig*, vied for readers. The *Whig*, though itself teetering on financial ruin, was the more intent on promoting Nashville's economic growth. As the year began, it invoked the watchword of the day according to the president's message—"the spirit of improvement is abroad upon the earth"—to announce that it favored, as neighboring Kentucky did, a stage route linking Nashville and Louisville, where no reliable road yet existed. "It is hoped that in its wanderings," the paper's sprightly editor appealed, "this benignant spirit [of improvement] will abide awhile with us, and infuse into the minds of the people, a disposition to emulate the most famed achievements, which have been accomplished in our country." Nashville's promoters did not want the tobacco- and cotton-baling town to lag behind others. In this vein, the *Whig* pleaded for "some man of sufficient means and capacity" to step forward and introduce a paper mill to the community, which boasted four printing establishments but no near source of paper. Business in southern Kentucky and Alabama was assured, if some entrepreneur would take advantage of the ready supply of hemp and rags.[31]

An active commercial spirit was conspicuous. The *Whig*'s front page on Dec. 12, 1825, advertised for journeymen to file and turn iron and brass, offering "liberal wages." Journeymen tailors were in demand, too. A Philadelphia hat manufacturer, "determined to sell at Philadelphia prices," announced the establishment of a local branch. A "Fashionable Hat Store" offered men's and boys' hats made in "the most elegant stile." Woolen socks went on sale, as did, uncomfortably, "A stout, hearty NEGRO WOMAN" of thirty, "a good cook, washer and ironer," with her eighteen-month-old child. This, too, was Jackson's Nashville as 1826 got under way.[32]

Grocers prospered. Stewart & Charter received a substantial shipment from New Orleans at the start of April, containing Holland gin, Jamaica rum, and "Cicily Madeira," kegs of almonds, some allspice, nutmeg, raisins, rice, and the "best Spanish segars," all of which they advertised "at small profits for cash, or on credit to punctual men, for negotiable paper at short date." Besides staples like nails, ropes, twine, shovels, spades, "dipt candles," "sweet flour," coffee, and sugar, the merchant John B. Burke, at the corner of College and Spring, was selling two bales of buffalo robes and 150 pairs of "coarse Shoes."[33]

Individuals took out ads for other reasons. One resident, Wilson Sanderlin, was in a bind, because he did not trust his wife. They had exchanged words, and she had vowed to ruin him. So he, in turn, cautioned the merchants of the town not to extend her any credit in the expectation of his covering her debts. "If she chooses to live with me," he stated unabashedly, "I will furnish her with all the necessaries and comforts of life myself; But as she intimates leaving my bed and board, and speaks how she could run me into debt, I am resolved to pay none of them, nor be accountable for her conduct in any way." The flustered Mr. Sanderlin may have envied the good fortune of one James Ogden, whose $170,000 in stolen bonds from the Mercantile Insurance Company of New York were found that same week under a rock outside of town.[34]

In the spring of 1826 the two rival newspapers came to a crossroads. The *Whig*'s publisher, Joseph Norvell, had sounded the death-knell of his paper at the start of the year, and was only saved by combining with a newcomer in town, the *National Banner, and Literary, Political and Commercial Gazette*. The *Nashville Republican* printed a parable poking fun at the new partnership, with a lengthy marriage announcement. The gist of it was that the old Kentucky gentleman Mr. Norvellius E. Whig had found a young and not so blushing bride, Simpsonia H. Banner, who had been reared in, of all places, Massachusetts.[35]

With this roguish satire, newspaper competition merged with presidential politics. The *Republican* narrated its little history, tracing the change in kindly old Mr. Whig's disposition to the traumatic election of 1824. Old Whig had wholeheartedly supported the candidacy of William H. Crawford of Georgia, the underdog Jeffersonian favorite, having nothing positive to say at the time about John Quincy Adams, "that vile old hypocrite! arch apostate! rank aristocrat! the last man on the list!" But after the "frightful monster" Adams assumed office, Mr. Whig "performed a complete somerset, knocked his heels together, clapped his hands, and cried Adams and liberty!"

The old gentleman had gotten "a little crabbed." This internal confusion had afflicted him with "all the humours and oddities of a crusty old bachelor," and drew to him a "malcontent" clientele, while he lost all his original friends. Miss Banner, meanwhile, had settled in the neighborhood and "conceived the idea of strengthening herself with some gentleman of fixed interest and influence." The "jolly old face of Mr. Whig caught her eye, and captivated her fancy." Fortunately for her, the awkward, aging Whig still had some of the "lustihood" of his youth, though even he could see by the way she "ogled" him that she had "designs" upon him.

Now the deed was done, the marriage sealed, and "like all old fellows, who marry young wives, he will be sadly, henpecked." It was clear to the *Republican* where things were headed. The new Mrs. Whig had put her name before his on the masthead: the weekly was being called the *National Banner and Nashville Whig.* More literary than political prior to their union, the new entity now promised to exhibit a political flavor. Its position had not yet been stated, but the *Banner*'s sentimental attachment to New England oratory was sufficiently suggestive to the staff at the *Republican.* Consequently, the *Republican* would establish itself more firmly as Nashville's lead voice in predicting a Jackson victory in 1828.[36]

The *Republican*'s bold motto, "Our Country,—Right or Wrong," was discontinued after the April 26, 1826, issue, the same week that the *Banner* and *Whig* merged. A simpler, motto-free masthead succeeded. The *Republican* had been reporting on activities in Congress for the first half of the jubilee year, elevating the "vivid" performances of George McDuffie, and faithfully reporting on the endearing, if not always easily decipherable, John Randolph. Henceforth, it would begin to focus more intently on Jackson himself.

Andrew Jackson's Nashville was hard to define. New York and New Orleans were characterized by their unquestioned commercial importance and diverse ethnic population. Washington was unassailable as the seat of national power, even if its physical environment still retained much of the stagnant and unwholesome character of its marshy infancy. Cincinnati might have appeared comparable to the Tennessee port, but its rapidity of growth and the impending canal boom rendered it unique. Although Nashville was a commercial way station linking the trans-Appalachian West to the international port of New Orleans, the town was situated on a quiet, shallow Mississippi tributary, the Cumberland River. It seemed to belong half to the wilderness, while aspiring to be another Cincinnati.

When it was incorporated in 1804, Nashville had a population of four hundred. Hardy men held the oak or ash poles that guided flatboats and barges loaded with tobacco, coal, whiskey—and later a good deal of cotton—out to the Mississippi. Strong currents conducted one south. Before the steamboat age, the boatman had to sell his vessel upon arrival in New Orleans, where the buyer dismantled the craft and used the wood in house building. From 1819, steamboats plied the waters between Nashville and the Mississippi Valley, and changed the economy of the town. The first steamboat to be seen in Nashville was part owned by William Carroll, who christened it *Andrew Jackson* after the commander he still admired at that time. In the one year 1819, the Louisiana port received over two million gallons of what was called Tennessee whiskey, nearly half of it from Tennessee and the remainder from stills in Ohio, Kentucky, and Indiana.[37]

Nashville's population in 1825 was given as 3,460, a respectable but not especially impressive figure. Yet it was considered the intellectual and cultural center of the South, west of the Appalachians. Booksellers did well: shipments of Cooper's newest novel, *The Last of the Mohicans,* at $2.00 each, were prominently advertised throughout the spring and summer of 1826, along with Washington Irving's *Sketch Book,* travelogues of India and Egypt, volumes relating to the law and astronomy, and a lesser-known but certainly captivating title: *Husband Hunting, or the Mother and Daughters, a Tale of Fashionable Life.* Performance arts flourished, too. A new theater, the third in a decade, was erected in the jubilee year. Nashville staged a medley of Shakespeare, which included the trial scene of Shylock in *The Merchant of Venice,* the assassination of Julius Caesar, and the closing scene of *Hamlet.*

The average Tennessean of the 1820s was efficiently characterized as the generic farmer "Jonathan." A clever local columnist wrote a poem celebrating Jonathan's visit to the playhouse, impersonating his use of an unpolished, countrified vocabulary:

> *Did y' ever go to the Playhouse?*
> *O lauks, what a nation fine place,*
> *By jing, but they make sitch a rouse*
> *To get in, that they near bumped my face.*

He marvels at the festive decor:

> *My stars, what a mighty fine ceiling,*
> *All be painted all over in streaks,*
> *That round thing in't, set me a reeling,*
> *I wonder, when it rains, if it leaks.*

He is next surrounded by "tarnation folks" and "darn'd handsome galls," dressed in colors. The stretch of the curtain impels him to estimate how many shirts could be made from that much material. He tries his best to enjoy the performance, and would have enjoyed it more had his view not been obscured by the "great fellar" who "stood right afore me," and whose looks threatened Jonathan with a beating, were he to have insisted that the man move.[38]

In Jonathan's community, the pioneering tongue was as raw and picturesque as Nashville's mainly one- and two-story log houses. A literal people, the original Tennesseans had named their small but essential waters Otter Creek, Duck River, Big Swan Creek, Fishing Creek, Big Sandy, and the like. The unassuming folk apparently found as curious the "Popular Similes" featured in the *Whig* in the early spring of 1826, providing symbolic attributes for the creatures that inhabited their backcountry world:

> *As wet as a fish—as dry as a bone;*
> *As live as a bird—as dead as a stone:*
> *As plump as a partridge—as poor as a rat*
> *As strong as a horse—as weak as a cat . . .*
> *As heavy as lead—as light as a feather,*
> *As steady as time—uncertain as weather.*[39]

In the rustic mind, something pleasant could be "tolerable good." Bad folk could "run to seed." Even the proper Englishwoman Frances Trollope repeated what she called the "Kentucky phrase," that one who refuses to hold back "goes the whole hog." Other natural metaphors peppered Western speech: it could be "milking time," "lambing time," or "dog-wood blooming time." Mud could be "fat" as well as thick. For boatmen, when the river called, the water was "answering." And a man suited for this environment might just be "tough as hickory"—such as the native son Andrew Jackson, who had become known popularly as Old Hickory.[40]

If they recognized their unfinished state of development, the people of Nashville regarded their town as no less a viable community, easily rescued by a few new industries and increased commerce. So that the most modest of their number were not forgotten, they counted on the moral support of Old Hickory, whom John Randolph in mid-1826 called "a man of strong and vigorous mind, of dignified deportment, and . . . *omni foenore solatus,*" a comfort to all those suffering under their debts.[41]

COURTED BY Vice President Calhoun, to whom he would assent as his own vice president, Jackson was on his way to celebrate the national jubilee south of Nashville when he received a letter from Washington marked "Private." Calhoun's letter was hand-carried by their mutual friend, Tennessee Senator John Eaton. In it, the anxious South Carolinian wrote of what he believed (and, more important, what he believed Jackson believed) to be of the utmost consideration at that moment:

> In my opinion liberty was never in greater danger; and such, I believe to be the impression of the coolest and most considerate of our citizens. An issue has been fairly made, as it seems to me, between *power* and *liberty;* and it must be determined in the next three years, whether the real governing principle in our political system be the power and patronage of the Executive, or the voice of the people. For it can scarcely be doubted, that a scheme has been formed to perpetuate power in the present hands, in spite of the free and unbiased sentiment of the country. . . . Let the Presidency be transmitted by the exercise of a corrupt patronage from hand to hand, and we shall soon consider the form of electing by the people a mere farce.[42]

Once again, it was the corrupt bargain, the pivot on which all anti-administration activism turned, and now Calhoun's tool for advancing his own interest. In the letter, he went on to flatter Jackson in even more transparent terms: "It will be no small addition to your future renown, that in this great struggle your name is found, as it always has been, on the side of liberty, and your country. Occupying the grounds that you do, there can be no triumph over you, which will not also be a triumph over liberty."[43]

When Jackson finally replied from the Hermitage a month later, he explained, more or less as he had to Polk, that he was leisurely viewing the passing scenes: "I have been an attentive observer of the interesting subjects brought into discussion in the last Congress." Without committing himself to anything specific, he repeated the democratic catechism, vowing to defend the people's liberties. He advised Calhoun to place his confidence in the people, too, and to count on the people's reason to expose selfish office-seekers and bring government back to the good and faithful. The most he would say in Calhoun's favor was to link the vice president with McDuffie and Randolph, as another whom the Adams Administration had "wantonly assailed." Less fawning than Calhoun's was the generous statement of John Randolph on the Senate floor in April, announcing his early intention to vote for Jackson in 1828 as "the only man on whom the people could safely unite to put down the present usurpers."[44]

The lines were drawn. There were no neutrals. Both the Adams Administration and the noisy opposition in Congress were expressing their prejudices openly and unreservedly, smelling conspiracy and claiming to unmask unprincipled designs. Jackson, described by the partisan *U.S. Telegraph* as a man of lofty purposes "whom neither prosperity can elate nor adversity press down," was attempting to discipline his mind and prepare for his elevation to commander-in-chief.[45]

It was widely felt that President Adams would follow in his father's footsteps, as an unpopular one-term president who did not communicate moderation. This may have been an accurate assessment, a quality of mind that masked his better attributes: wisdom, experience, and moral strength. And yet the jubilee approached, when citizens were expected to set aside their differences and revel in the perpetuation of liberty over the course of fifty years.

CHAPTER TEN

The People Salute Their
First Fifty Years

IN PHILADELPHIA, where it all began, the temperature already stood at 76° at 9:00 a.m. on Tuesday, the Fourth of July, 1826; seventy-six had been the high on July 4 fifty years earlier, according to Thomas Jefferson's personal measurement.[1] Diarist Deborah Norris Logan of that city noted a minor coincidence on the day of jubilee: once again she was "clearstarching"—stiffening fabric with starch—just as she recalled doing fifty years to the day earlier.[2]

Hers, of course, was not to be the most extraordinary coincidence to occur on this anniversary. While there was nothing to be deemed providential in clearstarching, something eerie and exhilarating was to strike men and women all across the country when, over the next days and weeks, they learned that Adams and Jefferson had each contrived to die natural deaths on that fiftieth Fourth, a mathematically improbable coincidence.

Among the many places that planned jubilee celebrations, Philadelphia, oddly, did not anticipate a particularly exciting Independence Day. Logan recorded that the jubilee was not to be ornamented with "any flowers of poesy or modes of eloquence that have not been used before." She occupied her own pen with somber suggestions of a misty 1776, forsaking all grand observances for private reflection on "the tide of human beings that at that period lived, and acted, and looked forward, as we do now, but have since dropped into the sea of oblivion."

The largest newspaper in Philadelphia confirmed that "all was quiet" this day. Indeed, "the apathy of the citizens" made it especially noteworthy that Colonel Patterson's Regiment had succeeded in maintaining its "discipline and martial appearance" throughout the "customary parade."[3]

While events were surprisingly subdued in the historic city of Philadelphia, the same day's observance roused millions of others around the nation, amplifying as news carried and imaginations fired. In various ways, patriotic sentiment acquired an independent life on the fiftieth Fourth. It sparked some passions that burst forth as spontaneously as fireworks, and some that recombined, once the deaths of Adams and Jefferson were known, into a force of eloquence—imagined, almost combatively, as a collective intuition. That is the meaning behind America's jubilee, and the consciousness of it will fill the rest of these pages.

On July 4, 1776, when his Declaration met with the final approval of the members of the Continental Congress, Thomas Jefferson was not celebrating. He recorded in his account book nothing more momentous than the shopping he did: a visit to the Second Street apothecary and bookstore operated by John Sparhawk, where he purchased a new thermometer. He also picked up seven pairs of ladies' gloves that day, either before or after overseeing the authentication of his not-yet-famous composition. He understood that the new United States was in the midst of a war, one that, the longer it went on, the underequipped American forces seemed more likely to lose than win. Jefferson could not be confident of victory. So over the next two days, he registered only the purchase of more paper, and a quantity of beer— a common table drink, not a celebratory indulgence.[4] Identifying himself as a Virginian first, the amiable, thirty-three-year-old legislator was at that moment eager to return home, and to proceed with work on revising the laws of his state. In other words, when he penned the Declaration of Independence, Thomas Jefferson did not imagine that he would someday become a national executive, let alone a national hero. Most Americans would not even learn of his association with that most cherished document until he was president a quarter-century later.[5]

But John Adams knew, somehow, what this moment would mean. The outspoken Adams had foreseen a glorious beginning for the independent nation on July 2, when the Declaration was still in the hands of congressional editors, if essentially agreed to. Though burdened by the very grave danger posed by an impending British invasion of New York, he wrote effusively to his wife Abigail that July 2, 1776, would be "the most memorable epocha in the history of America." If he miscalculated by two days, Adams was absolutely prophetic in recommending how Independence Day might be commemorated by future generations: ". . . with pomp and parade, with shows, games, sports, guns, bells, bonfires, and illuminations. . . ."[6]

A WEEK FROM his fifty-ninth birthday, the politically wounded son of John Adams awoke in the Executive Mansion. The thermometer read 78° at 7:00 a.m. on a day that would see occasional rain and little sun in the nation's capital. He met with Secretary of the Treasury Richard Rush and Secretary of War James Barbour at nine. They were joined by the postmaster-general. As Adams was greeting his cabinet officers, a procession for the Capitol was getting under way. Volunteer companies of militia, assembling at Lafayette Square across from the President's House, offered their passing salutes. First came trumpeters, then cavalry, then a military band and an infantry detachment, followed by the mayor of Washington, D.C., Roger C. Weightman, Orator of the Day Walter Jones (a distinguished member of the Washington bar, known locally as "Lawyer" Jones), and the two chaplains who would be delivering official prayers at the Capitol ceremony. This was the moment when Adams himself joined in the procession, taking his place in a carriage beside members of the Committee of Arrangements who had organized the day's festivities. High officers of the army and navy sat astride their horses in front of the president's carriage, holding the flag aloft. Vice President John C. Calhoun, politically divorced from his boss, rode in the next carriage behind the president. The cabinet fell in behind Calhoun, trailed by foreign diplomats who permanently resided in the city, more army and navy personnel, members of the clergy, and finally, "Citizens and Strangers."[7]

Salutes had begun firing at sunrise from several places: the Navy Yard, the Arsenal, the Capitol, and even the president's front lawn. Her father away in Annapolis, the attorney general's teenage daughter

Catharine Wirt wrote from Washington to her sister Lizzy, who was with their mother visiting family in Richmond:

> I arose at day break, the clouds indicated rain. I sat down at the window and watched for some time, but at length perceiving that my anxiety did not change this aspect I laid down again but I could not sleep. The cannons were roaring around me in every direction, which however did not at all disturb [sisters] Ellen or Agnes, my room-mates: they slept as soundly as ever did those wearied soldiers, the remembrance of whom the roaring artillery brought to my recollection.[8]

A majority of the "wearied soldiers" of the Revolution were already entombed, as many of the orators on this day were to mourn. But those who still survived, as if awakened from Rip Van Winkle's long sleep, were by their mere presence in the America of 1826 the cause of a new awareness. The past was acquiring greater meaning this day. The veterans of the Revolution had re-entered the nation's conscience.

First-term congressman Edward Everett of Massachusetts was one whose oratorical talent had been employed a few months earlier in support of the veterans. Anticipating the fiftieth Fourth, he had reminded his House colleagues in April of how easy—and how wrong—it had been to forget the self-sacrifice of those who had battled for Independence a half-century earlier: "Most devoutly do I hope, that when the silver trumpet of our political jubilee sounds, it may be with a note of comfort and joy to the withered heart of the war-torn veteran of the Revolution." As he spoke, it appeared that Congress was prepared to add pension money in order to remedy the situation of surviving Revolutionary veterans in need of relief. But Everett was not satisfied. "Our tardy provision," said the outraged representative, "will, indeed, come too late."[9]

Judge Dabney Carr of Virginia had cried out to a friend during Lafayette's tour, "Oh, these revolutionaries have something about them, that we look for in vain, in the every day men of the world—."[10] Had America let down its heroes? Who did not bear some guilt? Only a relative few among those who had once braved British bullets (and the even more lethal camp diseases) enjoyed easy lives in the post-

Revolutionary period. A restrictive pension system had been in place since 1818, but it left many veterans uncared for who were in desperate need.

Congress had heard individual cases, not always the most extreme ones. To the legislators of 1826, however, it seemed that there might still be time to remedy the sufferings of these old and forgotten men, and to allay some portion of the guilt that had accrued among the Revolutionaries' successors. The legislation before them would appropriate more than a million dollars for this general purpose. Introducing the bill, Representative Joseph Hemphill of Pennsylvania had chosen the most obvious symbol, the most powerful image Americans possessed, in order to bring attention to the plight of the veteran: he reminded his fellow House members how the stirring return of Lafayette had infused a "lively recollection" of 1776 as nothing else could, how it had produced "a glow of honest feeling" across America. Hemphill's Pennsylvania colleague, future president James Buchanan, added forthrightly: "I do not consider that the claim of the officers of the Revolution rests upon gratitude alone," he said. "It is not an appeal to your gratitude only, but to your justice. You owe them a debt, in the strictest sense of the word; and of a nature so meritorious, that, if you shall refuse to pay it, the nation will be disgraced."[11]

Joining the chorus, Representative Peleg Sprague of Maine contributed colorful language:

> Let gentlemen recur to our Revolutionary struggle, and consult their own hearts and their own judgments, and then say what is due to the soldier, who, feeble and sinking for want of food and sustenance, marched, during the day, through snow and ice, on naked feet, exposed unclad to the Winter's cold, with no resting place at night but the earth, and no covering but the skies, passing through sufferings which human nature could not sustain unbroken; and falling prey to a pestilence, more deadly and more terrific than the sword of the enemy. Cheerfully did he face the cannon's mouth, and dare a soldier's death on the field of honor.[12]

Everett was the last to speak before the vote. Praise was "sweet music," he pronounced. However, the compliments that would "fill the ears of these poor veterans" on the day of jubilee would not just be meaningless but unconscionable, if nothing were put in their pockets at the same time.

On the morning of July 4, 1826, as the president's carriage arrived at the Capitol, Congress had been out of session for over a month. Most of the legislators were at home. John Randolph had sailed to Europe. The *U.S. Telegraph* reported that the floor of the House chamber and gallery above were "filled to overflowing" with ordinary citizens, members of the military, and foreign guests, but few politicians. Ladies had been permitted to take their seats at nine, while gentlemen were obliged to wait until the procession formally entered the hall. The president made his entrance with Comptroller (Judge) Joseph Anderson, who was designated to read the text of the Declaration of Independence after the opening prayer and before the address of Walter Jones.[13]

Jones was just shy of fifty himself, born near the mouth of the Potomac on Virginia's eastern shore in the fall of 1776. His father, also Walter Jones, now twelve years in his grave, had been a Virginia congressman and a medical doctor. In his political prime, he was a staunch Jeffersonian. The son had read the law under Bushrod Washington, nephew of the first president and associate justice of the Supreme Court since 1798. He was a prodigy, having been admitted to the Virginia bar at the tender age of nineteen. Since then, Jones had distinguished himself as a U.S. attorney. Also of note, he was married to the granddaughter of Richard Henry Lee, a signer of the Declaration of Independence who held a special place in the process: it was Lee who, on June 7, 1776, submitted to Congress the definitive resolution to separate from Britain, which Jefferson had then drafted as the immortal Declaration.[14]

Conspicuous as he was in Washington, Jones was a small man, and he did not have a reputation for powerful oratory. On this day he delivered what Adams called an "ingenious" oration, "far wide from the commonplaces of the day," though, being an Adams—demanding as well as self-demanding—the president could not let the orator get away without the same kind of criticism he had once leveled at the actors in a performance of *Hamlet* he had witnessed in London in 1783, when the teenager had confided to his diary: "They lay an emphasis upon almost every word; yet in some places they speak, both too low and too slow." Jones's performance was, to Adams's taste, made up of "loose fragments, without much connection," for he had failed to commit his speech to memory. "So he read from his notes," Adams observed, "and commented upon them extemporaneously, which made a desultory composition, full of interesting matter, but producing little effect as a whole."[15]

After the ceremonies at the Capitol, the Adamses courteously opened the Executive Mansion for several hours to the general public, that is, to the "citizens and strangers" whom the newspaper referred to in its description of the anonymous paraders who had brought up the rear of the Capitol procession that morning. The president's formal obligations were now fulfilled.

The following day, newspapers around the country began publishing the letters that the Washington Committee for Arrangements had received from the four living ex-presidents and from Charles Carroll of Carrollton, Maryland, the only surviving signer of the Declaration of Independence besides Adams and Jefferson. On the day before the jubilee, President Adams had inspected the originals of these several letters, all apologetic declinations. Interested in the handwriting, he remarked in his diary: "Mr. Jefferson's is in the freest style; my father's is signed with his own hand."[16]

Jefferson had written movingly from Monticello on June 24: "It adds sensibly to the sufferings of sickness, to be deprived by it of a personal participation in the rejoicing of that day." And he pronounced, with the same eloquence he had displayed a half-century before, "All eyes are opened, or opening, to the rights of men." Adams, on the 22nd, expressed his gratitude for the invitation, as regretful as his Virginia comrade that "my health forbids me to indulge the hope of participating." Carroll, who would finally surrender to death in 1832 at the age of ninety-five, employed a different justification: New York had asked first, and having said no once already, it would have been improper for him to agree to Washington's offer. Monroe was vague, protesting the "many engagements which press on me at this time," and indicating that he would not leave home. (He was fêted in Richmond.) Madison, who would outlive all the rest, vied with Jefferson for the most elegant letter of refusal. He recalled the kindness showed him by the citizens of Washington during his two terms, and while citing the "instability of my health" in order to decline the journey, he assured that "all my feelings will be in sympathy with the sentiments inspired by the occasion."[17]

President Adams turned his attention to the planting of acorn, hickory, and chestnut trees in public places around Washington.[18] Elsewhere in America, the jubilee was celebrated with pageantry comparable to that which he had just experienced. In Boston, where the Revolution first took root, and where an old spirit of resistance to British rule could still be recalled to many minds, Mayor Josiah Quincy gave a rousing oration. This old friend of President Adams had had but a few days to prepare, having been selected to deliver the address only after the designated speaker, Reverend Henry Ware Jr. of Boston's Second Church, had taken ill.[19]

An accomplished speechmaker and former congressman who had welcomed Lafayette to Boston, Quincy began with sanctifying references to "our fathers' glory," to their "labours and sacrifices." He termed the Fourth of July assembly "a solemn, and somewhat a religious duty." He painted, too, a vivid picture of fifty years past, though he himself was only a toddler, unlikely to have remembered when "sentries, with fixed bayonets [were] at our State-house doors;—while Boston was but a garrison; its islands and harbours, possessed by a vindictive and indignant foe . . . and the blood of its slaughtered citizens flowed, like water, in its streets." Few orations around the country that day were as unforgiving of the British, with whom Americans now enjoyed a mild, if not exactly a warm, relationship.[20]

The mayor had not proceeded much beyond these chilling images before reminding his hearers of the Revolutionary patriarch, still among them, whose life was to be cherished. With poignancy and accustomed extravagance, he spoke of John Adams, his esteemed neighbor, who had been lifted into his carriage to pay a visit to the Quincy house just three days before:

> Especially shall not be forgotten—now, or ever—that ancient citizen of Boston . . . , [who] oppressed by years, sinking under the burdens of decaying nature, hears not our public song, or voice of praise, or ascending prayer. But the sounds of a nation's joy, rushing from our cities, ringing from our vallies, echoing from our hills, shall break the silence of his aged ear; the rising

blessings of grateful millions shall visit, with a glad light, his fading vision; and flush the last shades of his evening sky, with the
reflected splendours of his meridian brightness.[21]

Around the time of the address, George Washington Adams, eldest
son of John Quincy Adams, was being called from Boston to his
grandfather's bedchamber, to be present for his last hours.

Meanwhile, Mayor Quincy spoke more of his devotion to the
moral lessons of the Revolution:

> During the struggle our fathers displayed great strength and
> great moderation in purpose. In difficult times they conducted
> with wisdom. In doubtful times, with firmness. In perilous with
> courage. Under oppressive trials, erect. Amidst great temptation,
> unseduced. In the dark hour of danger, fearless. In the bright
> hour of prosperity, faithful.[22]

The litany he was conveying—much as he had professed at the start of
the address—was a religious model of adoration and supplication. It
was, in fact, a portrait of retrospective perfection.

Quincy's was an unduly embellished view of the Revolution. But
in the idiom of his day, pious devotion to the founding ideal was seen
as a valuable teaching tool that might be exaggerated without appearing disproportionate. As we have seen, literate Americans of 1826 were
highly self-conscious. They viewed themselves as a people prone to the
exercise of unhealthy passions who required sterner consciences and a
political tone of moderation to soften their enthusiasm. An almanac of
1826 quipped: "Our passions are like convulsive fits, which, though
they make us stronger for a moment, yet leave us much weaker after-
wards."[23]

Unmanaged passion was the weakness Jackson's detractors attributed to the general, as Quincy meant to suggest when he observed,
"There can be no surer sign that the liberties of a people are hastening
to a dissolution, than their countenancing those, who form parties on
men, and not upon principles." If only men could once again adopt the
stern virtues of the great Revolutionary leaders: "By the virtue of your
fathers," Quincy reminded, "you have been preserved from ignomin-
ious bondage. Beware lest you become subjected to a more grievous

bondage of base, ignoble passions." The Jackson phenomenon was unmentioned but inescapably present, just as it was in those parts of the country where the new Jackson was gentle and purposeful, and where the Revolution was being celebrated in a "Jacksonian" mode as the passionate exercise of the many, a common commitment that, in moral terms, knew no rank.

Quincy, from the Adams camp, closed his religiously inspired oration with more superlatives for the "fathers," paying homage to their "labours, councils, and virtues" and the "pillars" of a past "moral architecture" that they had erected. Their example, if followed, would lead to spiritual renewal, to a time of restored hope. Indeed, the whole world would prosper, if the new generation would preserve the inherited "temple of liberty" by adding the "purest faith" to its "glorious archings of celestial wisdom."[24]

A distance north and west of Boston, in the town of Pepperell, the Fourth of July oration was given by Reverend Ezekiel L. Bascom. It was a place just slightly more populous than Ashby, and he had ridden the fourteen miles east to it under threatening skies. It had rained every day for the past two weeks. Bascom's speech has not survived. But Pepperell was a town where Revolutionary heroism had lived in the hearts of the people for at least one very good reason: this had been the home of William Prescott, often called the bravest man at the Battle of Bunker Hill. Prior to June 17, 1775, the most famous son of Pepperell was only known as a tall, quiet farmer. But on the day of the momentous battle, as a colonel of a regiment of minutemen, the forty-nine-year-old strode across the earthen entrenchments overlooking Boston. Wearing a broad-brimmed hat, he stood out, unafraid. Distinguished, too, by the long coat he wore, he was an obvious target for the disciplined British troops, and in exposing himself, Prescott narrowly evaded a bayonet during one grand charge. As Pepperell's Luther Bancroft would tell it on the fifty-fifth anniversary of Bunker Hill in 1830, "shafts of death were aimed at him in every direction." If Bunker Hill remained for the people of Pepperell the greatest battle "ever fought on the globe," the heroic farmer Prescott was "the corner stone of our Independence."[25] Surely, the earnest and artful Reverend Bascom would have prepared his jubilee oration as carefully as Bancroft had; knowing that Prescott was buried at Pepperell, he, too, would have made the Revolutionary hero a cornerstone of his speech.

Perhaps Luther Bancroft, who was just twenty-two in 1826, was in the audience for Bascom's address. The young man had attempted his first publication some months earlier, titled *Bancroft's Agricultural Almanac*. Beholding the starry universe as God's "palace," he combined an Emersonian awe of nature—"I am lost in a labyrinth of suns and worlds"—with a Franklinian sense of humor. A clergyman's son was about to lift a glass of bitters. "Son, do not drink that filthy stuff, for ardent spirit is the worst enemy you have." Replied the son, "I know it, father, but we are commanded to love our enemies—so here it goes."[26]

There was not an ounce of humor or irony in the preserved speeches of Ezekiel Bascom or, for that matter, in Ruth Bascom's diary. She recorded nothing about her husband's oration, and she did not accompany him to Pepperell to hear it. He had steered his carriage home by sunset, driving through a mid-afternoon shower that brought with it considerable thunder and lightning, which his wife had sat out in the company of some neighbors.

In fact, though, one unusual visitor came to Ashby for the Fourth of July. After the Reverend Bascom had left for Pepperell, a "stranger" showed up at Ruth's door, and introduced himself as Jonathan Cato. He was a "pious black man," she wrote, "a preacher to his colour," and Ruth invited him in for breakfast. He bore appropriate "certificates" and letters of recommendation from several ministers of the Bascoms' acquaintance. Cato "conversed much," she said, but that was all she said. There were no black residents of Ashby. A soldier of the Revolution identified as "Prince Estabrook, Negro" was buried behind the Ashby church, but this was the first indication that either of the Bascoms had given thought to persons of color since Ruth was moved by an evening address at the church delivered by a Mr. Niles of the American Colonization Society in February. He had spoken boldly and left a considerable impression.

On the subject of human liberty, there were, in fact, a number of Fourth of July orations that did not forget the plight of American blacks. In most cases, though, rhetoric simplified understanding. Professor George W. Benedict in Burlington, Vermont, was typical in holding out hope for the colonization project. Liberia, he said, had become "our own happy colony . . . where formerly the slave-merchant received his victims" and where now, "the people, whom nature is said to have stamped with an imbecility incompatible with freedom, by one mighty effort burst their chains, and wrote in characters of blood and fire, their claims to the rights of men." Blacks' humanity was considered, but white superiority was assumed.[27]

In Newark, New Jersey, where the population was 6 percent black, William Halsey was more explicit: "It is in vain we boast of perfect liberty, whilst the degraded sons of Africa, still yoked to their iron car of slavery . . . are here driven on, merciless and remorseless. Slavery is the dark spot in the sun of our independence." Of the 511 blacks in Newark, a few dozen were still deemed "slaves for life" in 1826. In New Jersey as a whole, the number of slaves had peaked in 1800, with 12,422 counted—that was two years after the state legislature had prohibited traffic in slaves between New Jersey and other states. In 1820, there were still 7,557 slaves, and while an act of 1804 had decreed that all slaves born in the state after July 4, 1804, would be freed upon reaching the age of twenty-five, there would remain 2,254 slaves in 1830. Yet Halsey, too, ultimately banked on the colonizationists' solution of greatest convenience: "You have the assurance of nature," he said, "that the next return of this Jubilee will be effectual to the emancipation of every descendent of Africa in this portion of our country," and, he added, this event would "cause Liberia to rejoice, and Africa to be glad, because of the restoration of her sons."[28]

In John Adams's birthplace of Braintree, Massachusetts, Josiah Bent was differently transported: "But hark! what do I hear? It was a heavy groan; and it rose from the bosom of this happy land. It is repeated; more than a thousand thousand mingle into one. It gives utterance—it is the almost stifled prayer of the long oppressed. *'Spare injured Africa,'* it begs, *'the Negro spare!'*" Reverend Bent knew the biblical meaning of a jubilee, and did not shy from speaking it before his white congregation: "And, O my Country, is it so? Has thy Jubilee of freedom come; and brings it no Jubilee to those, who so long have sighed beneath a servitude an hundred fold more wretched than thou hast ever felt?" His passionate solicitation was just beginning to build.

Bent, like Harriet Beecher Stowe a quarter-century later, wanted to believe that the value of sympathy could cause a shift in national priorities. This was the moment, he urged, when true patriots could pause to "weep for suffering man . . . and the light of this Jubilee *shall* carry some cheering rays to the negro's disconsolate bosom, and flash conviction through the soul of those, who still remain willing to oppress." The pastor unreservedly called up the language of the Declaration that guaranteed human equality: "Can America be glorious in freedom with such a number of human beings so degraded, so oppressed, so wronged, and so bleeding in her bosom? Sons of Columbia, are you not this day happy in your freedom? and does not Liberty ask an offering worthy of your Jubilee?" He claimed that the spirit of Washington would "chide" those who shut their hearts: "Offer then your slaves," Bent demanded, "and it shall be a Jubilee indeed." Though he praised the charitable intent of the colonizationists, his message made clear that colonization did not offer enough. There was a purer compassion in Bent's address, such as would characterize later abolitionist writings and oratory, but even he did not effectively expose the false hope of colonization.[29]

The retired publisher of the *Massachusetts Spy*, Isaiah Thomas, who had founded the publication back in 1775, joined in celebrating the jubilee. Fifty years earlier he had had the distinction of being the first in the state to publicly read the Declaration of Independence. The express rider from Philadelphia had stopped in Worcester, handing Thomas a copy for publication in his newspaper. News of the document soon spread. "A large concourse of people collected," the *Spy* retold the printer's story. "To gratify their curiosity, Thomas ascended the portico of the South Meeting-House . . . and read it to those who were assembled."[30]

This nostalgic vignette was followed immediately by another kind of news, more reflective of prevailing social issues: "LIBEL SUIT," the headline read. In neighboring New York State, the lieutenant governor had sued another paper, the *New-York American*, for $1,400 in damages, after that newspaper reported him as "drunk, and filthy in appearance" when undertaking decisions in his role as president of the New York senate. Ten "highly respectable" witnesses testified that the state's number-two official had entered the senate "staggering, with tobacco juice running from the corners of his mouth." Other witnesses disagreed, saying that while he was often drunk, he was not drunk at that time. And here the presiding judge made a fine distinction between "drunkenness" and "the inferior grades of intoxication," finding for the public official. In commenting on the story, the *Spy* issued a warning to other newspapers lest they, too, court "pecuniary ruin" in taking a stand against intemperate politicians.

Moral lessons abounded on the occasion of the jubilee, the most unambiguous of which recited the contributions of those who had endured real privation in the Revolution. In Burlington, Vermont, George Benedict supplied florid phrasing. He praised "high-minded men of deathless memory" overall, but reserved special tribute for the underappreciated soldiers of the Continental Army, who had waged a war against unpropitious odds and for little financial remuneration. Here was the history of the War for Independence as he saw it:

> The long and unequal conflict had exhausted the means of Congress, and it was found necessary to disband the troops with the wages of many months, and in some cases, of years, unpaid. They were to be discharged destitute of the very necessaries of life,— without even money enough to bear them in their long-left and earnestly wished-for homes. Often, when hungry, naked, and wounded, they had thought of the solicitude of those who feared for the safety of a son or a brother . . . [and] they repressed the emotion with a hope that soon those anxieties would give place to joy—that soon they would bear to their destitute families the well-saved earnings of their toil and blood. . . . But the blast had swept across all those hopes and cheering anticipations.[31]

They had come home with smiles on their faces, but no money in their pockets. Reiterating what Representatives Everett, Buchanan, and Sprague had voiced in Congress the previous spring, Benedict attacked the general insensitivity toward the Revolutionary War veteran. Who could legitimately speak of the "general welfare" anymore without thinking of them? Day by day, as the nation moved ahead, one ancient hero after another was "gone to the land of silence." A grateful nation had to make up for years of forgetfulness, and treasure all that the Revolutionaries' lives stood for.[32]

Across Lake Champlain and down the Hudson River, Maryland-born William Maynadier, a nineteen-year-old cadet, was selected to give the jubilee oration at the United States Military Academy at West Point. He would graduate third in his class the following year. Though a good friend of fellow West Pointer Jefferson Davis, Maynadier was later to rise to the rank of colonel in the Union Army, and manage the ordnance bureau of the War Department in Washington during the Civil War.[33]

As Maynadier addressed his fellows, he naturally reflected on some of the military engagements that resulted in victory over England, but he did so less avidly than he addressed the motives of the civilian leadership in the Continental Congress in 1776: "What a subject for consideration!" he marveled, "either an open war with the proud Mistress of the World, without adequate resources—with but a bare possibility of success . . . or a tame submission." Steadfast resolution had fixed America's personality. On a host of battlefields, martyrs had fallen in the "Sacred Cause" so that the next generation, and citizens of future ages, could stand on "holy ground" and gaze reverently on the decayed scenes of founding glory, sensing what it had taken for freedom to be won.[34]

"The Jubilee has come, and found us—how?" he posed anxiously. "Does it find us as we were, when the glad tidings of Independence first went forth through the land . . . ? No! What fifty years have ever witnessed greater improvements in science, literature, and politics?" America, in a short half-century, had become respectable—and something even more profound, he imagined: "In every land, the name of a citizen of the United States is respected, and the hospitable Arab, when he sits down in his tent to repose, will speak of a free, a happy people beyond the sea, and tell deeds of Washington." The fantasy of a universally understood American purity and perfection led the cadet to his unifying prophecy: "The time shall come when the world shall behold the blissful reality. The bright star that appeared first in our own horizon, is shining on with increasing effulgence." As "unborn Washingtons in other climes" arose, that star would "shine on 'till its radiant brightness shall enlighten the universe," and all nations govern themselves after America's example.[35]

That "bright star" of America shining everywhere and "enlightening" the globe was perhaps the most often repeated allusion in jubilee oratory. Metaphors of light and glory had also proven a most effective turn of phrase for patriot propagandists in the Revolutionary age, when America was consistently drawn as "the Land of Light and Liberty." Pronounced the *Pennsylvania Gazette* in 1770: "Behold what a great Flame a small Spark kindleth!" And for the young Connecticut poet Timothy Dwight, in 1771, America was the "Land of light and joy!" John Adams in 1776 perceived "through all the Gloom . . . the Rays of a ravishing Light and Glory." Tom Paine, likewise: "The sun never shined on a cause of greater worth." In 1776 and 1826 alike, the idea of America as a grand political millennium, burying tyranny forever, was a powerful stimulant.[36]

Also along the Hudson, in the state capital of Albany, several balloons emblazoned with patriotic messages were sent aloft just as soon as the ceremonial reading of the Declaration was complete. The *Albany Argus & City Daily Gazette* printed a mild editorial on the morning of the Fourth urging citizens to differentiate between the necessarily harsh language of the historic Declaration and the "good feelings" now prevailing between the United States and its former political parent, as "becomes a wise and liberal people to strengthen and perpetuate." Two days later, the paper boasted that the jubilee festival had been a success: "much hilarity and rejoicing" and "little excess." That excess, however, required the *Argus* to rebuke those who played with firecrackers, in reporting "the loss of an eye by the imprudent and inexcusable habit of throwing lighted crackers, either without regard to their direction or with a mischievous intention."[37]

In New York City, the highlight of the day, according to the *New-York American,* was the huge banquet table set up to entertain eight hundred citizens. Oxen, roasted whole, filled the stomachs of the attendees, with "an endless quantity of hams and loaves of bread, interspersed with barrels of beer and cider on tap." The city's Horticultural Society saw that the oxen were decorated with garlands and ribbons and "green-house plants, and sweet shrubs." On the arrival of Governor DeWitt Clinton, "the oxen were attacked and cut up."

Newark, New Jersey, twice visited by Lafayette, was a township of eight thousand in the shadow of New York City. A special census undertaken by the jubilee planning committee had determined that only 2 percent of the inhabitants in 1826 were living there in 1776. Once this fact was known, the committee made arrangements for the fifty-six surviving Revolutionary veterans to be central to the celebration.

On the morning of the jubilee, the people of Newark awoke before the light to the "usual roar" of Fourth of July cannon, followed, on this extraordinary Fourth, by "a concert of horns." At sunrise, bells rang "a merry peal." Then, those fifty-six "Heroes of the Revolution" assembled under the command of eighty-seven-year-old Captain Obadiah Meeker. One of the company even wore his Revolutionary uniform complete, topped with his three-cornered cocked hat. Many shouldered their old rifles and carried canteens and powder boxes, and all marked time to the music of fife and drum, played by those of their number who had done so a half-century before.[38]

Thirteen of the men of '76 led thirteen oxen to the place where a tall column, a monument to America's jubilee day, was about to be erected. William S. Pennington, one of the veterans, addressed the assembled crowd. He reminded his hearers of what had been at stake fifty years before. Failure would have been "humiliating," he said, indeed, it would have made Americans indistinguishable from "the boors of Russia." He thanked God profusely for having led American troops "through our sea of difficulties and the wilderness of our affliction, to the consummation of our Independence." The foundation stone was laid. It read in part: "IN GRATEFUL COMMEMORATION OF THE FIFTIETH ANNIVERSARY OF AMERICAN INDEPENDENCE . . . WHEN THE DILAPIDATIONS OF TIME SHALL DISCOVER THIS INSCRIPTION TO FUTURE GENERATIONS, MAY THE LIGHT OF THE GOSPEL ILLUMINATE THE WHOLE WORLD." At the base of the monument, a time capsule, a lead box containing the day's proceedings, was sealed up and hidden. Instructions were left at a Newark bank that the box was only to be opened to add the Fourth of July orations of intervening years, and then opened publicly once more for America's centennial celebration in 1876.[39]

From here, a long procession led to the First Presbyterian Church. The "Heroes of '76" led the way, with their muskets. Behind them marched the modern military, accompanied by "an excellent Band of music." Newark's laborers directly followed: tailors, blacksmiths, quarrymen (carrying their tools in their hands), stonecutters and masons, carpenters, curriers (leather tanners), the "Ladies' Shoe and Men's Pump-makers' Benevolent Society," coach makers, cabinet makers and upholsterers, chair makers, saddlers, and painters. Behind the labor force marched Pennington; the orator of the day, William Halsey; and the town's clergy and civil authorities.[40]

Halsey's address recalled the flight of liberty from the Old World to the New. He was recurring to an idiom that the veterans remembered well, the same idiom that had prevailed in 1776, when the patriot press proclaimed that history was reaching its climax in America, "fugitive freedom" (in the words of Tom Paine) having crossed the Atlantic in the hope of lodging safely among a harmonizing people. With liberty wantonly assailed in this fabled place of last resort, the men who signed the Declaration of Independence had had to possess an "iron nerve," as Halsey put it, when they put their pens to that immortal document. And now the veterans, saviors of that liberty, were able to live out their years in a government that "furnishes protection as well to the poor as to the rich," a democracy yet in "infancy" that had already attained "a strength unparalleled for its age."[41]

Rather differently, the jubilee was celebrated in Chillicothe, Ohio, "with more than ordinary solemnity," and, it would appear, sedately, according to the *Supporter, and Scioto Gazette*. At dawn, a "federal salute" was fired from "a field piece" set up on a hill at the west end of town. At eleven, "a respectable number of citizens" formed a procession, the Declaration was read "in an impressive manner," an oration (not recorded, but "interspersed with solemn music") was given, and an outdoor banquet held in a nearby grove. There was no indication whether Mr. Atkinson's "old cheese" was on the menu. In Wooster, far more demonstratively, the *Ohio Oracle* reported on a celebration "worthy of the day." Dinner was styled "*a feast of fat things,* conferring much credit on the host." The festive spirit was enhanced by the presence of "a goodly number of ladies," and "a small number of aged veterans . . . heroes of '76—who had tested and knew the intrinsic value of *Liberty;* and whose venerable and whitened locks, joined with the remembrance of former days, heightened the interests of the occasion."[42]

The day's oration in Wooster was delivered by the Reverend Samuel Irvine, who stressed the value of civic education—"moral and political virtue, individual and national friendship"—and reminded his hearers that all political power was derived from the people. In America, he said, the only thing that set one individual above another was and ought to be "improvement of mind, conjoined with moral worth." Yet Irvine was also attuned to the rise of sectional conflict, and asked for greater understanding toward "the different states of the union." He called forth the adage, as Abraham Lincoln would more famously three decades later, that "A house divided against itself cannot stand." As he reached for his closing, the preacher returned to the most literal theme of the day: "This is called the year of Jubilee. Be it so. Let us imitate the Jew, and sound the trumpet, and proclaim 'liberty through-out all the land, and to all the inhabitants thereof.' Redeem the bond-man—and the distressed—assist the needy brother—exact not usury of a fellow citizen—and *restore* all things to their *proper condition.*"[43]

In rain-soaked Cincinnati, the Declaration of Independence was read by a Mr. Looker, a survivor of the Revolution. U.S. Senator William Henry Harrison gave the day's oration, which the *National Crisis* of that city only mildly praised, seeing something too ordinary in it. Harrison's message had been "received with general satisfaction," to be sure, but the moment was better suited for words from a Revo-lutionary hero, "to *have the image with the action, and the substance with the words.*" The newspaper had editorialized two weeks earlier that the power of the jubilee ought to match the growth of the country. The West, especially, "as if by enchantment, or by some supernatural agency," had arrived at "a tolerable stage of permanency and security" in a very short time, a truth meant to be woven somehow into the national creation story. To the *National Crisis,* human speech may not have been equal to the task of so transcendent an occasion as the "first Jubilee of our country's freedom," but the ceremonial six-pounders that exploded from cannon that morning, "announcing from their deep-toned mouths a nation's gratitude," were at least a fair reminder of what had come to pass in the last fifty years.[44]

Rain fell all day in Lexington, Kentucky, too, but this did not pre-vent the Light Infantry from parading at daybreak, and firing a salute of fifty guns. Dancing and feasting began early, and what the *Kentucky Reporter* called "rational amusements and interchanges of patriotic sentiment and heartfelt gratulations" were meant to suggest that the usual political antagonisms had ceased, at least for one day. Similarly, in tiny Dover, Kentucky, on the Ohio River, "the day was wet and unpleasant, but the presence of a number of ladies, whose smiles will turn the *darkest* hour into one of *sunshine,* added much to the enjoy-ments of the day." Kentuckians stressed their vaunted sociability.[45]

Although its favorite son was absent in the south-central part of the state, at the invitation of a friend in the town of Pulaski, Nashville still featured a military review. The highlight of the day was the parad-ing of assembled militia units from across the state, joining Nashville's own guard and Lafayette rifle corps. Received by "a brilliant concourse of ladies and gentlemen," the marchers displayed their colors and celebrated the blazing history of the west Tennessee frontier. Jackson stalwart, former congressman, and future U.S. senator Felix Grundy read the Declaration of Independence and toasted the intrepid founders of Nashville. Other celebrants joined in raising their glasses to their proud section of the western country, "a favored spot," as one judge put it, "where martial spirit has combined with the blandishments of peace to captivate the hearts of strangers." While Jackson was missed, his name was on many lips: in persistent toasts to the miraculous triumph in New Orleans eleven years earlier; in a predictable salute to "The pride of Tennessee and the man of the people. His public life is before the nation, his private character is cherished by his neighbors"; and in portents of *"The next presidential election*—All power is inherent in the people; their will be done." Six cheers, and six guns, were followed by a round of "Yankee Doodle."[46]

In Salem, Indiana, a pelting rain marred the day, as in so many other places. Harvard-educated John Farnum stood at the front of the modest town's Presbyterian church, and gave a learned address to men and women of the Western frontier that, as he worked his way along, grew from standard imagery to apocalyptic dread. Farnum, a lawyer who it was said "turned many an honest penny" writing speeches for others, had ghostwritten the welcoming address read before Lafayette a year earlier, when the French general, recovering from his shipwreck in the Ohio River, set foot on Indiana soil in the town of Jeffersonville, opposite Louisville, Kentucky.[47]

For Farnum, the spirit of the Revolution was magical sentiment, virtually impossible to rekindle amid the political trials of 1826. Launching into his speech, he expressed awe, as many other orators were doing that day, at the manner in which America had risen from insignificance: "Fifty years ago—the sun rose on a handful of brave and determined but dependent colonies.—*To-day*, it shines on twelve millions of freemen, composing a powerful, opulent, harmonious Empire!" Not so long ago languishing as the "remote and subservient appendages of the British Isles," America now stood "in the front rank of a galaxy of Republics." How fulfilling to the prophecies of the Revolutionary era, when Ezra Stiles, president of Yale College, had vowed: "Our population will soon overspread the vast territory from the *Atlantick* to the *Mississippi*, which in two generations will become a property superiour to that of *Britain*." Farnum was critically aware of the achievement.[48]

Enchantments evoked in other orations were especially alive in Farnum's address. Where the West Pointer Maynadier envisioned the "hospitable Arab" praising America from his tent in the desert, Farnum presumed that any American, from any spot in the world, instinctively knew when it was the Fourth of July:

> Wherever in the wide circuit of the globe his lot may be cast, whether buoyed in his progress by the Atlantic or Pacific wave, whether an Indian or an African sun mantle his cheek, whether he furrow the Northern Ocean to strike the Greenland whale, or plunge his harpoon into the scaly monster of the Antarctic seas, the 4th of July commands the suspension of his labors; the sacred fire of Amor Patriae burns in his bosom—the star spangled banner floats before his vision in new and brighter colors—the anniversary cannon strikes his thrilled nerves with Heaven-inspiring power. . . . He embraces *"The Land of the Free and the Home of the Brave."*

The epic quality of Farnum's patriotic tale kept unfolding:

> Our Revolution, like all great changes in the moral world, was gradual, and accomodated [*sic*] to the operation of natural causes. Its early dawning may be compared to the effect of a pebble cast into the bosom of a tranquil lake. . . . It has proceeded with an accelerated momentum, gaining new strength and resources in its progress, till it bids fair to encircle the globe, and to bless with the triumphs of philanthropy the inhabitants of the equator and the poles.[49]

As a Westerner with roots in the Adamses' New England, he easily invoked "the spirit of *Internal Improvement*" that had caused "these vast Western forests to bow to the genius of Civilization." Reminiscent of the claims of Ohioans, Farnum recalled southern Indiana as "a howling wilderness"—a phrase as old as the Puritans—once desolate and now "studded with farms and villages, teeming with a hardy and industrious population, all animated with the spirit of Liberty."

But all at once, his message became darker. Just as an individual could forfeit reason, the nation could forfeit the animating spirit of '76, its strong, "affectionate" union, through obstinacy, alienation—or something worse. An accusatory Farnum announced that all one had to do was to inspect "the mad ravings of disappointed ambition," the "half maniac, half incendiary politician of our days," whose "self-tormenting soul," whose "foul vapourings," whose "malignant spirit of envy and detraction," marred the nation's moral progress, to see that such destructive behavior had to be purged. The federal government needed to be "disenthralled and redeemed from prejudice and calumny" (its ungracious representatives) and returned to the people.[50]

His was certainly not the only note of caution on this day. In Charleston, South Carolina, even before the jubilee got under way, a spirit of rivalry divided the community. Forebodingly—whether a simple mistake or something else—a typesetter dated the front page of the *Charleston Courier* "Saturday, July 4, 1826" instead of "Saturday, July 1, 1826." Inside, an anonymous letter signed by "A Subscriber" sharply protested that the well-to-do had systematically excluded "THE PEOPLE" from all preparations. "It is strange," this individual wrote, "that common folks cannot even eat and drink together, without exciting the watchfulness of their assumed guardians." So the "common folks" had organized a defiant party and a table of their own, to toast the jubilee without seeking permission from the stuffy leaders of the city. "We expect nothing better than 'a well regulated mob,' " the writer challenged, "that is, we wish young and old, high and low, rich and poor, to sit down, governed by their own sense of propriety, and rejoice together." Their forefathers had been rebels, and so were they, even in their revelry: "We own we are rebels, plebians, common citizens," wishing simply to be left alone by the "aristocrats."[51]

Monitoring Charlestonians' interest in setting aside rank and fortune during the jubilee season, Boston's *Columbian Centinel* went further: What about the slaves? Will their plight be forgotten at the jubilee? This commentator prodded, "To what better purpose could we devote the Anniversaries of our struggle for liberty, than that of exciting a sympathy for the slaves"—one-sixth of the country's population in 1826. The jubilee was producing a mix of messages; among them, the seeds of sectional conflict were proving to have sprouted.[52]

All the same, the declaration of independence by Charleston's mildly oppressed white citizens had an appreciable effect. The four most publicized dinners all went off without a hitch, after last-minute advertisements encouraged broader participation. "On such an occasion," read an ad for the revamped dinner at City Hall, "the difference of fortune and of situation ought not to be forgotten, and all classes of Citizens should unite in the expression of their sentiment.... To afford an opportunity to all Citizens to join in the festivities of the day, Tickets of admission to the dinner can be obtained ... at $2.50 each." The ad for another dinner exhibited the same sensitivity: "The Surviving Officers and Soldiers of the Revolution, who may be in Charleston or its vicinity are respectfully invited.... This public invitation [substituting for individually addressed invitations] is dictated by the shortness of the intervening time, and the possibility of an omission." On July 6, the *Courier* reported on the affectionate sentiment that prevailed among the various dinners around the city. Many glasses were raised to the surviving veterans. A volunteer toast by the city sheriff hailed these often ignored men as "The war-torn and weather-beaten Soldiers of the Revolution—May they always be greeted with that grateful feeling which has characterized my fellow-citizens on the present glorious occasion."[53]

Innumerable odes were written for the occasion of America's jubilee. Some were sung in public, others printed in the newspapers. All were local in origin, entirely derivative in their allusions, and regrettably generic in the attempt to express Americans' passion. A few brief examples will suffice:

> *The day is Freedom's Jubilee!*
> *Her joyous song is swelling*
> *From every hill—from sea to sea—*
> *Her glorious triumphs telling.*

This particular ode went on to describe the spirit of friendship that was supposed to be shared by all Americans: "warm hands fondly meeting," "buoyant hearts" free from sorrow, the "patriot pride" that beat in every heart:

> *Swell high the song and fill the bowl*
> *We'll pledge, as on the bright hours roll,*

The brave, the beautiful, the free—
'Tis Liberty's high Jubilee![54]

It was common to refer in verse to the "bowl" of ceremonial drink by which modern patriots were meant to toast their Revolutionary predecessors, and especially "the health of the few who survive." Another song to the pride and vigilance of freedom-loving Americans ends with a quatrain:

> *Then pledge the bowl for the pleasure it gives,*
> *Let it sparkle up brimming and high;*
> *And here's to the Freeman where'er he lives,*
> *Who shall drink to the FOURTH OF JULY.*[55]

And that is precisely what citizens everywhere did to conclude their jubilee banquets. From the time of the Revolution, American newspapers had been routinely publishing toasts, with meaningful rankings, on every social occasion. A survey of newspapers during the week of July 4, 1826, yields a remarkably fixed order for the first three toasts publicly proposed in planned banquets:

Toast #1: the day itself: described either as "The Day" or "The ever memorable 4th of July 1776" or "To the present Anniversary—The Jubilee of our National Independence," or some variation on the same theme.

Toast #2: "The patriots and sages," or as often, "General George Washington and the other departed heroes" (alternately "the Memory of the Immortal Washington"). If he was not mentioned in toast #2, Washington generally commanded toast #3. In the *Kentucky Reporter,* the pro-Clay (and internal improvements) paper in Lexington, toast #2 at the principal celebration in the city was given to "The improvements within the first Jubilee of American Independence—where can History show a parallel?" Toast #3 was then accorded to "The Statesmen and Soldiers of the Revolution," not specifically mentioning Washington by name. In a few other cases, though, toast #2 was: "the Republican form of Government" or "the Constitution of the United States."

Toast #3: Either "the Constitution of the United States," or "the President of the United States," though Adams was rarely mentioned by name. The *Richmond Enquirer* rubbed it in a few weeks later: "The papers from the east, west, north, and south, are pouring in upon us, bringing with them the public opinion. . . . [I]n none of the set toasts, if we remember right . . . has a warm approbatory remark been extended to the President. . . . the toasts laudatory of his conduct are, 'like angels' visits, few and far between.' "[56]

After the top three salutes, ceremonial toasts ranged widely, and typically elevated a local or state figure. General Lafayette was rated highly at some jubilee dinners, entirely forgotten at others. At a Cincinnati banquet, a medical doctor coupled Lafayette and Jefferson: "The sages of La Grange and Monticello—although in the yellow leaf of life, yet are freshly blooming in the heart of America, and green in the memory of every Patriot."[57] In Charleston, Lafayette's highest place was toast #5, at the dinner sponsored by "The Charleston Riflemen." (Andrew Jackson was right behind him at toast #6, Jefferson at #7.) Here Lafayette was remembered in the context of generational transition: "In youth our Fathers knew him; in old age their descendents have not forgotten his distinguished and chivalrous darings in the cause of Liberty." Once the toast was presented, the revelers sang "Hail to the Chief." At "The People's Dinner," also in Charleston, the French hero received toast #13, immediately after "freedom of the press," and in this instance he came several places ahead of General Jackson (#16), who nonetheless received an equal nine cheers—and this time it was the future president who elicited a round of "Hail to the Chief."[58]

Other memorable or unusual toasts (some wonderfully cynical) were given at jubilee dinners:

"The American Eagle—May her wings be tipped with gold, and her talons with hardened steel; may she perch high, and with an eye of scrutiny, watch the monarchs of the earth" (Lexington, Kentucky).

"The political miracle—that bright sun, which on the 4th of July 1776, had its rising in the WEST,—may it keep above the horizon, until it shall have shown on all nations" (Daniel Webster, at Faneuil Hall in Boston).

"The First Session of the 19th Congress. So much has been said *by* it that we will say but little *of* it" (public banquet near the Schuylkill Ferry, in Philadelphia, as printed in the *United States Gazette*).

"The Senate of the United States—As it *was*, not as it *is*" (volunteer toast in Lebanon, Ohio, as printed in the *Kentucky Reporter*).

"The State of Ohio—One of the youngest sisters of the American Republic. She has no rival in the spirit of enterprise, and holds the fourth rank in the career of knowledge, population, and the improvement of her domestic resources" (a dinner "in the vicinity of" Dayton, Ohio, published in the *Dayton Watchman*).

"*Faction.* Small men, like little dogs, bark much but seldom bite" (John Charlton, Nashville).

"The Press—When not tainted by venality, the greatest living source of light and liberty" (toast #18 in Petersburg, Virginia).

"John Randolph of Roanoke against John Q. Adams and Henry Clay—Lay on Macduff, and damn'd be he who first cries hold, enough" (Louis C. Bouldin, also in Petersburg).[59]

"Virginia and her noble contributions to the day we celebrate" (William Wirt, in Annapolis).

Lively praise of American womanhood issued forth, at once patriarchal in tone and designed to amuse:

"The Fair—Although formed to obey, their charms are such formidable weapons as always secures them the command" (toast #13 of the Cincinnati Hussars and City Guards).

"The American Fair—Their minds are nobler sure, their charms perchance as great. May the single be married, and the married be happy" (toast #24 at "The People's Dinner," Charleston).

"The American fair—may they possess such a knowledge of the soldiery of their country, as to discern the coward from the brave man; and possessing such knowledge, may they never place their affections on unworthy members of the community" (toast in Bethlehem, New York, reprinted in the *Albany Argus*).

It was a variously celebrated day of national jubilee, but it can be summed up well in the sentiment expressed in the *Ohio Oracle*. Americans were a people distracted by the clashing viewpoints and malevolent passions of their leaders, but their republic seemed to these same people more secure than ever before in its fifty-year history. The *Oracle* was attempting to live up to its name by predicting a better future: of the several men who had vied for the presidency in 1824, it asserted, all were equally devoted to "the great principles of rational liberty." The federal Constitution, which had produced the political conditions of both election year 1824 and the jubilee year 1826, warranted as deep a respect as ever. "No government upon the earth is so safe as ours," the paper maintained, because "no other people are so well informed." The jubilee had served to encourage a greater diffusion of knowledge about the fundamental principles of the American republic, and in doing so promised to prolong the Revolutionary spirit and nourish peace.[60]

CHAPTER ELEVEN

Adams and Jefferson Have the Last Word

D URING THE 1824 presidential campaign, eighty-eight-year-old John Adams and eighty-year-old Thomas Jefferson inadvertently found themselves caught up in historical controversy. In 1803, just two years after his involuntary retirement from politics began, Adams had an exchange of letters with a relative named William Cunningham, the gist of which was the ex-president's intemperate denunciation of his popular successor as a conniving, disingenuous political operative. With some presence of mind, at least, Adams had insisted that Cunningham not print his comments about Jefferson until after Adams's death. But it was Cunningham who died first; he took his own life in May 1823. His son, a Jackson enthusiast, promptly published the correspondence in order to embarrass the Adams family and hopefully to deny John Quincy Adams the presidency.

The book was pure character assassination. Claiming a "deep solicitude for the welfare of our republic," the younger Cunningham introduced the malicious volume by declaring that the despotic Adams should have retired from politics at the end of the Revolution. As to Adams's distaste for Jefferson, readers would glean from the letters "that Mr. Adams' imagination was incessantly disturbed by the grisly goblin of Democracy," to the point of concocting a "herculean project" to sink his successor's reputation.[1]

Post-Revolutionary politics was the sort that had bred much distrust. Some of its most forceful practitioners were long-lived. Around the same time as Cunningham's book appeared, a common enemy of the second and third presidents, Timothy Pickering, delivered a Fourth of July oration in his hometown of Salem, Massachusetts. In it, he perversely proclaimed that Jefferson had had no original conceptions when he undertook to draft the Declaration. Pickering based his conclusions in part, he said, on the opinion of John Adams, who, in a recent communication, had enlarged his own role in the preparation of that nation-founding document, while diminishing Jefferson's.

This kind of sinister manipulation of language was typical of Pickering. In 1795, he had creatively translated a letter from the French to convince George Washington that his secretary of state, Edmund Randolph, was passing state secrets. It was pure political deception. Then, as Adams's secretary of state, Pickering refused to carry out the president's policy, forcing Adams to remove him in 1800. Later, in the middle of Jefferson's two terms, the quarrelsome Federalist initiated a desperate move to separate New York and New England from the Union. As a member of Congress during the War of 1812, he sympathized with Great Britain. When left to his own devices, Timothy Pickering was downright belligerent. Making trouble for Adams and Jefferson was nothing new for him.[2]

In 1823, however, the two old political warriors were not to be trapped by their former difficulties. Jefferson repelled Pickering's assault, at least in his own mind, by conferring with James Madison, and quietly insisting that his own recollection of the operations of the committee that he and Adams had served on together in preparing the Declaration was the more reliable. He had preserved "written notes," he said, "taken by myself at the moment and on the spot." Jefferson also insisted that the eventual publication of these notes would settle any controversy over how much he had contributed to the honored document. As to the question of originality, he easily acknowledged that his Declaration was never intended to be purely original, and yet he was also certain that he "turned to neither book or pamphlet while writing it." He added, "This however I will say for Mr. Adams, that he supported the Declaration with zeal and ability, fighting fearlessly for every word of it."[3]

Jefferson did not reopen the Pickering business in his correspondence with Adams. As to the late William Cunningham's revelations, however, a direct approach seemed in order. He composed a letter that began with a sigh—crippled wrists and fingers reminding him that their common concern was "how to get rid of our heavy hours until the friendly hand of death shall rid us of all at once." Jefferson then proceeded to alert Adams that Cunningham's volume, though not yet available in the South, was being excerpted in various newspapers, divulging its design to "draw a curtain of separation between you and myself." But, he assured, these "dark hints and mysterious innuendoes" would fail to have effect.

Even at this stage of retirement, Jefferson could still become quite agitated in contemplating how posterity would evaluate his political legacy, but he was about to show unusual generosity on a political subject here. "The circumstances of the times," he wrote, "placed us in a state of apparent opposition, which some might suppose to be personal also." In the most fundamental sense, Jefferson stated emphatically, it was not personal. Yes, they had each required the passage of time to see the passions of the past dissipate. Yes, they had once been responsive to others who had dressed up "hideous phantoms of their own creation . . . when we were off our guard." But, speaking for both, Jefferson proclaimed that true sight had been restored to them. "It would be strange indeed," he wrote Adams, "if, at our years, we were to go back to hunt up imaginary, or forgotten facts, to disturb the repose of affections so sweetening to the evening of our lives."[4]

Adams knew his favorite correspondent well enough to have expected Jefferson to pronounce on this matter. He had prepared his family for it, with greater confidence, one might suppose, than his protective loved ones were willing to muster. "There is no secrets [*sic*] between Mr. Jefferson and me," he had contended when the letter was announced, and urged someone to read it to him. "When it was done," Adams explained in his reply to Jefferson, "it was followed by an universal exclamation, The best letter that ever was written . . . , how generous! how noble! how magnanimous!"[5]

All of this is especially remarkable because Adams and Jefferson could just as easily have grown old bearing grudges. They had stopped talking to one another when the first was unseated by the second in the election of 1800. But in 1812 their mutual friend, the renowned Philadelphia physician and educator Benjamin Rush, after several failures, brought the two back together. A marvelous exchange of letters ensued, fourteen years' worth, for which history is much the richer. Rush had had a dream, he told Adams, in which the second and third presidents had renewed their old friendship. It was a dream, he most prophetically reported, in which they *"sunk into the grave nearly at the same time."* Be it a dream or a clever invention, Dr. Rush unwittingly contributed to the most singular curiosity of 1826.[6]

This good-hearted Pennsylvanian was two years younger than Jefferson, ten years younger than Adams, and himself a signer of the Declaration of Independence. But he sank into his own grave years before them, in the spring of 1813. He did not live to see the full measure of his prediction come true. But he lived long enough to see his friendly conspiracy succeed: Adams and Jefferson were on intimate terms again. When Rush died, Jefferson wrote sensitively to Adams of their late friend's benevolence and genius. Counting the number of signers left—only two that Jefferson knew of besides themselves—the Virginian sighed, "We too must go; and that ere long."[7]

In the correspondence of their late years, Jefferson affectingly proclaimed his nostalgia for the Revolution. He was pleased to recall the two of them as "fellow laborers in the same cause," self-government, who "rode through the storm with heart and hand, and made a happy port." As metaphoric mariners, they had frequently left their separate ports, where they might otherwise have enjoyed a happy domesticity, for the bustle of politics, and so they could speak yet of life as a voyage. Jefferson said in 1816: "My temperament is sanguine. I steer my bark with Hope in the head, leaving Fear astern." He had known great grief, he said, "some terrible convulsions" on that ocean, but he would not mind experiencing it all over again. For, as he had elsewhere written, the greater part of life was sunshine. The dauntless, whimsical Adams came aboard: "I admire your Navigation and should like to sail with you. . . . Hope with her gay Ensigns displayed at the Prow; fear with her Hobgoblins behind the Stern. Hope springs eternal," he quoted from Alexander Pope's *Essay on Man*, "and Hope is all that endures." Ten years from death, but unmistakably losing his eyesight, Adams was willing to play along, though ultimately he resisted his friend's fantasy. He preferred the thought of a happy future state, he said, to the imaginary prospect of living all over again.[8]

Late in 1825, John Adams received a visit at home from Jefferson's granddaughter, twenty-eight-year-old Ellen Wayles Randolph Coolidge, who had married a Boston businessman at Monticello in May of that year, and moved north.[9] Adams wrote of their conversation. Ellen had recounted for him how her grandfather continued to fancy that life was worth living over again. Hearing this, Adams revived the argument of 1816. "I had rather go forward and meet my destiny," he reminded Jefferson.[10]

Earlier in 1825 Adams had ruminated about past and future in a single letter. The first sentiment exulted over a time of political harmony: "I look back with rapture to those golden days when Virginia and Massachusetts lived and acted together like a band of brothers." The second sentiment ended the letter: "We shall meet again, so wishes and so believes your friend." Another signed off, "Your friend to all eternity." Jefferson tried to convince Adams one last time, in December 1825, that the pleasures of their earlier years outweighed the pain: "Why not taste them again, fat and lean together." It was as if this running debate was meant to serve as a distraction, to temper reports on the ailments and infirmities that neither could resist presenting, letter after letter, as the months and years advanced.[11]

Around the same time, a piece of Jefferson's past traveled as freight from Monticello to Boston. His granddaughter Ellen, still in the process of adapting to life in New England, was saddened by the loss of letters, books, and childhood memories that had been destroyed when the vessel transporting them sank. Slave John Hemings, a skilled woodworker, had painstakingly fashioned Ellen a writing desk, now at the bottom of the Atlantic. To compensate in part, Jefferson found a "substitute" for the one-of-a-kind desk, something that he supposed might before long acquire a "superstitious value"; it was the portable writing table, manufactured to his own specifications by a Philadelphia cabinetmaker in May 1776, on which he had written the Declaration of Independence. He described it to Ellen as "plain, neat, convenient."[12] It arrived safely.

In January 1826, Adams composed a letter of introduction for the use of Josiah Quincy, son and namesake of the Boston mayor, who was traveling south and planned to visit Monticello. By now his teeth were nearly gone, and while his hearing remained, his eyesight was poor and he walked with great difficulty.[13] "I am certainly very near the end of my life," Adams wrote Jefferson in the one-paragraph note. "I am far from trifling with the idea of Death which is a great and solemn event. But I contemplate it without terror or dismay, 'aut transit, aut finit [either it is a transformation, or it is the end].' " It was a letter Jefferson could not have seen, as the younger Quincy did not proceed past Washington on his trip.[14]

Jefferson undertook the same task, with better results. In March, he wrote out a letter of introduction to Adams on behalf of his grandson and namesake, Thomas Jefferson Randolph, who delivered it by hand. "Like other young people," Jefferson explained of the Boston-bound Randolph, "he wishes to be able, in the winter nights of old age, to recount to those around him what he has heard and learnt of the Heroic age preceding his birth, and which of the Argonauts particularly he was in time to have seen. . . . Theirs are the Halcyon calms succeeding the storm which our Argosy had so stoutly weathered." Another nautical metaphor, followed by a courtly request: "Gratify his ambition then by recieving [sic] his best bow." This prompted the final communication, Adams's report on the meeting: the new Bostonian Ellen Coolidge had joined her brother Jefferson, impressing the feeble patriarch with the quality of their conversation. Adams chose to conclude his brief letter, however, with a head-shaking observation on the state of politics in 1826: "perpetual chicanery and rather more personal abuse than there used to be." In particular Adams seemed offended by the nastiness shown toward his son by unpredictable Southerners with reputations as duelists, John Randolph and George McDuffie: "Mr. McDuffie seems to be swallowed up in chivalry. . . . Our American Chivalry is the worst in the World. It has no Laws, no bounds, no definitions; it seems to be all a Caprice." To the end, John Adams retained his dynamically caustic air.[15]

Newspapers all across America had announced in the early months of 1826 that Thomas Jefferson, hopelessly in debt, was struggling to preserve the well-ordered dreamworld of Monticello, his mountaintop plantation. Supporters from various parts of the country editorialized that the patriot-sage should not have to despair over such mundane matters in his last days. He had always put his country's interest above his own; his country should now take care of him. In March, as the legislature of Virginia contemplated whether to aid the embarrassed ex-president, the *United States Telegraph*, for one, urged that citizens make donations "without information from whom or from whence it comes." The newspaper lamented: "Our history should not be stained with the foul reproach of suffering the gray hairs of so distinguished a public benefactor to descend in sorrow to the grave."[16] Sensing the mood, Jefferson's relatives quietly advanced a plan to collect from "his Country" the $130,000 that he needed to pay off his debts, with particular attention to preventing "the obligation of selling the favorite Montic[e]llo." These were the words of a favorite nephew's widow, who instructed her son, living in Baltimore, to act with dispatch: "I cannot have the Idea that the grave yard of almost all my family should be sold . . . it should be kept as a grave yard for every descendant of the Jefferson race."[17]

Jefferson had lived well and on credit. He had lost income over the years in part by entrusting the management of his estate to others while he held national office. He had put off the inevitable too long. Relying on appreciative citizens to come to his aid was an uncertain proposition, so in order to raise funds he decided to offer up most of his properties in central Virginia by means of a lottery. At first, he gave thought only to parting with some lands of lesser value. When his grandson and executor, Thomas Jefferson Randolph, proposed including Monticello itself in the dispersal, "Mr. Jefferson turned quite white & set for some time silent."[18] The shock forced him to embrace a more comprehensive lottery, to include choice lands—but not Monticello. He came to consider the success of this dire plan, as he wrote a Virginia friend, "almost a question of life and death." Jefferson, who generally disapproved of gambling, undertook a careful review of the history of lotteries; he needed—for himself, for a mindful public, for posterity—to justify its use as a "salutary instrument." Still he acknowledged to his grandson, amid publicity of his financial affairs in February, that his spirits were low. His "mortification" over this "prostration of fortune," he said, was deepened by the knowledge that his devoted daughter Martha, the tireless mother of eleven, who was now fifty-three, would suffer. After several anxious weeks, the lottery bill passed, permitting Jefferson to hold on to a faint hope of financial rescue. Seriously impaired by chronic diarrhea that was slowly sapping his strength, he did not know that the lottery was destined to fall short of raising the necessary funds to save Monticello.[19]

In March, Jefferson composed his last will. He emancipated three of his most favored slaves immediately upon his death and provided for the apprenticeship of the two youngest sons of the house servant now presumed to have been his concubine, Sally Hemings. They would be freed upon reaching the age of twenty-one. To the younger children of his surviving daughter, Martha Jefferson Randolph, Jefferson bequeathed gold watches. In April, Martha wrote her daughter Ellen Coolidge that her grandpapa was expecting his end: "He said he had lived too long, that his death would be an advantage to the family." (Ellen would have received this letter just about the time of her visit with her brother to John Adams.) Yet in May, Jefferson must have rallied some, for he wrote to James Madison that he was feeling better than he had the year before and complained only of the "unceasing pain and peevishness" that a continued occupation with letter writing was inducing. Madison recommended that he shorten his replies to the many well-wishers who wrote him.[20]

During the second half of June, Jefferson took a decisive turn for the worse. He penned a note asking for his doctor, Robley Dunglison, a twenty-eight-year-old Englishman who taught medicine at the new University of Virginia. Dr. Dunglison came immediately and stayed at Monticello during his patient's final days. Also, Jefferson Randolph, back from Boston, was by his grandfather's side at most times. According to both witnesses, the dying man's mind remained clear, and he expressed no regrets about the "journey" that impended, but as the month of June disappeared, he found himself returning in his thoughts to the defining era of his life—the Revolution. "I am like an old watch," he said without protest, "with a pinion worn out here, and a wheel there, until it can go no longer." Jefferson Randolph marveled at his grandfather's composure as he visited with each of his other grandchildren for the last time, relaying practical advice and urging them all to pursue virtuous lives.[21]

The doctor administered the opiate laudanum, for pain, every day. On Sunday, July 2, his patient consumed a bit of rice, soup, tea, and brandy. Nothing seemed right for his digestion. On Monday, July 3, after refusing more laudanum, Jefferson awoke from a long bout of agitated sleep, during which he went through the motions of writing urgent letters. He was speaking deliriously of the Committee of Safety, which had been in place in 1775–76 to protect against the British onslaught. "Warn the Committee to be on the alert," he exhorted the imaginary people who were present in his mind. On the night of the third, according to another who attended him (Nicholas P. Trist, husband of a granddaughter, Virginia Randolph Trist), Jefferson whispered, "This is the Fourth?" The clock beside his bed had not struck twelve, and Trist remained silent rather than answer in the negative, until Jefferson asked a second time, at which point the young man deceived the dying man with an affirmative reply. "Ah," he recorded Jefferson's words. "Just as I wished."[22]

Dr. Dunglison registered this moment differently, although it is possible that there was more than one such moment in which Jefferson expressed an urgent consciousness of the approaching day of national jubilee. In an independent record of the dying man's concerns, Dunglison wrote that at 7:00 p.m. on the third, his patient, in a "husky and indistinct" voice, appealed to him: "Is it the Fourth?" to which the doctor replied: "It soon will be." At any event, among Trist, Dunglison, and grandson Randolph, the scene is described with similar facts and similar emotion.[23]

The most intriguing account remains that of Thomas Jefferson Randolph. He recalled that his grandfather slept through the midnight hour, regaining consciousness at 4:00 a.m. on July 4th, when, in full possession of his faculties, he called to his servants, "with a strong and clear voice, perfectly conscious of his wants." This was the last Thomas Jefferson spoke.

Importantly, then, while Jefferson's "last words" have come down in history as the question "Is it the Fourth?" his actual last words, apparently unrecorded, were those of a man long in the habit of issuing commands. They were words spoken to a slave, and probably undramatic. His body servant Burwell, who was to be freed under terms of Jefferson's will, had generally been close at hand during his master's final illness. Most likely he was there to receive the "strong and clear" words. After this, at 10:00 a.m., and again at 11:00, the master of Monticello "fixed his eyes intently" on his grandson and namesake, unable to utter a word. His pulse "barely perceptible," or, as his doctor put it, "his circulation . . . languid," Thomas Jefferson then lost consciousness, breathing his last at fifty minutes past noon.[24]

James Madison had prepared for the news upon receipt of Dr. Dunglison's "worst apprehensions" three days earlier, a letter stating that Jefferson's longtime gastrointestinal complaint had returned, while his "power of restoration" was fast fading. The fourth president received official word of Jefferson's death from Nicholas Trist (most likely delivered by private channels on July 5). Madison, who first met Jefferson in the autumn of 1776 and was destined to outlive his dear friend by a full decade, replied to Trist that there was consolation to be had, "by the assurance that he lives and will live in the memory and gratitude of the wise and good." The two statesmen had enjoyed a half-century of mutual devotion and trust, as Madison put it, "without interruption or diminution . . . in a single instance." In a letter to Madison on February 17, 1826, in which he went on at length about his indebtedness, Jefferson had prepared for the end: "And if I remove beyond the reach of attentions to the University, or beyond the bourne of life itself, as I soon must, it is a comfort to leave that institution under your care. . . . It has also been a great solace to me, to believe that you are engaged in vindicating to posterity the course we have pursued for preserving to them, *in all their purity,* the blessings of self-government." Jefferson closed this particular letter with an appeal to his staunch friend to protect his reputation from the political enemies who remained: "To myself you have been a pillar of support through life. Take care of me when dead."[25]

Andrew Jackson learned of Jefferson's approaching death earlier than most. He received a letter dated July 1 from Monticello, penned by the visiting Henry Lee, a fawning Jackson partisan who was the son of Revolutionary War hero "Light Horse Harry" Lee. Quoting Dr. Dunglison, Lee explained that the patriarch was "confined to his bed with a severe Dysentary, which cannot but place so old a patient in great danger." The dying man had expressed his willingness to see Lee, who indicated to Jackson that he was "surprised at the energy of his grasp and the alacrity of his conversation." Lee did not mention what was discussed other than that Jefferson saw death "as an event rather unpleasant than terrible—like a traveller expressing his apprehension of being caught in a rain." Still, the overeager partisan, seeking Jackson's approval, went on to assert that Jefferson's family confirmed for him that Jefferson "holds in contempt and abhorrence" the Adams Administration. Who might have hinted at such sentiments is not clear; the only person Lee mentioned by name was Martha Jefferson Randolph, as one who "hovers round his bed with grief at her heart."[26]

President John Quincy Adams learned of Thomas Jefferson's death on Thursday the sixth, three days before he knew that his own father had passed on. His secretary of war, James Barbour, delivered the news. On the seventh, newspapers in the nation's capital and in neighboring Baltimore ran "the melancholy intelligence" framed in black. Letters from Jefferson's neighborhood, printed in Washington on the eighth, immediately reckoned on a further coincidence, that the hour of his demise was the same hour of the day that the Declaration of Independence was read in Congress fifty years earlier. The *Richmond Whig* even reported that the Declaration was in the process of being read aloud in Charlottesville, as Jefferson expired just a few miles from the scene.[27]

On July 7, President Adams received Henry Lee, who described the state of Jefferson's health during his recent visit. The next day, according to his diary, Adams turned his attention to Quincy, Massachusetts, having received letters that gave him reason to suspect another death: his niece had written five days before, to advise him that "my father's end was approaching," and that the doctor was predicting that he could not survive two weeks, and perhaps not even two days. The president's brother Thomas had written on the morning of the Fourth itself, "announcing that, in the opinion of those who surrounded my father's couch, he was rapidly sinking; that they were sending an express for my son in Boston, who might perhaps arrive in time to receive his last breath." The president left for Boston on Sunday the ninth, and learned that day, before he had reached Baltimore, that he was already too late. He immediately noted the "visible and palpable marks of Divine favor," in the coincidence of the two ex-presidents' deaths on the day of national jubilee.[28]

Jefferson's grave was dug by his gardener Wormley, who, like the freed Burwell, was related to the biracial Hemings family. The Sage was quietly buried in the cemetery atop Monticello on a rainy July 5, amid those loved ones whose loss he had endured in his own lifetime. No advance notice of the time of the burial was given to the public, and yet neighbors from below the mountain streamed in to pay tribute. Reportedly, among those eyeing the fresh grave was a seventeen-year-old student from the university named Edgar Allan Poe.[29] A small monument, a granite obelisk of Jefferson's own design, was produced by builders at the university he had founded, and later placed above his remains.[30]

As the U.S. warship *John Adams* plied the waters of the Caribbean in search of pirates during 1826,[31] the original had remained at his home in Quincy. On June 30 Mayor Josiah Quincy and his wife Eliza paid him a visit. Still lucid, Adams conversed about the first American railroad, a small length of track then under construction nearby to carry granite to the Bunker Hill Monument. He wished to see it finished, he said, adding, "What wonderful improvements those will see in this country, who live fifty years hence! But I am thankful I have seen those which have taken place during the last fifty!" He went on to speak of the approaching jubilee, expressing the hope that his strength would be sufficient for him to attend Mayor Quincy's oration in Boston.[32]

The following day, Adams was lifted to his carriage for a return visit to the mayor's ("in opposition to the entreaties of his family"), but whether he left his room again after that day is not known. He had been too weak to write for some time and could barely see. His mental faculties, however, were unimpaired. A story later repeated by New York politician William Henry Seward quoted a conversation Daniel Webster was meant to have had with Adams on the day before his death, when the mentally agile patriarch made a wry reference to his physical decrepitude: "Mr. Webster said to the old statesman, 'How do you do, this morning, Mr. Adams?' 'Not very well,' he replied; 'I am living in a very old house, Mr. Webster, and, from all that I can learn, the landlord does not intend to repair.' " On the second Adams had evidenced a bad cough and on the night of the third, as Dr. Holbrook, who attended him, told his son the president, he "suffered much."[33]

On the morning of July 4, the last day of his life, John Adams woke hearing a bell ringing and cannon firing. A servant asked him if he knew what day it was, and he was said to have replied: "O yes, it is the glorious Fourth of July—God bless it—God bless you all." Later that morning, the orator of the day in Quincy, Reverend John Whitney, found Adams seated in a large armchair and requested a "sentiment" from him to be conveyed to the public on this festive occasion. "I will give it to you," the old man replied. "Independence forever." A granddaughter, Mrs. Susan B. Clark, the daughter of John Quincy Adams's brother Charles, next asked her grandfather if he had anything to add to the toast, and he reportedly said, "Not a syllable."[34]

A reputable writer recorded these historic events. He was Judge William Cranch (1769–1855), a Harvard classmate of John Quincy Adams. Cranch was appointed Chief Justice of the District Court of Washington, D.C., by President Jefferson in 1805, a position he would continue to hold until his death fifty years later. He wrote a sensitive biography of Adams in the months following the events, while those present at the dying man's bedside remained accessible. So, Adams's recorded answer to the last question—"Not a syllable"—suggests that an effort was being made to keep track of the old Revolutionary's precise wording on this day of jubilee.

Continuing his narrative, Cranch advanced the legend further:

> This passed an hour or two only before his dissolution. In the course of the day he said, "It is a great and good day." And that his thoughts were dwelling on the scenes of 1776, is evident from the last words he uttered, which were "Jefferson survives." But alas! at that very moment, the spirit of Jefferson had already flown.[35]

"Jefferson survives." Who heard these "last words"? Did Susan Clark, the granddaughter who had been at the old man's side earlier in the day? The sixth president's eldest son, twenty-five-year-old George Washington Adams, did not. He had been urgently summoned from Boston, and had returned, as he wrote to his father, "in time to see him but not to hear him speak."[36]

As for John Quincy Adams himself, the president only arrived in the town of Quincy on the seventeenth, after a weeklong journey, and spent that night at Mayor Josiah Quincy's home. At first, all were reluctant to dwell on the details of the patriarch's dying process. But then the president opened a frank discussion by alluding to his father's passing more in terms of history than private anguish. He marveled at the astronomical odds of the two founders' coincidental departures, which he termed "unparalleled in the history of the world." He reminisced about the first time he heard the Declaration read. It was a day on which he had taken ill. His mother kept him away from the "rejoicings on the Common—which I thought as great a misfortune as could befall me."[37]

The power of history was always very much alive in the restless mind of John Quincy Adams, especially now as he sat with his grieving family. It was on July 21 that he entered in his diary that his father had spoken the words "Thomas Jefferson survives" at about 1:00 p.m. on the Fourth. But, the diary entry goes on to contradict critically, "the last word was indistinctly and imperfectly uttered. He spoke no more." At approximately the same hour that Jefferson departed life, then, John Adams had indeed spoken the name "Thomas Jefferson."[38] But what word or words might have followed?

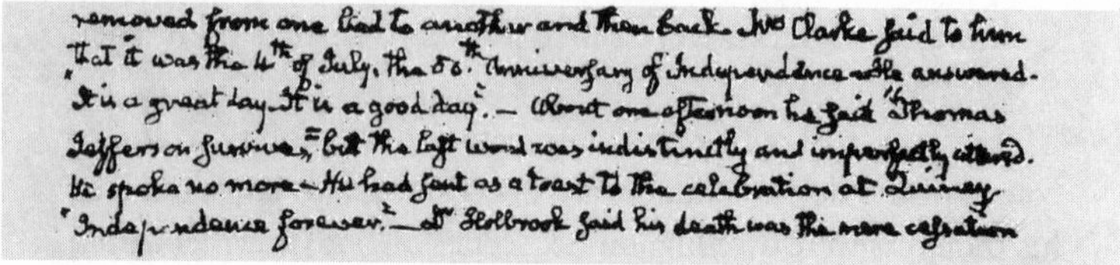
removed from one bed to another and then back. Mrs Clarke said to him
that it was the 4th of July, the 50th Anniversary of Independence—He answered.
"It is a great day. It is a good day."— About one afternoon he said "Thomas
Jefferson survives," but the last word was indistinctly and imperfectly uttered.
He spoke no more—He had sent as a toast to the celebration at Quincy
"Independence forever."—Dr Holbrook said his death was the mere cessation

Fig. 16. "Jefferson survives," John Adams's reputed last words, as recorded in the diary of his son. *(Courtesy, Massachusetts Historical Society.)*

In fact, the one person plainly identified as having been present at this moment was Louisa Smith, the never-married, fifty-three-year-old niece of Abigail Adams. Substantiation is provided by the unnamed editor of the 1861 memoir of Mayor Quincy's wife, Eliza, who died in 1850. In a footnote, he indicates having been told personally of the circumstances of Adams's last words: "Louisa Smith, the niece and adopted daughter of Mrs. Abigail Adams, who attended Mr. Adams on that day, informed the Editor, that the last words he distinctly spoke was the name 'Thomas Jefferson.' The rest of the sentence he uttered was so inarticulate, that she could not catch the meaning. This occurred at one o'clock—a few moments after Mr. Jefferson had died." But she does not explain what happened after, how "Jefferson survives" became the standard translation.[39]

It is obvious why the ironic construction "Jefferson survives" would be irresistible to patriotic mythmakers, but this is not at all the sort of thing that the earnest Adamses would manufacture and disseminate themselves. By the time Judge Cranch's 1827 biography was published, others had already made the "inarticulate" word or words distinct, so that they could not easily be taken back. We must do our best to trace the process by which such agreeable "last words" were used to amplify the already perfect deaths of Adams and Jefferson.

Of the joint eulogies read and published over the next months, many recounted the morning interview with Reverend Whitney and Adams's celebrated words, "Independence forever!" Some were faithful in their retelling while others embellished. The recent chaplain of the Senate, William Staughton, offered a sermon in the Capitol on July 16, while President Adams was still en route to Quincy. Staughton did the best he could at this early stage of legend-building: "Mr. Jefferson," he said, "expressed his wish to live until the day of Jubilee; his desire was granted him. Mr. Adams, on hearing the voice of the cannon, and being informed that it announced the Jubilee of our Independence, said, 'O IT IS A GREAT, A GLORIOUS DAY'; and spake no more."[40] Samuel Smith pronounced on July 20, in Baltimore: "The last words of the venerable Adams were '*Independence forever.*' The last words of our beloved Jefferson, (and let not his country forget them,) were, '*I resign my Soul to my God, and My daughter to my country!* and I humbly hope that this country will watch over and guard her, aid and cherish her.' "[41] William Thornton, speaking in Alexandria, Virginia, on August 10, stated of Adams: "When the measure of his days was full—he heard the trumpet sound the Jubilee of Freedom—and died with 'Independence forever,' quivering on his lips."[42]

It appears that the first eulogist to have popularized "Jefferson survives" as Adams's definitive last words was Congressman Edward Everett, closely followed by Joseph Sprague, postmaster of Salem, Massachusetts. In addition to the eulogists' specific phrasing, their personal and political relationships with Adams and Jefferson are worth exploring further, as we test the authority of Adams's last words.

Everett noted in his oration of August 1:

Mr. Adams' mind had also wandered back . . . and found rest on the thought of Independence. When the discharges of artillery proclaimed the triumphant anniversary, he pronounced it "a great and good day." The thrilling word of Independence . . . was now among the last that dwelt on his quivering lips; and when, toward the hour of noon, he felt his noble heart growing cold within him, the last emotion which warmed it was, that "Jefferson still survives." But he survives not; he is gone. Ye are gone together![43]

Sprague spoke in nearby Salem on August 10:

The Independence of his country was the ruling passion of Mr. Adams, and "he felt his ruling passion strong in death." His last sentiment to his country was "INDEPENDENCE FOR-EVER." And his last words show that when he was sensible that the scene was closing, his thoughts still lingered on this subject— "JEFFERSON SURVIVES." This is unquestionably the translation of this sentence: "I am going—but Jefferson, he who acted with me on the great day of our country's deliverance, outlives me." Heaven, however, had otherwise ordered it. . . .[44]

A few weeks earlier, Everett had given a jubilee oration in Cambridge in which he mentioned both Adams and Jefferson by name— the first as the "venerable survivor in our neighborhood," the second, in urging his financial relief, as the sage "who can show the original draft of the Declaration of Independence . . . in his own handwriting." It was, in general, a filial address, because, said Everett, "we owe it to our fathers and to our children" to mark each return of the Fourth of July and remember the year of America's birth as "an auspicious era."[45]

Everett was Boston-born and European-educated. The patriot even met Lord Byron in London after sending him one of his own poems, and while in Paris became close to Lafayette. He was a nationalist, and in the patriarchs' later years enjoyed good relations with both Adamses and with Jefferson.[46] While, as a Massachusetts congressman, Everett clearly gravitated to the politics of John Quincy Adams in 1826, he had also been Jefferson's recent correspondent on matters of shared intellectual interest. Sending the Virginian a Greek grammar in 1823, Everett received a warm reply on the subject of oratorical styles. Jefferson urged him to take caution in appropriating too much from classical models: "By analyzing too minutely," he observed, "we often reduce our subject to atoms, of which the mind loses its hold. . . . I readily sacrifice the niceties of syntax to euphony and strength." Jefferson's point, relevant in this case of "last words," was that the best writing and oratory was achieved by "boldly neglecting" grammatical purism, in favor of popular effect.[47]

The other New Englander who refused to ratify his section's general prejudice, who found much to admire in Jefferson, was Postmaster

Sprague. Indeed, no one brought quite the same flourish as Sprague to his public effort to establish Adams's last words as a commendation of Jefferson. "Unquestionably the translation," Sprague insisted in his modified version of "Jefferson survives."

Surely no crime was committed. Everett, if he took Jefferson's 1823 letter to heart, was keen on adding "euphony and strength" to his oratory when he settled on "Jefferson still survives." Sprague may not be a culprit any more than a number of others among his Romantic contemporaries. He, too, looked for effect, observing that Jefferson had died at the very hour that Congress had adopted his Declaration fifty years before. It is Sprague's political pedigree that is of special interest. For in the troubled 1810s, while Everett was earning a Ph.D. abroad, Sprague was an outspoken Jeffersonian living in the heart of Adams territory.

Born Joseph Sprague Stearns, he was an intimate of John Quincy Adams, writing the president familiarly in June 1826 with regard to their shared sympathies about state politics, while offering to make Henry Clay feel welcome if he should visit New England.[48] In 1810 and 1813, however, he gave Fourth of July orations in Salem that mentioned John Adams briefly or not at all, while loudly proclaiming Jefferson's achievements. In the 1810 address, given two years before Adams and Jefferson had reconciled through the mail, Sprague took particular aim at those embittered New England Federalists (Salem was also the home of arch-Federalist Timothy Pickering) who had taunted and defamed Jefferson during his just concluded presidency: "Calumny with her hundred tongues," he railed, "had attributed to him the blackest actions of which man is capable, and detraction had opened her flood-gates to overwhelm him." But the worthy Jefferson, he went on, rose and surpassed even "the fondest expectations of his friends."[49]

A curious aspect of Sprague's character is the fact that he twice changed his own name by an act of the legislature. The first time was in 1800, when he changed it from Stearns to Sprague, abandoning his physician-father's surname in favor of that of his maternal grandfather, "having always lived with my grandfather, Joseph Sprague"; the second time, in 1809, he simply added the middle initial "E."[50]

What are we then to conclude? Perhaps the longtime political supporters of John Adams who eulogized the second president were still so hostile that they refused to have Adams give any credit to Jefferson, even in death. This would explain why it was only those who had access to the Adams household but no animus toward the Virginian who propagated "Jefferson survives." And if this is the case, was the household in Quincy, though uncertain of its accuracy, somehow complicit in disseminating the narrative as fact? Were it not for the accepted sobriety of Congressman Everett and Judge Cranch, it might well appear that the enthusiastic partisan Sprague, who intentionally mixed up his own public identity, was once again acting from a personal motive in stealthily passing on to posterity the decidedly captivating "Jefferson survives." Was it, then, ultimately, the Romantic impulse that made the "maybe" of Adams's utterance something more, to bring forth this desirable phrase?

Indeed, beyond the Everett and Sprague eulogies, Judge Cranch's 1827 biography seems to have been the only prominent reference to "Jefferson survives" in the years immediately following the jubilee. Within a month after news of the near simultaneous deaths reached him in Alexandria, Virginia, Cranch wrote John Quincy Adams: "Shall we not now say that the finger of God has pointed to Adams & Jefferson?" It is likely, but hard to say for certain, that in doing his research the judge had felt the need to consult both Everett's and Sprague's texts. He wrote President Adams a second time in August, specifically requesting published copies of other Boston-area eulogies "as soon as published," and can be presumed to have had an interest in all. He stated in his letter that he desired as much information as the president could provide of his father, and to refer him to "any accessible sources . . . which may assist me in doing justice to a character I so much venerate."

His connection to the Adamses was direct. Cranch was Abigail Adams's nephew and an old Federalist. He was once present at a gathering in the company of John Adams, when the elder statesman had said: "It was the finger of God that pointed to Washington." It was the memory of this statement that had led the Adams biographer to attribute the finger of God to Adams and Jefferson: "Were they not both equally his care? both led on by the same heavenly impulse? both rewarded by the same manifestation of divine approbation?" Like Everett, though for different reasons, he held Jefferson in a certain esteem: Jefferson had set partisan politics aside when he elevated

Cranch on the bench at a time when Federalist jurists were quite vocal in their opposition to his administration.[51]

If we look closely at the language he uses, even Sprague knows that he is dealing with something that is muddied—a dying man's lingering thoughts. The verb "to linger" at this time meant principally "to remain long in languor and pain," and "to hesitate."[52] The word itself connotes uncertainty, so that when Sprague says of Adams, "his last words show . . . his thoughts still lingered" on the subject of the Revolution, he is not saying as explicitly as he could have that "Jefferson survives," the words that come down to us today, were words that Adams plainly uttered—even when Sprague "unquestionably" defends their meaning. By offering a "translation" of those words, he is encumbered; he in essence acknowledges to us that he is aiming for his words to achieve their Romantic effect.

The most credible authority to have made a record of Adams's final hours was his eldest son, the unceremoniously explicit John Quincy Adams, whose diary entry emphasizes the indistinctness of his father's last words. They might have been the garbled beginnings of a sentence, as in "Thomas Jefferson surmised . . ." or "Thomas Jefferson said . . ." or even something delirious. We will never know.

Over the years, as the politics which once separated Adams and Jefferson lost its emotional potency, "Jefferson survives" became widely accepted. Henry S. Randall's 1858 three-volume *Life of Thomas Jefferson* opened with the epigraph, " 'Thomas Jefferson still survives!'—the Last Words of John Adams." Boston-area author John T. Morse wrote in his 1884 biography, *John Adams:* "Before he died nearly all his old animosities had entirely disappeared, or had lost their virulence. . . . The familiar story goes that his last words were, 'Thomas Jefferson survives.' " The "familiar story" was by now part of the historical record.[53]

After all was said and done, John Adams died at half past five o'clock on the afternoon of July 4th. His grandson George Washington Adams supposed a connection to the "two days of suffering occasioned by an accumulation of phlegm in the throat which he was too weak to throw off." The ex-president was buried three days later, at a funeral service arranged by Mayor Quincy; the guns of an artillery corps fired throughout. Among the pallbearers were the president of

Harvard, the governor of Massachusetts, and Associate Justice of the Supreme Court Joseph Story. Despite his advanced age, Adams's death was momentously felt.[54]

IT IS IMPORTANT to bear in mind that in 1826 the Adams-Jefferson rift was still recent history, easily resurrected in newspaper stories and political conversations. Americans were zealous and opinionated, just as they were when these two larger-than-life patriots vied on the national stage. Indeed, their names had never ceased to provoke comment. Crusty John Adams was hard to warm up to, and no one held a neutral opinion on the subject of Thomas Jefferson either. Households were sometimes divided.

Take that of Attorney General William Wirt, who was briefly in Washington, his wife Elizabeth visiting her family in Richmond, when the death of his former benefactor became known. Elizabeth Gamble Wirt had grown up in a prosperous Federalist environment, where Jefferson was considered a man of mystery and deceit. Wirt wrote to her: "The news of Mr. Jefferson's death is too true—and I cannot tell you how it has made my heart sink—and, indeed, I will not tell you—for on this subject you cannot sympathize with me." It was a rare instance of a lack of shared sympathies between this affectionate couple. And yet, only one day before, she had written a letter containing kindlier sentiments, a letter that he had yet to receive:

The *bells have been tolling* all day for Mr. Jefferson—and the papers which announced his death this morning were all *in mourning*. I understand we are to have a mock funeral. What a glorious and well-timed exit he made! On the 4th of July and at the *very hour* in which the declaration of independence was first read. There is something very touching in this universal lament for one of our Fathers. We are continually reminded of our loss. The bell strikes every minute of the day and coming at such long intervals it sounds like choking suppressed *sobbing* breaking forth every now & then and [with?] long vibrations of the sound on the air like low [...] moanings. Every thing seems to have caught the *sombre* humour. Even Lizzy and I have not ventured to play [on piano] any thing but the Dead March.[55]

The tradition that Jefferson had died at the same hour that the Declaration was adopted in Philadelphia immediately gripped many of the nation's mourners, adding meaning to the already outstanding coincidence of the cooperatively timed deaths of two presidents. The Philadelphia-based *United States Gazette* attempted a clarification, and it was carried by other newspapers: 1:00 p.m., it said, marked the hour when the Declaration was "promulgated in the halls of Congress"; however, it was "first read, in the yard of the Philadelphia State-house" at "about a quarter before five o'clock."[56] On timing, the facts were carefully reviewed; on "last words," few questions were asked.

Baltimore's Hezekiah Niles published in the July 15 issue of *Niles' Weekly Register* a lengthy review of the events surrounding the fiftieth Fourth. To satisfy readers' desire for details, he extrapolated from his files the names of those signers who were actually present in Philadelphia when the Declaration was approved by Congress on July 4, 1776. It was, Niles asserted, concurring with the *United States Gazette,* "nearly if not precisely" the hour of Jefferson's death when the Declaration was approved, and "nearly, if not precisely" the same hour that Adams died when the Declaration was "first proclaimed" in the statehouse yard in Philadelphia. "With what pleasure do we dwell on the past?" he asked rhetorically, and in the next week's issue unwittingly answered himself: "the *fourth of July* will never be remembered without calling to mind the strange things we have witnessed."[57]

In the Romantic age, free minds were free to wander. From Lexington, Kentucky, Henry Clay offered the president "felicitations upon the illustrious death of your father," as soon as he learned the news. Felicitations? Condolence did not seem to fit. "Who would not have been willing to have died such a death?" he presumed. "Without indulging in a spirit of superstition, it is impossible to contemplate the dissolution of your father and Mr. Jefferson without believing that it has been so ordered to produce a great moral effect upon the American people[,] their liberty and their institutions." Always looking for the political silver lining, as he romanticized the founders' deaths Clay assured his president that Kentucky sentiment remained with the administration. Degrading pro-Jackson fervor, he noted the warm reception he had lately received at a series of public testimonials: "I believe other portions of the West to be quite well disposed towards your administration as we imagined."[58]

Though Clay could not put partisan politics aside, across the United States newspapers carried cleansed commentaries on the two departed Revolutionaries. Many provided detailed biographies; all were careful to explain away the years of enmity. The way the press learned of events, however, was not uniform—some knew of Jefferson's death days before Adams's, and vice versa. On July 7, a newspaper of Petersburg, Virginia, exclaimed: "It is too true! JEFFERSON IS NO MORE!" The *New-York American* on the same day cried out: "*'Then burst his mighty heart!'*—On the 4th of July, 1776, JOHN ADAMS signed, with others, the Declaration of Independence. On July 4th, 1826, after the revolution of fifty years, and amidst the 'bells, bonfires, and illuminations' which he had predicted would mark, in all time to come, the anniversary of that day, this patriot statesman breathed his last." A day later, word of Jefferson's death reached New York, and the same paper noted "a coincidence marvelous and enviable. . . . It cannot be all chance."

Philadelphians first began hearing of Jefferson's death on the seventh and, after the news was printed but not yet distributed, the first hint of Adams's death arrived. The *Gazette* appended these words: "There was a report in the city last evening that JOHN ADAMS, died at his residence Quincy, Mass. on the 4th instant.—We hope that this report is an error arising out of the affecting intelligence of Mr. Jefferson's death." In Newark, New Jersey, on July 11, William Halsey, who had given the town's jubilee oration a week earlier, was called upon again, to mourn Adams and Jefferson. "The sound of the Trumpet of Jubilee is reverberated in strange and mysterious echoes," he said, appreciating the two patriots' late years' reconciliation: "In one spirit they lived—in one affection they died." In Albany, New York, also on the eleventh, a moving editorial spoke to the same mystery: "We are free to believe, even at the hazard of incurring the charge of superstition, that for wise purposes, the Ruler of Events has chosen to manifest by a signal act of his Providence, not only the value of the fame of the Fathers of the Revolution, but to impress upon the minds of all men the importance and verity of the Principles asserted by them."[59]

In Chillicothe, Ohio, on July 20, the *Supporter, and Scioto Gazette* published news of Jefferson's "felicitous" death first. His spirit was on its winged flight to "the regions of immortality . . . while millions of his countrymen had his name on their lips." The article had been set in type when, just a few hours later, more "unexpected intelligence" came with the "eastern mail," announcing the death of the "venerable" Adams, "at the very advanced age of 90 years, 8 months, and 4 days." On July 22, a pithy statement was printed in the *Nashville Republican:* "Thomas Jefferson is no more: he expired at Monticello, his residence, on the 4th of July last. . . ." Though brief, the story closed with a timely maxim: "The day of his fame was the day of his death." And on July 26 in that town, slow to come by the news, local officials met and passed a resolution to take notice of the two ex-presidents' passing "under circumstances peculiarly calculated to awaken the noblest feelings of the human heart."

The *Charleston Courier* offered a profound tribute to Jefferson in its issue of July 12, terming him "the Sage, whose prophetic pen wrote on the walls of tyranny, sentiments that have shaken Despotism to its base, and are destined to crumble it into ruins." The commentator was moved to imagine this revelatory patriot, a man of "manly and fearless expressions," in his ascent to heaven "amid the grateful praises of assembled millions." When news of Adams's death reached Charleston in time for the July 17 issue of the *Courier,* it became clear that Jefferson's "illustrious associate" enjoyed with him "the peculiar favor of heaven." And from England on August 8, as always bearing his tortured soul—"I wear a window in my breast. . . . What an ill-starred wretch I have been through life"—John Randolph wrote to his favorite correspondent back home: "And so old Adams is dead; on the 4th of July, too, just half a century after our Declaration of Independence; and leaving his son on the throne. This is Euthenasia, indeed. They have killed Mr. Jefferson, too, on the same day, but I don't believe it."[60]

Still looking for amazing coincidences, a writer, dubbed "ingenious" by the Boston newspaper *American Statesman,* found an anagram in the name "Thomas Jefferson." The letters, jumbled, can be made to read: "Host of man is free," the meaning of "Host" here intended as "great numbers." The newspaper adds: "It is singular that the Declaration of Independence commences with the same sentiment—'All men are created equal.' "[61]

Of course, not all eulogies were created equal. President Adams was obliged to sit through six long-winded ones in and around Boston, including Everett's and Sprague's, in just eleven days. The first of the series was that of local attorney Horace Mann, on July 31, at the Dedham meetinghouse. In 1823, Mann had given a Fourth of July oration at the same location, rich in classical allusions and religious sentiment, but short on references to the American Revolution except for a concluding tribute to the "daring" of Adams and Jefferson. In 1826, Mann was about to begin a career in state politics, and to achieve renown for his efforts to improve public education. His eulogy was, Adams noted, "of splendid composition and lofty eloquence."[62]

The next day, August 1, Edward Everett spoke near Bunker Hill, where the president politely received a group of survivors of the 1775 battle that he himself had witnessed, at the age of not quite eight, from a prominence on his family's property. "We are assembled," Everett opened, "beneath the weeping canopy of the Heavens, in the exercise of feelings in which the whole family of Americans unites with us." The first-term congressman focused on the meaning of the coincidence: "They have not left us singly . . . but having lived, and acted and counselled, and dared, and risked all, and triumphed and enjoyed together, they have gone together to their great reward." Adams and Jefferson had been "permitted" to die on the day when "those who loved them best could have wished they might die." Why was the jubilee of America "turned into mourning?" he posed. Because it was meant to be celebrated in two ways: as a day of "joy and triumph" and a day on which Americans could experience a "chastised and tender recollection" of the higher purpose associated with the nation's destiny.[63]

On August 2, the president listened to two orations: first that of lawyer and author Samuel L. Knapp, and then the masterful address of Daniel Webster, whose tongue, Adams wrote, "held the whole assembly mute" for two and a half hours. Knapp's highlighted the modest means of the departed patriarchs: "Jefferson after all his opportunities to amass wealth died poor, and Adams was not rich." He compared intellectual faculties, observing: "Adams grasped at facts drawn from practical life," while the theoretical Jefferson "saw man and his nature through generalities." It was a balanced, though hardly a stirring address.[64]

At Webster's display, John Quincy Adams beheld "a greater concourse of people than I ever witnessed in Boston"—over four thousand, according to a reliable account. Understandably, the president complained that he was "overcome with fatigue" afterward, but he was also plainly moved by the spectacle. The hall was, as Harvard's George

Ticknor wrote, "very gracefully covered in black." Representative Webster, soon headed for the U.S. Senate, was already well known for his piercing dark eyes, his forensic ability, his literary style, his electricity, his mythmaking power. On this day, Webster was dazzling.[65]

Preceded by a funeral symphony, he extracted emotion from the audience in a way that was so commanding it was almost effrontery: "The tears which flow, and the honors that are paid, when the founders of the republic die, give hope that the republic itself may be immortal." Combining sentiment with symbolism, Webster was scarcely seen referring to his notes. "ADAMS and JEFFERSON are no more," the exhortation proceeded. "The great epic of their lives, how happily concluded! Poetry itself has hardly terminated illustrious lives, and finished the career of earthly renown, by such a consummation."[66]

Reverent and gladdened as he continued to cast his spell, Webster delivered a message of national religious significance: "A superior and commanding human intellect, a truly great man, when Heaven vouchsafes so rare a gift, is not a temporary flame, burning brightly for a while, and then giving place to returning darkness. It is rather a spark of fervent heat, as well as radiant light, with power to enkindle the common mass of human kind." Webster had taken the familiar patriotic metaphors of light and heat and, by associating them with the immortal spirits of Adams and Jefferson, enhanced their spiritual importance. The intellectual treasure bequeathed by the patriarchs "leaves the world all light, all on fire." A new sun shone—Adams and Jefferson *were* America, the America that other nations were meant to imitate. They had erased ignorance. They had descended below the visible horizon in "grateful, long-lingering light," like the mildness of a summer day, their characters enshrined among their grateful political offspring. They had insured the success of the Revolution, "one of the greatest events in history." They had insured "free representative government." They had insured America's greatness.

George Ticknor, who along with Lafayette had heard Webster's Bunker Hill address the year before, pronounced this speech "much more solemn, imposing, and sublime." He was no less amazed that the orator, who paid him a visit at home the night before, had behaved "entirely disencumbered and careless [carefree]." On the other hand, the overtaxed President Adams complained of "a night of broken rest" afterward. Yet he had further duties. Before he could recover from

Webster's much adorned address, he rode on August 3rd to his father's birthplace of Braintree, and listened to a eulogy given there by the Reverend Storrs. Without time to peruse the "large bundle of letters and dispatches" that had been sent to him there, the president was obliged to greet some two hundred citizens of adjacent towns who were presented to him. He made every effort to be courteous. Storrs, he wrote, "bore a warm and affectionate testimony to my father's character." A week later, Adams found himself in the North Church of Salem—"The ceremonies there were similar to those I had five times witnessed last week"—listening to Joseph Sprague's joint eulogy, nearly the length of Webster's. He offered no comment on anything Sprague said.[67]

The Jeffersonian Sprague wisely made no attempt to compete with former Federalist Daniel Webster. Indeed, he opened his address by praising Webster's "powerful eloquence." And rather than repeat or add to what had been said, he proposed to be a "rivulet" which "unites with the majestic river in its tribute to the deep." Of Jefferson, whose life history he delineated first, Sprague stressed a richness of intellect, "unequalled" powers of conversation, and an uncanny ability to convince others of his own point of view while by "magic" causing them to believe that he was "advocating theirs." He added that Jefferson's presidency was "peculiarly successful," and even the unpopular Embargo Act, he rationalized, "a wise expedient." As Sprague moved on to Adams, he praised the elder founder for his earnestness and unparalleled determination, his "resistless and overpowering eloquence" when the issue of independence was debated in the Continental Congress. He barely alluded to Adams's single term as president, generously remarking in this vein, however, that "Mr. Adams has deserved most where he has been most severely censured." It was near the end of the address that the Salem postmaster sought to rouse his audience with Adams's supposed last words of "Jefferson survives." Following that, he related the two July Fourths, fifty years apart, with corresponding sentimentalism: in 1776 "the Heavens were covered with weeping clouds—but beyond those clouds these patriots discerned the sunshine of their country's triumph"; in 1826, "the Heavens again wept," this time for the exquisite theater of the two patriots' timed departures. Sprague performed ably. It was as much as one could do coming on the heels of Daniel Webster's unsurpassable drama.[68]

Writing in his daily journal, John Quincy Adams recognized that *he* was now the elder Adams. This meant something to him. He remained in Massachusetts, on a somewhat less hectic schedule, until October. Then, on departure for Washington, he beseeched "the directing and effecting hand of Providence" for aid, confiding to his diary that he expected to return and occupy his father's home at the conclusion of a single term as president—moreover, he expressed a "consoling hope" of doing so. Adams did not seem at all regretful. He thought that in his projected retirement he might be able to demonstrate "usefulness" to his children, "benevolence to the neighborhood of my own and my father's nativity," and offer "improvement to the condition of my country."[69]

The president's son Charles Francis, nineteen years old in 1826, possessed something of his father's private eloquence, writing colorfully in his own diary about the vagaries of human nature. He lived in Washington and had been observing the Nineteenth Congress in session. He fathomed his father's character easily, and knew that the president had never developed a politically useful facility for appearing amiable. On July 4th, while being fêted in New York ("many foolish toasts, a great deal of holiday patriotism and some execrable singing"), the younger Adams reflected on the attachment shown by political backers of the president: "My father has unfortunately such a cold manner of meeting this sort of feeling that I am surprised at the appearance of it at any time." The youth judged that his father's support was "more impelled by a sense of his merit in the performance of his duty than by any art of personal popularity." Expressing some of the Adams acerbity himself, Charles Francis joined mild insouciance to a mild sarcasm.[70]

He also showed sobriety and strength of character, equally Adams traits. Learning on July 7, in Baltimore, of the death of Jefferson, and apprised in Washington, only on the afternoon of July 9, of the death of his grandfather (his father had departed for Boston hours earlier), Charles Francis Adams composed the following lines: "There are occurrences sometimes in the course of Human affairs, too great for words. The mind is already exalted that any attempt to shackle it by expression destroys the flight, and lets it down again to common place. . . . The greatest of all eloquence in the known world is the eloquence of *facts*." Adding that old John Adams, "always personally kind to me," had been "bold, energetic, ardent" and "sincere," he was also, wrote the grandson, "ignorant of the power of self restraint." Yet, the future politician and ambassador foretold, "the country will still do him justice." And to help the country along, Charles resolved do his utmost to "restore him" to his deserved place in history. As the editor, in later years, of both his father's and grandfather's papers, he would most assuredly do that.[71]

There were others, less remarkable perhaps, but equally citizens, who died on the fiftieth Fourth. They included, in rural Stamford, New York, the 101-year-old Catherine Harris, granddaughter of a governor of Rhode Island; in Albany, "a coloured boy," working as a waiter aboard the steamboat *Commerce*, who fell from a barge into the Hudson River and drowned; and in Philadelphia, Michael Baker Jr., a thirty-seven-year-old coppersmith. In fact, in the city where the Declaration of Independence was produced, statistics for the week of July 1 through July 8 gave the total deaths as ninety-four, forty-four of whom were under one year of age, sixteen others under the age of ten—thus two-thirds of the deaths were among the very young. Of adults who died, "consumption of the lungs" claimed more than any other single disease; two deaths were attributed to "insanity"; and the one suicide resulted from an overdose of laudanum.[72]

The president of the United States arrived back in Washington just in time to be a part of his attorney general's finest hour as a patriotic orator. His son Charles met him with his carriage in the early morning hours of October 19, after the president had docked in Baltimore, to take him to the Capitol. William Wirt had been selected back in July to give the official joint eulogy of Adams and Jefferson. He had expressed reticence about undertaking a dual eulogy, having been intimate with Jefferson without knowing John Adams. First Lady Louisa Catherine Adams implied in letters to her husband that Wirt's excuse was suspiciously weak. He had referred to his sense of failure in crafting *Patrick Henry,* as proof to himself that he could not succeed in capturing the life of one with whom he was personally unacquainted. The agitated Mrs. Adams termed Wirt's excuse "a bitter pill to swallow," noting further: "He says that every feeling in his soul would be glowing while speaking of Mr. Jefferson and that he could only speak of Mr. Adams political character and that it would be impossible to help it."[73]

Some others in Washington, including Treasury Secretary Richard

Rush (son of the late Dr. Benjamin Rush), were just as displeased with the attorney general over this matter. Wirt wished to speak to the Virginian's virtues and yield to someone else on the subject of the New Englander; Edward Everett seemed to him the likely choice. Rush preferred William Cranch, and offered the D.C. judge the honor "to perform the interesting duty." Cranch declined, and went on to solicit the president for personal information to convey directly to Wirt, who was eventually persuaded to tackle both subjects. Mrs. Adams remained displeased: "I see many flattering puffs in the papers," she had written, "calculated to rouse his vanity."[74]

As protective as his wife was, the president apparently did not express any measurable distrust toward his attorney general. The sensitive Wirt was more likely conveying the high standards he set for himself than he was posturing politically. His ego was engaged; he did not want to disappoint his audience. His often-voiced elocutionary model was, after all, the incomparable Patrick Henry. While researching his 1817 biography, Wirt had been full of advice for Francis Walker Gilmer, the younger brother of Wirt's first wife, as that novice attorney approached his first case. Be like Henry, he had prodded: Command the attention of as large an audience as possible. "Let it be such a cause as will ensure you a throng of hearers," and make the speech accessible, "*simple, strong,* and *manly.*" The orator's goal was always an ambitious one: to "insinuate yourself among the heart-strings, the bones and marrow, both of your jury and back-bar hearers."[75]

On October 19, it was Wirt's turn once again. He had long ago impressed the audience at Aaron Burr's Richmond trial, with his energy, fluency, and elocution. There was much going for him on this day, too: the same date on which the climactic Battle of Yorktown had ended, when the British had capitulated to the combined American and French armies. October 19, 1826, would have been the ninety-first birthday of John Adams.

In Washington, banks and shops were closed for the day (it was a Thursday). A procession to the Capitol described as "brilliant" by the *National Intelligencer* began late morning, featuring men in uniform, civil administrators, judicial authorities, and clergy. As the attorney general faced his audience in the House of Representatives, he insinuated himself among the collected heartstrings. He spoke lovingly of the two departed spirits, minimizing partisanship and their personal problems: "They met, and at once became friends—to part no more, but for a short season, and then to be reunited, both for time and eternity." This simplification made his next allusion seem natural: "They were, in truth, hemispheres of the same globe, and required only to be brought and put together, to prove that they were parts of the same heaven-formed whole."[76]

As an expert on language himself, Wirt described the power of the word in the well-earned reputations of Adams and, especially, Jefferson. Of Adams, he praised succinctly "the thought couched in the strongest words, and striking with a kind of epigrammatic force." As to Jefferson he was far more expansive: "Mr. Jefferson, flowing with easy and careless melody, the language at the same time pruned of every redundant word, and giving the thought with the happiest precision, the aptest words dropping unbidden and unsought into their places, as if they had fallen from the skies; and so beautiful, so felicitous, as to fill the mind with a succession of delightful surprises. . . ." Apparently, as his earlier reticence suggests, Wirt was largely unfamiliar with, or was indifferent to, Adams's rhetoric.[77]

Every mention of Jefferson was precise and bittersweet. The visitor to Jefferson's mountaintop was sure to be met "by the tall, and animated, and stately figure of the patriot himself—his countenance beaming with intelligence and benignity, and his outstretched hand, with its strong and cordial pressure, confirming the courteous welcome of his lips . . . he won every heart that approached, as certainly as he astonished every mind." And at Monticello itself, "the patriot could look down, with uninterrupted vision, upon the wide expanse of the world around." Clearly Wirt had been moved by the vista on his numerous pilgrimages. But, aware of Jefferson's finances, his tone became dire: "Monticello has now lost its great charm," he reported. He preferred to recall it as it used to be, an "enchanted landscape" looking out at "several detached mountains" that Jefferson would point to, where one could "watch the motions of the planets, and the greater revolutions of the celestial sphere. . . . It is indeed a prospect in which you see and feel, at once, that nothing mean or little could live. It is a scene fit to nourish those great and high-sounded principles which formed the elements of his character, and was a most noble and appropriate post, for such a sentinel, over the rights and liberties of man."

Monticello was to be sold, and Jefferson's white and black families (he referred to his slaves as family) dispersed.[78]

Wirt could not help but dwell on the grief that attended his thoughts. Near the end of his oration he reconstituted Jefferson's end as it provoked the deepest feelings in him. He clutched onto an image of the old man he had known, stretched out in bed and audibly wishing only to live to see the Fourth. "When that day came," Wirt breathed, "all that he was heard to whisper, was the repeated ejaculation,—*Nunc dimittas Domine*, Now Lord, let thy servant depart in peace! And the prayer of the patriot was heard and answered."[79]

All that he was heard to whisper? Wirt was being poetic rather than literal, repeating one of the phrases attributed to the dying Jefferson. Everett, in his joint eulogy on August 1, had as imprecisely referred to "*Nunc dimittas, Domine*" as Jefferson's "repeated exclamation, on the last great day." Of the few who had sat beside the dying Jefferson, none included in published accounts the Latin that Wirt quoted, though, along with other anecdotal material, Thomas Jefferson Randolph apparently conveyed the phrase to the editor of the *Richmond Enquirer*, which on July 7 noted the variant *Nunc demittas, Domine* as "his favorite quotation."[80]

The attorney general was unable to express sentiments concerning John Adams that even remotely approached his tribute to the singular world that Thomas Jefferson had created. One could only be struck, he said, at the two patriots' common prayer—that they might live until the day of national jubilee. Nothing bespoke a superior purpose so well as the last days of "the patriot of Quincy," who, "with the same certainty of death before him, prayed only for the protraction of life to the same day . . . and when a messenger from the neighboring festivities, unapprized of his danger, was deputed to ask him for the honor of a toast, he showed the object on which his dying eyes were fixed, and exclaimed with energy, 'Independence forever!' " Wirt was satisfied to convey Adams's much publicized salute to the jubilee. He said nothing of "Jefferson survives."[81]

He concluded by remarking one last time on the majestic coincidence. The Fourth of July had been celebrated for a half-century simply as an anniversary of Independence, its "votaries . . . merely human beings." But after "the great Jubilee of the nation," each subsequent anniversary observance would have to include the recognition that "Heaven, itself, mingled visibly in the celebration, and hallowed the day anew by a double apotheosis." Wirt looked out at his audience. "Is there one among us," he cried, "to whom this language seems too strong?" And again, "Is there a voice that was not hushed, is there a heart that did not quail, at the close manifestation of the hand of Heaven in our affairs!"[82]

The eulogy lasted nearly three hours, surprising the editor of Washington's *National Intelligencer*, "for it did not appear to us half so long." It was, he wrote, "a masterly production, worthy of the extraordinary occasion and character of the subject, and fully sustained the reputation of the gifted orator." The friendly *Baltimore Chronicle* referred to Wirt as a "magician," adding superlatives supplied by a member of the audience, fresh from the experience: "I am at this moment as I have often felt after landing from a vessel that had been tossed about by billows—not only giddy—but stupid."[83]

A few days after delivering his speech, Wirt was back in Annapolis, at work as a lawyer. Receiving a formal request from the Washington organizing committee to publish his remarks, he wrote back with the same formality:

> My own prayer is that the youth of our country may turn their eyes from that humble effort [his eulogy] to the far nobler models of chaste & classic Eloquence, as well as of patriotism & philosophy, furnished by the writings & speeches of Thomas Jefferson and John Adams, than whom I believe the world has never seen two greater men, if greatness consist in the soundest heads with the soundest hearts.[84]

By this expression of modesty, the orator graciously accorded Adams and Jefferson the last word.

Epilogue

A FEW DAYS after he listened to William Wirt's joint eulogy in the Capitol, President John Quincy Adams responded in writing to General Lafayette, whose two "kind and sympathizing" letters were waiting for him when he returned to Washington from three months in Quincy. "The removal of my father and Mr. Jefferson on the same day," he wrote, "the fiftieth Anniversary of our Independence, has produced as you would well imagine a great momentary sensation in thy Country. To a true hearted Son these is [*sic*] no consolation for the loss of a father. Acquiescence and resignation *is* all that Nature can yield or Heaven can require in such events." Referring to the two founders' public lives in the singular, as "their career," Adams went on to acknowledge that "among the fortunate incidents of their lives, was the opportunity by which each of them enjoyed of meeting again in person the associate of their momentary struggle for human liberty." In Adams's phrasing, there were two "momentary" events to record—the moment of "sensation" marked by the jubilee anniversary, and the preceding moment of "struggle for human liberty," represented by the rightful Revolution with which Lafayette was gloriously associated.[1]

One year later, as Adams was dressing in the dark, he noticed that his French chronometer had stopped. It had been the first reliable timepiece he had owned as a youth, and he was greatly disturbed by the sudden death—what he called the "desertion"—of this old "friend." All at once, the second President Adams was reminded of a comparable loss that had occurred to his late father, who at one point years earlier had misplaced a particular souvenir, the seal he had affixed to the 1783 Treaty of Paris, which affirmed American Independence. "He told me," recalled the younger Adams, "that the loss of that seal had affected him more than so trifling an incident ought to have done." The seal was soon recovered and later came into the son's possession. Of his own relic, the chronometer, Adams wrote: "It now betrays my confidence, and I can take no true note of time. And what says the moral? 'Lean not on friendship or time.' "[2]

It was the Adams way to analyze even the most minute occurrences. Father and son alike were proud, intense, temperamental men, whose political fortunes rose because their minds were respected and whose political fortunes fell because they would not court popularity. But it is equally curious that both had attached themselves to objects possessing the power to produce nostalgic reveries about a period when time was alive with friendly suggestions and Hope had yet to turn into betrayal.

If a most atypical American, John Quincy Adams nonetheless reflects the time consciousness of his generation, the successor generation, for whom the Revolution lived on as a fond and distant memory. The hopes of the old Revolutionaries had been realized on one level: evidence of prosperity. But they were being betrayed on other levels: illusions of equality, the tenuousness of political union—that is, disharmony among the states. In the jubilee year, there was no greater pursuit of purity, no greater gift of perfection, than the Revolution as it was being revived in the collective imagination. No one quite wanted to suggest that the nation's promise or the people's virtuous character as embodied in these reveries of 1776 was irretrievable. In 1826, it was a severe enough deduction to regard the present as suspect. Who would dare to brand memory a lie?

Marvelous coincidences continued to unfold. Ex-President James Monroe died on July 4, 1831, five years to the day after Adams and Jefferson. Another five years passed, and James Madison tried to time his own death in like fashion, or so it would seem, but he miscalculated ever so slightly, taking his last breath on June 30, 1836.

.   .   .

AMERICANS SAW the course of world history very much in terms of their own prospective achievements. The condescending English visitor Frances Trollope, who toured the United States between 1827 and 1830, concluded of these provincials: "No people appear more anxious to excite admiration and receive applause than the Americans." Disparaging them for their lack of taste and their "money-getting" obsession, she tried to grasp what it was that had produced their crude self-absorption and unfounded confidence, their resistance to acquiring the Old World's politesse.

For her answer, Mrs. Trollope turned to the reception of General Lafayette and the extraordinary "feeling of enthusiasm" and "national pride" that his visit occasioned. Americans' ultimate fixation was "the triumph of their successful struggle for national independence." She wished that they would come to realize how limited the durability of their glorious moment of self-creation was: "Their children inherit the independence; they inherit too the honour of being the sons of brave fathers; but this will not give them the reputation at which they aim." While Mrs. Trollope had hit upon the successors' enduring frustration, she clearly did not appreciate the American capacity for patriotic mythmaking, which indeed proved durable.[3]

It did not salvage the presidency of John Quincy Adams, however. As early as May 1827, the president wrote in his diary: "My own career is closed. My duties are to prepare for the end, with a grateful heart and unwavering mind." The day before this he had received New York's Senator Martin Van Buren, the activist Democrat, on that gentleman's return from a swing through the South, where he had been promoting the candidacy of Andrew Jackson. Identifying easily with his late father's political isolation during the last year of his single term, Adams could not help but consider Van Buren as a reincarnation of the New Yorker Aaron Burr, who had insured John Adams's defeat and Thomas Jefferson's election by engineering a North-South alliance for his candidate.[4]

Henry Clay of Kentucky wanted desperately to be president. The skillful, influential nationalist was obsessed with Jackson's greater popularity, and fussed about it often. He saw the Tennessean as a simple man of mean, ungovernable passions, a tyrant in waiting. He did not think that the nation could survive a Jackson victory. Furthermore, as a relatively young secretary of state (forty-nine years old in 1826), Clay had convinced himself that his chance of succeeding Adams after two terms was good. After all, President Madison had first been Jefferson's secretary of state, and Monroe and the younger Adams each in his turn had occupied the same cabinet post. But Clay simply could not shake the corrupt bargain charge. If Jackson had his own reputation as the impetuous commander to overcome, he could at least rely on his battlefield exploits to overwhelm this other reputation. Clay, on the other hand, did not possess the magic (or a comparable number of committed backers) needed to undo the damage to his reputation caused by the election of 1824.

He would not quit. No, indeed, "Harry of the West" was just digging in. As an accomplished political manipulator, he cultivated partisan journalists who were willing to smear Jackson by printing lurid stories defaming not only the brutal, imperious general, but also casting doubts on the morals of his mother and his wife. The offensive was led by Charles Hammond, editor of the *Liberty Hall & Cincinnati Gazette*, who called Jackson's mother a "common prostitute," and Jackson's wife Rachel "a convicted adulteress." Jackson supporters branded Adams, among other things, a "pimp," claiming that while U.S. minister in St. Petersburg, he had procured an American virgin for the lustful appetite of his friend the Russian tsar.[5]

When the ailing Rachel Jackson's heart finally gave out just after the election, a Jackson campaign biographer called her accusers the "vile assailants" of a truly virtuous woman. She had simply loved the "manly heart" of her husband and "the patriot flame that warmed his breast."[6] Jackson showed how much he despised Clay by writing to Tennessean Sam Houston in December 1826: "I am determined to . . . lay the perfidy, meanness, and wickedness, of Clay, naked before the american people. . . . I will curb my feelings until it becomes proper to act."[7]

Directly after the jubilee, the editor of Boston's pro-Jackson newspaper, the *American Statesman and City Register,* sorted through newspaper commentaries from around the country and published his findings: "The demonstration of respect and attachment to the Hero of New-Orleans, at the late celebration of Independence, pour in from all quarters," he assured. "The American people seemed determined, as this distinguished patriot had a *trick* played upon him at the last election, that he shall have *fair play* the next."[8] It was precisely "fair play," or justice, that Jacksonian Democrats felt they achieved in 1828. Their champion defeated Adams by receiving 178 electoral votes to the incumbent's 83. This time there was no question about the outcome. Notably, all the states but two—South Carolina and Delaware—awarded their electoral votes by means of the popular vote. Jackson commanded 56 percent of this total, and Adams won no state outside the Northeast. Despite limitations that were obvious to many who operated on the public stage, the old war hero personified something that the majority cherished: courageous honor, the *appearance* of utter honesty, homeliness, bluntness, a desirable inelegance, cordiality, familiarity. Those who saw the worth, or thought they heard the heartbeat, of the democratic masses identified with Jackson.

For helping Jackson to secure the basis of a North-South consensus, Martin Van Buren was awarded the post of secretary of state, just as Henry Clay had been when he "made" Adams president under more unusual circumstances. For four years, at least, Clay was stopped. And despite having anticipated his retirement to Quincy, the defeated John Quincy Adams did what only an Adams could do: he went back to Congress, and proudly, doggedly, served his Massachusetts constituents in the House of Representatives for the next twenty years.

Meanwhile, as the jubilee and the deaths of Adams and Jefferson receded from view, the most sensational issue to grip the country in the autumn of 1826 was the anti-Masonic movement. Questions concerning the self-sanctioned brotherhood's need for secrecy had existed before, but a single, unexplained death now brought a new and intensified focus on the meaning of Masonry to the American identity. The episode even touched on the Clay-Jackson feud.

In bustling Batavia, New York, fifty miles east of Niagara Falls, a stonemason named William Morgan was kidnapped and presumed murdered after having broadcast his plan to publish time-honored secrets of the brotherhood. Not only had Washington, Hamilton, and Lafayette been brothers, but Jackson and Clay were as well. After Morgan's mysterious disappearance, resentful citizens began grumbling louder than before, and in larger numbers. They complained that Masonry was elitist, that it had no place in democratizing America. An exclusive fraternity that wallowed in its puzzles and mystifying ceremonies, a group that excluded common people from membership, was not to be trusted—and not to be left alone. Its self-declared affinity with the "pure principles" of Christianity was irksome, as was its apparent conspiracy to monopolize political power. The fraternity's arcane practices began to be ridiculed. To belong suddenly became a political liability; both Jackson and Clay, who held high positions in their state lodges, found it prudent to acknowledge their involvement, while protesting the innocence of their own activities connected with the secret order.[9]

Anti-Masonry did not go away. In fact, it grew in its appeal from 1826 to 1832, especially in the states of New England, New York, and Pennsylvania. By this time, as a manifestation of anti-Jackson partisanship, well-coordinated members founded the Anti-Masonic party, a national political party, and nominated as their candidate none other than the honorable William Wirt. In the election of 1832, the ex-attorney general received the support of former President John Quincy Adams, who fumed that oaths and secrecy undermined a free society. Though a reluctant candidate, Wirt received one hundred thousand popular votes and the electoral votes of one state—Vermont.[10] Democrat Jackson easily won reelection and the National Republican candidate Henry Clay, as he would one more time (to the Jacksonian James K. Polk in 1844), came in second.

As TO THE other individuals who have taken the stage in this drama of the jubilee year, we begin again with Eliza Foster. On October 28, 1826, in the Boston newspaper *American Statesman*, the following brief notice appeared: "A new novel entitled 'Yorktown,' by a citizen of Massachusetts, is announced as being in the press and shortly to be published by Wells & Lilly, of Boston. Report speaks favorably of its merit."

There are no descriptions of the author, no reflections from which we might know the level of her disappointment at the unexceptional reception given to her sentimental novel about the Revolutionary triumph of 1781. Indeed, we can glean little more of her character than what we already have extrapolated from her book, and to suppose from the influence of her mother and the long-standing position of her father that she was responsive to the liberal Christian patriotism of the period, idealizing social harmony.

While her character Maude dies from exhaustion and heartbreak in the novel, the cross-dressing Continental soldier Deborah Sampson died near Boston at age sixty-seven, in the spring of 1827, just months after the publication of *Yorktown*. As a veteran, she had collected a congressional pension. Her obituary listed her as a "heroine," for having performed her duty with "more than ordinary alertness, gallantry, and courage having been in several severe engagements, and twice dangerously wounded but sustaining a character unsullied." In spite of the daring that had led her to trade gender roles, she had recovered—the point was that she had in fact never surrendered—the qualities that enabled her to live out her life as a "proper" woman. She bore her husband (described as an industrious farmer) "a reputable family of children." Thus she merited the name "amiable wife."[11]

There are yet a few pieces of biographical information that enhance our appreciation for the mother-daughter novelists. In Hannah Foster's *Coquette,* the heroine Eliza is a headstrong single woman until, unwed at thirty-seven, she finally succumbs to the seduction scheme of Major Sanford, and spirals into disrepute. Hannah's real-life daughter Eliza, it seems, was intent on remaining unmarried herself until *she* was ready, and that day did not arrive until she was nearly thirty-four. Like Eliza Foster and Ruth Henshaw Bascom, another eldest daughter who was single until the age of thirty-two, there were significant numbers of women, particularly in New England, who preferred to rely on their own good sense and carefully weigh the future rather than be directed toward an early, ill-matched union.[12] In 1828, a brief wedding notice in the *Columbian Centinel* announced the marriage of Eliza L. Foster, in her hometown of Brighton, Massachusetts, to Dr. Frederick Cushing of Durham, New Hampshire, on the always-auspicious date of July 4th.[13]

Dr. Cushing was two years older than Eliza and, like her minister father, a graduate of Dartmouth College. He had attended Harvard Medical College, receiving his degree there in 1817, before opening a practice in Durham. How he came to be acquainted with Eliza is unknown, and there is a gap of a few years after their wedding, during which time they apparently resided in both New Hampshire and Vermont. Eliza's copy of Samuel L. Knapp's 1821 *Biographical Sketches of Eminent Lawyers, Statesmen, and Men of Letters* has turned up (Knapp was one of the several Boston-area speakers whose joint eulogies of Adams and Jefferson President John Quincy Adams was obliged to sit through). Eliza signed her new name inside the book: "E. L. Cushing, Charlestown N.H." Her handwriting is plain, not beautiful, large but not ostentatious. The book was probably acquired sometime around 1829, the year of Reverend John Foster's death, as the couple left Brighton with the widow Hannah Webster Foster, and moved gradually north.[14]

The Cushings were apparently residing in Burlington, Vermont, in 1833, when they left the United States and settled in Montreal. They were joined there by Eliza's younger sister Harriet and her husband. Dr. Cushing practiced medicine in Montreal, and was said to have exhibited remarkable devotion to his work. In 1834, his successful treatment of cholera was publicized, and his humane conduct toward the afflicted poor applauded. He volunteered his services to the Montreal Emigrant Hospital, treating sufferers of "ship fever." Eliza's husband then contracted the dread disease himself and died of it in 1847. They had one child, Harriet, who died in youth.[15]

In Canada, Eliza continued to write. Two dramas, the romantic *Fatal Ring* and the religious *Esther*, were published in 1840, the year her mother died at the age of eighty-one. After her husband's death seven years later, she was obliged to make her living as a writer, and for six years, with her sister, coedited the monthly *Snow Drop*, the first children's literary magazine with U.S. and Canadian distribution. And so, what we know beyond this is that Eliza Foster Cushing remained in Montreal, surrounded by the French language, for the rest of her ninety-one years. If not exactly swept off her feet by an invincible French knight, like the fictional Helen Leslie, she had been at one time loved by a heroic healer and, presumably, found contentment. Her obituary in the *Montreal Gazette* in the spring of 1886 made no note of her writing career, identifying her merely as the widow of Dr. Cushing, already four decades in his grave.[16]

In Ashby, Massachusetts, Ruth Henshaw Bascom read of the death of John Adams in the *Spy* on July 11, 1826, learning of the fabulous coincidence when Jefferson's death was reported in that paper the next week. She wrote in her diary on July 22 that Adams had died "suddenly & happily" and that Jefferson had died "suddenly." On that day, while her husband was in the next town visiting, the daughter of patriot William Henshaw "took a northerly walk" and had tea with the prolific clockmaker Abraham Edwards, sixty-four. He had been a lad of fourteen in 1775 when his hometown of Concord received an unwanted visit from a large detachment of British troops. This was the first time that Ruth had called at the Edwards home, and so the profile artist doubtless was taken with the craftsman's wood movements and distinctively painted birch dials, that have since made Ashby tall clocks modern collectibles. As they sipped their tea, the clockmaker and the diarist must have shared a consciousness of time.[17]

Reverend Ezekiel Bascom, who had a history of stomach ailments, continued to minister to the people of Ashby until his health began to deteriorate in 1832. Each year thereafter, he spent the cold months with his married daughter, Elvira, in Savannah, Georgia, and even journeyed to Cuba. Though he began to feel hardier, a new minister took over in Ashby, and so the Bascoms removed to Fitzwilliam, New Hampshire, twenty miles to the northwest, where he apparently preached irregularly. Ruth began her diary for the year 1841 referring to her "invalid husband," who had "almost lost his voice for public speaking." The entry for Friday, April 2, sounds ominous: "cloudy warm sprinkles of rain thunder shower"—the mixture of weather conditions seeming to mirror the confusion of her own emotions—and then: "Mr. B. had the most quiet sleep of any night for two weeks past."

She did not write for the next several days. Wednesday, April 7, reads:

> . . . cloudy after a bright morn . . . A dark and trying scene has past over us since penning the last log—for on that afternoon of Friday last when we all thought & he himself that he was more comfortable than for many days past, fell asleep & when we endevored in vain to wake him (to see Dr. Hobb who had walked in) and at length raised him up he breathed but a few short moments & without any movement, the vital spark was gone! Thus my dear husband after a life of much suffering, particularly the last 3 years, was taken from us . . . when we thought him in a refreshing sleep.

It remained only for Ruth to comment five days later on the first death of a president while in office, coinciding with the death of her husband. William Henry Harrison's death was, she wrote, "a great and irreparable loss to the Nation; but we richly deserve this and still greater calamities!"

In fact, though, Ruth's life had changed dramatically long before this. Necessity—the absence of her husband for the better part of six years and the loss of his pulpit—had left her to her own devices. During these years, she took up her scissors, adding crayons and pastels, and earned her living as an itinerant profile artist, traveling on her own as far as Kennebunk, Maine, and sleeping at the homes of friends, relatives, and strangers. Though she had cut silhouettes for her neighbors from early in her married life (many of which were children's faces and bereavement souvenirs, such as the Wallis one of 1826), beginning in 1829, when she produced a remarkable 155 portraits, her avocation grew into a far-reaching enterprise.[18]

Thus Ruth Henshaw Bascom, whose diary for so long expressed the resignation of a dutiful wife organizing church activities and hosting teas, spent her declining years at a far more strenuous trade. Profoundly conscious of the plight of women, she composed a will in 1841, just after her husband's death, that declared her independence from the past: "My object is," she wrote, "that *if* I leave any property at my decease, it may *eventually* descend to such of my *female* relatives, to whom it will probably be the most beneficient—for their own personal use & under their *sole control*."[19]

Her diary stops in December 1846, in Ashby, where she was living at the home of Mr. and Mrs. Pearly Gates. December 12: "sun shone brightly, but snow blew about ¾ of the day + wind whistled round my house *whew whew whew* day + evening." On her seventy-fourth birthday, December 15, she noted, with traditional humility, of her own "unprofitable life how frail is man—his life a *span!*" Her days ended on February 19, 1848, the same week that ex-President Adams breathed his last.

The Ohio canal system was inaugurated on July 4, 1827, with a scant thirty-eight-mile voyage. Citizens lined the banks and applauded the buoyant *State of Ohio*, as the ceremonial canal boat was named. Ethan Allen Brown was aboard, along with the other Ohio canal commissioners. In February 1828, Brown was saddened by the unexpected death of his friend Governor DeWitt Clinton. Life moved on, and in March he was able to toast the first barges to ply the length of the Ohio-Erie canal and dock in Cincinnati. That year, too, Brown became an active Jackson supporter, and in 1830 received an appointment as U.S. chargé d'affaires in Brazil, where he remained for four years before retiring to his farm in Rising Sun, Indiana. The man born on the same day as his nation, July 4, 1776, died of a cerebral hemorrhage at the age of seventy-six, a lifelong bachelor. The stone shaft that marks his grave lists the offices he held and commends his "purity of heart."[20]

The canal craze continued. Eastern capital, state aid, and local promoters combined to extend the canal system to all parts of Ohio. Where the canals ran, population and farm output increased. Travelers opted for the comfortable canals, at three miles per hour and three cents per mile (meals included), over the faster but bumpier stagecoach. In the 1840s the new Mahoning canal, which ran east from Akron, awakened the long unexploited coalfields of Youngstown, while linking Ohio dairy lands with fast-growing Cleveland. The Yankee settlers of decades past were now able to transport their cheese efficiently. Nine million pounds of cheese traveled the Mahoning to Cleveland in the year 1851 alone, with expectant buyers for Ohio cheese in New York, Canada, and even distant California. At about this time, however, excitement over the profitable canals began to fade. It was in 1826 that railways had first been proposed for Ohio, and in 1848 the first regular train service between Cincinnati and Lake Erie opened, speeding the canals on a course toward obsolescence.[21]

The obsolete politician John Randolph sailed to England at the close of the first session of the Nineteenth Congress in May 1826, and did not partake in any celebration of America's jubilee. Even in England, though, the wayward Virginian made sure that he was noticed. Standing aboard a river-going vessel, he was hailed by a group of curious onlookers. Given "three cheers," Randolph doffed his hat and exclaimed: "Old England and young America, united forever! Who shall divide them!" Dressed in a blue coat, with a yellow silk scarf, he remarked that their two nations had been on the same political course ever since 1776, "without tacking or taking in sail[.] Only we have thrown the king overboard. God bless him!"[22] Stories about Randolph abounded and, as always, found their way into American newspapers. Coming home, he was defeated in his bid for the Senate, only to be returned to his old House seat for one final term. He grumbled about his "feeble" health all during 1827–28, but still found a way to cheer on Jackson's candidacy. On the subject of slavery, he wrote of his belief that "Congress will liberate our slaves in less than twenty years" (he was fifteen years off) and aimlessly queried: "Where now could we find leaders of a revolution?"[23]

President Jackson appointed Randolph as his ambassador to Russia in the autumn of 1829. The oddly proportioned, sickly man sailed the Atlantic again in mid-1830. When he arrived at his post, he complained of the "nauseous" summer insects, and "flies innumerable, gigantic as the empire they inhabit." He was home again after a year, announced his retirement from Congress, and took to using opium. All the while, Randolph continued to protest the degeneration of the American political scene.

He died in 1833, in his sixtieth year, while on a visit to Philadelphia, but not before stopping in Washington. He needed to see his old nemesis Henry Clay one last time and, if his mid-nineteenth-century biographer is accurate, only so that he might take the hand of the canny Kentuckian and bid him a final farewell. The Philadelphia Quaker physician who tended to Randolph in his last days recalled a conversation with his patient: "There are idiosyncracies in many constitutions," observed the doctor. "I wish to ascertain what is peculiar about you." And Randolph replied: "I have been an idiosyncracy all my life."[24]

John C. Calhoun's slow, steady transformation from nationalist to sectionalist was motivated by a series of rejections. Rejected as a result of Clay's apparent manipulation of Adams, he in turn had rejected Adams by 1826, and veered toward his fellow Southerner Jackson. But in 1829, as Jackson's vice president, Calhoun almost immediately became disappointed in Jackson and his cabinet as well. Unable to be effective from the second position within the executive under two administrations, he was, consciously or not, awaiting the issue that would compel him finally to an obsessive protectiveness of Southern culture, against the federal government he had so long served. He would reject Jackson for, in his mind, rejecting the South. Thus, oddly, Calhoun's future lay in Randolph's past: the more Randolph had regarded himself as a man cast off from the mainstream, the more he projected that *he* was the South, and that the South was similarly being cast off. In a way, Randolph started it all, the move toward disunion that Calhoun went on to insure.

George McDuffie married late, in 1829, when he was about forty, to the twenty-four-year-old daughter of a wealthy planter, who sometimes watched her husband from the House gallery. She died a scant two years later. They had a daughter, and he never remarried. In the 1830s, McDuffie stood by his fellow South Carolinian Calhoun when their state protested the morality and legality of a tariff passed by Congress that seemed to ignore Southern economic interests. Historians see the nullification controversy—the debate over a state's right to nullify an act of Congress that it finds odious—as a benchmark in the drift toward the Civil War. McDuffie was as much as Calhoun incensed by an "oppressive tyranny" directed against the South; he termed the Union at this time the "foul monster" of an unfair majority. Still, the fist-shaking orator sought compromise. The possibility of violent confrontation between forces of the federal government and the state of South Carolina greatly alarmed him.[25]

Like his mentor Calhoun, who felt muted as vice president and resigned in order to enter the Senate, McDuffie came to express the view that the Southern Unionist Andrew Jackson was as much a tyrant as the combined North. In a particularly poignant speech, McDuffie noted with amazement on the floor of the House that President Jackson, "in his old age, when his passions have survived the vigor of his intellect, intoxicated with those everlasting draughts of flattery which the cringing sycophants around him are forever administering, should imagine himself to be the chosen instrument of Heaven to inflict its vengeance upon the people of the United States."[26]

McDuffie served as Governor of South Carolina during Jackson's second term and was a U.S. senator from 1843 to 1846. By this time, though, his health was in decline. He leaned heavily on a cane and sometimes had to be helped to his Senate seat. In his last years, he was cared for by his teenage daughter while suffering from periodic nerve ailments that were attributed to the duels he fought with the Georgian Cumming early in his career. He died in 1851.[27]

Henry Clay died in 1852, as the successor generation was nearing the time when it would yield to the next generation of post-Revolutionary Americans, who would prosecute the bloody Civil War. After losing to

Polk in 1844, the disquieted old warhorse appeared finished in politics, and retired to his six-hundred-acre estate of Ashland, in Lexington, Kentucky. When his son and namesake died in combat in 1847, during the Mexican War, the long irreverent Clay, at seventy, turned to religion. Continuing as president of the American Colonization Society, he manumitted a number of his own slaves, meanwhile angering abolitionists with his insistence that any more far-reaching act of emancipation would be to the detriment of African Americans. As it turned out, Clay could not stay retired, and returned to the Senate in 1849. His last effort as a nationalist was to help forge the Compromise of 1850, and moderate the ever-deepening North-South conflict.

After Clay's death, his casket lay in state in the Capitol Rotunda. Kentucky's other senator, Joseph R. Underwood, called him "ardent, fearless, and full of hope," and found it fitting that Clay was to be buried in Lexington: "In our Revolution, liberty's first libation blood was poured out of a town of that name in Massachusetts." In Springfield, Illinois, Abraham Lincoln praised Clay's magnetic quality: "The spell—the long enduring spell—with which the souls of men were bound to him, is a miracle." He attributed to Clay what others would ultimately attribute to the martyred Lincoln, saying that the Kentuckian's eloquence was not an "elegant arrangement of words and sentences; but rather of that deeply earnest and impassioned tone, and manner, which can proceed only from great sincerity and a thorough conviction. . . . This it is, that truly touches the chords of human sympathy." The jaunty Clay would go down in history as the man who famously said, "I would rather be right than be President."[28]

Another failed presidential aspirant, William Wirt, had to endure the loss of his precious daughter Agnes, from dysentery, in 1830. This favorite child, to whom he blew kisses through the mail, was only sixteen at the time of her death. A pamphlet published by the American Tract Society noted how, two days before, she claimed to have heard "sweet . . . heavenly music" in her sleep. Though absent on "important professional business" while Agnes suffered, Wirt arrived at her deathbed to receive delirious sounds in French, as she expressed fears of being trapped in a crowded boat. The grieving father wrote afterward to his old friend Dabney Carr that he was a changed man: "There is a better world of which I have thought too little—to that world she is gone—and thither my affections have followed her." Indeed, during the suffocating winter of 1831–32, he felt his own death approaching, spending anguished months bedridden. By the time Wirt agreed to stand for president as an Anti-Mason, he had grown religious and, arguably, viewed his legal practice as a less governing feature of his life's outlook. Ironically, then, it was as he ran for president that William Wirt's ambition softened.[29]

After the 1832 election, still planning Supreme Court appearances for one more season, the designing Wirt more urgently envisioned settling his Florida cotton plantation. He hoped to use free German laborers rather than African American slaves, if possible. Experiencing persistent premonitions of death, he wanted to make prompt arrangements in Florida to secure a better life for those he was to leave behind. Daughter Lizzy was getting married; daughter Catharine had dismissed her fiancé after he revealed himself irreligious. Wirt still had debts to work out, and sold his Washington, D.C., property, moving with his wife into a Baltimore boardinghouse. The remaining young ones went to live with their Richmond relatives. Around this time, their oldest, Laura, died of tuberculosis.[30]

Despite his stable law practice, William Wirt was unable to hold everything together. In the winter of 1833–34, he tried to maintain his spirits, writing wistfully to Dabney Carr of the felicity he had known: "I believe the happiest time of a man's life is after he marries and sees a family of young children growing all around him . . . and he has an excellent and affectionate wife, and a circle of friends who admire and love him. This happy state we have both known. Our hopes and imaginations were all bright and buoyant, and painted the future in colors of love and joy." But what had been the result? he opposed plaintively. "Where are all those dear children? Where are all those friends? What is our condition? The world is the same, the planet keeps its place, the seasons revolve, and the young world still smiles. But, what are we!" The pained writer could not stop himself from saying one thing more to his best friend: "my song ends in a sigh that shakes my inner man."[31]

His song ended only weeks later, on February 18, 1834, as his wife calmly assured the dying man he would be meeting "our dear angels [five children] in heaven." Receiving the doleful intelligence, the justices of the Supreme Court adjourned for the day. On the twentieth both houses of Congress adjourned as well, in order to accompany the body of William Wirt to the national cemetery. There gathered Andrew Jackson and Henry Clay, John Quincy Adams and John C. Calhoun, justices and cabinet members, congressmen and generals. A squat monument was placed above the coffin.

On February 21, in the House of Representatives, Adams rose unofficially to pay tribute to the merits of his longtime colleague. He noted that William Wirt was a man of learning, an able attorney, an orator who combined elocution with "a sportive vein of humor, an inoffensive temper, and an angelic purity of heart." Beyond this, Adams affirmed, the determined advocate was also a "husband and father in the bosom of a happy, but now most afflicted family." Realizing that the deceased had never served in Congress and therefore might not ordinarily be considered for state honors, the former president conceived an inscription worthy of any future statue or painting commissioned for the Capitol that would make Wirt its subject: "Nothing was wanting to *his* glory," Adams said. "*He* was wanting to ours."[32]

Lafayette, too, died in 1834. The novelist James Fenimore Cooper, who had sailed from New York in June 1826, remained in Europe for seven years, living mostly in Paris. While there, he formed an affectionate friendship with the marquis, and the two found a common purpose in correcting the commonly dismissive views most Europeans still had about American culture.[33] When news of the general's death reached Washington, Congress promptly voted Representative John Quincy Adams to deliver a eulogy on the Revolutionary hero who had so galvanized Americans on the eve of the jubilee.

Adams continued in Congress, the perfect picture of an elder statesman. Fourteen years to the day after he rose to address his colleagues on the subject of William Wirt's virtues, the sixth president, at the age of eighty, collapsed at his desk on Capitol Hill. It was a Monday afternoon. He had attended public worship the day before and, wrote one contemporary, cheerfully ascended the Capitol steps at the start of a new week, to cast his vote on two routine measures. He had even taken time that morning to pen a few lines of poetry for a friend. But around one o'clock, he slumped in his chair; as he did, an Ohio representative sitting beside him caught "Old Man Eloquent" in his arms. Another lawmaker applied ice water to his face. Congress adjourned, as physicians and relatives were called to the scene. It was said that Adams revived long enough to call out for Henry Clay, and to utter last words of sermonic eloquence: *"This is the end of earth, but I am composed."* He died the next day, February 23, 1848.[34]

On the twenty-fourth, the Speaker of the House, Robert Winthrop of Massachusetts, announced what everyone in attendance already knew. All eyes took in the conspicuously vacant seat of their late colleague. "A voice has been hushed forever in this Hall," he said, "to which all ears have been wont to listen with profound reverence." In the Senate, John Davis of Massachusetts, who had been a naive freshman representative in the Nineteenth Congress, stood up as a veteran in this Thirtieth Congress, and demonstratively spoke of origins: "His parentage is too well known to need even an allusion; yet I may be pardoned if I say, that his father seemed born to aid in the establishment of our Government, and his mother was a suitable companion and co-laborer of such a patriot. The cradle hymns of the child were the songs of liberty." Detailing Adams's accomplishments, Davis mused that it had been his "earnest wish" to die amid his labors. "It was a sublime thought, that where he had toiled in the house of the nation, in hours of the day devoted to its service, the stroke of death should reach him, and there sever the ties of love and patriotism which bound him to earth."[35]

The statesman's body was transported back to Quincy. Edward Everett was on hand to eulogize Adams at Faneuil Hall in Boston. In the same hall, Revolutionaries plotted their resistance to British tyranny. Here, too, in August 1826, Daniel Webster mustered "the largest concourse of people" that President Adams could ever recall having seen in Boston, on that summer day when the gifted orator extolled the virtues of the recently departed second and third presidents. Now it was the successor's turn to be promoted.

Everett's address stood as a vindication of both the man and his much maligned administration. John Quincy Adams was a Puritan in the best sense, he intoned, once Puritanism had "laid aside much of its sternness and intolerance, and had begun to reconcile itself with the milder charities of life." Crediting Abigail Adams for having united female and Christian virtues in bringing up her son, Everett attributed

John Quincy's combined erudition and simplicity of manners to this particular environment.[36]

As to his administration, the orator was straightforward. Although Adams had sought merely to continue those principles and policies that had brought a measure of success to his predecessor, James Monroe, he had added a "special object" to distinguish his own brand of government—"to bind the distant parts of the country together, and promote their mutual prosperity, by increased facilities of communication." Unlike Monroe, then, Adams encountered, "from the outset, a formidable and harassing opposition" to his program of improvement. Yet, these years later, the Adams Administration could be viewed apart from former prejudices, "generally admitted to have been honest, able, and patriotic."

After his defeat, Adams had done a most remarkable thing: "It was a step never before taken by a retiring chief magistrate," said Everett. His return to Congress arose from "an inward, all-controlling sense of duty. He was conscious of his capacity to be useful, and his work was not yet done." This was the sum of John Quincy Adams: "A person of truer courage, physical and moral, I think never lived." In words similar to those which others had used to celebrate John Adams's nerve, Everett now memorialized the second President Adams: "No man laid hold, with a firmer grasp, to the realities of life."[37]

That was a fitting way to condense what it meant to be an Adams in a society that was already warm with desire for a simpler view of democracy. He was hard to appreciate at a time when popularity alone dictated political fortunes. But, if in the highest character of nineteenth-century Americans is seen a combination of grit and humanity, it could rightly be said that such an outlook, to a significant degree, issued from something strong and mindful that lodged in the person of John Quincy Adams—the vividness of his perceptions, the coherence of his calculations, his depth of awareness, his critical edge, his agility as a student of history, his love for the noblest ideas of the Revolutionary generation.

WHAT IS THERE, finally, to be said of the Americans of 1826? They were, first and foremost, acutely aware of themselves as the immediate successors of the founding generation. In making their parents immortal, they celebrated what were in effect emotionally chaotic connections to their past, connections that often made them feel their own prodigality. But these romantically muddled people were also an ingenious and industrious people, who defined their generation equally in terms of nostalgia and newness.

They wished to author moral progress on a scale comparable to their predecessors. Sometimes they believed they would succeed. But the ever-widening reach of newspapers, and the political alienation they routinely read about in those newspapers, gave them ample reason to doubt themselves. The progress they perceived, frontier expansion and grand technological innovations like steamboats and canals, did not liberate them from their troubles. And so, the power of the past—specifically, the unifying power of fifty years past—loomed large for them. When they visualized a democratic achievement growing directly from the spirit of 1776, they glowed, they crowed, they took credit for sustaining what they calculated made them as good and virtuous as their forebears. But their consciousness of time in 1826 had a humbling effect as well. Insufficiently appreciating that the founders themselves had lamented a loss of control over the future, and despite the unprecedented level of energy that directed them, the successors were unsure of their ability to steer ahead.

They felt superior to other nations, other cultures, on the strength of their system of government, but time consciousness, no less, weighed on them. It is why James Fenimore Cooper criticized conventionality by looking to the eighteenth century for uncorrupted morals and national promise. As the present was understood to be morally complex, the past was made pristine. And the future was seen through anxious eyes, or at best enshrouded in a tremulous mist. As the orator in Newark, New Jersey, William Halsey, taunted on July 4, 1826, "Who in this assembly will celebrate the Centurial Jubilee? *Not one in fifty!*"[38]

History is the politics of memory, the enterprise of creating the memories that offer special meaning to the present. "Jefferson survives" is certainly one of these. There remains no memory of 1826 more potent and enduring in the modern American imagination than the "act" that in and of itself immortalized the Revolution: the nearly simultaneous deaths of the founding geniuses Adams and Jefferson. This stands as a kind of symbol, evidence that nothing the successors ever did could equal the sublime achievements they themselves attributed to their parents. As the canals that they delighted in began to operate on annual deficits, the waterways were poorly maintained and gradually fell into disuse. More catastrophically, the successors' inability to find a pacific solution to the problems that divided North and South made their generation appear well-intentioned but unquestionably wanting to *their* successors.

Of course, this is not a fair appraisal. They were a fascinating body of Americans, who embraced modernity even as they were celebrating the Revolutionary moment. They were vigorously attached to the land, and to every enterprise bent on improving it. Among them were deeply concerned men and women possessed of acute minds and agreeable manners. They spoke an American English that was more easily differentiated from the parent English, and they were taking a more noticeable pride in their own literature.[39] They understood political democracy, even if they could not control its ruinous tendencies. Their emotional extravagance was matched by their solid sense of community.

All this leads to one final reflection. The stanza written by Lord Byron that is offered as an epigraph at the opening of this book is actually the second stanza in a song of three stanzas. The entire composition is reprinted below.

I.

They say that Hope is happiness;
But genuine Love must prize the past,
And Memory wakes the thoughts that bless:
They rose the first—they set the last;

II.

And all that Memory loves the most
Was once our only Hope to be,
And all that Hope adored and lost
Hath melted into Memory.

III.

Alas! it is delusion all:
The future cheats us from afar,
Nor can we be what we recall,
Nor dare we think on what we are.

We of the twenty-first century are faced with an old question: Where does cultural identity come from? A fanciful memory of the past? If so, we stand only to mock ourselves. For if memory is delusion, and love of the past a faint hope at best for rescue from some present moral predicament, then what progressive value can the reconstitution of old lives possess? The Romantic might respond this way: We will never breathe the air they breathed, but we can still appreciate that facet of their spirit which may not have entirely disintegrated. Even if we do not know what the next day will bring, there is, after all, something we recognize, something prophetic, in the seasons.

To the same dilemma—the task of discovering value in the reconstruction of past lives—the reformed, rational historian might answer: We need not recur to the past for guidance (strong though the temptation always is), because heroes are never real. They are, inevitably, the creative result of our need for emotional anchoring, as faith in God is.

There is a third solution, part Romantic, part rational: Even if memory is delusion, who can deny that there is an innocent joy in wandering? In 1826, Daniel Webster thrilled Bostonians with his masterfully delivered joint eulogy of Adams and Jefferson, and in the process of recapturing the scene in Philadelphia in 1776 improvised a debate over the issue of Independence. He accorded Adams eloquent opening lines—"Sink or swim, live or die, survive or perish, I give my hand and my heart, to this vote." These lines would be recited so often during the nineteenth century that many believed them to be genuine. Treasury Secretary Richard Rush read the published oration and wrote Webster that it "made my hair rise. It wears the character of a startling historical discovery." Untroubled by the fiction Webster had issued by putting words in Adams's mouth, Rush averred, "Nothing but success could have justified it, and you have succeeded."[40] Success in recasting history to serve the present, while something less than truth, continues to animate American political culture; it is at once as quaint as romance and as insidious as ideology.

Romance and ideology are unavoidable, and today's historians are engaged in an uphill battle—perhaps a fruitless battle—to encounter an objective reality. Let us acknowledge who we are, then, as we critically examine past subjects. They were purveyors of an ideology, and we are as well. They represented the connection between an environment and a universe of emotions, and so do we. They vacillated between certainty and self-doubt, just as we alternately ignore and prepare for the consequences of our historic actions. They looked as we look for symmetry, only to find chaos. Here, there, and everywhere, human beings are engaged with an unseen presence. By conjuring the ghosts of the past, we seek signs of life in ourselves.

Notes

I am grateful to the following institutions for the manuscript sources cited in this book:

American Antiquarian Society
Library of Congress
Maryland Historical Society
Massachusetts Historical Society
McGill University
Monticello
Ohio Historical Society
University of Virginia
Virginia Historical Society
Wisconsin State Historical Society

Newspapers and journals consulted, encompassing original issues and microfilm editions:

The African Repository, and Colonial Journal
Albany Argus & Daily City Gazette (Albany, N.Y.)
American Statesman and City Register (Boston)
The Charleston Courier
Columbian Centinel (Boston)
Kentucky Reporter (Lexington)
Liberty Hall & Cincinnati Gazette
Massachusetts Spy (Worcester)
Montreal Gazette
Nashville Republican

Nashville Whig
National Crisis (Cincinnati)
National Intelligencer (Washington, D.C.)
New-York American
New-York Mirror, and Ladies' Literary Gazette
Niles' Weekly Register (Baltimore)
North American Review
The Ohio Oracle (Wooster)
Richmond Enquirer
The Supporter, and Scioto Gazette (Chillicothe, Ohio)
United States Gazette (Philadelphia)
United States Telegraph (Washington, D.C.)

NOTES TO INTRODUCTION

1. John Quincy Adams's inaugural address, in James D. Richardson, *A Compilation of the Messages and Papers of the Presidents* (New York, 1897), 2:860–65; on the original "Old Glory," so named by a merchant seaman, Captain William Driver of Salem, Massachusetts, in 1824, and displayed in ports around the world, see William Rhea Furlong and Byron McCandless, *So Proudly We Hail: The History of the United States Flag* (Washington, D.C., 1981), 190. A rare example of "Old Glory" is preserved at the Smithsonian Institution.

2. *Kentucky Reporter* (Lexington, Ky.), Mar. 21, 1825. Without acknowledging the contradiction, the *Reporter* followed its explanation by heralding "our confirmed institutions of freedom" and "just and equal laws."

3. *Compact Edition of the Oxford English Dictionary* (Oxford, 1971), 1517. In the first edition of Noah Webster's *American Dictionary of the English Language* (New York, 1828), the Jewish jubilee tradition is described, noting as the *Kentucky Reporter* does, the liberation of slaves and return of alienated lands. On July 3, 1826, the *United States Telegraph*, a Washington, D.C., newspaper, would print immediately below the full text of the Declaration of Independence the words of Holy Writ: "Then shall thou cause the trumpet of the Jubilee to sound throughout the land. And ye shall hallow the fiftieth year, and proclaim LIBERTY throughout all the land to all the inhabitants thereof. Ye shall not therefore oppress one another; but thou shalt fear thy God—and the land shall yield her fruit, and ye shall eat your fill, and dwell therein in safety."

NOTES TO CHAPTER ONE

1. A[uguste] Levasseur, *Lafayette in America in 1824 and 1825; or, Journal of a Voyage to the United States,* 2 vols. (Philadelphia, 1829), 1:10. A modern facsimile was issued by Research Reprints, New York, 1970.

2. The details of the Yorktown campaign have been given by generations of American historians, beginning with David Ramsay, *The History of the American Revolution*, ed. Lester H. Cohen (Indianapolis, Ind., 1990 [1789]); a particularly readable account is Christopher Ward, *The War of the Revolution* (New York, 1952); overall, the best compact study of Washington is John E. Ferling, *The First of Men: A Life of George Washington* (Knoxville, Tenn., 1988).

3. On Washington's efforts to reconstitute a domestic life and add to the amenities at Mount Vernon, see esp. Robert F. Dalzell Jr. and Lee Baldwin Dalzell, *George Washington's Mount Vernon: At Home in Revolutionary America* (New York, 1998).

4. Washington to Lafayette, Dec. 8, 1784, in *The Papers of George Washington*, ed. W. W. Abbott et al., Confederation Series (Charlottesville, Va., 1983), 2:175.

5. See Lloyd Kramer, *Lafayette in Two Worlds: Public Cultures and Personal Identities in an Age of Revolutions* (Chapel Hill, N.C., 1996), 112. My exposition of the real and symbolic dimensions of Americans' romance with Lafayette, in this and the next chapter, owes a debt to Kramer's excellent study. The report in the *New-York American* was published on Aug. 18, 1824, and described Lafayette's modest bearing: "His manners are plain, but pleasing; and he appears to return with equal cordiality, the warm and heartfelt congratulations of all classes."

6. Levasseur, *Lafayette in America*, 1:123–24. Levasseur's descriptions were painstakingly recorded at the scene and represent a valuable resource. Yet it is important to recognize that for literary aims, and consistent with the style of the period, they are understandably embellished.

7. Ibid., 16–17.

8. Ibid., 37–38.

9. Paul Revere Frothingham, *Edward Everett, Orator and Statesman* (Boston, 1925), 82–87.

10. Levasseur, *Lafayette in America*, 1:38; Edmund Quincy, *Life of Josiah Quincy of Massachusetts* (Boston, 1869), 402–03.

11. Quincy, *Life of Josiah Quincy*, 405.

12. Levasseur, *Lafayette in America*, 1:65; Adams to Jefferson, Nov. 15, 1824, Lester J. Cappon, ed., *The Adams-Jefferson Letters* (Chapel Hill, N.C., 1959), 604; Quincy, *Life of Josiah Quincy*, 406–07.

13. Wirt to Dabney Carr, Aug. 27, 1824, William Wirt Papers, Maryland Historical Society; also in John P. Kennedy, *Memoirs of the Life of William Wirt* (Philadelphia, 1849), 2:174.

14. *New-York American*, Sept. 15, 1824, reprinted in *The Letters and Journals of James Fenimore Cooper*, ed. James Franklin Beard (Cambridge, Mass., 1960), 1:114–19.

15. *New-York American,* Sept. 25, 1824; Levasseur, *Lafayette in America,* 1:134, 142–43.

16. Levasseur, *Lafayette in America,* 1:174–77; Constance McLaughlin Green, *Washington: Village and Capital, 1800–1878* (Princeton, N.J., 1962), 90–97.

17. Levasseur, *Lafayette in America,* 1:181–82; on George Washington Lafayette's sojourn in America, 1795–97, see Ferling, *The First of Men,* 444.

18. Letter reprinted in the *New-York American,* Aug. 31, 1824; Levasseur, *Lafayette in America,* 1:183.

19. Ibid., 183–84.

20. Ibid., 185.

21. Henry S. Randall, *The Life of Thomas Jefferson* (New York, 1858), 3:503–04; also Dumas Malone, *Jefferson and His Time* (Boston, 1948–81), 6:403–08.

22. Carr to David Watson (of Louisa City, Virginia), Dec. 8, 1824, in Watson Family Papers, Manuscripts Division, University of Virginia Library.

23. Jefferson's statement in *Niles' Weekly Register,* Oct. 23, 1824; Virginia's situation, Washington's letter of June 8, 1781, and Tarleton's activities, in Randall, *The Life of Thomas Jefferson,* 1:330–41, 3:503–04.

24. Randall, *The Life of Thomas Jefferson,* 3:504.

25. Levasseur, *Lafayette in America,* 1:217–19.

26. Ibid., 220–22.

27. For a compelling discussion of Madison's late-life views on slavery, see Drew R. McCoy, *The Last of the Fathers: James Madison and the Republican Legacy* (Cambridge, 1989), esp. chap. 7.

28. *Niles' Weekly Register,* Dec. 18, 1824.

29. Margaret Bayard Smith, *Forty Years of Washington Society,* ed. Gaillard Hunt (New York, 1906), 189.

30. On Jackson's sudden popularity and the rise of America's spirits in 1815, see in particular "The Retreat of the English," a poem written for the *New Orleans Gazette* and reprinted in the *New-York Evening Post,* Mar. 22, 1815; Levasseur, *Lafayette in America,* 2:89–90.

31. Levasseur, *Lafayette in America,* 2:90–91.

32. Ibid., 91–94; [A Citizen of New-Orleans], *Visit of General Lafayette to Louisiana, Containing the Speeches Addressed to Him, With His Answers* (New Orleans, 1825), 42–43.

33. Levasseur, *Lafayette in America,* 2:136–47.

34. Ibid., 148.

35. Ibid., 150–52.

36. Ibid., 156–57; *Niles' Weekly Register,* Apr. 9, 1825.

37. Levasseur, *Lafayette in America*, 2:158–69. Unlike her politician husband, Lucretia Hart Clay, it was said, never made an enemy. She is characterized by Margaret Bayard Smith early in their long acquaintance, as "a woman of strong natural sense, very kind and friendly." See Smith, *Forty Years of Washington Society*, 85.

38. *Kentucky Reporter*, May 23, 1825.

39. Levasseur, *Lafayette in America*, 2:172–78.

40. Ibid., 182–83.

41. Ibid., 188–99.

42. Ibid., 202–03; Sarah Harvey Porter, *The Life and Times of Anne Royall* (New York, 1972 [1908]), 68–70. After Lafayette's visit to Boston in August 1824, Edward Everett had led a subscription drive for the Bunker Hill monument. It was his intent to ascribe the whole sum collected to Lafayette alone, so as to make Lafayette the monument's symbolic benefactor. See Everett broadside at the American Antiquarian Society. Anne Royall met Everett, and described his face as "angelic."

43. "The Bunker Hill Monument Address," in *The Writings and Speeches of Daniel Webster* (Boston, 1903), 235–54.

44. Levasseur, *Lafayette in America*, 2:217–18.

45. Entry of Feb. 21, 1785, in *Diary of John Quincy Adams* (Cambridge, Mass., 1981), 1:225; entries of May 2–5, 1815, in Charles Francis Adams, ed., *Memoirs of John Quincy Adams* (Freeport, N.Y., 1969), 3:187, 189.

46. Levasseur, *Lafayette in America*, 2:245.

47. Ibid., 248–50.

48. Ibid., 251–52.

49. Ibid., 254–57.

NOTES TO CHAPTER TWO

1. As of the year 2000, no attorney general has served as many years as Wirt. The only cabinet member to serve longer was Harold Ickes, secretary of the interior during the Roosevelt and Truman Administrations, who held that post from 1933 to 1946.

2. William Wirt, *The Letters of the British Spy* (Chapel Hill, N.C., 1970 [1803]), Letter III, 143; Wirt to Dabney Carr, June 8, 1804, William Wirt Papers, Maryland Historical Society (henceforth MHS). In serialized newspaper essays published as *The Old Bachelor* (Richmond, 1814), Wirt had praised the Revolutionary generation as "plain, honest, hardy sons of virtue," while noting already that Americans stood at the "isthmus" between two generations (Essay #17, p. 105).

3. Wirt to Dabney Carr, Aug. 20, 1815, in Kennedy, *Memoirs of the Life of William Wirt*, 1:388.

4. William Wirt, *The Life of Patrick Henry* (Hartford, Conn., 1832), v–xv. For a recent analysis of Wirt's approach to writing biography, see Scott E. Casper, *Constructing American Lives: Biography and Culture in Nineteenth-Century America* (Chapel Hill, N.C., 1999), 46–47.

5. Kennedy, *Memoirs of the Life of William Wirt*, 1:15.

6. Kennedy employed euphemism to describe Wirt's behavior: "A certain boyishness of character, if I may call it so, did not altogether desert his mature age, and, indeed, often disputed the mastery in it." See ibid., 91–92.

7. Ibid., 185.

8. *Reports of the Trials of Colonel Aaron Burr (Late Vice President of the United States), for Treason* (New York, 1969 [Philadelphia, 1808]), 2:59–60.

9. Jefferson to Wirt, Jan. 10, 1808, and Wirt to Jefferson, Jan. 14, 1808, in Kennedy, *Memoirs of the Life of William Wirt*, 1:227–28.

10. Wirt to Dabney Carr, Aug. 20, 1815 in ibid., 344–48.

11. Ibid; Wirt, *Life of Patrick Henry*, xvi, 32–33.

12. William Wirt to Elizabeth Wirt, July 7, 1826, in William Wirt Papers, MHS.

13. Ibid.

14. Jefferson to Wirt, Aug. 4, 1805, Jefferson Papers, Library of Congress (henceforth DLC).

15. Wirt, *Life of Patrick Henry*, 37–47.

16. Ibid., 48, 52–53.

17. Ibid., 69–85. In the chapter-ending footnote, which recounts Henry's role in promoting crosscolonial resistance to the Stamp Act, Wirt rekindles the metaphorical fire: "after Mr. Henry had touched with his match the train of American courage, its scintillations were seen, sparkling and flashing, on every page of this paper" (i.e., the *Pennsylvania Gazette*, hitherto undone by a "drooping spirit").

18. Ibid., 111–12.

19. Ibid., 123–25, 131.

20. Ibid., 132–42.

21. Ibid., 149–65; Jefferson to Maria Cosway, Oct. 12, 1786, *The Papers of Thomas Jefferson*, ed. Julian Boyd, et al. (Princeton, N.J., 1950), 10:443–453.

22. From George Ticknor Curtis, *Life of Daniel Webster* (New York, 1872), cited in William R. Taylor, *Cavalier and Yankee: The Old South and American National Character* (New York, 1961), 68.

23. Wirt, *Life of Patrick Henry*, 417–43.

24. Wirt to Adams, Jan. 12, 1818; Adams to Wirt, Jan. 23, 1818, in Kennedy, *Memoirs of the Life of William Wirt*, 2:46–54.

25. William Robert Taylor, "William Wirt and the Legend of the Old South," in *William and Mary Quarterly* 14 (Oct. 1957): 481.

26. Wirt to Dabney Carr, Aug. 23, 1813, in Kennedy, *Memoirs of the Life of William Wirt*, 1:357–58. Wirt had dreamed of military glory as early as 1807, when the aggressive posture of the British navy off the coast of Virginia first produced the war fever that finally resulted in the War of 1812. See Kennedy, vol. 1, chap. 15.

27. Wirt to Francis W. Gilmer, Apr. 1, 1816, and to Dabney Carr, Apr. 7, 1816, in Kennedy, *Memoirs of the Life of William Wirt*, 1:400–07.

28. Anya Jabour, *Marriage in the Early Republic: Elizabeth and William Wirt and the Companionate Ideal* (Baltimore, Md., 1998), 105, 130–31. William Pinkney died in 1822, but something of his overconfidence apparently lived on in his son, also a lawyer. When President Adams met the son in 1825, he described his attitude as "peevish," and an arrogant remark Pinkney made as "conspicuous . . . [in] its absurdity or its impertinence." See Adams, *Memoirs of John Quincy Adams*, 7:45. On the culture of the duel, see in particular Joanne B. Freeman, "Dueling as Politics: Reinterpreting the Burr-Hamilton Duel," in *William and Mary Quarterly* (Apr. 1996): 289–318; Bertram Wyatt-Brown, *Southern Honor: Ethics and Behavior in the Old South* (New York, 1982); and Steven M. Stowe, *Intimacy and Power in the Old South: Rituals in the Lives of the Planters* (Baltimore, Md., 1987), chap. 1.

29. Elizabeth Wirt to William Wirt, Dec. 3, 1818; William Wirt to Elizabeth Wirt, Dec. 5, 1818, cited in Jabour, *Marriage in the Early Republic*, 131.

30. The Wirts' marriage, and especially Elizabeth Wirt's frustrations, forms the centerpiece of Jabour, *Marriage in the Early Republic*. One of his most captivating letters to his wife is an 1811 example that contains this conscious declaration: "Beloved of my soul, that I have ever loved you most tenderly and respected you most deeply, no one who reads these letters can ever doubt; for they bear a stamp of love that no human power can counterfeit." See Jabour, 5. For another view of Virginia marriages in this period, see Melinda S. Buza, " 'Pledges of Our Love': Friendship, Love, and Marriage among the Virginia Gentry, 1800–1825," in Edward L. Ayers and John C. Willis, eds., *The Edge of the South: Life in Nineteenth-Century Virginia* (Charlottesville, Va., 1991), 9–36.

31. William Wirt to Elizabeth Wirt, Sept. 9 and 12, 1814, cited in Jabour, *Marriage in the Early Republic*, 83, 95.

32. The brick house was bought from Tobias Lear, who had been at one time President Washington's personal secretary. See ibid., 101.

33. William Wirt to Elizabeth Wirt, Dec. 24, 25, and 26, 1825; Elizabeth Wirt to William Wirt, Dec. 26, 1825, in William Wirt Papers, MHS.

34. William Wirt to Elizabeth Wirt, Dec. 27, 1825, in William Wirt Papers, MHS.

35. William Wirt to Elizabeth Wirt, May 23 and July 2 and 4, 1825; Elizabeth Wirt to William Wirt, May 19 and July 1 and 3, 1825, in William Wirt Papers, MHS.

36. William Wirt to Elizabeth Wirt, Nov. 25, 1825, in William Wirt Papers, MHS.

37. Smith, *Forty Years of Washington Society,* 239, 244.

38. Kennedy, *Memoirs of the Life of William Wirt,* 1:136.

39. Jabour, *Marriage in the Early Republic,* 112–13; Catharine Wirt to William Wirt, May 27, 1826, in William Wirt Papers, MHS.

40. William Wirt to Elizabeth Wirt (daughter), Nov. 1, 1825, in William Wirt Papers, DLC.

41. William Wirt to Elizabeth Wirt (daughter), Dec. 2, 1825, in William Wirt Papers, DLC.

42. Elizabeth Wirt (daughter) to William Wirt, Dec. 8, 1825, in William Wirt Papers, DLC.

43. Elizabeth Wirt (daughter) to William Wirt, Dec. 25, 1825, in William Wirt Papers, DLC.

44. Adams, *Memoirs of John Quincy Adams,* 7:98; William Wirt to Elizabeth Wirt (wife), Jan. 4, 1826, in William Wirt Papers, MHS.

45. William Wirt to Elizabeth Wirt (daughter), Jan. 22, 1826, William Wirt Papers, DLC. Letter-writing style was as germane to a female's as to a male's education. Modern scholarship that effectively deals with intimacy and epistolary culture in the nineteenth century includes Karen Lystra, *Searching the Heart: Women, Men, and Romantic Love in Nineteenth-Century America* (New York, 1989), and Ellen K. Rothman, *Hands and Hearts: A History of Courtship in America* (New York, 1984).

46. Kennedy, *Memoirs of the Life of William Wirt,* 2:189–90; Jabour, *Marriage in the Early Republic,* 117–19; William Wirt to Robert Wirt, Nov. 14, 1824, in William Wirt Papers, MHS.

47. School advertised in the *United States Telegraph,* various issues between February and July 1826; Catharine Wirt to William Wirt, May 27, 1826, in William Wirt Papers, MHS.

48. William Wirt to Agnes Wirt, Aug. 12, 1825, in William Wirt Papers, MHS.

49. Agnes Wirt to William Wirt, Dec. 4, 1825; William Wirt to Elizabeth Wirt, Dec. 5, 1825, in William Wirt Papers, MHS.

50. William Wirt to Elizabeth Wirt, Jan. 7, 1826, in William Wirt Papers, MHS.

51. William Wirt to Agnes Wirt, Jan. 21 and May 8, 1826; Agnes Wirt to William Wirt, May 7, 1826, William Wirt Papers, DLC.

52. Kennedy, *Memoirs of the Life of William Wirt,* 2:203, 207–08; Kennedy vaguely indicates that Wirt and Jefferson had a meeting, which the author presumes to have been "melancholy," but the surviving record of

Wirt's papers does not specifically indicate this. This was also the time of Lafayette's second visit to Monticello, and Wirt was seated on the general's right during a Charlottesville dinner. He marveled at the level of dignity he had attained: "They toasted the Marquis—They toasted Monroe and they toasted—*me*!!!" See William Wirt to [unnamed], Aug. 20, 1825 [not dated, but clearly the twentieth], in William Wirt Papers, MHS. For Wirt's comments on his visit with Laura to Monticello, see William Wirt to Elizabeth Wirt, Aug. 26, 1825, in William Wirt Papers, MHS. The office of president of the University of Virginia was not reestablished until early in the twentieth century.

53. Wirt to Benjamin Edwards, Mar. 17, 1805, in Kennedy, *Memoirs of the Life of William Wirt*, 1:135.

NOTES TO CHAPTER THREE

1. *North American Review* (July 1825), 98–99. The reviewer found fault with "the crowding of persons and plots, and the last exceedingly complicated"—a criticism as easily applied to *Yorktown*. "Still," the reviewer went on, "we should call it a respectable novel."

2. Hannah Webster Foster, *The Coquette*, ed. Cathy N. Davidson (New York, 1986), 9, 13, 22, 29. The full title of the first edition is: *The Coquette; or, the History of Eliza Wharton; a Novel; Founded on Fact. By a Lady of Massachusetts* (Boston: Samuel Etheridge, 1797).

3. *The Sunday School or Village Sketches* was published in Andover, Massachusetts, by Flagg & Gould. Harriet Vaughn Foster (Cheney) also wrote the historical novel *A Peep at the Pilgrims*, published by Wells and Lilly in 1824, the same year that *Saratoga* appeared. *A Peep at the Pilgrims* takes place in Plymouth in the 1630s and concerns Indians, kidnapping, and timely rescues. The critic for the *North American Review* rated it a mediocre work. See *North American Review* (July 1825), 95–96. A valuable analysis appears in Linda K. Kerber, *Women of the Republic: Intellect and Ideology in Revolutionary America* (Chapel Hill, N.C., 1980), 272–74.

4. *North American Review* (Oct. 1825), 300–59. On the growth of Byron's reputation, see esp. Peter X. Accardo, "Byron in America to 1830," *Harvard Library Bulletin* 9 (Summer 1998). I thank Brad Bradley for bringing this special issue to my attention. For a powerful biography, see Benita Eisler, *Byron: Child of Passion, Fool of Fame* (New York, 1999).

5. The text of *Childe Harold's Pilgrimage* used here is from *The Works of Lord Byron* (Ware, England, 1994), 174–244. Note that the epigraph in *Yorktown* does not specifically identify where the quote is taken from other than to state that they are lines of Byron.

6. [Eliza Foster], *Yorktown: An Historical Romance* (Boston, 1826).

7. Levasseur, *Lafayette in America*, 1:189.

8. Foster, *The Coquette*, 22, 82.

9. [Herman Mann], *The Female Review: Or, Memoirs of an American Young Lady* (Dedham, Mass., 1797), v–vi.

10. Ibid., viii, 62–67, 85–86. On the importance of dress in defining gender roles, see Nancy Isenberg, *Sex and Citizenship in Antebellum America* (Chapel Hill, N.C., 1998), chap. 3.

11. *The Female Review*, 119, 129, 132–33.

12. Ibid., 151–52, 171–75, 230–38. For the determination that Deborah Sampson did not fight at Yorktown, as well as the fact that her live performances in 1802–03 were advertised in the Boston press, I owe a debt to the novelist Jan Nelson, who has conducted extensive research into Sampson's life. Note, too, the popularity of *The Female Marine*, a work of fiction first published in 1815. Eliza Foster certainly would have been familiar, too, with this reputed true account of one Lucy Brewer (a.k.a. Louisa Baker) of Plymouth, Massachusetts, a seduced woman who, disguised as a man, fled a life of prostitution and served commendably on the frigate *Constitution* during the War of 1812. See Daniel A. Cohen's introduction to Cohen, ed., *The Female Marine and Related Works: Narratives of Cross-Dressing and Urban Vice in America's Early Republic* (Amherst, Mass., 1997).

13. The point here concerns both the writing of history and understandings of female roles. Within what has been called "domestic feminism," early-nineteenth-century women like Eliza Foster (in part through her character Helen Leslie) could relate moral lessons of history without outreaching themselves, or overstepping gender boundaries then in place. Mercy Otis Warren, a patriotic dramatist-satirist during the War for Independence, went on to compile a three-volume history of the American Revolution in 1805, without challenging patriarchal assumptions. Susanna Rowson, another successful female novelist of Hannah Foster's generation, turned from novel writing to promoting the study of history, and wrote in her 1811 work, *A Present for Young Ladies:* "History is the common school of mankind, equally open and useful to all; every age, condition, and sex may derive advantages from its study." See Nina Baym, *American Women Writers and the Work of History* (New Brunswick, N.J., 1995), chap. 2; Andrew Burstein, *Sentimental Democracy: The Evolution of America's Romantic Self-Image* (New York, 1999), 311–15.

14. An extended analysis of Cooper's role in establishing the trend in American historical romance novels appeared in the *North American Review*. Lamenting an obligation to report on "the trash which appears under this disguise," the reviewer gave Cooper his due: "Mr. Cooper, however, has the almost singular merit of writing American novels which everyone reads. . . . No one has yet appeared among us who has been wholly able to cope with him in his proper walk." See *North Amer-*

ican Review (July 1826), 150–51. Cooper's first such novel was *The Spy* (1821), followed by *The Pioneers* (1823) and *The Pilot* (1824).

15. James Fenimore Cooper, *The Last of the Mohicans: A Narrative of 1757* (New York, 1962), 257–58.

16. Ibid., 92, 152–53.

17. *New-York Mirror, and Ladies' Literary Gazette,* May 27, 1826.

18. Levasseur, *Lafayette in America,* 1:127.

19. *New-York Mirror, and Ladies' Literary Gazette,* Jan. 14, 1826.

20. "Retort," in *New-York Mirror, and Ladies' Literary Gazette,* Jan. 7, 1826.

21. The pose expected of women like Eliza Foster is particularly well explored in Mary Kelley, *Private Women, Public Stage: Literary Domesticity in Nineteenth-Century America* (New York, 1984).

22. *New-York Mirror, and Ladies' Literary Gazette,* Mar. 4, 1826.

23. Lord Byron's premature death fulfilled the romantic imagination, adding fuel to Americans' constant longing to extract larger meaning from the course of human events. For example, the Apr. 29, 1825, issue of the *Liberty Hall & Cincinnati Gazette* called Byron's death a "strange and singular destiny," traceable to some lines in Canto IV of his *Childe Harold:*

> *Have I not had to wrestle with my lot?*
> *Have I not suffer'd things to be forgiven?*
> *Have I not had my brain sear'd, my heart riven,*
> *Hopes sapp'd, name blighted . . . ?*
> *But I have lived, and have not lived in vain:*
> *My mind may lose its force, my blood its fire,*
> *And my frame perish even in conquering pain;*
> *But there is that within me which shall tire*
> *Torture and Time, and breathe when I expire.*

The forces that had caused the real Byron to be "flung upon the world" and then "betrayed into regretted excesses" taught universal lessons, according to this interpretation.

NOTES TO CHAPTER FOUR

1. Dorothy T. Wilder, *A History of the First Parish Unitarian-Universalist Church of Ashby, Massachusetts* (Ashby, Mass., 1967); Edwin P. Conklin, *Middlesex County and Its People: A History* (New York, 1927), 2:481–83.

2. *Vital Records of Leicester, Massachusetts* (Worcester, Mass., 1903), 48, 165; Henshaw to General Artemus Ward and commissioned officers, Jan. 2, 1775, in Henshaw Family Papers, American Antiquarian Society (henceforth AAS). (Subsequent letters of Mar. 6, 1775, from Henshaw

to Ward and Mar. 27, 1775, from Asa Baldwin to Henshaw distinguished the "Minute Men" from the general militia); William to Phebe Henshaw, July 14, 1775, and Jan. 7 and May 5, 1776; Phebe to William Henshaw, July 16 and Aug. 9, 1775.

3. Specific references here are from 1789 and 1790 volumes of the Diary of Ruth Henshaw Bascom, which is owned by the American Antiquarian Society, Worcester, Massachusetts.

4. Ruth Bascom, Diary, Feb. 22, June 1, and July 4, 1800.

5. Ruth Bascom, Diary, Feb. 22–27 and May 26, 1820, and Apr. 28 and July 4, 1790.

6. *Vital Records of Westminster, Massachusetts* (Worcester, Mass., 1908), 61, 166, 236.

7. But first, Ruth needed to come to terms with her most recent loss. She wrote of Catherine again: "Saw her consigned to the gloomy mansions of the dead—May this scene of affliction be made subservient to our everlasting good. . . . May we be enabled to make daily preparations for the solemn period when this mortal shall put on immortality!"

8. *Vital Records of Phillipston, Massachusetts* (Worcester, Mass., 1906), 11, 98; various diary entries.

9. E. L. Bascom to Horatio Gates Henshaw, Aug. 17, 1811, Jan. 27, 1812, and Mar. 20, 1814; Ruth Bascom to Horatio Gates Henshaw, Oct. 12, 1812, and Feb. 9, 1814, in Henshaw Family Papers, AAS.

10. Ruth Bascom, Diary, Nov. 2–10, 1808, and Feb. 24, 1820.

11. Wilder, *A History of the First Parish Unitarian-Universalist Church of Ashby, Massachusetts;* "disaffection" was the word used in the published sermon given by Rev. John Foster before the Ecclesiastical Council on the occasion of Reverend Bascom's installation as Ashby's minister on January 3, 1821. It mentions April 1819 as the time when "disaffection" in Phillipston was expressed toward Bascom. The "subjects of difficulty" were investigated, and Bascom cleared. See *Results of Council, SERMON, Charge to the Pastor, Address to the Church and People, and Right Hand of Fellowship, at the Installation of Rev. Ezekiel L. Bascom . . .* (Worcester, Mass., Mar. 1821), 19; see Daniel Walker Howe, *The Unitarian Conscience: Harvard Moral Philosophy, 1805–1861* (Cambridge, Mass., 1970), 218*ff,* concerning the 1820 schism between New England liberals and Calvinists. That year, a Massachusetts Supreme Court ruling made it feasible for a community to settle a minister of its choosing, even if a majority in the church itself opposed such change—this is what happened in the case of Reverend Bascom's appointment in Ashby.

12. The marquis is thought to have had a connection to a Masonic lodge in France even before coming to America; see Maurice de la Fuye and Emile Babeau, *The Apostle of Liberty: A Life of La Fayette* (New York, 1956).

13. Levasseur, *Lafayette in America*, 1:210.

14. Steven C. Bullock, *Revolutionary Brotherhood: Freemasonry and the Transformation of the American Social Order, 1730–1840* (Chapel Hill, N.C., 1996), 137, 152, 223.

15. Ibid., chap. 1, and 140–42.

16. *Richmond Enquirer*, Oct. 24, 1826, reprinting an address of June 24, 1826.

17. *Supporter, and Scioto Gazette* (Chillicothe, Ohio), June 8, 1826.

18. *Supporter, and Scioto Gazette,* July 20, 1826. Similarly, the same paper, July 27, 1826, citing a June address at the Scioto Lodge: "Free-Masonry has been a means in all ages of preserving the literature of antiquity from destruction."

19. Ezekiel L. Bascom, *Masonic Discourse Spoken at Greenfield, Massachusetts, Before the Officers and Brethren of the Republican Lodge of Free and Accepted Masons . . .* (Greenfield, Mass., 1800), 8, 12.

20. Ezekiel L. Bascom, *A Sermon, Delivered at Westfield, (Mass.) at the Request of the Officers and Members of Friendly Society Lodge, of Ancient Masons* (Hartford, Conn., 1815), 7–8, 10–12.

21. Ezekiel L. Bascom, *An Address, Delivered at Leicester, (Mass.), Before King Solomon's R.A. Chapter, in Conjunction with Several Lodges . . .* (Leicester, Mass., 1817), 6–7, 13, 16.

22. Ezekiel L. Bascom, *Farewell! A Discourse, Delivered at Phillipston, December 31, 1820* (Worcester, Mass., 1821), 8.

23. Ibid., 9–12.

24. Ruth Bascom, Diary, Dec. 31, 1820.

25. *Results of Council, SERMON, Charge to the Pastor,* 9–20, 27–28.

26. Ruth Bascom, Diary, Feb. 12 and 19, 1826.

27. *Massachusetts Spy, and Worcester County Advertiser,* Jan. 4, 1826.

28. *Massachusetts Spy,* Mar. 1, 1826; *New-York Mirror, and Ladies' Literary Gazette,* Jan. 28, 1826.

29. *Massachusetts Spy,* Mar. 15, 1826. Around the country, other newspapers were printing odes on death at the same time. In the *National Crisis* (Cincinnati) of March 9, for example, under the simple heading "DEATH," a paragraph asserted the importance of humility in life: death was the inevitable "sovereign cure of human pride." This paragraph was followed by a poem titled "Death-Bed of the Pious," that promised "a holy, vested calm,/That breathes of bliss and heaven."

30. Ruth Bascom, Diary, March 31, 1826.

31. *Massachusetts Spy,* Mar. 29, 1826; Ruth Bascom, Diary, Feb. 20, 1820, and Mar. 31, 1826.

32. Ruth Bascom, Diary, various entries of April–May 1826; *Massachusetts Spy,* Apr. 5, 1826.

33. Caroline F. Sloat, ed., *Meet Your Neighbors: New England Portraits, Painters, & Society, 1790–1850* (Sturbridge, Mass., 1992), 84, 100; Clara

Endicott Sears, *Some American Primitives: A Study of New England Faces and Folk Portraits* (Boston, 1941), 118–24; Mary Eileen Egan, "Ruth Henshaw Bascom: New England Portraitist," Honor's Thesis, Holy Cross College, 1980; Georgia Brady Bumgardner, "The Early Career of Ethan Allen Greenwood," in Peter Benes, ed., *Itinerancy in New England and New York* (Boston, 1986), 212–25; Greenwood owned a physiognotrace box, used in making silhouette profiles, but Ruth most likely drew and cut freehand. See Greenwood Diary, 1806, memo no. 29, at the American Antiquarian Society.

34. Ruth Bascom, Diary, May 11–25, 1826; Sloat, ed., *Meet Your Neighbors*, 32.

35. Washington Irving, "The Widow and Her Son," and "Rural Funerals," in *The Sketch Book*, part of *The Works of Washington Irving*, 1:146–53, 176–88.

36. Jan Lewis, *The Pursuit of Happiness: Family and Values in Jefferson's Virginia* (Cambridge, 1983), chap. 3, quote at 95.

37. Ibid., 69; Barry Schwartz, *George Washington: The Making of an American Symbol* (New York, 1987), esp. 101–02.

38. Lewis, *The Pursuit of Happiness*, 82–85.

39. Ibid., 86.

40. *Childe Harold's Pilgrimage*, Canto III, 207.

NOTES TO CHAPTER FIVE

1. John Samuel Still, *The Life of Ethan Allen Brown, Governor of Ohio*, Ph.D. dissertation, Ohio State University, 1951, chap. 1.

2. Michael A. Bellesiles, *Revolutionary Outlaws: Ethan Allen and the Struggle for Independence on the Early American Frontier* (Charlottesville, Va., 1993).

3. Still, *The Life of Ethan Allen Brown*, chap. 2.

4. Ibid., chaps. 3–5.

5. Ibid., chaps. 4 and 5; *The Papers of Henry Clay*, ed., James F. Hopkins (Lexington, Ky., 1959–1991), 2:720–23; *The Papers of Daniel Webster, Legal Papers*, ed. Andrew J. King (Hanover, N.H., 1989), 3:291–93.

6. *North American Review* (Oct. 1826), 459–60. According to the 1820 census, there were also a comparable number of towns in the state named after military heroes William Henry Harrison and Andrew Jackson.

7. R. Douglas Hurt, *The Ohio Frontier: Crucible of the Old Northwest, 1720–1830* (Bloomington, Ind., 1996); Andrew R. L. Cayton, *The Frontier Republic: Ideology and Politics in the Ohio Country, 1780–1825* (Kent, Ohio, 1986).

8. William T. Utter, *The Frontier State, 1803–1825*, Volume II of Carl Wittke, ed., *The History of the State of Ohio* (Columbus, Ohio, 1942), 34, 334–37. Politics surrounding canal construction were deemed more

important to Ohioans than the election of 1824, according to the *Liberty Hall & Cincinnati Gazette.* See Harry B. Scheiber, *Ohio Canal Era: A Case Study of Government and the Economy, 1820–1861* (Athens, Ohio, 1968), 24. The complex roots of the state's political alignment are detailed in Donald J. Ratcliffe, *Party Spirit in a Frontier Republic: Democratic Politics in Ohio, 1793–1821* (Columbus, Ohio, 1998).

9. Utter, *The Frontier State,* 6–12, 213–14, 392–93.

10. *Boston News-Letter* article, reprinted in the *Ohio Oracle* (Wooster, Ohio weekly), May 26, 1826. With a stab at wry humor, the writer went on to observe that he might even forget the "ingratitude of human beings" for a precious while—*"though one wonders how"*—by perusing the speech of a long-winded member of Congress reprinted in the papers.

11. "For the Ladies," in the *Supporter, and Scioto Gazette,* Jan. 5, 1826.

12. Ads variously from late 1825 through summer 1826. A Cincinnati piano-maker established a shop around 1818, before which time pianos had to be imported from New Orleans. See Utter, *The Frontier State, 1803–1825,* 408.

13. *The Compleat Housewife* in 1742 gave directions for cheese making: "Take the new milk of twelve cows in the morning, and the evening cream of twelve cows, and put to it three spoonfuls of rennet: and when it is come, break it, and whey it [remove the liquid]." See T. A. Layton, *The Cheese Handbook* (New York, 1973), 69–71; David Kolatch, ed., *Completely Cheese* (Middle Village, N.Y., 1978), 10–14. Defined simply as a "ferment" in Samuel Johnson's *Dictionary* (Philadelphia, 1813), and thus an organic catalyst speeding up chemical changes in the milk, rennet was the dried inner membrane of a calf's stomach.

14. Dumas Malone, *Jefferson the President: First Term, 1801–1805* (Boston, 1970), 106–08; Kolatch, ed., *Completely Cheese,* 11–12. Even before Leland's "mammoth cheese," German butchers in Philadelphia had sent President Jefferson what might be called a "mammoth veal," the hind quarter of the largest calf ever seen in that part of Pennsylvania. Unfortunately, it arrived at Jefferson's door too late to be safely ingested.

15. Sally McMurry, *Transforming Rural Life: Dairying Families and Agricultural Change, 1820–1885* (Baltimore, Md., 1995), 6–15.

16. An 1826 example of the mobility of Ohio drovers is found in the May 19 issue of the *Ohio Oracle.* The Baltimore market is the subject of this particular appeal to drovers to announce their intentions to sell cattle.

17. McMurry, *Transforming Rural Life,* 16–22, 46.

18. William Cooper Howells, *Recollections of Life in Ohio, from 1813 to 1840* (Cincinnati, Ohio, 1895), 125–26. The author is the father of the writer William Dean Howells; *Liberty Hall & Cincinnati Gazette,* Jan. 13, 1826.

19. Richard Osborn Cummings, *The American and His Food* (Chicago, 1940), chap. 2; Richard J. Hooker, *Food and Drink in America: A History*

(Indianapolis, Ind., 1981), chap. 8; Frances Trollope, *Domestic Manners of the Americans* (New York, 1927 [1832]), 51.

20. John S. Wright, *Letters from the West; or a Caution to Emigrants* (Salem, N.Y., 1819), 21–25.

21. Cummings, *The American and His Food*, chap. 2; Richard Pillsbury, *No Foreign Food: The American Diet in Time and Place* (Boulder, Colo., 1998), 31–39; Sarah N. Randolph, *The Domestic Life of Thomas Jefferson* (Charlottesville, Va., 1978 [1871]); Barbara McEwan, *Thomas Jefferson, Farmer* (Jefferson, N.C., 1991). Where vegetables were routinely used in cooking, particularly in New England, they were most often dried (as peas and green beans) and combined in soups or porridges.

22. Trollope, *Domestic Manners of the Americans*, 42; Ian M. G. Quimby, ed., *The Craftsman in Early America* (New York, 1984), 234–37, part of a chapter that primarily concerns the transmission of shoemaking skills in Massachusetts, where a shoe factory culture would emerge by mid-century.

23. June Swann, *Shoes* (London, 1982), chap. 4; R. Turner Wilcox, *The Mode in Footwear* (New York, 1948), 131–32, 147–48. Drawings of men's boots in newspaper ads generally bore the appearance of the Wellington style. Note that in Newark in 1826, according to a special census relative to preparations for the jubilee celebration, there were counted a remarkable 685 shoemakers in a town with a total population of eight thousand. See *The First Jubilee of American Independence . . .* (Newark, N.J., 1826), 36.

24. Howells, *Recollections of Life in Ohio*, 115–19; I. T. Frary, *Early Homes of Ohio* (Richmond, Ind., 1936); Trollope, *Domestic Manners of the Americans*, 41–43, 73.

25. Trollope, *Domestic Manners of the Americans*, 50–55, 72; Hooker, *Food and Drink in America*, 118, 134; Utter, *The Frontier State, 1803–1825*, 169–70.

26. B. Drake and E. D. Mansfield, *Cincinnati in 1826* (Cincinnati, Ohio 1827), 33–37, 40–45, 52, 57, 64–65; *National Crisis*, Mar. 13, 1826; various issues of *Liberty Hall & Cincinnati Gazette* for 1825–26.

27. Utter, *The Frontier State*, 32–34; Carter G. Woodson, "Negroes of Cincinnati Prior to the Civil War," *Journal of Negro History* 1 (Jan. 1916). Woodson describes the period up to 1826 as a time of "toleration" of blacks, succeeded by a period of greater controversy owing in some measure to abolitionist agitation elsewhere in the Union. Business-minded white citizens of the city who traded extensively with the South found it preferable to placate Southerners than for their city to acquire the reputation as a haven for runaways. In the decade of the 1820s, Cincinnati's black population more than tripled, and particular Virginians who manumitted their slaves (sometimes hundreds at a time, as stipulated in their wills) looked to Ohio for resettlement, causing alarm among Ohio's whites. See Francis P. Weisenburger, *The Passing of the*

Frontier, 1825–1850, Volume III of Wittke, ed., *The History of the State of Ohio* (Columbus, Ohio, 1941), 42–47, and Utter, *The Frontier State*, 396–97. More recently, Donald Ratcliffe has assembled materials that indicate a level of intolerance for blacks in the pre-1826 period as well as efforts to assist black settlement. See Ratcliffe, *Party Spirit in a Frontier Republic*, esp. 231–34.

28. Trollope's quintessential encounter with a milkman explores the relationship of newspaper reading and Americans' embrace of political democracy. If not for the papers, the milkman quips, "How should freemen spend their time, but looking after their government, and watching that them fellers as we gives offices to, doos their duty . . . ?" The one day on which Trollope put aside her disparagement of Americans' "coarse familiarity" was the Fourth of July, 1828, in Cincinnati. "[I]t was indeed a glorious sight to behold a jubilee so heartfelt as this," she wrote. While she understandably disapproved of the reading of "the warlike manifesto called the Declaration of Independence," she found the people on that day more "high-spirited, gay, animated, social, generous" than she had previously seen them. If only, she lamented, they would "refrain from spitting on that hallowed day," she might eventually regard them as "an amiable people." Trollope, *Domestic Manners of the Americans*, 71, 85.

29. *Ohio Oracle*, May 4 and June 9, 1826.

30. Newspaper carrier's address, in the *New-York Mirror, and Ladies' Literary Gazette*, Jan. 7, 1826.

31. Frank Wilcox, *The Ohio Canals* (Kent, Ohio, 1969); Review of the *Report of the Canal Commissioners to the General Assembly of Ohio, Dec. 12th, 1825*, in *North American Review* (Apr. 1826), 459.

32. See esp. Scheiber, *Ohio Canal Era*, chap. 3, and Ronald E. Shaw, *Canals for a Nation: The Canal Era in the United States, 1790–1860* (Lexington, Ky., 1990), chap. 6. When Secretary of State Henry Clay was honored at a public dinner in Cincinnati in July 1825, he noted that of all the toasts drunk none revealed greater popular sentiment than the salute to "their Great Canal." Clay to John Quincy Adams, July 21, 1825, *Papers of Henry Clay*, 4:546–47.

33. Scheiber, *Ohio Canal Era*, 3–25, 61–87; Alvin F. Harlow, *Old Towpaths: The Story of the American Canal Era* (New York, 1926), 241; March 1826 issues of the *Liberty Hall & Cincinnati Gazette*; Drake and Mansfield, *Cincinnati in 1826*, 45.

34. Ibid., 74–75, 83; Ophia D. Smith, "Cincinnati: From Keelboat to Steamboat," *Historical and Philosophical Society of Ohio Bulletin* 15 (Oct. 1957): 259–89.

35. Drake and Mansfield, *Cincinnati in 1826*, 79, 84–86.

36. *Commencement of the Ohio Canal at the Licking Summit, July 4, 1825*, copy

of original text of 1825 in the archives of the Ohio Historical Society. Porter, *The Life and Times of Anne Royall,* 66–67.

37. Shaw, *Canals for a Nation,* 19–29, quote at 29. Few recalled that George Washington himself had been a canal promoter, desiring to extend the Potomac River west, linking it with smaller waterways and eventually meeting Lake Erie. He had hoped to strengthen nationalist sentiment through economic ties, fearing that if this were not done Western settlers would desire to separate from the Union. See Ferling, *The First of Men,* 333–34.

38. Carol Sheriff, *The Artificial River: The Erie Canal and the Paradox of Progress, 1817–1862* (New York, 1996), 19–26, 64; Scheiber, *Ohio Canal Era,* 88–91.

39. *National Crisis,* May 18, 1826.

40. *Richmond Enquirer,* Feb. 7, 1826.

41. *Liberty Hall & Cincinnati Gazette,* June 16, 1826; first appearing in the *New-York American,* May 30, 1826, also the *Albany* (New York) *Argus & Daily City Gazette,* June 1, 1826.

42. See especially the argument advanced in John McWilliams, *The Last of the Mohicans: Civil Savagery and Savage Civility* (New York, 1995), chap. 4. Also see Blake Nevius, *Cooper's Landscapes: An Essay on the Picturesque Vision* (Berkeley, Calif., 1976) and Kay Seymour House, *Cooper's Americans* (Columbus, Ohio, 1965). On romantic nature and the pioneer ethos, see Andrew Burstein, *Sentimental Democracy: The Evolution of America's Romantic Self-Image* (New York, 1999), 274–87.

43. Utter, *The Frontier State,* 30, 326–27; synopsis of a biography of Governor Morrow by S. Winifred Smith, at the Ohio Historical Society; Still, *The Life of Ethan Allen Brown,* 204.

44. As recounted in the *Kentucky Reporter,* July 31, 1826.

45. Still, *The Life of Ethan Allen Brown,* 19–20.

46. Ibid., 160–61.

47. Clinton to Brown, Dec. 29, 1825, and Feb. 6, 1826, Ethan Allen Brown Papers, Ohio Historical Society.

48. Clinton to Brown, Apr. 26, 1826, Ethan Allen Brown Papers, Ohio Historical Society. The discomfort of nineteenth-century Americans with bachelorhood and childlessness is nicely brought out in John W. M. Hallock, *The American Byron: Homosexuality and the Fall of Fitz-Greene Halleck* (Madison, Wisc., 2000).

NOTES TO CHAPTER SIX

1. John Davis to Elvira Davis, Dec. 3, 1825, John Davis Correspondence, American Antiquarian Society; *Nashville Whig,* July 30, 1825, citing an article in the *New Hampshire Patriot.*

2. James Sterling Young, *The Washington Community, 1800–1828* (New York, 1966), chap. 2; Green, *Washington*, 93–94; Harriet Martineau, *Retrospect of Western Travel* (New York, 1838), 1:143–44; Davis to Elvira Davis, Dec. 3, 1825.

3. Davis to Elvira Davis, Dec. 4 & 7, 1825, John Davis Correspondence, AAS.

4. Ibid; advertisements in the *United States Telegraph*, Feb. 8, 18, and 23, 1826.

5. Davis to John Bancroft Davis, Dec. 21, 1825, John Davis Correspondence, AAS. "Young Master John" (1822–1907) would later serve as a member of the U.S. diplomatic corps in London from 1849 to 1853.

6. Davis to Elvira Davis, Jan 9, 1826, John Davis Correspondence, AAS.

7. Davis to Elvira Davis, Jan. 13, 1826, John Davis Correspondence, AAS. For a discussion of nineteenth-century New Englanders' sense of their provincialism in the context of social dinners, see Catherine E. Kelly, " 'Well Bred Country People': Sociability, Social Networks, and the Creation of a Provincial Middle Class, 1820–1860," *Journal of the Early Republic* 19 (Fall 1999): 451–79.

8. Hiller B. Zobel, *The Boston Massacre* (New York, 1970), 220–21. The ensuing discussion draws upon thoughts and events conveyed in the published diaries and papers of both John Adams and John Quincy Adams, and also neatly synthesized in Lynn Hudson Parsons, *John Quincy Adams* (Madison, Wisc., 1998).

9. John Adams to Abigail Adams, July 3, 1776, in C. F. Adams, ed., *Familiar Letters of John Adams and His Wife Abigail, During the Revolution* (New York, 1876), 193–94.

10. Entries of Aug. 27, Oct. 28, and Nov. 11, 1783, *Diary of John Quincy Adams* (Cambridge, Mass., 1981), 1:187, 197, 202, 262.

11. Ibid., 2:260–61.

12. Entry of Aug. 12, 1788, in ibid., 441.

13. On the personal dimension of the Adams-Jefferson rift, see Andrew Burstein, *The Inner Jefferson: Portrait of a Grieving Optimist* (Charlottesville, Va., 1995), 173–80. Jefferson, himself quite thin-skinned, confronted the evidence underlying Adams's anger in an exchange with Abigail Adams—letters that she wrote without consulting her husband. See especially Abigail Adams to Jefferson, July 1, 1804, and Jefferson's reply of July 22, 1804, *Adams-Jefferson Letters*, 271–76.

14. Hugh A. Garland, *The Life of John Randolph of Roanoke* (New York, 1857), 242–44.

15. Adams, *Memoirs of John Quincy Adams*, 3:40. Adams's quintessential account of Clay's belligerence and resort to "brag," is in ibid., 101.

16. Cited in Parsons, *John Quincy Adams*, 117.

17. Robert V. Remini, *Henry Clay: Statesman for the Union* (New York, 1991), 130–31.

18. Adams, *Memoirs of John Quincy Adams,* 3:565.
19. Henry S. Randall, *The Life of Thomas Jefferson* (New York, 1858), 3:441. On Jefferson's psychologically complex relationship with Monroe, see Andrew Burstein, "Jefferson's Madison versus Jefferson's Monroe," *Presidential Studies Quarterly* 28 (Spring 1998): 394–408.
20. Text as reprinted in *Niles' Weekly Register,* July 21, 1821, 326–32.
21. For the bright career of Crawford, see Chase C. Mooney, *William H. Crawford, 1772–1834* (Lexington, Ky., 1974) and Philip Jackson Green, *The Life of William Harris Crawford* (Charlotte, N.C., n.d.).
22. This number would fall to two by the election of 1828.
23. Neal R. Peirce and Lawrence D. Longley, *The People's President: The Electoral College in American History and the Direct Vote Alternative* (New Haven, Conn., 1981), 50.
24. Adams, *Memoirs of John Quincy Adams,* 6:492–93, 499–500; Henry R. Warfield to Henry Clay, July 5, 1826, *Papers of Henry Clay,* ed. James F. Hopkins et al. (Lexington, Ky., 1959–91), 5:523–24. This was written in the context of decrying Adams's stubborn insistence of appearing fair to the point where he was denying patronage jobs to those who supported him and "promoting his Enemies." Warfield reckoned that Adams was losing his friends in so doing.
25. Webster to William Gaston, May 31, 1826, *Papers of Daniel Webster, Correspondence* (Hanover, N.H., 1976), 2:116–17.
26. Smith, *The First Forty Years of Washington Society,* 186–87.
27. Jefferson to Gallatin, Aug. 2, 1823, in *The Works of Thomas Jefferson,* ed. Paul Leicester Ford (New York, 1905), 12:299–300; Jefferson to Lafayette, Nov. 4, 1823, in Randall, *Life of Thomas Jefferson,* 3:495.
28. Jefferson to Smith, Aug. 2, 1823, *Works of Thomas Jefferson,* 12:301–02.
29. Adams to Jefferson, Jan. 22, 1825; Jefferson to Adams, Feb. 15, 1825, *Adams-Jefferson Letters,* 606–09.
30. *National Intelligencer,* March 5, 1825.
31. *National Intelligencer,* March 5, 1825; *Niles' Weekly Register,* Mar. 12, 1825; public dinner in Baltimore, as detailed in the *Kentucky Reporter,* March 14, 1825.
32. Smith, *Forty Years of Washington Society,* 248.
33. Adams, *Memoirs of John Quincy Adams,* 7:97.
34. Ibid.
35. Diary entry of Nov. 26, 1825, in ibid., 63.
36. Ibid., 63–64.
37. *Register of Debates,* Nineteenth Congress, First Session (Washington, D.C., 1826), vol. 2, Appendix, 2–5.
38. Ibid., 5–9; *Liberty Hall & Cincinnati Gazette,* Dec. 23, 1825.
39. This discussion, and the ensuing paragraphs, are drawn in large part from the argument presented in Young, *The Washington Community,*

esp. chap. 11; for a thorough discussion of Jefferson's relations on Capitol Hill, see Dumas Malone, *Jefferson the President*, volumes 4 and 5 of *Jefferson and His Time*.

40. Review of Francis Wayland's published discourse, *The Duties of an American Citizen*, in *North American Review* (Oct. 1825), 366. For general works of merit on the circumstances surrounding Adams's accession to the presidency and his conduct in office, see esp. Mary W. M. Hargreaves, *The Presidency of John Quincy Adams* (Lawrence, Kans., 1985) and Samuel Flagg Bemis, *John Quincy Adams and the Union* (New York, 1956).

41. Levasseur, *Lafayette in America*, 2:24–25, 241–44. In the opinion of Levasseur, Adams was unchanged by his elevation to the presidency, his countenance "open and modest"—his opponents, indeed, having unfairly branded him.

NOTES TO CHAPTER SEVEN

1. *Register of Debates*, Nineteenth Congress, First Session (Washington, D.C., 1826), 797.

2. Ibid., Feb. 15, 1826, 1370–71.

3. The separate districts, added together, would equal the number of electoral votes the state had been awarded on the basis of the most recent national census.

4. Peirce and Longley, *The People's President*, 46. The general ticket system has evolved, but it has never been replaced by the district system. Still today, electors are awarded to the party that receives a plurality (the highest number, as opposed to a majority) of that state's votes; and in this way, all of a state's electoral votes generally go to a single national candidate. This means that every voter is voting for every elector in the electoral college to which that state is entitled. By law, the electors meet in each state capital on a specified date to vote by ballot for president and vice president. They then transmit the sealed results to Congress, to be opened and read before a joint session of Congress.

5. The vast majority of today's Americans are accustomed to the manner in which the president is elected, because for a long time the leading candidate in the popular vote has been the same individual to win with the most electoral votes. Today the presidential electors who comprise the electoral college are understood to vote according to the people's choice; that is, an elector identifies himself or herself with a particular party and a particular candidate. Technically, the voters of each district today vote not for president but for their presidential elector, who in virtually every case abides by the prescribed presidential choice the voters expect when they indicate on their ballots the specified elector. In many places, the elector's name does not even appear anymore.

6. *Register of Debates,* Nineteenth Congress, First Session, Feb. 17, 1826, 1405; Lucius Wilmerding Jr., *The Electoral College* (New Brunswick, N.J., 1958), 43, 46–48, 53–58, 73.

7. The district system had been the most talked about alternative to the general ticket plurality system ever since 1800. Representative John Nicholas of Virginia introduced the idea at that time, when reformers conceived that the district system would be the most fair, given a population in flux. Depending on how the system was standardized, qualified voters in each district would cast their votes either for an elector who would be expected to ratify their presidential choice (this was Madison's preference), or directly themselves, for the president. Either of these two options within the district system would enable a state's electoral vote to be split among leading candidates. See Peirce and Longley, *The People's President,* 29, 132–34; *Register of Debates,* Nineteenth Congress, First Session, Mar. 13, 1826, 1628–29.

8. Edwin L. Green, *George McDuffie* (Columbia, S.C., 1936), chap. 1.

9. Ibid., 23–24, 74.

10. *Nashville Republican,* Mar. 25, 1826; Green, *George McDuffie,* 139–40, 237; William W. Freehling, *Prelude to Civil War: The Nullification Controversy in South Carolina, 1816–1836* (New York, 1965), 146–47.

11. Green, *George McDuffie,* chap. 2; William Cumming, *Conduct of George M'Duffie, Esq. in Relation to an Intended Meeting Between Himself and Col. William Cumming* (Augusta, Ga., 1822), 3–5.

12. Green, *George McDuffie,* chap. 3; *Speech of George M'Duffie on the Proposition to Clear the Galleries During the Election of President by the House of Representatives* (Washington City, 1825).

13. *Register of Debates,* Nineteenth Congress, First Session, Feb. 16, 1826, 1380–86.

14. Ibid., Feb. 17, 1826, 1405–17.

15. Ibid., Feb. 23, 1826, 1438–60.

16. Ibid., Feb. 24 and Mar. 8, 1826, 1464, 1554.

17. Frothingham, *Edward Everett, Orator and Statesman,* 100–01.

18. *Register of Debates,* Nineteenth Congress, First Session, Feb. 16, 1826, 1387–90.

19. Ibid., Mar. 9, 1826, 1589–96. On the nature of political oratory and public response during this period, see Kimberly K. Smith, *The Dominion of Voice: Riot, Reason, and Romance in Antebellum Politics* (Lawrence, Kans., 1999), esp. chap. 3; Kenneth Cmiel, *Democratic Eloquence: The Fight Over Popular Speech in Nineteenth-Century America* (Berkeley, Calif., 1990); Andrew W. Robertson, *The Language of Democracy: Political Rhetoric in the United States and Great Britain, 1790–1900* (Ithaca, N.Y., 1995).

20. *Register of Debates,* Nineteenth Congress, First Session, Mar. 13, 1826, 1625–26.

21. Henry Adams, *John Randolph* (Boston, 1882), 17–19.
22. Ibid., 22.
23. Ibid., 170–71.
24. George S. Hillard, *Life, Letters, and Journals of George Ticknor* (Boston, 1876), 1:15, 27–28.
25. Garland, *The Life of John Randolph of Roanoke*, 235.
26. Irving to Henry Brevoort, June 11, 1822, in Ralph M. Aderman, et al., eds., *Washington Irving: Letters* (Boston, 1978), 1:677.
27. Quincy, *Life of Josiah Quincy,* 123.
28. Ibid., 88, 146.
29. Ibid., 94–95, 266–70.
30. Ibid., 421–22.
31. *Register of Debates,* Nineteenth Congress, First Session, Mar. 2, 1826, 116–17.
32. *Massachusetts Spy,* Mar. 15, 1826.
33. *Massachusetts Spy,* Mar. 22, 1826.
34. *Supporter, and Scioto Gazette,* May 11, 1826. Randolph's assistant Tims subsequently wrote to the *Boston Gazette,* disputing a story it had disseminated with respect to Randolph's consumption of liquor. The "six bottles of porter, two glasses of gin, and one of brandy," which were reportedly imbibed in the course of one speech, represented, according to Tims, "a base and infamous falsehood." As reported in the *Albany Argus & Daily City Gazette,* July 3, 1826.
35. *Nashville Republican,* May 13, 1826, citing the *United States Telegraph.*
36. *Liberty Hall & Cincinnati Gazette,* Mar. 17, 1826.
37. "To John Randolph, Esq.," in the *Cape Fear Recorder,* May 17, 1826, reprinted in the *United States Gazette* (Philadelphia), July 4, 1826.
38. *Register of Debates,* Nineteenth Congress, First Session, 405–07.
39. Ibid., May 18, 1826, 2659.
40. Webster to John Evelyn Denison, May 3, 1826, *Papers of Daniel Webster, Correspondence,* 2:107.

NOTES TO CHAPTER EIGHT

1. On Clay's popularity and early development, see Robert V. Remini, *Henry Clay: Statesman for the Union* (New York, 1991), chap. 2. When he first arrived in Washington in 1806, as a Kentucky senator, Clay struck his colleague from New Hampshire, William Plumer, as congenial and honest, but also a "man of pleasure," out most nights gambling, and making a name for himself among the ladies of the capital. Yet his national ambitions were immediately noticed. See *William Plumer's Memorandum of Proceedings in the United States Senate, 1803–1807,* ed. Everett S. Brown (New York, 1969), 547.

2. Clay to Blair, Jan. 8, 1825, *Papers of Henry Clay,* 4:9–10.

3. Ibid.

4. Clay to Lafayette, Dec. 13, 1825, ibid., 905.

5. On Clay and Kremer, and the "Corrupt Bargain" generally, see Remini, *Henry Clay,* chap. 15; the letter naming McDuffie was from Philadelphia; see John Binns to Clay, Feb. 27, 1826, *Papers of Henry Clay,* 4:84–85.

6. Clay to Francis Brooke, Feb. 18, 1825; and to Hammond, Apr. 4, 1825; *Papers of Henry Clay,* 73, 211. To Brooke, he wrote again just after the letter to Hammond: "I find my office no bed of roses. With spirits never more buoyant, 12 hours work per day are almost too much for my physical powers. An entire harmony as to public measures exists between Mr. Adams and me." See Clay to Brooke, Apr. 6, 1825, in ibid., 221.

7. Adams, *Memoirs of John Quincy Adams,* 5:325.

8. Ibid., 325–26.

9. Smith, *Forty Years in Washington Society,* 185–86.

10. In later years, the historian Henry Adams, grandson of John Quincy Adams, wrote of Randolph's approach to the two Adams presidents: "For thirty years he never missed a chance to have his fling at both the Adamses, father and son; the 'cub,' he said, 'is a greater bear than the old one.'" See Adams, *John Randolph,* 26, 294.

11. The standard secondary work on the tangle of issues that comprised the Missouri question in Congress is Glover Moore, *The Missouri Controversy* (Lexington, Ky., 1953); see also Merrill D. Peterson, *The Great Triumvirate: Webster, Clay, and Calhoun* (New York, 1987), 59–65.

12. Cooper, *The Last of the Mohicans,* 21; *North American Review* (July 1826), 162–63.

13. Gary Nash, *Forging Freedom: The Formation of Philadelphia's Black Community, 1720–1840* (Cambridge, Mass., 1988), chaps. 4 and 5; on Madison's support for the American Colonization Society, see Drew R. McCoy, *The Last of the Fathers: James Madison and the Republican Legacy* (Cambridge, 1989), chap. 7.

14. Nash, *Forging Freedom,* 246–60; *Liberty Hall & Cincinnati Gazette,* Apr. 22, 1825.

15. *New-York Mirror, and Ladies' Literary Gazette,* Feb. 19, 1825; Nash, *Forging Freedom,* 184–85, 235–45; P. J. Staudenraus, *The African Colonization Movement, 1816–1865* (New York, 1961), 9–11, 81–87.

16. Philip C. Hay, *Our Duty to our Coloured Population. A Sermon for the Benefit of the American Colonization Society . . .* (Newark, N.J., 1826), 13–15. On Liberia at this time, see Staudenraus, *The African Colonization Movement.* Similar to Hay, a reviewer of *A Plea for Africa* (a Fourth of July oration published in New Haven, Connecticut, in 1825) deemed colonization a cause "of great and lasting importance," by which moral African Americans stood to transform a continent long marked by

"misery and desolation" into one that respected human happiness. See the *North American Review* (Oct. 1825), 462–63.

17. Charles Caldwell, *Introductory Address on Independence of Intellect* (Lexington, Ky., 1825), 7–8, 15–16. He would temper (without dismantling) his prescription a few years later in urging the powerful white majority to shelter rather than demolish lesser peoples: "The Caucasians are not justified in either enslaving the Africans or destroying the Indians, merely because their superiority in intellect and war enables them to do so." Different races were entitled to different rights, and lesser peoples ought to be accorded those rights that they were qualified to enjoy. See Caldwell, 22–23, 40–42; Caldwell, *Thoughts on the Original Unity of the Human Race* (New York, 1830), vii. Caldwell was later described as "not a social man . . . He was proud, and bore the *appearance* of personal vanity, but was singularly candid and confiding to . . . his friends." See *The Biographical Dictionary of Kentucky* (Cincinnati, 1878), 145–46.

18. "To Electors of Fayette County," Apr. 16, 1798, *Papers of Henry Clay* 1:4.

19. Powhatan Bouldin, *Home Reminiscences of John Randolph of Roanoke* (Richmond, Va., 1878), 203; Randolph to Dr. John Brockenbrough, Feb. 20, 1826, in Garland, *The Life of John Randolph*, 266–67.

20. Ibid. Understanding, as the slave-owning Randolph did, the paradox presented by the American Colonization Society, abolitionist William Lloyd Garrison would vocally protest the unintended effects of the society's philanthropy. He saw it as "a scheme which directly tends to increase the value of the slaves, to degrade and persecute the free people of color, to quiet the consciences of slave-holders, and to perpetuate the system of slavery." See Garrison to Henry Brougham, Aug. 1, 1832, in *The Letters of William Lloyd Garrison,* ed., Walter M. Merrill (Cambridge, Mass., 1971), 1:69. Garrison's strongest indictment of the society was addressed to its agent, Elliott Cresson, as part of a challenge to debate. See Garrison to Cresson, June 4, 1833, in ibid., 235.

21. See John M. Grammer, *Pastoral and Politics in the Old South* (Baton Rouge, La., 1996). In keeping with Randolph's life of paradox, Grammer argues that Randolph defended the agrarian life with passion, but was bored with country people and constantly sought to remedy his isolation by surrounding himself with sharp, contentious minds like his own.

22. See Peter S. Onuf, *Jefferson's Empire: The Language of American Nationhood* (Charlottesville, Va., 2000). I have compressed Onuf's argument in my book *Sentimental Democracy*, 160–61.

23. In an especially revealing letter, Calhoun wrote a former New York congressman of the "secret manner" in which Adams and Clay affiliated. "Mr. Clay," he wrote, "governs the President. The latter is in his power. He has thought proper to consider me his rival; and while Mr. Adams is left to struggle with Gen Jackson as he can, the weight of the Executive

is made to bear, as Mr. Clay desires, and for his own ends." See Calhoun to Micah Sterling, Feb. 4, 1826, *Papers of John C. Calhoun,* 10:72.

24. In a letter to Dr. John Brockenbrough in March 1826, he terms himself a "passionate admirer" of Byron. See Garland, *Life of John Randolph,* 268.

25. See *Register of Debates,* Nineteenth Congress, First Session, 111–32, 152–343.

26. Ibid., 399, 401.

27. Clay to Randolph, Mar. 31, 1826, *Papers of Henry Clay,* 5:208.

28. Thomas Hart Benton, *Thirty Years' View; or, a History of the Working of the American Government for Thirty Years, From 1820 to 1850* (New York, 1883), 70. The best recent analysis is Kenneth S. Greenberg, *Honor and Slavery* (Princeton, 1996), chap. 3.

29. Harriet W. Stern, "William Carroll," in Charles W. Crawford, ed., *Governors of Tennessee, 1790–1835* (Memphis, Tenn., 1979), 125–26; William Nisbet Chambers, *Old Bullion Benton: Senator from the New West* (Boston, 1956), 13–53; Memorandum about Jackson's Duels (written by Jackson), approx. Sept. 1824, in John Spencer Bassett, ed., *Correspondence of Andrew Jackson* (Washington, D.C., 1928), 3:267.

30. Chambers, *Old Bullion Benton,* 63–75.

31. Ibid., 76.

32. Benton, *Thirty Years' View,* 70. From this point, Randolph communicated through his second. He wanted Clay to understand his position: he supported the Kentuckian's *private* right to have "satisfaction" for what he deemed an injury. But he wanted it made just as clear that he "protests against the right of any minister of the Executive Government of the U.S. to hold him responsible for words spoken in debate as a Senator of Virginia." It was essential to Randolph that the challenger see the duel only as the conspicuous act of a man of private honor who acknowledged having giving offense to another gentleman. In his memoir, Benton did his best to make this distinction, while observing that it was a subtle one, "not very clear to the common intellect." See Benton, 70–71; Randolph to Clay, Apr. 1, 1826, *Papers of Henry Clay,* 5:211–12.

33. Benton, *Thirty Years' View,* 74.

34. Ibid., 75–76.

35. Adams, *Memoirs of John Quincy Adams,* 7:51–52.

36. Benton, *Thirty Years' View,* 76.

37. Ibid., 77. Among the many newspaper reports of the duel, Randolph's privately spoken words to Benton, "that he would not have seen Mr. Clay fall dangerously wounded, not for all the land upon the King of Rivers," strongly suggests that it was Benton who served as the unnamed, reliable source used by the antiadministration *United States Telegraph,* which originated the popular account.

38. Ibid. A blackguard was one for whom crime was virtually an addiction, seen as the lowest sort of violent street criminal in the middle decades of the nineteenth century.

39. See Isenberg, *Sex and Citizenship in Antebellum America,* chap. 5. The value of retributive justice and justification for aggressive expansion of the American Union were not significantly questioned until the anti–capital punishment campaign and opposition to the Mexican War emerged in the 1840s. Note, too, that in peacetime, gentlemen officers in the South typically retained their militia rank—he was General Jackson more often than Senator Jackson, Colonel Tattnall and not Representative Tattnall. Such designations would have tended to afford some protection to one's sense of manhood that neither Clay nor Randolph could rely on.

40. *New-York Mirror, and Ladies' Literary Gazette,* Apr. 15, 1826; Washington newspaper accounts reprinted side by side in the *Nashville Republican,* Apr. 29, 1826.

41. Hughes to Clay, Apr. 12, 1826, *Papers of Henry Clay,* 5:231–32.

42. Clay to Hammond, Apr. 19, 1826, ibid., 253–54.

43. A model defense of the duel is provided in Moses Tabbs (of Indianapolis) to Clay, May 6, 1826, ibid., 309. The letter writer ritually regrets and ritually understands the "extremity" which provoked the interview. An equally strong expression of the belief that duels rarely solved anything is in James Brown (hearing a report while in Paris) to Clay, May 10, 1826, ibid., 354.

44. Clinton to Brown, Apr. 19, 1826, Ethan Allen Brown Papers. Clinton's comment on Clay actually reads: "Clay's conduct verifies on this and other occasions, the 'Quem Deus vult pendere,'" an anonymous old Latin saying, to which is ordinarily appended the words *prius dementat* and translates as "Whom God would destroy, he first makes mad." I am indebted to Jay Lees for identifying and translating the Latin quotation.

45. "Extract of a letter from Washington, April 11," in the *Richmond Enquirer,* Apr. 18, 1826.

46. Garland, *Life of John Randolph,* 261, 264, 268.

47. William Cabell Bruce, *John Randolph of Roanoke, 1773–1833* (New York, 1922), 318–19, 322–30.

48. I am indebted to Elizabeth Reis and Dr. Joan Witkin for their help on this subject. A clinical description of Klinefelter's syndrome is in M. H. Beers and R. Berkow, eds., *Merck Manual of Diagnosis and Therapy,* 17th edition (Whitehouse Station, N.J., 1999); Hillard, *Life, Letters, and Journals of George Ticknor,* 1:27.

49. Bruce, *John Randolph of Roanoke,* 319–21.

50. Bouldin, *Home Reminiscences of John Randolph of Roanoke,* 124.

51. Ibid., 45–46, 218. A modern, absorbing treatment is Robert Dawidoff, *The Education of John Randolph* (New York, 1979).
52. *Kentucky Reporter*, Mar. 18, 1825.

NOTES TO CHAPTER NINE

1. Jackson to Polk, May 3, 1826, *Correspondence of James K. Polk*, ed. Herbert Weaver (Nashville, Tenn., 1969), 1:41–42.
2. Ibid., 42–43.
3. Polk to Jackson, Apr. 3, 1826, ibid., 38–39.
4. Robert V. Remini, *Andrew Jackson and the Course of American Empire, 1767–1821* (New York, 1977), 136–43. See also Bertram Wyatt-Brown, "Andrew Jackson's Honor," *Journal of the Early Republic* 17 (Spring 1997): 1–36.
5. Burr, in turn, credited Jackson for providing him with transportation and the promise of men and equipment for his planned expedition. The shadowy vice president wrote his daughter of his welcome in Nashville on May 23, 1805: "One is astonished at the number of sensible, well-informed, and well-behaved people which is found here. I have been received with much hospitality and kindness, and could stay a month with pleasure." Mark Van Doren, ed., *Correspondence of Aaron Burr and His Daughter Theodosia* (New York, 1929), 210.
6. Remini, *Andrew Jackson and the Course of American Empire*, chap. 10.
7. *Niles' Weekly Register*, Mar. 6, 1819. Recall from chapter six that when authorized by the Monroe Administration to cross into Spanish Florida to punish Seminole Indians responsible for cross-border attacks on Georgia settlements, Jackson created an international incident by capturing the Spanish fort in Pensacola and putting to death two British subjects under the powers he took on through an aggressive interpretation of his instructions. The final result, however, was American acquisition of Florida from a weakened Spain, and it was accomplished through the astute diplomacy of Secretary of State Adams, who, unlike Secretary of War Calhoun, expressed consistent support for Jackson's controversial actions. Jackson would not fully appreciate Adams's support, nor his vice president's betrayal, until his presidency, years later, when he examined relevant documents.
8. Harriet W. Stern, "William Carroll," in Crawford, ed., *Governors of Tennessee, 1790–1835;* Lorman A. Ratner, *Andrew Jackson and His Tennessee Lieutenants* (Westport, Conn., 1997), 65–72; Stanley J. Folmsbee, et al., *Tennessee: A Short History* (Knoxville, Tenn., 1969), 163–66.
9. A letter from Carroll to Clay in 1823 informs him of political movements, which he calls "strange and uncertain," resulting in Jackson's election to the U.S. Senate. At this critical political juncture, Carroll's

tone suggests that he is hopeful Tennesseans will mount a resistance to Jackson that would obviously benefit Clay's presidential chances. See Carroll to Clay, Oct. 1, 1823, *Papers of Henry Clay,* 3:492.

10. *Liberty Hall & Cincinnati Gazette,* Aug. 1, 1826; [Charles Hammond], *View of General Jackson's Domestic Relations, in Reference to His Fitness for the Presidency* (Washington, D.C., 1828).

11. Jackson to Coffee, Feb. 15, 1824; to Samuel Swartwout, Mar. 4, 1824; to Rachel Jackson, Mar. 6, 1824, in Bassett, ed., *Correspondence of Andrew Jackson,* 3:229, 233–34, 237.

12. Jackson to Coffee, June 18, 1824, ibid., 255–56.

13. Jackson to John Coffee, Dec. 27, 1824, and Jan. 9 and 23, and Feb. 19, 1825; to Samuel Swartwout, Dec. 14, 1824, and Feb. 22 and Mar. 5, 1825, ibid., 268–70, 273–75, 277–81.

14. See especially letter to the editor of New York's *National Advocate* by Samuel Swartwout, published in *Niles' Weekly Register,* Mar. 12, 1825, accompanying a statement from Jackson constituting an honorable defense against Clay's published attacks on his character.

15. John H. Marable to Jackson, Apr. 3, 1826, in Bassett, ed., *Correspondence of Andrew Jackson,* 3:300. On Jackson and evolving concepts of masculinity, see Burstein, *Sentimental Democracy,* chap. 9.

16. Jackson to Willis Alston (of North Carolina), May 18, 1826, in Bassett, ed., *Correspondence of Andrew Jackson,* 3:301.

17. Clay to Benjamin Leigh, Oct. 20, 1823, *Papers of Henry Clay,* 3:501. On Clay's reaction to the Battle of New Orleans, see Remini, *Henry Clay: Statesman for the Union,* 125–26.

18. "Address to the People of the Congressional District," Mar. 26, 1825, *Papers of Henry Clay,* 4:152–53.

19. *National Crisis,* Apr. 27, 1826.

20. Wharton, *Social Life in the Early Republic,* 196–97.

21. Jackson to Polk, May 3, 1826, *Correspondence of James K. Polk,* 1:42–43.

22. The Battle of Germantown is early told in David Ramsay's 1789 *History of the American Revolution* (rept. Indianapolis, 1990), 2:349–51; see also Thomas J. McGuire, *The Surprise of Germantown* (Philadelphia, 1994), and biographical information on Nash in *Dictionary of American Biography.*

23. Colin Calloway, *The American Revolution in Indian Country* (New York, 1995), chap. 7; Folmsbee, et al., *Tennessee: A Short History,* 145–52.

24. See especially Jefferson's second Inaugural Address.

25. Michael D. Green, *The Politics of Indian Removal: Creek Government and Society in Crisis* (Lincoln, Neb., 1982), esp. 42–43; Anthony F. C. Wallace, *Andrew Jackson and the Indians* (New York, 1993), 27–29; John Ehle, *Trail of Tears: The Rise and Fall of the Cherokee Nation* (New York, 1988), chap. 6.

26. Harry Ammon, *James Monroe: The Quest for National Identity* (New York, 1971), 474–75; Green, *The Politics of Indian Removal,* 49. For a compelling analysis of the evolution of this policy, see James P. Ronda, " 'We Have a Country': Race, Geography, and the Invention of Indian Territory," *Journal of the Early Republic* 19 (Winter 1999): 739–55.

27. Adams, *Memoirs of John Quincy Adams,* 7:90, 113.

28. Ibid., 73–74, 78–79. In early 1826, one chief in the delegation attempted suicide, as Adams and Secretary of War Barbour adjusted their hopes for agreement to an expedient treaty. See ibid., 106. For details of the Adams administration policy toward the Creeks, see Green, *The Politics of Indian Removal,* chaps. 5 and 6.

29. Cooper, *The Last of the Mohicans,* 236–37, 397–400.

30. *Hobomok, a Tale of Early Times* was printed by the Boston firm of Cummings, Hilliard & Co., as was Eliza Foster's *Saratoga,* both in the same year. *Hobomok* takes place in Salem (also given as Naumkeak, its Indian name) in the 1630s. Hobomok is meanly treated by the whites, but remains a man of honor and discernment. For a facsimile reprint modern edition, see *Hobomok* (New York: Garrett Press, 1970).

31. *Nashville Whig,* Jan. 2, 1826.

32. *Nashville Whig,* Dec. 12, 1825.

33. *Nashville Republican,* Apr. 22, 1826; *Nashville Whig,* Mar. 18, 1826.

34. *Nashville Whig,* Apr. 15, 1826.

35. *Nashville Whig,* Jan. 2, 1826; *Nashville Republican,* May 6, 1826.

36. *Nashville Republican,* May 6, 1826.

37. Harriette Simpson Arnow, *Flowering of the Cumberland* (Lexington, Ky., 1984), 152–54, 366–68; Folmsbee, et al., *Tennessee: A Short History; Nashville Whig,* Jan. 28, 1826; Joseph Earl Dabney, *Mountain Spirits: A Chronicle of Corn Whiskey From King James' Ulster Plantation to America's Appalachians and the Moonshine Life* (New York, 1974), 72–73.

38. *Nashville Republican,* March 18 and 25, Apr. 1 and 22, and June 17, 1826; *Nashville Whig,* Jan. 2 and 28, 1826.

39. *Nashville Whig,* March 11, 1826.

40. Arnow, *Flowering of the Cumberland,* chap. 5; F. Garvin Davenport, *Cultural Life in Nashville on the Eve of the Civil War* (Chapel Hill, N.C., 1941), chap. 1; Trollope, *Domestic Manners of the Americans,* 322.

41. Randolph to Dr. John Brockenbrough, Aug. 8, 1826, in Garland, *Life of John Randolph of Roanoke,* 272.

42. Calhoun to Jackson, June 4, 1826, *Papers of John C. Calhoun,* 10:110.

43. Ibid., 111.

44. Jackson to Calhoun, July 18, 1826, ibid., 158–60; Randolph, as reported in the *Nashville Republican,* Apr. 29, 1826.

45. *United States Telegraph,* Feb. 24, 1826.

NOTES TO CHAPTER TEN

1. *United States Gazette,* July 14, 1826. The thermometer would reach 80° that day. On Jefferson's measurements, see Dumas Malone, *Jefferson the Virginian* (Boston, 1948), 229.

2. Cited in Len Travers, *Celebrating the Fourth: Independence Day and the Rites of Nationalism in the Early Republic* (Amherst, Mass., 1996), 218–19.

3. Ibid; *United States Gazette,* July 7, 1826.

4. James A. Bear Jr. and Lucia C. Stanton, eds., *Thomas Jefferson's Memorandum Books* (Princeton, N.J., 1997), 420–21.

5. On Americans' slowness to celebrate Jefferson's role in writing the Declaration, see Robert M. S. McDonald, "Thomas Jefferson's Changing Reputation as Author of the Declaration of Independence: The First Fifty Years," in *Journal of the Early Republic* 19 (Summer 1999): 169–95.

6. John Adams to Abigail Adams, July 3, 1776, *Familiar Letters of John Adams and His Wife Abigail Adams . . . ,* 193–94.

7. *United States Telegraph,* July 5, 1826; Adams, *Memoirs of John Quincy Adams,* 7:120.

8. *United States Telegraph,* July 5, 1826; *Richmond Enquirer,* July 25, 1826; Catherine Wirt to Elizabeth Wirt, July 6, 1826, William Wirt Papers, DLC.

9. *Register of Debates,* Nineteenth Congress, First Session, Apr. 25, 1826, 2571–72.

10. Carr to David Watson, Dec. 8, 1824, in Watson Family Papers, Manuscripts Division, University of Virginia Library.

11. *Register of Debates,* Nineteenth Congress, First Session, Apr. 24, 1826, 1058–59, 2520*ff;* Hemphill and Buchanan quotes at 2531, 2540, respectively.

12. *Register of Debates,* Nineteenth Congress, First Session, Apr. 25, 1826, 2562.

13. *United States Telegraph,* July 3 and 5, 1826.

14. "Walter Jones," in *Dictionary of American Biography;* Burstein, *The Inner Jefferson,* 235–36.

15. Adams, *Memoirs of John Quincy Adams,* 7:121. The July 13 issue of the *American Statesman and City Register* of Boston called Jones's delivery "impressive and argumentative," but "imperfectly heard in many parts of the hall."

16. Adams, *Memoirs of John Quincy Adams,* 7:120.

17. *United States Telegraph,* July 5, 1826.

18. Adams, *Memoirs of John Quincy Adams,* 7:121–22.

19. Quincy, *Life of Josiah Quincy,* 417–18.

20. Quincy, *An Oration, Delivered on Tuesday, the Fourth of July, 1826 . . . ,* 3–5.

21. Ibid., 5–6.
22. Ibid., 7–8.
23. David Young, *The Citizen's and Farmer's Almanac, for the Year of Our Lord 1826* . . . (Morristown, N.J., 1825), n.p.
24. Quincy, *An Oration, Delivered on Tuesday, the Fourth of July, 1826* . . . , 24–30.
25. Luther S. Bancroft, *An Address Delivered to the Prescott Guards, and to the Inhabitants of Pepperell* (Groton, Mass., 1830), 6–9.
26. Luther S. Bancroft, *Bancroft's Agricultural Almanack, Calculated on a New and Improved Plan, for the Year of Our Lord 1826* (East Chelmsford, Mass., 1825), 34–35, 53.
27. George W. Benedict, *An Oration, Delivered at Burlington, Vt. on the Fourth of July 1826. Being the Fiftieth Anniversary of American Independence* (Burlington, Vt., 1826), 17–21.
28. Irving S. Kull, ed., *New Jersey: A History* (New York, 1930), 2:639; *The First Jubilee of American Independence; and Tribute of Gratitude to the Illustrious Adams and Jefferson* (Newark, N.J., 1826), 23, 26.
29. Josiah Bent Jr., *National Jubilee. An Oration Delivered at Braintree, July 4, 1826* . . . (Boston, 1826), 14–15, 19–21. Another Bostonian, Rev. Knowles of the Second Baptist Church, reminded: "We ought to look at this subject as Americans. If there is guilt, we all have our share." See *American Statesman and City Register,* July 13, 1826.
30. *Massachusetts Spy,* July 5, 1826.
31. Benedict, *An Oration, delivered at Burlington, Vt.* . . . , 3, 6–8.
32. Ibid., 9–10, 16.
33. Biographical sketch of Maynadier in *The National Cyclopedia of American Biography* (New York, 1940), 28:448.
34. William Maynadier, *An Oration Prepared for Delivery Before the Corps of Cadets at West Point, on the Fiftieth Anniversary of American Independence* (Newburgh, N.Y., 1826), 5–7.
35. Ibid., 14–16.
36. Burstein, *Sentimental Democracy,* 74, 76, 84–85, 100, 113. In a 1793 Fourth of July oration, John Quincy Adams himself urged citizens never to forget the Revolution, and to work to retrieve the "rapturous glow of patriotism." See Burstein, *Sentimental Democracy,* 168. A younger William Wirt had also expressed the cosmic significance of 1776: "The very sound of the 4th of July, gives rise to a train of thought and feeling so interesting to mankind . . . , so august as might strike into silent astonishment the most sublime genius which the world ever knew." Wirt, *An Oration Delivered in Richmond on the Fourth of July, 1800* (Richmond, 1800), 3.
37. *Albany Argus & Daily City Gazette,* July 4 and 6, 1826.
38. *The First Jubilee of American Independence; and Tribute of Gratitude to the Illustrious Adams and Jefferson,* 3–6, 33–36.

39. Ibid., 13.
40. Ibid., 8.
41. Ibid., 15–20, 27–28. The Revolutionary idiom is fully characterized in Burstein, *Sentimental Democracy*, chaps. 3 and 4.
42. *Supporter, and Scioto Gazette*, July 6, 1826; *Ohio Oracle*, July 14, 1826.
43. *Ohio Oracle*, July 14, 1826.
44. *National Crisis*, June 22 and July 6, 1826.
45. *Kentucky Reporter*, July 8 and 24, 1826.
46. *Nashville Republican*, July 8, 1826.
47. Warder W. Stevens, *Centennial History of Washington County, Indiana* (Indianapolis, 1916), 200–02, 212–13, 615–16. Farnum and his wife Evelyn both died during the cholera epidemic that decimated Salem's population in 1833, culminating on July 4th of that year. The sister of Evelyn Marie (Leonard) Farnum survived the epidemic and in 1838 in Salem gave birth to a son, John Hay, who went on to distinguish himself as Abraham Lincoln's personal secretary (1860–65) and U.S. secretary of state (1898–1905). On the Farnum/Leonard/Hay genealogy, see also *Abstract of Wills of Washington County, Indiana, 1814–1900*, copy at the Salem Public Library. I am grateful to Eric Eubank, director of the library, for the details of Farnum's life.
48. John H. Farnham, *Oration Delivered at Salem, Indiana. On the Fiftieth Anniversary of American Independence* (New Albany, Ind., 1826), 3; Ezra Stiles, *The United States Elevated to Glory and Honour* (Worcester, Mass., 1783), 12–13.
49. Farnham, *Oration Delivered at Salem, Indiana*, 4, 10.
50. Ibid., 11, 15–16.
51. *Charleston Courier*, July 1, 1826.
52. *Columbian Centinel*, June 24, 1826.
53. *Charleston Courier*, July 3 and 6, 1826.
54. *Massachusetts Spy*, July 12, 1826.
55. *Charleston Courier*, July 4, 1826.
56. *Richmond Enquirer*, Aug. 1, 1826.
57. *National Crisis*, July 6, 1826.
58. *Charleston Courier*, July 7, 1826.
59. This quote from the final act of Shakespeare's *Macbeth* no doubt combined a salute to Randolph's persistence with support for the efforts of George McDuffie.
60. *Ohio Oracle*, July 21, 1826.

NOTES TO CHAPTER ELEVEN

1. [William Cunningham], *Correspondence Between the Hon. John Adams, Late President of the United States and the Late William Cunningham,*

Esq. Beginning in 1803, and Ending in 1812 (Boston, 1823), iii–vi. Cunningham's grandmother was the sister of John Adams's mother.

2. For a clear summary of the Cunningham and Pickering matters, see Dumas Malone, *Jefferson and His Time: The Sage of Monticello* (Boston, 1981), 432–35; on Pickering and Randolph, see Ferling, *The First of Men*, 458–62. More broadly, on Pickering's bitterness, see Gerard H. Clarfield, *Timothy Pickering and the American Republic* (Pittsburgh, Pa., 1980). John Adams had good reason to be wary of Pickering and had suggested as much to Jefferson in 1818, if somewhat obliquely—when lightheartedly construing what the afterlife might be like, Adams ultimately considered that he was just open-minded enough to entertain the prospect of reencountering his sworn enemies, to wit, "I believe I could get over all my Objections to meeting Alec Hamilton and Tim Pick, if I could perceive a Symptom of sincere Penitence in either." See Adams to Jefferson, May 29, 1818, *The Adams-Jefferson Letters*, 526. Pickering, born in 1745, would live to 1829.

3. Jefferson to Madison, Aug. 30, 1823, in James Morton Smith, ed., *The Republic of Letters: The Correspondence between Thomas Jefferson and James Madison, 1776–1826* (New York, 1994), 1875–77. Madison's reply to this letter was greatly supportive; a subsequent mention of Pickering by Jefferson described him as a person of "malignity" whose testimony history would not fail to consider as irrelevant, because it was colored by a spiteful passion. See Madison to Jefferson, Sept. 6, 1823, and Jefferson to Madison, Oct. 18, 1823, in Smith, 1877–78. Also see Robert E. McGlone, "Deciphering Memory: John Adams and the Authorship of the Declaration of Independence," *Journal of American History* 85 (Sept. 1998): 411–38.

4. Jefferson to Adams, Oct. 12, 1823, *The Adams-Jefferson Letters*, 599–601.

5. Adams to Jefferson, Nov. 10, 1823, ibid., 601.

6. Rush to Adams, Oct. 17, 1809, *Letters of Benjamin Rush*, ed. L. H. Butterfield (Princeton, N.J., 1951), 2:1021–22. Benjamin Rush's son, Richard Rush, was President J. Q. Adams's secretary of the treasury.

7. Jefferson to Adams, May 27, 1813, *The Adams-Jefferson Letters*, 323.

8. Jefferson to Adams, Jan. 21, 1812, and Apr. 8, 1816, ibid., 291, 467; Adams to Jefferson, May 3, 1816, ibid., 470–71.

9. Ellen's new husband, Joseph Coolidge, was a graduate of Harvard and had been to Europe, where, at one point, he had been able to visit with Lord Byron. Jefferson met his future grandson-in-law for the first time in May 1824, and was so impressed with the young man that he invited him to the dinner given in honor of Lafayette that autumn. Ellen herself, a favorite correspondent of her grandfather during his second term as president, had grown into a graceful, mature writer, advising Jefferson from Boston of "the flourishing state of things" in the North and her

grievous disappointment that the Southern states were doomed "whilst the canker of slavery eats into their hearts." She had earlier broken the heart of a former suitor whose erudition, at least, Jefferson credited— William Wirt's good friend Francis Walker Gilmer. See Malone, *Jefferson and His Time: The Sage of Monticello,* 456–58, and Ellen Coolidge to Jefferson, Aug. 1, 1825, *The Family Letters of Thomas Jefferson,* 454–55.

10. Adams to Jefferson, Dec. 1, 1825, *The Adams-Jefferson Letters,* 611.

11. Adams to Jefferson, Feb. 25, 1825, ibid., 610–11; Jefferson to Adams, Dec. 18, 1825, ibid., 612.

12. Jefferson to Ellen Coolidge, Nov. 14, 1825, *The Family Letters of Thomas Jefferson,* 461–62.

13. Adams's physical condition is described by Virginian Anne Royall, who paid a visit in April 1825, and called the patriarch a "dear old man" who could not speak of his son or late wife for the tender emotion that overcame him. See Porter, *The Life and Times of Anne Royall,* 71.

14. Adams to Jefferson, Jan. 14, 1826, *The Adams-Jefferson Letters,* 613; Quincy, *Life of Josiah Quincy,* 417; *Memoir of the Life of Eliza S. M. Quincy* (Boston, 1861), 205, confirms that Jefferson never saw the letter.

15. Jefferson to Adams, Mar. 25, 1826, *The Adams-Jefferson Letters,* 613–14; Adams to Jefferson, Apr. 17, 1826, ibid., 614.

16. *United States Telegraph,* March 3, 1826. See a similarly sympathetic plea in the *New-York Mirror, and Ladies' Literary Gazette,* Apr. 15, 1826.

17. Hetty Smith Stevenson Carr to Dabney Smith Carr, Mar. 10 and 13, 1826, in Carr-Cary Family Papers, Manuscripts Division, University of Virginia Library. Hetty Carr was the widow of Peter Carr (1770–1815), the son of Jefferson's sister.

18. Hetty Smith Stevenson Carr to Dabney Smith Carr, Mar. 13, 1826, in Carr-Cary Family Papers.

19. Randall, *The Life of Thomas Jefferson,* 3:527–37. The most sound and thorough study of Jefferson's finances is Herbert Sloan, *Principle and Interest: Thomas Jefferson and the Problem of Debt* (New York, 1995).

20. Martha Randolph to Ellen Coolidge, Apr. 5, 1826, Ellen Wayles Coolidge Correspondence, University of Virginia Library; Jefferson to Madison, May 3, 1826, and Madison to Jefferson, May 6, 1826, in Smith, ed., *The Republic of Letters,* 1970–71.

21. Randall, *The Life of Thomas Jefferson,* 3:543.

22. Ibid., 544, 546; James A. Bear Jr., "The Last Few Days in the Life of Thomas Jefferson," in *Magazine of Albemarle County History* 32 (1974): 72–73.

23. Randall, *The Life of Thomas Jefferson,* 3:548. Joseph C. Cabell, a Virginia legislator and Jefferson associate, had heard from both Dr. Dunglison and T. J. Randolph that the patient was "sinking rapidly" on the 2nd.

Presuming on the 4th that Jefferson had succeeded in putting off death until the day of jubilee, Cabell wrote: "His great wish throughout his illness has been to live till the 4th July and to be buried on that day. . . . Is there not something very impressive in the circumstances of his dying on the 50th anniversary." Cabell to John Hartwell Cocke, July 4, 1826, Cocke Papers, Manuscripts Division, University of Virginia Library.

24. Randall, *The Life of Thomas Jefferson,* 3:544, 3:548. Burwell would be freed and given $300 under the terms of his master's last will, dated March 17, 1826, which referred to him as "my good, affectionate, and faithful servant." See ibid., 666.

25. Dunglison to Madison, July 1, 1826, in John M. Dorsey, ed., *The Jefferson-Dunglison Letters* (Charlottesville, Va., 1960), 66–67; Madison to Trist, July 6, 1826, in Randall, *The Life of Thomas Jefferson,* 3:550; Jefferson to Madison, Feb. 17, 1826, in Smith, ed., *The Republic of Letters,* 1965–67.

26. Lee to Jackson, July 1, 1826, in Bassett, ed., *Correspondence of Andrew Jackson,* 3:305–06. Henry Lee would go on to assist Jackson in the preparation of his Inaugural Address in 1829. Dr. Dunglison, who also advised James Madison, successfully treated President Jackson for a pain in his side in 1837. See Dorsey, ed., *The Jefferson-Dunglison Letters,* 78–79.

27. Adams, *Memoirs of John Quincy Adams,* 7:122; *National Intelligencer,* July 7, 1826; *United States Telegraph,* July 7, 8, and 10, 1826.

28. Adams, *Memoirs of John Quincy Adams,* 7:123–25; Thomas B. Adams to John Quincy Adams, July 4, 1826, Adams Papers, Massachusetts Historical Society, microfilm reel #476.

29. Bear, "The Last Few Days in the Life of Thomas Jefferson," 77–78. Reported in a newspaper story some years later, Poe's presence cannot be confirmed.

30. Malone, *Jefferson and His Time: The Sage of Monticello,* 499n77. The original obelisk was chipped at by souvenir hunters over the years, and replaced in the 1870s with the taller version that stands at the Monticello grave site today.

31. *Register of Debates,* Nineteenth Congress, First Session, Appendix pp. 12, 16.

32. *Memoir of the Life of Eliza S. M. Quincy,* 206.

33. Ibid; Adams, *Memoirs of John Quincy Adams,* 7:132; Olive Risley Seward, ed., *William H. Seward's Travels Around the World* (New York, 1873), 125; William Cranch, *Memoir of the Life, Character, and Writings of John Adams* (Washington, D.C., 1827), 57.

34. Cranch, *Memoir of the Life, Character, and Writings of John Adams,* 57–58. The *Boston Evening Gazette* faithfully reprinted the unnamed servant's question and Adams's answer, an irresistible vignette picked up by the *Massachusetts Spy* and disseminated. On July 8, John Quincy Adams noted his receipt of a letter from Susan Clark (he spells the name

"Clarke"), dated July 3, anticipating her grandfather's death. See Adams Papers, microfilm reel #38.

35. Cranch, *Memoir of the Life, Character, and Writings of John Adams*, 58.

36. George Washington Adams to John Quincy Adams, July 5, 1826, Adams Papers, microfilm reel #476.

37. *Memoir of the Life of Eliza S. M. Quincy*, 207–08.

38. Adams, *Memoirs of John Quincy Adams*, 7:133.

39. *Memoir of the Life of Eliza S. M. Quincy*, 207. Note that both this source and John Quincy Adams's diary give both first and last names, "Thomas Jefferson," and not simply "Jefferson survives," as Judge Cranch and many later chroniclers do. Louisa Catherine Smith (1773–1857) was the daughter of Abigail Adams's brother William Smith, a man of modest means who died at a fairly young age. She first came to live with Abigail while John Adams was abroad in the late 1770s, and in later years served unofficially as the ailing John Adams's secretary. Presumably, the editor of Eliza Quincy's memoir is one of her sons.

40. William Staughton, *Sermon, Delivered in the Capitol of the United States; on Lord's Day, July 16, 1826; at the Request of the Citizens of Washington, on the Death of Mr. Jefferson and Mr. Adams* (Washington, D.C., 1826), 17.

41. *A Selection of Eulogies, Pronounced in the Several States, in Honor of Those Illustrious Patriots and Statesmen, John Adams and Thomas Jefferson* (Hartford, Conn., 1826), 88. Samuel Smith's quote of Jefferson on the subject of his daughter Martha was given in many newspaper accounts—though not usually as "last words." The eulogy given by Congressman Churchill C. Cambreleng in New York City on July 20 contains the same quote: "I have done, said he [Jefferson], for my country, and I now resign my soul, without fear, to my God, my daughter to my country." See *A Selection of Eulogies*, 66. The source of the quote is Thomas Jefferson Randolph, who recorded it in these words to his cousin Dabney Smith Carr: "On my recieving [*sic*] a letter from McIntire containing a most liberal and kind message from the Nyork committee, he [Jefferson, during his final illness] observed that 'he cheerfully committed his soul to his god, his child to his country.' " Randolph to Carr, July 11, 1826, in Carr-Cary Family Papers.

42. *A Selection of Eulogies*, 345.

43. Edward Everett, *An Address Delivered at Charlestown August 1, 1826 in Commemoration of John Adams and Thomas Jefferson* (Boston, 1826), 34.

44. *A Selection of Eulogies*, 257.

45. Edward Everett, *An Oration Delivered at Cambridge on the Fiftieth Anniversary of the Declaration of Independence* (Boston, 1826), quotes at 3, 10.

46. Everett even showed himself tolerant of Andrew Jackson, visiting Nashville after Jackson's inauguration and then exchanging friendly

greetings with the new president at the White House. See Frothing-ham, *Edward Everett, Orator and Statesman,* 119–20.

47. Jefferson to Everett, Feb. 24, 1823, in Andrew A. Lipscomb and Albert Ellery Bergh, eds., *The Writings of Thomas Jefferson* (Washington, D.C., 1904), 15:410–15. Everett had to have appreciated the thought-ful response, knowing that Jefferson, turning eighty, had recently broken a wrist and was writing the long letter "with both hands crippled." And not inconsequentially, Harvard's Professor George Ticknor, Everett's close friend since youth, was also a great favorite of Jefferson. See Hillard, *Life, Letters, and Journals of George Ticknor,* passim.

48. Sprague to Adams, June 9, 1826, Adams Papers, microfilm reel #476.

49. Joseph E. Sprague, *An Oration, Delivered at Salem, On the Fourth of July, 1810* (Salem, Mass., 1810), esp. 8–10; and Joseph E. Sprague, *An Oration, Delivered in Salem, on the Fifth of July, 1813, in Commemoration of our Naval Victories, and National Independence* (Salem, Mass., 1813).

50. *Catalogue of Portraits in the Essex Institute, Salem, Massachusetts* (Salem, Mass., 1936), 209–10.

51. Cranch to Adams, Aug. 8 and 11, 1826, Adams Papers, microfilm reel #477. The eulogies he requested from Adams were those of Daniel Webster and Samuel Knapp. Cranch was appointed a federal judge by John Adams on the eve of Jefferson's inauguration. Though Jefferson thus secured his career by elevating rather than removing him, Cranch often reached decisions against Jefferson's interest in important cases. See Dumas Malone, *Jefferson the President, Second Term, 1805–1809* (Boston, 1974), 275. Cranch's predisposition to accept "Jefferson sur-vives" and promulgate it is further suggested by phrasing in his August 8 letter: "A great political lesson also may be drawn from a connected view of their characters—that however parties may conflict with each other the Republic will be safe." What could constitute a more "connected view" (for patriotic purposes) than the unquestioned attribution of the desirable last words to Adams? Adams's confidence in Cranch is sug-gested in a letter to his son Charles Francis on September 15, 1826, urg-ing him to decide upon a profession. If his son were to choose to become a lawyer, "I should advise you to attend the course of Lectures to be delivered by Judge Cranch."

52. Samuel Johnson, *A Dictionary of the English Language* (Philadelphia, 1813), n.p.

53. Elaborating at the end of volume 3, Randall writes of Adams: "his last words, uttered in the failing articulation of the dying, were 'Thomas Jef-ferson still survives.'" Randall's choice of "failing articulation" subtly suggests the indistinctness John Quincy Adams recorded. The biogra-

pher's source is Charles Francis Adams. See Randall, *The Life of Thomas Jefferson*, 3:542; Clarks F. Adams, *The Life of John Adams* (New York, 1968), 2:405; John T. Morse, *John Adams* (Boston, 1884), 330.

54. George Washington Adams to John Quincy Adams, July 5, 1826, also confirmed in Benjamin Waterhouse to John Quincy Adams, July 4, 1826; Josiah Quincy to John Quincy Adams, July 7, 1826, Adams Papers, microfilm reel #476; *Boston Centinel,* July 8, 1826.

55. William Wirt to Elizabeth Wirt, July 7, 1826; Elizabeth Wirt to William Wirt, July 6, 1826, in William Wirt Papers, MHS.

56. *Albany Argus & Daily City Gazette,* July 10, 1826.

57. Indeed, Niles was right. Just after the Fourth of July conclusion to the critical Battle of Gettysburg, another point in time fraught with providential yearnings, President Abraham Lincoln would respond to citizens' "serenade" of him by appearing in person to recollect for them the "peculiar recognitions" that the national birthday conjured. "The two most distinguished men in the framing and support of the Declaration," he said, "the only two of the fifty-five" signers to have been president, met their end at the most consequential moment: "Precisely fifty years after they put their hands to the paper it pleased Almighty God to take both from the stage of action. This was indeed an extraordinary and remarkable event in our history." See "Response to a Serenade," July 7, 1863, in *The Collected Works of Abraham Lincoln,* ed. Roy P. Basler (New Brunswick, N.J., 1953), 6:319–20.

58. Clay to Adams, July 25, 1826, *Papers of Henry Clay,* 5:567–68.

59. *United States Gazette,* July 11, 1826; *The First Jubilee of American Independence,* 45–46; *Albany Argus & Daily City Gazette,* July 11, 1826.

60. Garland, *The Life of John Randolph of Roanoke,* 273.

61. *American Statesman & City Register,* Nov. 2, 1826. Note that "i" was an acceptable substitution for "j" in printing.

62. Horace Mann, *An Oration, Delivered at Dedham, July 4, 1823* (Dedham, Mass., 1823); Adams, *Memoirs of John Quincy Adams,* 7:133.

63. Everett, *An Address Delivered at Charlestown August 1, 1826,* 5, 8–11.

64. *A Selection of Eulogies,* 185, 187.

65. Adams, *Memoirs of John Quincy Adams,* 7:137–40; Adams to Louisa Catherine Adams (wife), Aug. 5, 1826, Adams Papers, microfilm reel #477; Hillard, *Life, Letters, and Journals of George Ticknor,* 1:378. Of modern treatments undertaking to explain Webster's charismatic power, see especially Irving H. Bartlett, *Daniel Webster* (New York, 1978); also see Robert V. Remini, *Daniel Webster: The Man and His Time* (New York, 1997) and Peterson, *The Great Triumvirate.*

66. "Adams and Jefferson," in *The Papers of Daniel Webster: Speeches and Formal Writings,* ed. Charles M. Wiltse, 1:237–71.

67. Hillard, *Life, Letters, and Journals of George Ticknor,* 1:378–79; Adams, *Memoirs of John Quincy Adams,* 7:140–41; Adams to Louisa Catherine Adams, Aug. 5 and 9, 1826, Adams Papers, microfilm reel #477.

68. Joseph E. Sprague, "Eulogy, Pronounced at Salem, Massachusetts," in *A Selection of Eulogies,* 235–58; for the order of services, see "Funeral Honors by the Town of Salem," in Adams Papers, microfilm reel #477.

69. Adams, *Memoirs of John Quincy Adams,* 7:150.

70. *Diary of Charles Francis Adams,* eds. Aida DiPace Donald and David Donald (Cambridge, Mass., 1964), 2:62.

71. Ibid., 65–66.

72. *Albany Argus & Daily City Gazette,* July 6, 1826; *United States Gazette,* July 7 and 14, 1826.

73. Louisa Catherine Adams to John Quincy Adams, July 15, 17, and 20, 1826, Adams Papers, microfilm reel #476. Concerning the president's arrival, see the note from the Washington Committee of Arrangements, two of whose delegates waited in vain for him at the Executive Mansion on the previous day, in Adams Papers, microfilm reel #478.

74. Richard Rush to Adams, July 15 and 24; Louisa Catherine Adams to Adams, July 17, 1826, Adams Papers, microfilm reel #476; William Cranch to John Quincy Adams, Aug. 11, 1826, Adams Papers, microfilm reel #477. Cranch urged Adams to provide Wirt with personal information on his late father, especially the formative years. "I have promised to give Mr. Wirt all the information in my power," Cranch wrote, while expressing the limits of his own knowledge.

75. Wirt to Gilmer, July 23, 1815, in Kennedy, *Memoirs of the Life of William Wirt,* 1:386.

76. Ibid., 2:215; Adams, *Memoirs of John Quincy Adams,* 7:153–54; *A Selection of Eulogies,* 401–04.

77. Ibid., 423.

78. Ibid., 419–21.

79. Ibid., 424–25.

80. Everett, *An Address Delivered at Charlestown August 1, 1826,* 34; *Richmond Enquirer,* July 7, 1826.

81. *A Selection of Eulogies,* 425.

82. Ibid.

83. *National Intelligencer,* Oct. 21, 1826; *Baltimore Chronicle* article by T. L. McKinny, as reprinted in the *Richmond Enquirer,* Oct. 27, 1826.

84. Wirt to Roger C. Weightman, Oct. 26, 1826, in William Wirt Papers, MHS. The oration was published by Gales & Seaton in Washington the following month, under the title *A Discourse on the Lives and Character of Thomas Jefferson and John Adams, Who Both Died on the Fourth of July, 1826.*

NOTES TO THE EPILOGUE

1. Adams to Lafayette, Oct. 25, 1826, in John Quincy Adams Letterbook, Adams Papers, microfilm reel #148.

2. Entry of Oct. 26, 1827, in Adams, *Memoirs of John Quincy Adams,* 7:345–46.

3. Trollope, *Domestic Manners of the Americans,* 284–85.

4. Adams, *Memoirs of John Quincy Adams,* 7:272–73. Both Burr and Van Buren went on to be their candidate's vice president, though for Van Buren the reward was put off until Jackson's second term, once first-term Vice President John C. Calhoun was thoroughly repudiated by Jackson and saw his president as a traitor to Southern interests.

5. [Charles Hammond], *View of General Jackson's Domestic Relations, in Reference to His Fitness for the Presidency* (Washington, D.C., 1828); on Hammond's political background, see Ratcliffe, *Party Spirit in a Frontier Republic,* chap. 7; *A Voice from the Interior. Who Shall Be President? The Hero of New-Orleans, Or John the Second of the House of Braintree* (Boston, 1828).

6. Robert Walsh Jr., *The Jackson Wreath, Or National Souvenir* (Philadelphia, 1829), 82–85.

7. Remini, *Henry Clay,* chap. 18.

8. *American Statesman and City Register,* July 13, 1826.

9. William Preston Vaughn, *The Antimasonic Party in the United States, 1826–1843* (Lexington, Ky., 1983); Bullock, *Revolutionary Brotherhood.*

10. The spread of Anti-Masonry into Vermont is nicely illustrated in Henry Swan Dana, *The History of Woodstock, Vermont, 1761–1886* (Taftsville, Vt., 1980), 527–35.

11. Obituary in *Village Register* (Dedham, Mass.), May 3, 1827. I thank Jan Nelson for providing me with a copy of this document.

12. See especially Lee Virginia Chambers-Schiller, *Liberty, a Better Husband. Single Women in America: The Generations of 1780–1840* (New Haven, Conn., 1984), chap. 1.

13. *Columbian Centinel,* July 4, 1828.

14. Copy of Knapp's *Biographical Sketches* owned by the American Antiquarian Society, Worcester, Massachusetts; Rev. George T. Chapman, *Sketches of the Alumni of Dartmouth College* (Cambridge, Mass., 1867), 32, 164–65.

15. James S. Cushing, *The Genealogy of the Cushing Family* (Montreal, 1905), 178–79, 308–09.

16. Anton Wagner, "Eliza Lanesford Cushing," in W. H. New, ed., *Canadian Writers Before 1890: Dictionary of Literary Biography,* vol. 99 (Detroit, Mich., 1990), 85–86; *Montreal Gazette,* May 6, 1886.

17. In 1834, Ruth Bascom would paint the portraits of Abraham and Lydia Edwards.

18. Mary Eileen Fouratt, "Ruth Henshaw Bascom, Itinerant Portraitist," in Peter Benes, ed., *Itinerancy in New England and New York* (Boston, 1986), 190–211.

19. Ibid.

20. Still, *The Life of Ethan Allen Brown*, 196–202, 236.

21. Scheiber, *Ohio Canal Era*, chaps. 9 and 11.

22. *Nashville Republican*, Aug. 26, 1826.

23. Letter of Jan. 12, 1829, in Garland, *The Life of John Randolph of Roanoke*, 317.

24. Ibid., 337, 369–71.

25. Green, *George McDuffie*, 110, 117.

26. Ibid., 133–34.

27. Ibid., 224 and chap. 11.

28. *Obituary Address on the Occasion of the Death of the Hon. Henry Clay* (Washington, D.C., 1852), 7, 15, 55; "Eulogy on Henry Clay," July 6, 1852, in *Collected Works of Abraham Lincoln*, 2:125–26; Peterson, *The Great Triumvirate*.

29. Jabour, *Marriage in the Early Republic*, 145–47; "Agnes C. Wirt" (New York, n.d.), 15–22.

30. Jabour, *Marriage in the Early Republic*, 151–61. Curiously, Wirt's preference for German laborers was identically expressed by Thomas Jefferson in a private communication of 1788. See William Howard Adams, *The Paris Years of Thomas Jefferson* (New Haven, Conn., 1997), 140.

31. Kennedy, *The Life of William Wirt*, 2:422–23.

32. Ibid., 425–29; letter from Catharine G. Wirt to her aunt, Eliza Carlton, dated Feb. 22, 1834, published as a pamphlet, "Death of Mr. Wirt," in Manuscripts Division University of Virginia Library.

33. Kramer, *Lafayette in Two Worlds*, 122–23.

34. William H. Seward, *Life and Public Services of John Quincy Adams, Sixth President of the United States* (Port Washington, N.Y., 1971 [1849]), 332–37. Seward was governor of New York when his book was printed, and it contained the text of his eulogy of Adams before the New York legislature.

35. House of Representatives, First Session, Thirtieth Congress, Feb. 24, 1848, in *The Congressional Globe*, (Washington, D.C., 1848); Seward, *Life and Public Services of John Quincy Adams*, 338–43. John Davis had left the House in 1834, when he became governor of Massachusetts. He then became a U.S. senator (1835–41), and was governor a second time (1841–42), before returning to the Senate (1845–53). Davis was at one point considered a possible running mate for Henry Clay when the latter ran against Polk in 1844. He died in 1854.

36. Edward Everett, *Eulogy on the Life and Character of John Quincy Adams* (Boston, 1848), 11.

37. Ibid., 41–43, 65–66.

38. *The First Jubilee of American Independence,* 60.

39. H. L. Mencken, *The American Language: An Inquiry into the Development of English in the United States* (New York, 1938), chap. 4. Mencken wrote that "there arose a national consciousness so soaring and so blatant that it began to dismiss every British usage and opinion as puerile and idiotic." See Mencken, 136.

40. Peterson, *The Great Triumvirate,* 110.

Index

FACES OF REVOLUTION
Personalities and Themes in the
Struggle for American Independence
by Bernard Bailyn

In this collection of essays, Bernard Bailyn combines lucid portraits of participants in the American Revolution with deft explorations of the ideas that moved them, the circumstances that shaped them, and their goals, fears, and aspirations. Bailyn offers character studies of figures such as John Adams, Thomas Jefferson, and Thomas Paine. *Faces of Revolution* is a fresh vision of the forces that shaped our country, one that is at once sweeping and filled with intimate detail.

American History/0-679-73623-9

THE AMERICANS
by Daniel J. Boorstin

Spanning the tumultuous history of the United States from the first Puritan settlers through the Revolution, the Civil War, and into the twentieth century, Librarian of Congress Emeritus Daniel J. Boorstin presents a dazzlingly comprehensive examination of the American nation and people. Boorstin's critically acclaimed trilogy includes the Pulitzer Prize–winning third volume, *The Democratic Experience*, which analyzes the American character through the last 100 years of economic, cultural, and social change.

The Colonial Experience, 0-394-70513-0
The National Experience, 0-394-70358-8
The Democratic Experience, 0-394-71011-8

FOUNDING BROTHERS
The Revolutionary Generation
by Joseph J. Ellis

Founding Brothers illuminates the intertwined lives of the founders of the American republic—George Washington, John Adams, Aaron Burr, Benjamin Franklin, Alexander Hamilton, Thomas Jefferson, and James Madison. In a lively and engaging narrative, Joseph J. Ellis recounts the sometimes collaborative, sometimes archly antagonistic interactions between these men, and shows us the private characters behind the public personas of the politicians who defined the young democracy and directed its course for the coming centuries.

American History/0-375-70524-4